BOOKS BY JUDITH VIORST

POEMS

The Village Square

It's Hard to Be Hip Over Thirty and Other Tragedies of
Married Life

People and Other Aggravations

How Did I Get to Be Forty and Other Atrocities

If I Were in Charge of the World and Other Worries

CHILDREN'S BOOKS

Sunday Morning

I'll Fix Anthony

Try It Again, Sam

The Tenth Good Thing About Barney

Alexander and the Terrible, Horrible, No Good, Very
Bad Day

My Mama Says There Aren't Any Zombies, Ghosts,
Vampires, Creatures, Demons, Monsters, Fiends,
Goblins, or Things

Rosie and Michael

Alexander, Who Used to Be Rich Last Sunday

OTHER

Yes, Married

A Visit from St. Nicholas (to a Liberated Household)

Love and Guilt and the Meaning of Life, Etc.

Necessary Losses

THE LOVES, ILLUSIONS, DEPENDENCIES
AND IMPOSSIBLE EXPECTATIONS
THAT ALL OF US HAVE TO GIVE UP
IN ORDER TO GROW

Necessary Losses

Judith Viorst

SIMON AND SCHUSTER   New York

Library of Congress Cataloging in Publication Data
Viorst, Judith.
     Necessary losses.

Bibliography: p.
     Includes index.
     1. Loss (psychology)   2. Self-actualization (Psychology)   I. Title.
BF575.D35V56   1986   155.9   85-26072
ISBN: 0-671-45655-5

The author is grateful to the following for permission to reprint:

From *Collected Papers*, Vol. 4, by Sigmund Freud. Edited by James Strachey.
Published by Basic Books, Inc., by arrangement with The Hogarth Press, Ltd.,
Sigmund Freud Copyrights, Ltd., The Institute of Psycho-Analysis, London, and
W. W. Norton & Co., Inc.

From *Collected Papers*, Vol. 2, by Sigmund Freud. Authorized Translation under
the supervision of Joan Riviere. Published by Basic Books, Inc., by arrangement
with The Hogarth Press Ltd. and The Institute of Psycho-Analysis, London. Reprinted by permission.

From *The Anatomy of Bereavement* by Beverley Raphael, © 1983 by Beverley
Raphael. Reprinted by permission of Basic Books, Inc., Publishers, and Century
Hutchinson, Ltd.

From *Haywire* by Brooke Hayward. Reprinted by permission of Jonathan Cape,
Ltd., and Random House, Inc.

From *archy and mehitabel* by Don Marquis. Copyright 1927, 1930, by Doubleday
& Co., Inc. Reprinted by permission.

From the poem by Ernest Dowson "Non sum qualis eram bonae sub regno Cynarae" in *The Norton Anthology of Poetry*. Reprinted by permission of Fairleigh
Dickinson University Press.

From the English translation of the poem "Self Portrait 2," by Tove Ditlevsen
from *The Other Voice: Twentieth Century Women's Poetry in Translation*, edited by
Joanna Bankier, et al. Translation copyright © 1976 by Ann Freeman. Reprinted by
permission of Ann Freeman and Gyldendal, © 1969 by Tove Ditlevsen.

From the poems "The Sunlight on the Garden" and "Les Sylphides" by Louis
MacNeice in *The Collected Poems of Louis MacNeice*. Reprinted by permission of
Faber and Faber, Ltd.

From the poem "Next Day" in *The Complete Poems of Randall Jarrell*. Copyright
© 1965 by Mrs. Randall Jarrell. Reprinted by permission of Farrar, Straus & Giroux, Inc., and Faber and Faber, Ltd.

From the poem "Seed Leaves" in *Walking to Sleep* by Richard Wilbur. Copyright
© 1964 by Richard Wilbur. Reprinted by permission of Harcourt Brace Jovanovich,
Inc., and Faber and Faber, Ltd.

(continued on page 430)

To my three sons

Anthony Jacob Viorst

Nicholas Nathan Viorst

Alexander Noah Viorst

Acknowledgments

This is a book that was built on the wisdom and help of many people. I am enormously grateful to them.

I am grateful to the Washington Psychoanalytic Society and to its Institute, where I studied for six intellectually thrilling years; to Doctors Joseph Smith, Oscar Legault, Marion Richmond and John Kafka, for guiding me to, and through, the Institute; to the Institute's Mary Allen, Jo Parker and, most especially, Pat Driscoll, for helping me—in the years I worked on this book—to track down countless elusive books and references; and to Dr. Donald Burnham, for small miracles.

I am grateful to my friend Silvia Koner for pointing me toward the theme of my book and to Dr. Louis Breger and Dr. Gerald Fogel for their immensely valuable critiques of my first draft.

I am grateful to the following psychoanalysts, who shared their expertise with me: Doctors Justin Frank, Robert Gillman, Pirkko Graves, Stanley Greenspan, Robert King, Susan Lazar, Glenn Miller, Nancy Miller, Frances Millican, Betty Ann Ottinger, Gerald Perman, Earle Silber, Stephen Sonnenberg, Richard Waugaman and Robert Winer.

I am grateful to the editors of *Redbook* magazine for providing me, for some eighteen years, with the opportunity to write about a wide range of human concerns, some of which are reflected in the pages of this book.

I am grateful to several friends who were involved with me in this book from beginning to end—to Leslie Oberdorfer for reading and discussing my chapters with me as they came rolling hot off my word processor; to Ruth Caplin, Li Schorr and Phyllis Hersh for always being available to explore issues and offer encouragement; and to Dr. Harvey Rich for his intelligence, clarity and loving heart.

I am grateful to Maria Niño of the Cleveland Park Library for three years of gracious helpfulness.

I am grateful to my husband Milton and our three sons for their sustaining love and good will during my years of consuming involvement in research and writing; to my friend and agent Robert Lescher for, as usual, help and guidance far above and beyond the call of duty; to my editor Herman Gollob for his consistent supportiveness; and to Dan Green, who said let's do this book.

Finally, I am grateful to a great many people who cannot be thanked by name—the men and women and children whose experiences appear in this book and whose privacy I have promised to protect. *Necessary Losses* would not exist without them.

Contents

It is the image in the mind that binds us to our lost treasures, but it is the loss that shapes the image.

—Colette

The library is not open to the public but we are offering curbside pick-up! You may place holds for items online using your library card number and PIN (default is OCLN).

When you receive the pick-up notification email please call the library at **781-447-7613 to schedule your pick-up time.**

Staff and curbside pick-up are available Monday-Friday 10 am - 4 pm.

Introduction

After almost two decades of writing essentially about the inner world of children and adults, I decided that I wanted to learn more about the theoretical underpinnings of human psychology. I sought my education at a psychoanalytic institute because I believe that, with all of its imperfections, the psychoanalytic perspective offers the most profound insights into what we are and why we do what we do. At its best, psychoanalytic theory simply teaches us in another way what we have already been taught by Sophocles and Shakespeare and Dostoevsky. At its best, psychoanalytic theory offers us illuminating generalizations while maintaining an exquisite respect for the complexity and uniqueness of each of us astonishing human beings.

In 1981, after six years of study, I became a research graduate of the Washington Psychoanalytic Institute, which belongs to that international network of teaching and training institutes spawned by Sigmund Freud. During those years I also underwent an analysis and worked in several psychiatric settings—as an aide in a children's psychiatric ward, as a creative-writing teacher for emotionally disturbed adolescents and as a therapist at two clinics doing individual psychotherapy with adults. It seemed to me that wherever I looked, both inside and outside of hospitals, people—all of us—were struggling with issues of loss. Loss became the subject I had to write about.

When we think of loss we think of the loss, through death, of people we love. But loss is a far more encompassing theme in our life. For we lose not only through death, but also by leaving and being left, by changing and letting go and moving on. And our losses include not only our separations and departures from those we love, but our conscious and unconscious losses of romantic dreams, impossible expectations, illusions of freedom and power, illusions of safety—and the loss of our own younger self, the self that thought it always would be unwrinkled and invulnerable and immortal.

Somewhat wrinkled, highly vulnerable and non-negotiably mortal, I have been examining these losses. These lifelong losses. These necessary losses. These losses we confront when we are confronted by the inescapable fact . . .

that our mother is going to leave us, and we will leave her;

that our mother's love can never be ours alone;

that what hurts us cannot always be kissed and made better;

that we are essentially out here on our own;

that we will have to accept—in other people and ourselves—the mingling of love with hate, of the good with the bad;

that no matter how wise and beautiful and charming a girl may be, she still cannot grow up to marry her dad;

that our options are constricted by anatomy and guilt;

that there are flaws in every human connection;

that our status on this planet is implacably impermanent;

and that we are utterly powerless to offer ourselves or those we love protection—protection from danger and pain, from the inroads of time, from the coming of age, from the coming of death; protection from our necessary losses.

These losses are a part of life—universal, unavoidable, inexorable. And these losses are necessary because we grow by losing and leaving and letting go.

This book is about the vital bond between our losses and gains. This book is about what we give up in order to grow.

For the road to human development is paved with renunciation. Throughout our life we grow by giving up. We give up some of our deepest attachments to others. We give up certain cherished parts of ourselves. We must confront, in the dreams we dream, as well as in our intimate relationships, all that we never will have and never will be. Passionate investment leaves us vulnerable to loss. And sometimes, no matter how clever we are, we must lose.

An eight-year-old was asked to provide a philosophical commentary on loss. A man of few words, he answered, "Losing sucks." At any age we would surely agree that losing tends to be difficult and painful. Let us also consider the view that it is only through our losses that we become fully developed human beings.

In fact, I would like to propose that central to understanding our lives is understanding how we deal with loss. I would like to propose in this book that the people we are and the lives that we lead are determined, for better and worse, by our loss experiences.

Now I am not a psychoanalyst and I have not tried to write like one. Nor am I a strict Freudian, if that term is intended to describe someone who hews rigorously to Freud's doctrines and resists any modification or change. But I do unhesitatingly embrace Freud's conviction that our past, with all of its clamorous wishes and terrors and passions, inhabits our present, and his belief in the enormous power of our unconscious—of that region outside our awareness—to shape the events of our life. I also embrace his belief that consciousness helps, that recognizing what we're doing helps, and that our self-understanding can expand the realm of our choices and possibilities.

In preparing this book I have relied not only on Freud and a wide range of other psychoanalytic thinkers but on many of the poets and philosophers and novelists who have concerned themselves—directly or indirectly—with aspects of loss.* In addition, I have drawn heavily on my own personal experiences as a girl and a woman, as a mother and a daughter, as a wife and a sister and a friend. I have talked with analysts about their patients, with patients about their analyses, and with large numbers of the kind of people to whom this book is addressed: marriage-and-the-family people who worry about their mortgage payments, their periodontal problems, their sex life, their children's future, love and death. Virtually all of the names have been changed except for those of a handful or so of "famous" people, whose stories are identified as some sort of public testimony to the pervasiveness of issues of loss.

For our losses—the losses successively examined in the four parts of this book—are indeed pervasive.

* Those interested may turn to the "Notes and Elaborations" section for information on all source materials and for further—sometimes extensive—elaboration on many of the themes discussed in this book.

The losses entailed in moving away from the body and being of our mother and gradually becoming a separate self.

The losses involved in facing the limitations on our power and potential and deferring to what is forbidden and what is impossible.

The losses of relinquishing our dreams of ideal relationships for the human realities of imperfect connections.

And the losses—the multiple losses—of the second half of life, of our final losing, leaving, letting go.

Examining these losses does not make for merry remedies like *Winning Through Losing* or *The Joy of Loss*. Our junior philosopher said it: Losing sucks. But to look at loss is to see how inextricably our losses are linked to growth. And to start to become aware of the ways in which our responses to loss have shaped our lives can be the beginning of wisdom and hopeful change.

JUDITH VIORST
Washington, D.C.

I The Separate Self

There is no ache more
Deadly than the striving
to be oneself.

—Yevgeniy Vinokurov

1

The High Cost of Separation

Then there is the matter of my mother's abandonment of me.
Again, this is the common experience. They walk ahead of us,
and walk too fast, and forget us, they are so lost in thoughts of
their own, and soon or late they disappear. The only mystery
is that we expect it to be otherwise.

—Marilynne Robinson

We begin life with loss. We are cast from the womb
without an apartment, a charge plate, a job or a car. We are sucking, sobbing, clinging, helpless babies. Our mother interposes herself between us and the world, protecting us from overwhelming
anxiety. We shall have no greater need than this need for our
mother.

Babies need mothers. Sometimes lawyers, housewives, pilots,
writers and electricians also need mothers. In the early years of
life we embark on the process of giving up what we have to give
up to be separate human beings. But until we can learn to tolerate
our physical and psychological separateness, our need for our
mother's presence—our mother's literal, actual presence—is absolute.

For it's hard to become a separate self, to separate both literally
and emotionally, to be able to outwardly stand alone and to inwardly feel ourselves to be distinct. There are losses we'll have to
sustain, though they may be balanced by our gains, as we move
away from the body and being of our mother. But if our mother
leaves us—when we are too young, too unprepared, too scared, too

helpless—the cost of this leaving, the cost of this loss, the cost of this separation may be too high.

There is a time to separate from our mother.

But unless we are ready to separate—unless we are ready to leave her and be left—anything is better than separation.

A young boy lies in a hospital bed. He is frightened and in pain. Burns cover 40 percent of his small body. Someone has doused him with alcohol and then, unimaginably, has set him on fire.

He cries for his mother.

His mother has set him on fire.

It doesn't seem to matter what kind of mother a child has lost, or how perilous it may be to dwell in her presence. It doesn't matter whether she hurts or hugs. Separation from mother is worse than being in her arms when the bombs are exploding. Separation from mother is sometimes worse than being with her when she is the bomb.

For the presence of mother—our mother—stands for safety. Fear of her loss is the earliest terror we know. "There is no such thing as a baby," writes psychoanalyst-pediatrician D. W. Winnicott, observing that babies in fact can't exist without mothers. Separation anxiety derives from the literal truth that without a caretaking presence we would die.

A father, of course, can be that caretaking presence. We'll look at his place in our life in Chapter Five. But the caretaking person I'll speak of here will be—because it usually is—our mother, from whom we can endure anything but abandonment.

Yet all of us are abandoned by our mother. She leaves us before we can know that she will return. She abandons us to work, to market, to go on vacation, to have another baby—or simply by not being there when we have need of her. She abandons us by having a separate life, a life of her own—and we will have to learn to have one too. But meanwhile, what do we do when we need our mother—we need our mother!—and she is not there?

What we doubtless do is survive. We surely survive the brief and temporary absences. But they teach us a fear that may set its mark on our life. And if, in early childhood, most especially within the first six years, we are too deprived of the mother we need and long for, we may sustain an injury emotionally equivalent to being doused with oil and set on fire. Indeed, such deprivation in the first few years of life has been compared to a massive burn or wound. The pain is unimaginable. The healing is hard and slow. The damage, although not fatal, may be permanent.

Selena must confront the damage every weekday morning when her sons leave for school and her husband leaves for work and, hearing her apartment door slam shut for the final time, "I feel lonely, abandoned, petrified. I need hours to compose myself. What would happen if people didn't come back?"

In the late 1930s, in Germany, when Selena was six months old, her mother began the struggle to keep them alive, departing each day to queue up for food and negotiate with the bureaucracy that was making it harder and harder for Jews to survive. Out of desperate necessity, Selena was left all alone, fed by a bottle, penned up in a crib—and if she cried, her tears had dried when, several hours later, her mother came home again.

Everyone who knew her then agrees that Selena was quite wonderfully good—a placid, undemanding, sweet-natured child. And if you encountered her now you might believe that you were seeing a bright, blithe spirit, happily untouched by what must have been experiences of harrowing loss.

She has been touched.

Selena is prone to depression. She is terrified of the unknown. "I don't like adventure. I don't like anything new." She says that her earliest memories are of anxiously wondering what would happen next. "I am frightened," she says, "of whatever is not familiar."

She also is frightened of too much responsibility—"I'd like someone to take care of me all of the time." And while she functions quite adequately as good mother and dutiful wife, she has also arranged—through a strong, steady husband and numerous older friends—for some surrogate mothering.

Women often envy Selena. She is funny and charming and warm. She can bake, she can sew, she likes music, she likes a good laugh. She has a Phi Beta Kappa key, two masters' degrees, a part-time teaching job. And with her narrow child's body, enormous brown eyes and elegant cheekbones, she strikingly resembles the young Audrey Hepburn.

Except that, in her late forties, she remains the *young* Audrey Hepburn, rather less a woman than a girl. And she finally has identified what she says "wakes me up every morning of my life with a bad taste in my mouth and pains in my stomach."

It is anger, she says—"lots of anger. I think I feel cheated."

This thought is not acceptable to Selena. Why isn't she simply grateful to be alive? She observes that six million Jews died and that all she suffered was the absence of her mother. The damage, she says, although permanent, is not fatal.

It is just in the last four decades, in the years since Selena's birth, that attention has fully been paid to the high cost of mother-loss, to both the immediate suffering and the future consequences of even fairly short-term separations. A child apart from his mother may show separation reactions which can last long after they are together again—problems with eating and sleeping, breakdowns of bladder and bowel control and even a decline in the number of words he uses. Furthermore, as early as six months old he may become, not merely weepy and sad, but gravely de-pressed. And tied in with the above is that painful feeling known as separation anxiety, which includes both the fear—when mother is gone—of the dangers he faces without her, and the fear—when they are together—that he will lose her again.

I am intimately acquainted with some of these symptoms and some of these fears, for they followed my spending three months —at age four—in a hospital, three virtually motherless months because the hospitals of that time rigidly restricted visiting hours. Years after I had recovered from the illness for which I'd been hospitalized, I suffered from the effects of the hospitalization. And among the manifestations of my separation anxiety was my newly acquired habit—which continued until my middle teens—of sleepwalking.

An example: One balmy autumn night, when I was six years old and my parents—to my distress—had gone out for the evening, I climbed out of bed without waking up from my sleep. Wandering into the living room, I slipped right past my dozing baby sitter, opened the front door and left the house. And then, still sound asleep, I walked to the corner and crossed the busy intersection, arriving at last at the goal of my somnambulistic journeying—the fire station.

"What do you want, little girl?" asked an astonished but extremely gentle fireman, trying not to frighten me awake.

I am told that, still in my sleeping state, I answered, loud and clear and without hesitation, "I want the firemen to find my mommy."

A six-year-old can desperately want her mommy.

A six-month-old can desperately want mommy too.

For by six months or so a child can form a mental image of his absent mother. He remembers and wants her specifically and the fact that she isn't present gives him pain. And swept with insistent needs that only his mother, his missing mother, can fulfill, he feels profoundly helpless and deprived. The younger the child the less time it takes—once he tunes in to his mother—before her absence is felt as a permanent loss. And while familiar substitute care will help him to tolerate everyday separations, it is not until age three that he gradually comes to understand that the mother who is not there is alive and intact in another place—and will return to him.

Except that the wait for mother's return may feel interminable —may feel like forever.

For we need to keep in mind that time accelerates with the years, and that once we measured time in a different way, that once an hour was a day and a day was a month and a month was surely an eternity. Small wonder then that as children we may grieve our missing mother the way that as adults we grieve our dead. Small wonder then that, when a child is taken from his mother, "the frustration and longing may send him frantic with grief."

Absence makes the heart grow frantic, not fonder.

Absence, in fact, produces a typical sequence of responses: protest; despair; and, finally, detachment. Take a child from his mother and put him with strangers in a strange place and he will find the living arrangements intolerable. He will scream, he will weep, he will thrash about. He will eagerly, desperately search for his missing mother. He will protest because he has hope, but after a while, when she doesn't come . . . and doesn't come . . . protest will turn to despair, to a state of muted, low-key yearning that may harbor an unutterable sorrow.

Listen to Anna Freud's description of Patrick, three years and two months, who was sent during World War II to England's Hampstead Nursery, and who

> assured himself and anybody who cared to listen with the greatest show of confidence that his mother would come for him, that she would put on his overcoat and would take him home with her again. . . .
>
> Later an ever-growing list of clothes that his mother was supposed to put on him was added: "She will put on my overcoat and my leggings, she will zip up the zipper, she will put on my pixie hat."
>
> When the repetitions of this formula became monotonous and endless, somebody asked him whether he could not stop saying it all over again. . . . He stopped repeating the formula aloud but his moving lips showed that he was saying it over and over to himself.
>
> At the same time he substituted for the spoken word gestures that showed the position of his pixie hat, the putting on of an imaginary coat, the zipping of the zipper, etc. . . . While the other children were mostly busy with their toys, playing games, making music, etc., Patrick, totally uninterested, would stand somewhere in a corner, [and] move his hands and lips with an absolutely tragic expression on his face.

Because the need for a mother is so powerful, most children emerge from despair and seek mother-substitutes. And because of this need it makes sense to assume that when the beloved long-lost mother returns, her child will throw himself joyously into her arms.

This isn't what happens.

For surprisingly enough, many children—especially under age three—may greet their returning mother very coldly, treating her with a distance, a blankness, that almost seems to say, "I never saw this lady before in my life." This response is called detachment—it is a shutdown of loving feelings—and it deals with loss in a number of different ways: It punishes the person for having left. It serves as a masked expression of rage, for intense and violent hatred is one of the chief responses to being abandoned. And it also may be a defense—which can last for hours, or days, or a lifetime—a defense against the agony of ever loving, and ever losing, again.

Absence makes the heart grow frozen, not fonder.

And if this absence is, in fact, the absence of any stable parent figure, if childhood is a series of such separations, what then? Psychoanalyst Selma Fraiberg describes a sixteen-year-old boy who filed a lawsuit in Alameda County, seeking a half million dollars on the grounds that in sixteen years he had been placed in sixteen different foster homes. What is it, exactly—the damage for which he is suing? He answers that "it's like a scar on your brain."

One of the funniest men in the world, the astute political humorist Art Buchwald, is an expert on foster homes and scars on the brain. He discussed them with me in his Washington office— an office as unpretentious as its owner—where, in the course of the afternoon, I found myself moved less to laughter than to tears.

Art's is, in a way, a classic story of separation and loss in households with little money and few family resources. His mother died while Art was still an infant. His father was left with three daughters and one baby boy. He did what he could—he tried to find safe placements for his children and he visited conscientiously once a week, becoming a "Sunday father" while Art "decided very young that I was not going to get too involved with anybody."

In his first sixteen years Art lived in seven households, all in New York, beginning with a Seventh-Day Adventists home, where, he says, "there was hell and damnation and going to church on Saturday, and my father coming with kosher every Sunday. It was very confusing."

Next was a home in Brooklyn and then a stay at the Hebrew Orphan Asylum which are, Art deadpans, "the three worst words in the language. *Hebrew* means you're Jewish. *Orphan* means you don't have any parents. And *asylum* . . ." After the HOA there was a placement with a lady who initially took in all four Buchwald children and then, a year or so later, decided that four was two too many and that Art and one of his sisters would have to go. Thus followed another foster home, and another foster home, and then a final year in his own father's house. And then he ran away to join the Marine Corps where, he says, he first found a sense of belonging, of being cared for.

At an early age Art concluded that life was "me against the world." He also learned early to hide behind a smile. He says he quickly discovered that "if I put a big smile on my face, people were nicer to me. And so," he says, quite matter-of-factly, "I smiled."

Years later—long after the foster homes, and the Marine Corps, and the struggle to make it as a writer—the anger beneath that smile could no longer be leashed. Looking for an object to attack, to hurt, to destroy, Art found . . . himself. Depression, in one definition, is anger turned inward. Midway into his thirties, Art, that funny fellow, became severely depressed.

The depression had followed a move, "a very emotional move," from Paris, where he had lived and worked for fourteen years. Settled in Washington, D.C., with his wife and three children, he was famous, successful, admired, liked and—in pain. "In everybody's mind I had it made, except mine," he says. "I was really desperate. I really needed help."

Recognizing that the time had come for ironing certain things out, Art decided to enter psychoanalysis, in the course of which he began to examine some of the early experiences which continued to cast their shadow on his life. Making him a loner. Making him unable to trust. Making him feel guilty for what he'd achieved— "Who am *I* to have *this?*" And making him afraid that sooner or later it would all be taken away from him. He also examined his rage, eventually coming to understand that "it wasn't a sin to be angry at my father" and that "it also wasn't irrational to be angry at a mother I never knew."

Art says now of the analysis that it saved his life, even though in a twist which sounds almost like fiction—trashy fiction—his analyst unexpectedly died of a heart attack. "I finally trust someone," says Art, "and he dies!" But the work that they did together has continued to reverberate through the years. ("A good analysis," Art observes, "is when five years later something happens and you suddenly say, 'Oh, yeah, *that's* what he meant.' ") In his fifties Art finally feels at peace with himself.

"I'm better at trusting. I'm not so fearful of people hurting me. I'm closer to my wife and to my kids." He still has problems with intimacy—"One-on-one is the toughest. One-on-a-thousand," he says, "is much easier." And he still is afraid of anger. "I don't handle it very well. I'll do anything to avoid getting angry."

But Art is less angry these days. He is enjoying his success. Standing on stage at the Kennedy Center, entertaining the President of the United States and assorted other power brokers and superstars, he smiles his winning smile and tells himself, "Oh, if my Jewish father could see me now." He says that in part his success represents "revenge on about ten people, all dead and buried."

He says that he understands about scars on the brain.

Severe separations in early life leave emotional scars on the brain because they assault the essential human connection: The mother-child bond which teaches us that we are lovable. The mother-child bond which teaches us how to love. We cannot be whole human beings—indeed, we may find it hard to be human— without the sustenance of this first attachment.

And yet it has been argued that the need for others is not a primary instinct, that love is merely a glorious side effect. The classic Freudian view is that babies find, in the feeding experience, relief from hunger and other oral tensions and that, in repeated encounters of sucking and sipping and sweet satiation, they begin to equate satisfaction with human contact. In the early months of life a meal is a meal and gratification is gratification. Interchangeable sources can fill all needs. In time the who—the mother— becomes as important as the what—the body relief. But love for mother begins with what Anna Freud calls "stomach love." Love for mother, or so this theory has it, is an acquired taste.

There is an alternative view, which holds that the need for human connection is fundamental. It argues that we are wired for love from the start. "The love of others comes into being," wrote psychotherapist Ian Suttie some fifty years ago, "simultaneously *with the recognition of their existence*." In other words we love as soon as we learn to distinguish a separate "you" and "me." Love is our attempt to assuage the terror and isolation of that separateness.

The best-known spokesman today for the view that mother-need is innate is the British psychoanalyst John Bowlby, who notes that babies—like calves and ducklings and lambs and young chimpanzees—behave in ways that keep them close to their mother. He calls this "attachment behavior" and says that attachment has the biological function of self-preservation, of keeping the young safe from harm. By remaining close to mother the baby chimp finds protection from predators that might kill him. By remaining close to mother, baby humans find protection from danger too.

It is generally agreed that by six to eight months most babies have formed a specific mother attachment. It is then that we all, for the first time, fall in love. And whether or not that love is linked, as I am convinced it must be, to a fundamental need for human attachment, it possesses an intensity which will make us exquisitely vulnerable to the loss—or even the threat of loss—of a loved one.

And if, as I am convinced it must be, a reliable early attachment is vitally important to healthy development, the cost of breaking that crucial bond—the cost of separation—may be high.

The cost of separation is high when a too-young child is left too long alone, or is passed from foster home to foster home, or is placed in a nursery—even Anna Freud's nursery—by a mother who says that she will (but will she?) come back. The cost of separation is high even in caring family situations when a divorce, a hospital stay, a geographical or emotional pulling away fragments a child's connection with his mother.

The cost of separation may also be high when working mothers cannot find or pay for adequate child care—and more than half of those with children under the age of six now go to work! The women's movement and simple urgent economic necessity are sending millions of women into the job market. But the question,

"What shall I do with my kids?" requires better answers than are offered by twelve-hour custodial day-care centers.

"In the years when a baby and his parents make their first enduring human partnerships," writes Selma Fraiberg, "when love, trust, joy and self-valuation emerge through the nurturing love of human partners, millions of small children in our land may be learning . . . in our baby banks . . . that all adults are interchangeable, that love is capricious, that human attachment is a perilous investment and that love should be hoarded for the self in the service of survival."

The cost of separation is often high.

Now of course there will be separations in early childhood. And they may indeed produce distress and pain. But most normal separations, within the context of a stable, caring relationship, aren't likely to leave us with scars on the brain. And yes, working mothers and babies can establish a loving, trusting human bond.

But when separation imperils that early attachment, it is difficult to build confidence, to build trust, to acquire the conviction that throughout the course of our life we will—and deserve to—find others to meet our needs. And when our first connections are unreliable or broken or impaired, we may transfer that experience, and our responses to that experience, onto what we expect from our children, our friends, our marriage partner, even our business partner.

Expecting to be abandoned, we hang on for dearest life: "Don't leave me. Without you I'm nothing. Without you I'll die."

Expecting to be betrayed, we seize on every flaw and lapse: "You see—I might have known I couldn't trust you."

Expecting to be refused, we make excessive aggressive demands, furious in advance that they will not be met.

Expecting to be disappointed, we make certain that, soon or late, we are disappointed.

Fearful of separation, we establish what Bowlby calls anxious and angry attachments. And frequently we bring about what we fear. Driving away those we love by our clinging dependency. Driving away those we love by our needy rage. Fearful of separation, we repeat without remembering our history, imposing upon new sets, new actors and a new production our unrecollected but still-so-potent past.

For no one is suggesting that we consciously remember experiences of early childhood loss, if by remember we mean that we can summon up a picture of mother leaving, of being alone in a crib. What stays with us instead is what it surely must have felt like to be powerless and needy and alone. Forty years later, a door slams shut, and a woman is swept with waves of primitive terror. That anxiety is her "memory" of loss.

Loss gives rise to anxiety when the loss is either impending or thought to be temporary. Anxiety contains a kernel of hope. But when loss appears to be permanent, anxiety—protest—gives way to depression—despair—and we may not only feel lonely and sad but responsible ("I drove her away") and helpless ("I can do nothing to bring her back") and unlovable ("There is something about me that makes me unworthy of love") and hopeless ("Therefore I'll feel this way forever!").

Studies show that early childhood losses make us sensitive to losses we encounter later on. And so, in mid-life, our response to a death in the family, a divorce, the loss of a job, may be a severe depression—the response of that helpless and hopeless, and angry, child.

Anxiety is painful. Depression is painful. Perhaps it is safer not to experience loss. And while we indeed may be powerless to prevent a death or divorce—or our mother from leaving us—we can develop strategies that defend us against the pain of separation.

Emotional detachment is one such defense. We cannot lose someone we care for if we don't care. The child who wants his mother and whose mother, again and again and again, isn't there, may learn that loving and needing hurt too much. And he may, in his future relationships, ask and give little, invest almost nothing at all, and become detached—like a rock—because "a rock," as a sixties song tells us, "feels no pain. And an island never cries."

Another defense against loss may be a compulsive need to take care of other people. Instead of aching, we help those who ache. And through our kind ministrations, we both alleviate our old, old sense of helplessness and identify with those we care for so well.

A third defense is a premature autonomy. We claim our independence far too soon. We learn at an early age not to let our survival depend on the help or love of anyone. We dress the helpless child in the brittle armor of the self-reliant adult.

These losses we have been looking at—these premature separations of early childhood—may skew our expectations and our responses, may skew our subsequent dealings with the necessary losses of our life. In Marilynne Robinson's extraordinary novel *Housekeeping*, her desolate heroine ponders the power of loss, remembering "when my mother left me waiting for her, and established in me the habit of waiting and expectation which makes any present moment most significant for what it does not contain."

Absence, she reminds us, can become "gigantic and multiple."

Loss can dwell within us all our life.

2
The Ultimate Connection

For he on honey-dew hath fed,
And drunk the milk of Paradise.

—Samuel Taylor Coleridge

All of our loss experiences hark back to Original Loss, the loss of that ultimate mother-child connection. For before we begin to encounter the inevitable separations of everyday life, we live in a state of oneness with our mother. This ideal state, this state of boundarylessness, this I-am-you-are-me-is-she-is-we, this "harmonious interpenetrating mix-up," this floating "I'm in the milk and the milk's in me," this chillproof insulation from aloneness and intimations of mortality: This is a condition known to lovers, saints, psychotics, druggies and infants. It is called bliss.

Our original bliss connection is the umbilical connection, the biological oneness of the womb. Outside the womb we experience the gratifying delusion that we and our mother share a common boundary. Our lifelong yearning for union, so some psychoanalysts say, originates in our yearning to return—to return, if not to the womb, then to this state of illusory union called symbiosis, a state "for which deep down in the original primal unconscious . . . every human being strives."

We have no conscious memories of being there—or leaving. But once it was ours, and we had to let it go. And while the cruel game of giving up what we love in order to grow must be replayed at each new stage of development, this is our first, perhaps hardest, renunciation.

The losing, leaving, letting go of paradise.

And although we do not remember it, we also never forget it. We acknowledge a paradise and a paradise lost. We acknowledge a time of harmony, wholeness, unbreachable safety, unconditional love, and a time when that wholeness was irretrievably rent. We acknowledge it in religion and myth and fairy tales and our conscious and unconscious fantasies. We acknowledge it as reality or as dream. And while we fiercely protect the boundaries of self that clearly demark the you from the me, we also yearn to recapture the lost paradise of that ultimate connection.

Our pursuit of this connection—of the restoration of oneness—may be an act of sickness or of health, may be a fearful retreat from the world or an effort to expand it, may be deliberate or unaware. Through sex, through religion, through nature, through art, through drugs, through meditation, even through jogging, we try to blur the boundaries that divide us. We try to escape the imprisonment of separateness. We sometimes succeed.

Sometimes in fleeting moments—moments of sexual ecstasy, for instance—we find ourself returned to oneness again, though it may not be until after, "After Love," as Maxine Kumin's fine poem would have it, that we can begin to sort out where we have been:

> Afterwards, the compromise.
> Bodies resume their boundaries.
>
> These legs, for instance, mine.
> Your arms take you back in.
>
> Spoons of our fingers, lips
> admit their ownership.
> . . . .
>
> Nothing is changed, except
> there was a moment when
>
> the wolf, the mongering wolf
> who stands outside the self
>
> lay lightly down, and slept.

It is argued that this experience—the physical merging that

sexual union may bring—takes us back to the oneness of our infancy. Indeed, analyst Robert Bak calls orgasm "the perfect compromise between love and death," the means by which we repair the separation of mother and child through the momentary extinction of the self. It is true that few of us consciously climb into a lover's bed in the hope of finding our mommy between the sheets. But the sexual loss of our separateness (which may scare some people so badly they cannot have orgasms) brings us pleasure, in part, because it unconsciously repeats our first connection.

Certainly Lady Chatterley provides us, for all time, with a vision of self-dissolving orgastic bliss as "further and further rolled waves of herself away from herself," until "the quick of all her plasm was touched, she knew herself touched . . . and she was gone." Another woman, describing a similar loss-of-self experience, says, "Coming makes me feel that I've come home."

But orgasm isn't the only means of extinguishing the self, of putting the watchful mongering wolf to sleep. There are many different highways that can carry us beyond our personal boundaries.

I, for example, have frequently sat (or is it *levitated?*) in my dentist's chair, adrift in a happy haze of nitrous oxide, feeling—as another user of this gas has put it—"as if the opposites of the world, whose contradictoriness and conflict make all our difficulties and troubles, were melted into unity." The man I'm quoting here is the philosopher/psychologist William James, but a variety of respectable—and not so respectable—types have also testified to the power of drugs to bring them to this condition of . . . melted unity.

For others, harmonious oneness can best be achieved through the natural world, through a breaking down of the wall between man and nature, permitting some of us—some of the time—"to return from the solitude of individuation into the consciousness of unity with all that is. . . ." There are those who have never felt this union with earth and heaven and sea, and those who—like Woody Allen—have always stoutly maintained that "I am two with nature." But some men and women find solace and joy not only in *seeing* but also in *being* nature—in being, temporarily, a part of "one vast world-encircling harmony."

Great art can also—sometimes—erase the line between viewer and viewed in what writer Annie Dillard calls "pure moments," astonishing moments she says that "I'll bear with me to my grave," moments during which "I stood planted, open-mouthed, born, before that one particular canvas, that river, up to my neck, gasping, lost, receding into watercolor depth . . . buoyant, awed, and had to be literally hauled away."

There are special religious experiences that can also re-create a state of oneness. Indeed, religious revelation can so irrefutably penetrate the soul that—these are Saint Teresa's words—"when she [the soul] returns to herself, it is wholly impossible for her to doubt that she has been in God, and God in her."

Mystical union is possible through a variety of transcendental experiences. Mystical union puts an end to self. And whether this union occurs between man and woman, man and cosmos, man and artistic creation or man and God, it repeats and restores—for brief, exquisite moments—the oceanic feeling of that mother-child connection where "the *me,* and the *we,* the *thou,* are not found, for in the One there can be no distinction."

Still, we try to make some distinctions: Between the psychotic and the saint. Between the moonstruck fanatic and the truly religious. We may challenge the legitimacy of drug- or drink-inspired cosmic union, and doubt the soundness of robed and sandaled cultists who exclaim: "Ecstatically, I merged into the mass, tasting the glorious pleasure that accompanies the loss of ego."

In other words, we may feel that oneness is fine if it isn't crazy, desperate or permanent—fine for folks to temporarily vanish into a painting, not fine if they vanish forever into a cult. We also may feel more accepting of Saint Teresa's divine experiences than we do of some pothead's stoned apprehension of God. And we may want to differentiate the sex life of a more-or-less healthy adult from sex which is just symbiosis, from sex which is nothing more than a fearful flight from separateness.

For analysts now tell us that vaginal orgasm, once regarded as the hallmark of female sexual maturity, may be rapturously experienced by severely troubled women who are merging in fantasy not with a man but a mother. Men also seek mommies through sex: A male patient reports that whenever he found himself "thinking crazily," he could relieve his "craziness" by paying a prostitute to lie in a nude embrace with him until he felt himself "melting into her body."

Clearly, merging can sometimes be no more than symbiosis—a desperate return to clinging, helpless infancy. Indeed, to be stuck —fixated—at the symbiotic phase or to return—regress—to this phase in ways that take over our life would indicate that we were emotionally ill. The severe mental illness called childhood symbiotic psychosis, and most adult schizophrenia as well, are believed to involve a failure to build or maintain the boundaries that separate self from others. The result is that "I am not I, You are not You, also You are not I; I am at the same time I and You, You are at the same time You and I. I am confused whether You are I or I You."

At its very craziest, this merger of You and I may be frantic and frightened and furious, colored more with hatred than with love. The feeling is: "I can't live with—or without—her." The feeling is: "She is smothering me but her presence makes me real, lets me survive." At its very craziest, with intimacy intolerable and a separate existence seemingly impossible, oneness may be not bliss, but raging necessity.

We are looking at serious illness—at psychosis. But problems with symbiosis can also produce less extreme emotional difficulties.

Consider Mrs. C, attractive and childlike at age thirty, who slept with her mother until she was twenty years old, after which she found herself a tolerant and womanly man to marry. Mrs. C lives in the apartment above her mother, who does all her housework and generally runs her life, and she cannot contemplate moving to a more convenient location without becoming physically ill. Mrs. C has a symbiotic *neurosis*, for unlike symbiotic psychotic children, important parts of her development were quite normal. And yet in other parts of her life she behaves and unconsciously views herself as only one half of a symbiotic duo. She also unconsciously fears that if this duo were broken up, neither she nor her mother could survive.

Mrs. C and her mother shared from the start of Mrs. C's life an anxious and clinging symbiotic relationship. No wonder, we sagely observe, that she can't leave. But even the healthiest mother-child union may stand in the way of subsequent separateness, for as analyst Harold Searles observes: "Probably the greatest reason why we tend to rebel against our developing individual identity is because we feel it to have come between, and to be coming increasingly between, ourself and the mother with whom we once shared a world-embracing oneness."

We must count among our necessary losses the giving up of this world-embracing oneness.

We will never give up wanting to retrieve it.

Yes, we all have oneness wishes, but for some—not especially crazy—men and women these wishes may secretly dominate their life, penetrating all their important relationships and influencing all their important decisions. A woman, trying to choose between two attractive marriage proposals, made her choice while out to dinner one night when her escort scooped up a morsel of food and spooned it—like a mommy—into her mouth. This man's compelling, tacit promise of infantile gratifications immediately brought an end to her indecision. He was her choice.

Analyst Sydney Smith says that for such people—in contrast to the rest of us—the universal longing for oneness has not been benignly cordoned off. Instead it establishes itself as a central, tenacious, life-shaping "golden fantasy" which, in the course of psychoanalytic treatment, may slowly and reluctantly be revealed.

"I have always felt," says one of Dr. Smith's patients, "there is a remote person somewhere who would do everything for me, somebody who would fulfill every need in some magical fairylike manner and see to it I would be able to get whatever I want without putting out any effort for it. . . . I have never lived without all this stuff being there in the background. I don't know if I can."

Living with golden fantasies of an endlessly nurtured infancy can be a neurotic refusal to grow up. But the yearning for moments of oneness, the yearning to now and then suspend the differences between the other and self, the yearning to recapture a mental state that resembles our early union with mother, is not in itself abnormal or undesirable.

For experiences of oneness can give us a respite from the solitude of separateness.

And experiences of oneness can help us transcend our former limits, can help us grow.

Analysts call the constructive return to some earlier stage of development "regression in the service of the ego." They mean that we are thereby enriched and enhanced. They mean that by taking a backward step we sometimes are able to forward our development. "To merge in order to reemerge," writes psychoanalyst Gilbert Rose, "may be part of the fundamental process of psychological growth. . . ."

In an intriguing book called *The Search for Oneness*, three psychologists make some dazzling claims for the potential benefits of oneness experiences. They present a hypothesis, supported by laboratory experiments, that the inducement of symbiotic-like fantasies—fantasies of oneness—can help schizophrenics to think and act less crazy and, in conjunction with behavior-modification techniques, can improve students' school performance, ease the fears of phobics and help smokers give up cigarettes, drinkers alcohol and dieters food!

These results were actually produced, write the authors, in controlled experiments in which subjects were exposed to a subliminal message (a message flashed before a viewer's eyes so fast that he isn't aware of seeing it), a message that said:

MOMMY AND I ARE ONE.

What were the experimenters doing? And why exactly do they think it worked?

We have already seen that oneness wishes persist into adult life and that—as Mrs. C and the spoonfed lady and Dr. Smith's patients clearly show us—they often can powerfully motivate behavior. The authors therefore argue that if unfulfilled yearnings for oneness can produce psychotic and other disturbed behavior, then perhaps the fulfillment—in fantasy—of this wish to be nurtured, protected, perfected, safe could have a wide range of beneficial effects.

The trick, then, is to arrange for fulfillment in fantasy. How?

Like a dream we forget upon wakening but which leaves us feeling good or bad all day, some fantasies work upon us outside our awareness. And the fantasy of oneness may be stirred, the authors say, by the subliminal message that MOMMY AND I ARE ONE. The authors go on to demonstrate that, with several important exceptions, this message produces good feelings and positive change, which, whether or not these good feelings and changes endure, may offer proof of the psychic value of oneness fantasies.

An example: Two groups of obese women went through a diet-counseling program. Both of the groups succeeded in losing weight. But the group of women exposed to the subliminal oneness message lost more weight than the women who were not.

Another example: Disturbed adolescents treated in a residential center took reading tests; their scores were compared with the scores of the previous year. The entire group had improved but the scores of those who had been exposed to the oneness message had improved four times as much as those who had not.

And another example: One month after the end of a program to help smokers give up cigarettes, a check was made on how many still abstained. The figure was 67 percent for those exposed to the MOMMY AND I ARE ONE message. It was 12½ percent for those who were not.

I don't think we need to conclude from all this that MOMMY AND I ARE ONE subliminal messages are destined to be the therapy of the future. Nor, as we have seen, are they required to get some oneness into our life. In bed, in church, in art museums, in unexpected boundary-softening moments, we gratify our lifelong wish for oneness. These fleeting fulfillments, these fusions, are experiences of grace that can deepen, rather than threaten, our sense of self.

"No one," writes Harold Searles, "becomes so fully an individual, so fully 'mature,' as to have lost his previously achieved capacity for symbiotic relatedness." But sometimes it feels that we have. Sometimes the wolf, the mongering wolf who stands outside the self, will not drop its guard, will not lie down and sleep. Sometimes we are too terrified to allow it to.

Certainly a union that involves annihilation of the self can generate annihilation anxiety. To give ourself up, to surrender ourself —in love or any passion—may feel to us like loss instead of gain. How can we be so passive, so possessed, so out of control, so . . . won't we go crazy? And how will we ever find ourselves again? Consumed by such anxieties, we may establish barricades, not boundaries. Shutting ourselves away from any threat to our inflexible autonomy. Shutting ourselves away from any experience of emotional surrender.

Yet the yearning to restore the bliss of mother-child oneness— that ultimate connection—is never relinquished. All of us live, at some unconscious level, as if we had been rendered incomplete. Though the rupture of primary unity is a necessary loss, it remains "an incurable wound which afflicts the destiny of the whole human race." And speaking to us through the dreams that we dream and the tales that we create, images of reunion persist and persist, and persist and persist—and bracket our life.

The force behind the movement of time is a mourning that will not be comforted. That is why the first event is known to have been an expulsion, and the last is hoped to be a reconciliation and return. So memory pulls us forward, so prophecy is only brilliant memory —there will be a garden where all of us as one child will sleep in our mother Eve. . . .

3

Standing Alone

This plant would like to grow
And yet be embryo;
Increase, and yet escape
The doom of taking shape. . . .

—Richard Wilbur

Oneness is bliss. Separation is dangerous. And yet we pull and pull and pull away. For the need to become a separate self is as urgent as the yearning to merge forever. And as long as we, not our mother, initiate parting, and as long as our mother remains reliably *there*, it seems possible to risk, and even to revel in, standing alone.

To crawl from the lap of paradise, and explore.

To stand erect on two feet, and walk out the door.

To leave for school, for work, for a married life.

To dare to cross the street, and all the continents of the earth, without our mother.

The poet Richard Wilbur addresses our oneness-separateness conflict in his little poem about plant, and human, development. And while Wilbur clearly acknowledges the urge to remain inchoately attached, "something at the root," he writes, "more urgent than that urge," presses outward.

It is the striving to be a separate self.

But separateness is, ultimately, a matter of inner perception, not geography. It rests on the knowledge that I am distinct from thou. It recognizes the boundaries that restrict and contain and limit and define us. It is linked to a core of self that cannot be altered or taken away like a piece of clothing.

Becoming a separate self is not a sudden revelation but an unfolding. It evolves, slowly slowly slowly, over time. And during our first three years, in predictable stages of separation-individuation, we venture upon a journey as momentous as any we will ever take —the journey out of oneness into separateness.

All subsequent departures from the familiar to the unknown may stir up echoes of this original journey. Alone in a strange hotel room, far from everyone we love, we may suddenly feel endangered and incomplete. And every time we move from the safe to the risky, expanding the boundaries of our experience, we will— in our act of breaking away—repeat some of the joys and terrors attendant upon that initial loss:

When we discovered the heady freedom and the panic-stricken aloneness of human separateness.

When we embarked on what psychoanalyst Margaret Mahler has termed our "psychological birth."

Our psychological birth begins at around five months of age, when we enter a stage called differentiation: A time when we display a "hatched" alertness. A time when we form a specific child-mother bond. And a time when we draw our body away from the body of our mother in the dawning recognition that our mother, and indeed an entire world, exists outside our boundaries —to be looked at, to be touched, to be enjoyed.

Stage two, at nine or so months, is an audacious practicing time when we start to physically crawl away from our mother, continuing, however, to return to her as a bountiful home base from which we obtain "emotional refueling." It is scary out there in the world, but we must practice our newfound talent for locomotion —and besides, there are all these marvels to explore. And as long as mother is there as a body to touch, as a lap to lay a weary head in, as a here-I-am-and-you're-fine encouraging smile, we exuberantly continue to expand our physical universe and our self.

Practice makes perfect, crawling yields to walking, and at this momentous point in the practicing stage, upright locomotion permits such vistas, such possibilities, such triumphs, that a child can grow drunk on omnipotence and grandeur. We turn into flaming narcissists. And megalomaniacs. Imperial. The masters of all we survey. The view from the top of two moving legs has seduced us into a love affair with the world. It, and we, are wonderful.

Somewhere in us today there lives that solo pilot, that African explorer, that navigator of uncharted seas. Somewhere in us there lives that dauntless adventurer. Somewhere in us, if we were allowed to engage in the normal pursuits of the practicing stage, there lives an exultant being who once was capable of finding wonders everywhere. We are chastened today, and restrained, but if we are lucky we make contact now and then with that self-intoxication, that sense of wonder. When Whitman roars: "I celebrate myself, and sing myself . . . Divine am I inside and out . . ." we can hear the barbaric yawp of the practicing child.

Practicing is perilous, but we are too eagerly on the move to notice. We bruise and we bleed and we keep coming back for more. And as we walk run climb jump fall and stand again, we appear so at home in this world, so cheerfully confident, so impervious to harm, that we almost seem oblivious to our mother.

But in fact her available presence hovering somewhere in the background is what permits this elated breaking away. And although there is distance now between us and our mother, we regard her as ours in some appendage-like way. At eighteen or so months of age, however, our mind gains the capacity to grasp the implications of our separateness. It is then that we see what we are: a small and vulnerable and helpless one-and-a-half-year-old. It is then that we are confronted with the price we have to pay for standing alone.

Imagine it this way: Here we are walking airily on a tightrope, and perhaps showing off with a jaunty trick or two, when suddenly we glance down and discover—"Oh, my God! Look at that!"— that we are walking our tightrope without a net.

Lost is the sense of perfection and power that comes from the illusion of being the king of the world, the star of the show.

Lost is the sense of security that derives from the illusion that a child always has a safety net for a mother.

Stage three, then, of the process of separation-individuation is confronting and trying to solve a great dilemma: How can we high-stepping toddlers, having known the buoyant pleasures of standing alone, retreat from autonomy? Yet how can we sobered toddlers, having grown aware of the hazards of autonomy, stand alone? This stage, called rapprochement, is our first attempt to reconcile separateness, closeness and safety.

If I leave, will I perish?

And, will she let me come home again?

At several points in our life we will be troubled again by this rapprochement dilemma. At several points we will ask, Should I go? Should I stay? At several turning points—with our parents, our friends, our partners in passion, our partners in marriage—we will struggle with questions of intimacy and autonomy.

How far away can I go and still be connected?

What can I—and do I—want to do for myself?

And exactly how much of me am I prepared to give up for love, or simply for shelter?

At several points in our life we may insist: I'll do it myself. I'll live by myself. I'll solve it myself. I'll make my own decisions. And, having made *that* decision, we then may find ourselves scared to death of standing alone.

We also then may find ourselves replaying some adult version of rapprochement.

For in the first weeks of rapprochement we turn back to our mother. We clamor for her attention. We woo, pester, charm. We are striving to repossess her in order to banish the anxiety of separateness. We are feeling: Don't stop loving me. I may not be able to make it out here on my own.

We are feeling: Help!

On the other hand, we don't want help. Or rather, we both want it and don't want it. And, besieged by contradictions, we hold tight and push away, we follow and flee. We insist on our all-powerfulness and rage—rage!—at our helplessness, and our separation anxiety intensifies. Craving that old sweet oneness yet dreading engulfment, wishing to be our mother's and yet be our own, we stormily swing from mood to mood, advancing and retreating—the quintessential model of two-mindedness.

Toward the end of our second year, each one of us, each in our own unique way, has to begin to resolve the rapprochement crisis: By establishing for ourself a comfortable distance, an optimal distance, from our mother. By finding a distance—not too close and not too far apart—where we can psychologically stand alone.

At every stage of separation-individuation, we flourish or falter, we grow or get stuck or retreat. At every stage there are tasks that need to be done. And although each act of our life is determined by many different forces—is multi-determined—we live in part today by what we learned then.

Consider the wary Alice, who holds her friends and her lovers at bay and who thinks intrusion is the real word for intimacy and who still may be defending herself against the mother of the practicing stage, that pesty, ubiquitous mother who kept rushing in to direct and restrain and assist and—control her.

And consider the passive Ray, who fears that any claim to autonomy would injure and even destroy the people he loves, a man whose happily symbiotic, huggy, kissy mother grew bleak and suicidal just as soon as her little boy started wriggling away.

And consider Amanda, whose overwhelmed and ineffectual mother was far too helpless to help her stand alone. Amanda, a grown woman now, is still unable to move away from her mother's house. And in dreams she is climbing a stairway with a terrible blankness behind her, with nothing behind her, nothing, nothing at all.

What happens to us if we're pushed from the nest by a mother who cannot endure our infant dependencies? Or if—with a quite different mother—we're treated as good when we stay and bad when we go? Or if our first explorations are viewed with alarm, as threats to our health, to our very survival? Or if, when we say, "To hell with you. I'm going exploring anyway," we fall on our face and our mother will not pick us up?

What happens is that we adapt, or crumple, or compromise. What happens is that we give in, or make do, or prevail. Whatever solutions we find will be reshaped and elaborated by later experiences. But in some form or other they will continue to mold us.

It is true, of course, that people sharing strikingly similar histories may emerge from them in strikingly different ways. It also is true that people who are very alike today have arrived there from entirely different places. There are, in human development, no sweepingly simple A-equals-B correlations. Because, in addition to nurture, there is nature. Because we bring to bear on all the experiences of our life the unique and specific qualities we are born with.

This concept of inborn qualities helps explain why Dave, with a mother much like Ray's, withstood her don't-ever-leave-me-you'll-kill-me smothering, fending her off at home and getting out of that home as quickly as he could, working after school at an early age, swooping out of reach at a distant college—"College ruined you for me," she once told him—and eventually picking a wife who had a self-contained and busy life of her own and who could love him at an undemanding distance.

"Every once in a while," Dave admits, "I miss the soft breast and the soothing, comforting closeness. When my mother took care, she really knew how to take care." He is quite aware of the losses that he has sustained in order to gain and preserve his autonomy. He lives—sometimes well, sometimes not so well—with these losses.

By the end of our second year we have made a remarkable journey from oneness into separateness, moving from differentiation on to practicing and then to rapprochement. These overlapping stages of separation-individuation conclude with a fourth but open-ended stage during which we stabilize our inner pictures of our self and others.

This takes some doing.

For in our immature state we cannot hold in our head the strange notion that those who are good can sometimes also be bad. And so our inner images—of mother and of self—are split in two.

There is an all-good self—I'm a totally wonderful person.

And an all-bad self—I'm a totally rotten person.

There is an all-good mother—she gives me whatever I need.

And an all-bad mother—she gives me nothing I need.

Early in childhood we seem to believe that these different selves and mothers are different people.

There are grown-up women and men who never stop doing this, who engage in some form of splitting all their lives, who—to a greater or lesser extent—dwell in a rigid world of black-and-white categories. They may alternate between an excessive self-love and just as excessive a self-hatred. They may idealize their lovers and their friends. And then, when their lovers or friends behave like normal, flawed human beings, they may cast them out of their lives: "You aren't perfect. You have failed me. You are no good."

Splitting is also done by parents who choose one son to be Cain and one to be Abel. And by lovers whose women are either madonnas or whores. And by leaders who brook no dissent: You're either for me or against me. And sometimes by those genial gents with murder in their heart—the Jekylls and Hydes.

Splitting is thought to be universal during early life. We defend the good by keeping the bad away. We quarantine our anger, afraid that our hateful feelings will wipe out those we cherish. But gradually we learn—if there is love and trust enough—to live with ambivalence. Gradually we learn to mend the split.

Now certainly a good-bad, right-wrong, yes-no, on-off universe provides a reassuring simplicity. And certainly even we so-called normal people indulge in splitting now and then. But letting go of our fearful and childish black-and-white simplifications for the difficult ambiguities of real life is another of our necessary losses. And there are, in this letting go, some valuable gains:

For the hated mother who leaves us, and the loved and loving mother who holds us tight, are understood to be one, not two different mothers. The bad, unworthy child and the good, deserving, lovable child are united into a single image of self. Instead of parts of people we begin to see the whole—the merely but magnificently human. And we come to know a self in which feelings of hate can intermingle with feelings of love.

The task is never complete—throughout our lives we will cut and splice these inner pictures. And at times we will see only black and only white. And until the day we die we will continue to edit our "I." But between ages two and three our internal world will begin to possess some measure of constancy.

Self-constancy: An integrated enduring mental picture of an "I."

And object constancy: An inner image of a whole and good-enough mother, an image that can survive our anger and hate, an image—and this is crucial—that can provide the sense of love, of safety, of comfort that our actual mother-in-the-flesh once supplied.

In our early daily encounters with a loving, good-enough mother, we feel safely held, both physically and emotionally. And as we build up memories of being benignly cared for, they become so much part of ourself that our actual mother is gradually needed less and less. We cannot stand alone until we come to possess this inner holding environment, furnished by mother and then by others as well. And although the clusters of memory which create our internal world are often out of reach of our awareness, they can sometimes—as in this experience—be recaptured:

A woman in psychoanalysis had started to discover and savor her strengths. There were resources there which she never knew she possessed. Somewhat to her surprise she found herself literally able to visualize those strengths. But the picture that formed in her mind was, oddly enough, an unknown four-sided wooden structure, pressing just inside her upper chest.

In the mode of psychoanalysis she let herself associate to this picture, and what came to mind, she found, was a tennis press, an image which, because she neither played nor liked the game, left her temporarily perplexed. But further associations led her from tennis press . . . to pressed flowers . . . to pressed butterflies, and a memory suddenly blossomed in her brain: Of a hospital nurse who had tended her when she was a desperately ill and terrified child. Of a gentle, comforting nurse who showed her each day how the gathering shadows of afternoon would cast, on the wall of her room, the shape of a butterfly.

That butterfly pressed inside her has remained an enduring memory—the memory of her nurse's consoling love. Sustaining her as a child in a hospital room with pains—that's right—in her upper chest.

Sustaining me now in my efforts to stand alone.

4

The Private "I"

When I say "I" I mean a thing absolutely unique, not to be confused with any other.

—Ugo Betti

Who is that presumptuous creature daring to stand alone? We answer—proudly, uneasily—"It is I." This "I" is a declaration of a consciousness of self—of some of the selves that we are or once were or might be. Our body and mind, our goals and roles, our lusts and limits, our feelings and capabilities: All and more are contained within that solitary but always upper-case letter.

Our "I"—the "I" we are now—may be making a beef stew, making love; running for office, running in a marathon; being wise in the courtroom and rude at the cleaner's and scared to death at the periodontist's; and knowing that all of these selves, and the six-year-old face in our photograph album, and the sixty-year-old that we sooner or later shall be, are one coherent entity, are part of a single identity, are "I."

In becoming this self, this "I," we have had to let go of the peerless paradise of oneness, the happy illusion of being untouchably safe and the comforting simplicities of a neatly split-off universe where good was only good and bad only bad. In becoming this self we have stepped into a world of aloneness and powerlessness and ambivalence. Aware of our terror and glory we say, "It is I."

As you doubtless already know, there is a model of the mind which divides it into three hypothetical structures: The id, the province of our infantile wishes. The superego, our conscience, our inner judge. And the ego, the seat of perception, memory, action, thought, emotion, defense and self-consciousness—the place where "I" as an inner self-image lives.

This "I"—this self-representation—is built from fragments of experience which our ego integrates into a whole: Experiences of harmony and joyful validation. Experiences of our early human relationships. The theory here is that gradually an image of "psychic self" coalesces around an earlier "body self" image so that, at about eighteen months, we begin to refer to ourself by name, as well as by that unique first person singular.

The "I" to which we refer has taken into itself—has internalized —a picture of I, the lovingly mothered child. But it also has taken in—by becoming like, by an identification with—various aspects of the loving mother.

Identification is one of the central processes by which we build a self.

Identification is why I am bossy, cautious and a lover of books —like my mother.

Identification is why I am superorganized and stubborn—like my father.

Identification is why—since my husband and I are accustomed to showering every day—our once unwashed sons have turned into daily showerers.

Identification is why the apple probably doesn't fall too far from the tree.

Our first identifications tend to be global, all-encompassing. But in time we identify partially and selectively. And as we go on to say, in effect, "I'll be like *this* part of you but not like *that* part," our identifications grow ever more depersonified. In this way we become—not clones of our mother or father or others—but soft-spoken, hard-working, funny, a dancer or prompt. Like Tennyson's Ulysses, we can claim, "I am a part of all that I have met." But these parts have been transformed: We each are artists of the self, creating a collage—a new and original work of art—out of scraps and fragments of identifications.

The people with whom we identify are, positively or negatively, always important to us. Our feelings toward them are, in some way, always intense. And although we may clearly recall a conscious decision to emulate some teacher or movie star, most identifications take place outside of our awareness, take place unconsciously. (It strikes me as I'm writing this that I'm probably still wearing bangs because they were worn by my seventh-grade idol—Pat Norton.)

We identify for many different reasons and usually for several reasons at once. And we often identify to deal with loss, preserving within ourself—by acquiring, say, the style of dress, the accent, the mannerisms—someone we must leave or someone who dies.

And so a middle-aged man starts growing a mustache, soon after his mustachioed father dies.

And a college sophomore switches his major from Government to Psychology, soon after his psychologist mother dies.

And a wife who has always been troubled by her husband's terrible table manners acquires the same rotten manners, soon after he dies.

And a non-churchgoing husband starts attending services regularly, soon after his devoutly religious wife dies.

But our losses needn't be mortal; the everyday losses of growing up will often promote important identifications. For identification can serve us simultaneously as a way to hang on and let go. Indeed, the act of identification often seems to imply "I don't need you to do it; I'll do it myself." It allows us to relinquish important aspects of relationships by taking in these aspects as our own.

Our early identifications are, for the most part, the most influential ones, limiting and shaping all that come later. And while we will identify, permanently or fleetingly, with those we love or envy or admire, we also may identify with those whom we are angry at or scared of.

This so-called "identification with the aggressor" may occur in situations of helplessness and frustration, when someone bigger, stronger or more powerful than we are has us under his or her control. In a spirit reminiscent of "if you can't beat them, join them," we try to resemble the people we fear and hate, hoping in that way to gain their power and thus defend ourselves against the danger that they represent.

Thus the kidnapped heiress Patty Hearst becomes the gun-toting revolutionary Tania.

Thus, through this defensive "identification with the aggressor," the abused child may grow up to be the child abuser.

Identifications can be both active and passive, loving and hating, for better and worse. They can be identifications with someone's impulse, emotion, conscience, achievement, skill, style, goal, hairdo, pain. And over the years, as we modify and harmonize these different identifications—including, of course, our gender identifications as a female or a male; and including, perhaps, a major identification with some religion, profession or class; and including, alas, identifications with terrible as well as excellent qualities—there are possible other selves we will have to discard.

Giving up these possible other selves is one more of our necessary losses.

"Not that I would not, if I could," writes William James,

> be both handsome and fat and well-dressed, and a great athlete, and make a million a year, be a wit, a *bon-vivant*, and a lady-killer, as well as a philosopher; a philanthropist, statesman, warrior, and African explorer, as well as a "tone poet" and saint. But the thing is simply impossible. . . . Such different characters may conceivably at the outset of life be alike possible to a man. But to make any one of them actual, the rest must more or less be suppressed. So the seeker of his truest, strongest, deepest self must review the list carefully, and pick out the one on which to stake his salvation. All other selves thereupon become unreal. . . .

Our failure to more or less harmonize our different identifications—our failure to integrate our separate selves—can lead at the extreme to that bizarre derangement called multiple personality, where (do you remember a movie called *The Three Faces of Eve*?) a number of contradictory selves dwell regularly within a single person. But everywhere around us—managing households, law firms, the country—are people with lesser disorders of the self. Everywhere around us, women and men with disturbances in their sense of wholeness populate our world with emotional casualties.

And we doubtless all have met the kind of people that Winnicott calls false-self personalities.

Or those people that psychoanalyst Helene Deutsch has given the name of as-if personalities.

Or those residents on the edge of the neurotic-psychotic boundary, literally termed the borderline personalities.

Or those current darlings of psycho- and sociological explorations, the self-starved narcissistic personalities.

Each of these names can be used as a way of talking about distortions of self and self-image. Each of these names is attached to slightly different but often overlapping descriptions of damage that has been done to the private "I."

Psychoanalyst Leslie Farber describes what happens to a person when he builds his entire existence around a false self, believing that he must "toy with his own presentation of himself . . . to earn the attention and approval he craves. . . ." Not only does he suffer from the pain and shame of possessing "a secret, unlovely, illegitimate self." He suffers as well from "the spiritual burden of not appearing as the person he 'is,' or not 'being' the person he appears to be. . . ."

Now certainly all of us, some of the time, will tinker with our public presentation. We wish to impress, to please, to placate, to win. And certainly all of us, some of the time, will engage in a certain measure of self-deception, giving ourself a B-plus for what any fair and impartial observer would barely grade C. But certainly most of us, most of the time, will attempt to maintain a reasonable connection between the self that we are and the self we display. For when that connection is broken, the self that we present to the world may be a false self.

Like the woman who, achieving success in a highly competitive field, insists, "What I really am is a poor girl from Brooklyn."

Like the man who speaks about having "two me's, the real me . . . petrified to reveal itself" and "the other me . . . which complied with social demands."

And maybe like Richard Cory, a man "who glittered when he walked"; who was envied for the golden life he led; who was handsome, rich, a gentleman; and who, one summer night, "went home and put a bullet through his head."

People who live their life as a false self.

The true self, as Winnicott talks about it, originates in our earliest relationship, in the sensitive attunement of mother to child. It begins with responses that, in effect, tell us, "You are what you are. You are feeling what you are feeling." Allowing us to believe in our own reality. Persuading us that it is safe to expose our early, fragile, beginning-to-grow true self.

Picture it this way: We reach for a toy, but in the process of reaching we glance for one split second at our mother. We are seeking, not permission, but something more. We are seeking confirmation that this wish, this spontaneous gesture, truly belongs to us. That we feel what we feel.

In that delicate, subtle moment our mother's responsive—and also unintrusive—presence allows us to trust our wish: "Yes, I want this. I do." Confirmed in our budding new sense of self, confirmed in our "self-consciousness," we continue reaching our hand out for the toy.

But when, instead, our mother responds to the question in our eyes by misreading our needs, or replacing them with her own, we can't trust the truth of what we feel or do. Her lack of attunement can make us feel that we have been repudiated, assaulted. And we then may defend our true self by forming a false self.

This false self is compliant. It has no agenda. It seems to be saying, "I'll be what you want me to be." Like a tree that has been espaliered so that spontaneous growth is forestalled, it conforms to a shape imposed upon it from outside. This shape is sometimes attractive, sometimes marvelously attractive, but it is unreal.

The as-if personality, as Helene Deutsch describes him, is more chameleon-like than the false self, for the "readiness to pick up signals from the outer world and to mold oneself and one's behavior accordingly," makes for frequently shifting—but highly persuasive—imitations, first of this kind of person and then of that. The as-if personality is not aware of the hollowness at his core. He lives his life "as if" it were a whole. The expressions he uses, the ties that he chooses, his values, his passions, his pleasures, merely mimic other people's realities. And eventually we are uneasy—we will look at him and think, "Wait: Something is wrong"—in spite of the brilliant show he is putting on. For without his even knowing it, like some humanoid in a science-fiction film, he duplicates only the forms of being human. He acts as if he experiences, but he has no corresponding inner experience.

A funny and brilliant caricature of the as-if personality is presented in Woody Allen's movie *Zelig*, where the hero is a man who has so little sense of himself that he turns into whomever he is with. Leonard Zelig—eager to fit in, to be accepted, to be liked—turns black, Chinese, obese and Indian chief, and appears as a look-alike member of Hitler's brown shirts, the Pope's entourage and Babe Ruth's ball team. Adopting not only their physical but their mental characteristics, Zelig becomes the company he keeps. "I'm nobody: I'm nothing," he tells his psychiatrist. What he is is Leonard Zelig—human chameleon.

The borderline personality divides the good and the bad in himself and in others by the process of splitting described in Chapter Three. Early in childhood he starts to fear that the rage that he (that we all) sometimes feels toward mother will surely destroy her—and then where will he be? But if the woman he hates and the woman he loves can be perceived as two different women, he then will be able to hate with impunity. And so he splits.

The borderline, according to psychoanalyst Otto Kernberg, lives a fragmented, moment-to-moment life, "actively cutting off the emotional links between what would otherwise become chaotic, contradictory, highly frustrating and frightening emotional experiences. . . ." Although the borderline feels love and hate, he never can bring them together, for fear that the bad is going to poison the good. And threatened with the unbearable guilt and anxiety such imagined destruction would bring, he may love you on Mondays and Wednesdays, and he may hate you on Tuesdays and Thursdays and alternate Saturdays, but he will not do both simultaneously. He splits.

Not surprisingly, the borderline is unstable in his moods and in his relationships. He is often impulsive and physically self-damaging. He may find it difficult to be alone. But the borderline's outstanding trait is the splitting which lets him tolerate profound contradictions in his thoughts and his deeds, with different aspects of his self disconnected—like separate islands—from each other.

The narcissist is commonly viewed as excessively self-adoring. (How do I love me? Let me count the ways.) But in fact it is the absence of a stable internal self-love—a healthy narcissism—that inspires in him such consuming concern about it. Pressing him to use other people for pure self-enhancement. Pressing him to use them as reflections and extensions of himself.

I must be attractive—see the beautiful women on my arm.

I must be important—I hang around with celebrities.

I must be exciting—I'm always the star, the center of attention.

I must be—mustn't I?

Something has gone awry in the development of a confident inner self-love.

Freud said that the love that we had for ourself before we knew that anyone else existed was original narcissism—primary narcissism. He said that later on, when we withdrew our love from others to love ourself, we were displaying secondary narcissism. He said that the more we loved ourself, the less we could love another. He said love of self and other were opposed. And he left us with the impression that narcissism most certainly wasn't a good thing.

In recent years, however, some psychoanalysts—particularly Heinz Kohut—have challenged this negative, polarized view of narcissism. Narcissism, says Kohut, is normal, is healthy, is important, is a good thing. And a hearty love of self will enrich and complement—not deplete—our love of others.

How do we acquire a desirable—but not overweening—self-love?

Kohut seems to be saying that we begin with a sense of being and possessing all that is perfect and powerful and good. And in order for us to come to terms with the limits of human grandeur, we first require a narcissistic fix.

For there is a time in our life when we need to strut our stuff and groove on grandiosity, when we need to be viewed as remarkable and rare, when we need to exhibit ourself in front of a mirror that reflects our self-admiration, when we need a parent to function as that mirror.

(What this means is the simple delight that a parent is able to take in her child, the pleasure she feels, the praise she is able to offer, the ability to respond to an exhibitionistic "Hey, ma, look at me!" with pride and encouragement. What it certainly doesn't mean is total indulgence and an absence of all frustration. Everybody needs some frustration to grow on.)

There is also a time in our life when we need to participate in the perfection of another, when we need to say, "You're wonderful and you're mine," when we need to enlarge ourself through our connection with some flawless omnipotent being, when we need a parent to function as that ideal.

(What this means is the calmness and confidence that a parent can offer his child, a parental infusion of glory and power and strength, a protectiveness that says, in effect, "I am here—you don't have to do it all by yourself," a willingness to be an invincible ally. What it certainly doesn't mean is that a parent has to be a superhero.)

There is a time in our life—in our early childhood—when we need to be larger than life, a golden self. And we need to believe that our actual self—the eager, jubilant, preening self we reveal—is accepted, at least for a little while, as golden.

When our mother and father can do this for us—not all of the time, just some of the time, just . . . enough—they are serving as parts of ourself which we can make ours. And supplied with these vital ingredients in the making of a self, we then can let them go —we then can modulate and transform them into something more realistic, more human-dimensioned:

A positive self-image.

A sturdy self-esteem.

And a love of self that sets us free to love others.

But without this narcissistic fix, we are stuck at a stage of archaic, infantile narcissism. We cannot move on. We cannot let it go. Others may then become for us, not human partners in a caring relationship, but ways of providing those missing pieces of self.

And so the narcissist seeks admiring people, hoping to make that admiration his own. And so the narcissist looks for powerful people, hoping that he can make that power his own. However, as Kohut observes, these sought-for people are "not loved or admired for their attributes, and the actual features of their personality . . . are only dimly recognized." Indeed, they are not truly friends or lovers or marriage partners or children, but parts of the narcissist's self—merely "self-objects."

A composite portrait of one kind of narcissistic personality— call her Peggy—might show her to be vital and intense, romanticizing and sexualizing all of life's daily events, overenthusiastic and overdramatic. Beneath all this pseudo-vitality, though, is an inner deadness and emptiness, a fill-me-up hunger, a what's-it-all-about dread. And behind the gestures and garments that insistently scream "Look at me!" are feelings of inauthenticity and worthlessness.

Peggy avoids dependency. She is terrified of intimacy. She goes through people like purse-size packets of Kleenex. Always on the move, she tries to flee her fear of aging and mortality. And without real ties to the future and past, those caring investments in others, those loving memories, she lives in an anxiety-haunted now.

Checking her face for wrinkles every morning.

Keeping her calendar filled every night of the week.

Constantly running to doctors with a chronic, nagging case of hypochondria.

And filled with boundless rage, the rage of the disappointed unempathized-with child.

I knew a man—call him Don—who was another kind of narcissist: He compulsively conquered women and took them to bed. His proudest boast was that in the course of one exhausting night he had slept with three different women in three different neighborhoods, "using"—it was during a gasoline shortage—"only public means of transportation."

In his relationships with women Don would convert them, again and again, into idealizations. They had beauty, brilliance and— always!—spiritual depth. His subsequent, often immediate, disillusionment sent him searching for replacements. He had many wives, many lovers, and he knew none of them.

My favorite fictional narcissist is not a man but a toad. He can be found in *archy and mehitabel*. His name is warty bliggens, and he sits beneath a toadstool in glossy contentment and he

> considers himself to be
> the center of the . . .
> universe
> the earth exists
> to grow toadstools for him
> to sit under
> the sun to give him light
> by day and the moon
> and wheeling constellations
> to make beautiful
> the night for the sake of
> warty bliggens

How's that for grandiosity!

Some narcissists display an "I'm the greatest" grandiosity. Others are grandiose in more indirect ways. But their haughtiness and contempt, or their promiscuity and antisocial behavior, or their lies about their accomplishments, or their inability ever to say "I don't know," hint at a fantasy world where they believe they know and control and are allowed *everything*, and where they are very special. *Very* special.

For a glimpse of this sense of specialness, take a look at this dream, reported by a patient to his psychiatrist:

"The question was raised of finding a successor for me.

I thought: How about God?"

The trouble with grandiosity is that it is vulnerable. It is relentlessly and inevitably vulnerable. For no matter how triumphant we are, no matter how high we may climb, the course of a normal life will lead us to losses. To illness. To age. To both physical and mental limitations. To separation and loneliness and death. These are difficult experiences—even with family and philosophy and religion, even with links to something beyond our frail flesh. Without such links, however, without some larger meaning beyond the "m" and the "e," the passage of time can only bring horror on horror. In the face of this long-term reality it is astounding how long the narcissist can deny it, convinced that youth and beauty, health and power, admiration and confirmation will endure forever.

Of course they do not.

When the talent flags, when the beauty fades, when the brilliant career declines, the world no longer reflects Narcissus's perfection. And because the mirrored self is the only self that he has acknowledged, he loses that self and sinks into depression. Depression—the other, dark side of grandiosity—is a likely response to the narcissist's hurt self-esteem, triggered by a trivial slight or a minor disappointment as well as by life's harsher inevitabilities.

"All her substitute mirrors were broken," an analyst writes of an aging depressed woman patient, "and she again stood helpless and confused, like the little girl once did before her mother's face in which she did not find herself. . . ."

The narcissist may also feel depleted and depressed whenever he loses his idealized self-objects. For having made them his source of all that is powerful and blissful, how powerless, how empty he is without them. And he may attempt to flee emptiness through drug or alcohol highs, through frenetic sexual conquests, through perilous hobbies. Or he may seek the shared narcissistic retreat of some religious cult, where "the total involvement, the endless routine, the compulsive chanting and the ritual meditation" help fill "the almost unimaginable voids. . . ."

As part of a magical, mystical whole with claims to perfect enlightenment, he tries to find an augmentation of self. As part of a joyful, blissed-out whole which banishes "negative thoughts," he tries to retrieve the rapture of infantile narcissism.

At the heart of these narcissistic lacks are experiences with unempathic parents; with parents who could not or would not be available; with parents who were rejecting or disapproving or disappointing or simply uninterested. Cynthia Macdonald, in her chilling poem "Accomplishments," captures a daughter's frenzy as she tries to wrest confirmation from her mother:

> I painted a picture—green sky—and showed it to my mother.
> She said that's nice, I guess.
> So I painted another holding the paintbrush in my teeth,

Look, Ma, no hands. And she said
I guess someone would admire that if they knew
How you did it and they were interested in painting which
    I am not.

I played clarinet solo in Gounod's Clarinet Concerto
With the Buffalo Philharmonic. Mother came to listen and said
That's nice, I guess.
So I played it with the Boston Symphony,
Lying on my back and using my toes,
Look, Ma, no hands. And she said
I guess someone would admire that if they knew
How you did it and they were interested in music which
    I am not.

I made an almond souffle and served it to my mother.
She said, that's nice, I guess.
So I made another, beating it with my breath,
Serving it with my elbows,
Look, Ma, no hands. And she said
I guess someone would admire that if they knew
How you did it and they were interested in eating which
    I am not.

So I sterilized my wrists, performed the amputation, threw away
My hands and went to my mother, but before I could say
Look, Ma, no hands, she said
I have a present for you and insisted I try on
The blue kid gloves to make sure they were the right size.

Sometimes the troubled narcissist had parents who did offer love, except—the love they offered was of the wrong kind. Their love was not for the child as himself but only for child-as-ornament, a self-adorning flower in their lapel.

Narcissists are often the children of narcissists.

Such narcissistic parents unconsciously use and misuse their children. Do well. Be good. Make me proud. Don't aggravate me. The unspoken deal is this: If you will bury the parts I don't like, then I will love you. The unspoken choice is this: Lose yourself or lose me.

It is important to keep remembering that sometimes good-enough parents fail to mesh with a particular child and that, if there is damage, it may result from a sorrowful mismatch and not from indifference, incompetence or villainy. But whatever the cause, the lack of these crucial mirroring and idealizing experiences endangers the cohesiveness of self. Defending against the threat to that self, and urgently trying to compensate for its lacks, the pathological narcissist is born.

Now we all have had experiences, in the course of normal development, of being false, as if, split, narcissistic. We all have had experiences of being unconnected with our self. We all have had experiences of thinking, "Why did I say that? I don't really mean that," of harboring distinctly contrary selves, of trying to hide our unacceptable selves, of being quite different selves with different people.

But the people described in the pages above are exhibiting more than everyday distortions, or par-for-the-course confusions and uncertainties. They are suffering from important impairments in their early development which interfere with their necessary losses—with the giving up of the needs, defenses, delusions that stand in the way of a robust, integrated sense of self.

For healthy growth involves being able to give up our need for approval when the price of that approval is our true self.

It means being able to give up defensively splitting and to integrate our good with our bad self.

It means being able to give up our grandiosity and make do with a human-proportioned self.

It means that although we may, in the course of our life, be beset by emotional difficulties, we possess a reliable self, a sense of identity.

What we call our sense of identity is our sense that our truest, strongest, deepest self persists over time in spite of constant change. It is a sense of selfsameness that is deeper than any differences, a true self on which all our other selves converge. This steadying sameness includes both what we are and what we are not. It includes our identifications and our distinctiveness. And it also includes both our private, inner "I am I" experiences and the recognition by others that "Yes, you are you."

This support and response from others is important at any time, but it is of special importance in our infancy. For none of us can possibly begin to have an "I" without some early assistance from an "other." All of us, in the beginning, need a mother who helps us be, a mother who helps us reach out and claim what is ours, a mother who helps us establish a central certainty—as unquestioned as our heartbeat—that our wishes and our feelings are our own. In the beginning we cannot fulfill and, furthermore, cannot recognize our needs. Our mother helps us fulfill and helps us recognize them.

In recognizing our needs, and in claiming our feelings as our own, we start to have a sense of our self *being*. We lose our unselfconsciousness, an existence without a self, without an identity.

We begin to create and discover our private "I."

5

Lessons in Love

For love . . . is the blood of life, the power of reunion in the separated.

—Paul Tillich

Being a separate self is a most glorious, most lonely proposition. Loving oneself is nice but . . . incomplete. Separateness is sweet but connection with someone outside ourself is surely sweeter. Our daily existence requires both closeness and distance, the wholeness of self, the wholeness of intimacy. We reconcile oneness and separateness through ordinary earthbound human love.

Our mother—our first lover—gives us our earliest lessons in love. She is our succor and shelter. She is our safety. Our mother loves without limits, without conditions, without self-interests or expectations. She lives for us. She unquestioningly would die for us.

What are we talking about?

For surely our flesh-and-blood mother was no such paragon. She wearied and resented and complained. She certainly loved other people and she didn't always love us, and there must have been times when we bored, annoyed and enraged her. And yet, if a mother is good enough, so Winnicott has argued, that goodness is experienced as perfection. If she is simply *good enough*, our wishes and dreams and fantasies confirm, she gives us a taste of unconditional love.

But when the mother of oneness becomes the mother of separation, we learn about the limitations of love. We learn the prices we have to pay, the prices we cannot pay, that sometimes love fails us, that sometimes we want and don't get. And by reconciling all this into life-size images of others and of self, we begin to give up what we have to give up—we begin to accept the necessary losses which are the precondition of human love.

Not everyone does.

And some of us will continue demanding unconditional mother love dressed in the guise of adult love relations, furious when a partner expects some mutual giving and taking, furious when he expects *his* needs to be met. Some of us will keep demanding unconditional mother love and then, if our partner should ask, "What's in this for me?" we may actually find the question incomprehensible.

For infantile love, remember, is experienced as harmony, is experienced as "her needs and mine are one." It is when we start to separate that we learn that mothers and babies have different agendas. It is when we start to separate that we learn to love the mother-who-is-not-me.

While grown-up love must begin with the separation of self from other, the wish to undo that separation persists. And being in love, it is argued—no matter how wonderfully mature we lovers may be—contains the wish to return to our mother's arms. We will never relinquish that wish, but we can infuse it with the capacity to be loving as well as loved, to give—not just get. "The more I give to thee," says Juliet, "the more I have, for both are infinite." We need not be star-crossed lovers, or masochistic, or oppressed by male chauvinist pigs to recognize the truth in Shakespeare's poetry.

Psychoanalyst Erich Fromm, in his little book *The Art of Loving*, distinguishes between childish and grown-up love. And although it is a distinction more easily made in print than in life, it suggests a spectrum on which we all can place ourselves:

"Infantile love follows the principle 'I love because I am loved.'

"Mature love follows the principle 'I am loved because I love.'

"Immature love says 'I love you because I need you.'

"Mature love says 'I need you because I love you.' "

But we cannot get to mature without passing through infantile.

We cannot love unless we know what love *is*. We cannot love others as others unless we possess sufficient self-love, a love we learn from being loved in infancy. And we cannot talk about love, about love that is infantile or mature, unless we are also prepared to talk about hate.

Hate is a word that makes most people uncomfortable. Hate can be ugly, excessive, out of control. Hate is a substance poisonous to the soul. Hate is not nice.

Far worse than not nice is the notion that we harbor feelings of hate toward the people we love, that we wish them some ill along with wishing them well, that even our purest love is something less than purest love, is stained with ambivalence. Freud writes that "With the exception of only a very few situations, there adheres to the tenderest and most intimate of our love-relations a small portion of hostility. . . ." It is doubtful that you and I are among the exceptions.

The presence of hate in love is commonplace but is only reluctantly acknowledged. On occasion, however, we face it in ourselves. Soaked to the skin as I wait in the rain for a husband who is twenty minutes late, I shriek with complete sincerity, "I could kill you." And when, on the stage, a tragedienne sighs, "Ah, I have loved too deeply not to hate," I am able to confess I have felt that way too.

But when Winnicott lists eighteen reasons why, in his view, all loving mothers hate their baby, I—and most mothers—tend to recoil with horror. Wrong! we insist. Not true! we insist. No, no! He asks us to pause for a moment and consider a nursery rhyme, a rhyme we have crooned as we rocked our loved baby to sleep. "When the bough breaks the cradle will fall. Down will come baby, cradle and all," is not, he convincingly notes, a friendly message. Indeed, it expresses some motherly feelings very far removed from sentimentality. Which is all right with Winnicott.

For sentimentality, Winnicott writes, serves no useful purpose. It harms because "it contains a denial of hate. . . ." And such a denial, he argues, will prevent the developing child from facing and learning to tolerate his own hatred. ("My *parents* never have such horrid feelings. What kind of monster am *I* to have such feelings?") We need to learn to tolerate our hate.

A four-year-old boy, whose parents we might presume to be unsentimental, sings this song to himself in his tub every evening:

He will just do nothing at all.
He will just sit there in the noonday sun.
And when they speak to him, he will not answer them.
Because he does not care to.
He will stick them with spears and put them in the garbage.
When they tell him to eat his dinner, he will just laugh at them . . .
He will not speak to nobody because he doesn't have to.
And when they come to look for him they will not find him,
Because he will not be there.
He will put spikes in their eyes and put them in the garbage,
And put the cover on.
He will not go out in the fresh air or eat his vegetables
Or make wee-wee for them, and he will get thin as a marble.
He will not do nothing at all.
He will just sit there in the noonday sun.

I expect there will be no dispute about the claim that this song conveys a certain . . . hostility. Spikes in the eyes are, all would agree, not nice. But what still seems up for debate is whether hostility and hate are expressions of a basic aggressive instinct, or whether human aggression is nothing more than our expression of disappointed, deprived or frustrated love.

Freud took the first position and argued that all of us are fueled by two basic instincts—an aggressive instinct just as well as a sexual one. However—and this is absolutely central to his thesis —sex and aggression are normally intermixed. Thus the most vicious and violent act also possesses some unconscious sexual meaning. Thus the most gentle and loving act always possesses some element—"We'll eat you up—we love you so!"—of hate.

Freud writes:

It is indeed foreign to our intelligence as well as to our feelings thus to couple love and hate; but Nature, by making use of this pair of opposites, contrives to keep love ever vigilant and fresh, so as to guard it against the hate which lurks behind it. It might be that we

owe the fairest flowerings of our love to the reaction against the
hostile impulses which we sense within us.

In other words, we can fend off the hate by emphasizing the
love. But in our unconscious, says Freud, we are all still murderers.

There are those who claim, on the other hand, that human
beings are intrinsically loving and good. Aggression is a reaction;
it isn't innate. This imperfect world into which we are born is the
cause of our rage and cruelty and hostility. Improve the world—
through Christ, through Marx, through Freud, through Gloria
Steinem—and eventually we will do away with hate.

Meanwhile, however, hate—in its innate and/or environmental
form—is alive and well and mixing it up with love. Indeed, psychoanalyst Rollo May contends that both are part of what he characterizes as the daimonic, which includes sex *and* aggression, the
creative *and* the destructive, the noble *and* the vile.

The daimonic May talks about is "the urge in every being to
affirm itself, assert itself, perpetuate and increase itself." It is a
force beyond good and evil. It is a force which—if unchanneled—
can drive us blindly to copulate and kill, a force which—if repudiated—can leave us apathetic and half alive, a force which—if
integrated into our self—can vitalize all of our experience.

Thus love is not threatened by the daimonic, but by our denial
of it, by our failure to greet it—aggression and all—as our own.
May quotes the poet Rilke who fears, "If my devils are to leave
me, I am afraid my angels will take flight as well." Rilke is right,
says May. We must embrace both.

The luminous Liv Ullmann, who has been called the world's
most charismatic actress, smiles when she hears about Rilke's
angels and devils, telling me that she always ("it's because of the
way I looked") was asked to play "angel" roles. She describes a
moment of revelation when she was rehearsing *The Chalk Garden*,
a play in which she portrayed a woman who, fleeing the ravages
of revolution, finds an infant abandoned by its mother.

"My interpretation was to sit down and look tenderly and softly at the baby. Sing to it, pick it up and then take it with me." But her director, she recalls, told her to dig deeper, to show the woman's doubts, her cowardice, her ambivalence in the face of such responsibility. Don't be so noble, she was advised. You don't have to represent goodness all the time.

In her final interpretation of the role, Liv, as the woman Grusha, picks up the baby "but puts it down as she realizes what a hindrance it will be. . . . She stands up and walks away. Stops. Doubts. Turns back. Reluctantly sits down again. Looks at the little bundle. Looks away. Then, finally, she picks it up with a gesture of resignation and runs on. . . .

"Only then," concludes Liv, "when no situation or character is obviously good or evil, is it truly interesting to act."

Liv talks about how fascinating this was to her—"to show both, to show the struggle"—for she had always been taught that "good children had no bad thoughts." Liv says that now, in her life and in her art, she knows that "we have to *work* to be good people, that goodness always involves the *choice* to be good."

To acknowledge our aggression is not an argument for brutality or, God forbid, for letting it all hang out. Nor does it challenge the view that, even in spite of our ambivalence, loving feelings will frequently prevail. The point is simply that yes, we also can hate our beloved mate, child, parents, dear friend. The point is that trying to say to ourselves, "This nasty stuff has nothing to do with me," depletes and in the long run may endanger us.

We too once used to be four-year-olds with hateful words on our tongue. Perhaps we were told, "You don't really feel that way." Perhaps we were taught that love means never having the wish to put spikes in your true love's eye.

That is a lie.

Our mother gives us our earliest lessons in love—and its partner, hate. Our father—our "second other"—elaborates on them. Offering us an alternative to the mother-baby relationship. Pulling us out of oneness into the world. Presenting a masculine model which can supplement and contrast with the feminine. And providing us with further and perhaps quite different meanings of *lovable* and *loving* and *being loved*.

It is time now to pause and take note of the fact that *fathers* and babies can form early, strong attachments, and that short of providing milk from their breasts, fathers can do whatever mothers can do. Fathers can be, and some of them are, their infant's primary caretaker. But having said this, are we saying that mothers and fathers are readily interchangeable?

The answer seems to be a qualified no.

Michael Yogman of Harvard Medical School and Boston Children's Hospital, whose research has been contributing valuable new information about the father-infant relationship, argues that "the father's role with young infants is far less biologically constrained than once thought." He writes that studies show fathers to be as sensitive as mothers to their infant's emotional cues and as skillful at responding to them. Furthermore, he notes, studies of the development of attachment with infants of ages six to twenty-four months "provide conclusive evidence . . . that infants are attached to fathers as well as to mothers."

However—and there are some crucial howevers, he notes—mothers and fathers respond to their infants, and infants respond to their mothers and their fathers, in clearly and consistently different ways:

Our fathers are more physical and more stimulating. Our mothers are more verbal and more soothing. Our fathers spend less of their time with us in caretaking tasks—the greater part of their time is spent in play. Our fathers tend to provide us with more novelty, more excitement, more events outside the routine of the everyday, and we, in turn, react with more arousal. We also (though more so if male) are more inclined to play with our fathers but we would rather have mommy than daddy when we feel stressed. And although both our mother and father can very very deeply invest in their relationship with us, biology may set the stage for a level of mother-child intimacy that fathers can only develop over time.

Dr. Yogman concludes that fathers and mothers give us "qualitatively different" experiences in infancy and that the roles of mothers and fathers are not interchangeable, not identical, but reciprocal. And while noting the benefits to everyone of fathers' increased involvement with their babies, he also makes the point that the "biological component of parenting may well prove to be weaker in men than women."

Comparing his role as father to his wife Susan's role as mother of Amanda, journalist Bob Greene makes a similar point:

> "We're not very happy today," Susan said to Amanda this morning. "You only slept from eleven to five. . . ."
> I think Susan means exactly that: "*We're* not very happy today." She uses the first person plural so much that it can't be a slip of the tongue; when she thinks of Amanda, she thinks of herself; when she thinks of herself, she thinks of Amanda. As much as I love Amanda, the relationship is not the same; in my mind we are still separate people. In this era of new attitudes on the part of men, I wonder if other fathers are different? . . .
> Somehow I don't think so. I think there's a built-in distance there that, if you're a man, you can never quite close. You can try all you want, but it won't happen.

A lot of feminists will disagree.

But sociologist Alice Rossi, in a dazzling analysis of parenting and sex roles, supports Dr. Yogman's research and Bob Greene's experiences. Indeed, she maintains that "no known society replaces the mother as the primary infant-tender except in cases of small and special categories of women," and that there are good "biosocial" reasons for this. ("A biosocial perspective," she explains, "does not argue that there is a genetic determination of what men can do compared to women; rather, it suggests that the biological contributions shape what is learned and that there are differences in the ease with which the sexes can learn certain things.")

Dr. Rossi argues that in the course of a long human history spent in hunting and gathering societies, women developed (and still in part possess) the selective adaptations which have made them better than men at raising young. (Yes, of course there are exceptions; she is speaking only of women as a group.) She also argues that hormonal cyclicity, pregnancy and birth may establish a biologically based predisposition in mothers to relate to their infants, at least in the first few months, more intensely than fathers do. And she speculates that important residues of this stronger maternal attachment may continue well beyond infancy.

What does she make of all this? She concludes that even early education on fathering, and even the most earnest equal-opportunity household, may not succeed in undoing our evolutionary heritage or in equalizing the intensity of mother-baby and father-baby attachments. She then goes on to predict that our mother will probably remain the parent who is emotionally most important to us.

This isn't meant to suggest that fathers aren't important to our early development. They are, without any question, hugely important. As constructive disrupters of the mother-child unit. As fosterers of autonomy and individuation. As models of masculinity for their sons. As confirmers of femininity for their daughters. And as the other-than-mother figure who provides a second source of steadfast love.

Our father presents an optional set of rhythms and responses for us to connect to. As a second home base, he makes it safer to roam. With him as an ally—a love—it is safer, too, to show that we're mad when we're mad at our mother. We can hate and not be abandoned, hate and still love.

Our father is someone to turn to when we need to resist the lure of re-merger with mother—and when we need to mourn that paradise lost. We cannot let go successfully of symbiotic union unless we can feel the sadness of letting go. Our father—concerned and supportive—makes that mourning less intense, and therefore possible.

Psychoanalyst Stanley Greenspan pictures our father on the shore as we struggle from the symbiotic waters. He holds out a hand and helps us climb out and move on. He is there as our second beloved, as a further and entirely other experience, adding richness and range to our understanding of what love is all about.

And if we have no father, we will long for him.

Indeed, there is a condition we might label father hunger, a yearning for that further, other love. Achievement and beauty, family and friends, even a cherished child may not suffice to chase that hunger away. On a quiet summer day Liv Ullmann speaks of the death of her father and of her continuing search for father love.

There is anger in her voice as she recalls her "mother and grandmother, screaming and crying, in competition for which one grieved the most." For Liv, who was six when her father died, was never granted the status of a mourner. Her grief was unacknowledged and uncomforted.

Nor was this grief really integrated into Liv's experience, because, she recalls, "I didn't believe he had gone. I would sit there at the window, thinking he would come. I wrote letters to him in heaven. I would put his picture under my pillow, take my animals into bed and then we would go off on a long fantasy journey to meet him."

It is not difficult to summon up the dreaming child in the freckle-faced, unintimidatingly beautiful woman with the direct blue eyes and long taffy-colored hair. It is not difficult to imagine her as a child, waking from nightmares to wish on the moon "that no one I loved would leave me." Nor is it difficult to imagine her, raised in a household of women, embracing the mother-made myth of a godlike dead man who was "kind, wise, protective, wonderful, perfect." Liv has written:

> I tried for a long time to remember Papa . . . who was in my life for six years and did not leave me with one real memory of him. Just a great lack. That cut into me so deeply that many of life's experiences relate to it. The void Papa's death left in me became a kind of cavity, into which later experiences were to be laid.

At twenty-one, Liv married a psychiatrist who "was everything I thought my father was, everything my mother told me about him." A few years later she left him for another protector, the great Swedish director, Ingmar Bergman. "My connections with men," says Liv, "are all about trying to reach my father, about trying to fill a childhood void, about believing that such a man exists and getting angry at poor innocent men for not being that man."

Her connections with men are still about father hunger.

But Liv is in her forties now. The affair with Bergman ended years ago. The daughter they had together is almost grown up.

She has known other men. My question: Since Liv is so clearly able to see what she does with men, and since she is so substantial, such a *mensch*, isn't it possible now to start doing things differently? Liv's honest, unabashed answer: Probably not.

"I can take it out and look at it," she explains, "but I think it will always be there. It is so deeply rooted, so basic, that it will not be resolved."

What will she do with it then? She answers, "Live with it. And try to be forgiving with myself."

We discover, from early experiences of passionate intensity, the pleasures love can offer, and the pain. We repeat and repeat our lessons all our life. And maybe, like Liv Ullmann, we may even be able to say, "Hey, there I go again."

But sometimes the repetitions are outside of our awareness.

And sometimes the lessons we learn are not too terrific.

I play with a little girl who has traumatically lost her mother and her father. In the midst of our fun she stops, stands up, says "Bye." Her style seems to be: "I'm leaving you first, before you go off and leave me." And I wonder if she will grow up compelled to always leave what she loves before it can hurt her, a practitioner of relationship interruptus.

I know a little boy whose mother pushes him away. "I'm busy," she tells him. "Not now. You're bothering me." Watching him pester and whine and plead and ragingly kick at her always locked bedroom door, I wonder what he will be doing with women twenty years from now and what he will want, need, women to do to him.

There is in human nature a compulsion to repeat. Indeed it is called the repetition compulsion. It impels us to do again and again what we have done before, to attempt to restore an earlier state of being. It impels us to transfer the past—our ancient longings, our defenses against those longings—onto the present.

Thus whom we love and how we love are revivals—unconscious revivals—of early experience, even when revival brings us pain. And although we may play Iago instead of Othello, Desdemona instead of Iago, we will act out the same old tragedies unless awareness and insight intervene.

That little boy, for instance, may play out his helplessness as a passive, submissive husband. He may play out his murderous rage as a wife-beating husband. He may choose his mother's role and become a cold you-have-to-beg-me-for-it husband. Or he may, like his absent father, simply abandon his wife and his own son to their fate.

That little boy may marry the psychological spitting image of his mother. He may work his wife over until she becomes that mother. He may ask his wife the impossible and then, when she refuses him, he may rail, "You always refuse me—just like my mother."

In repeating the past that boy might repeat his fury or humiliation or grief. Or he might repeat the tactics by which he beat back fury, humiliation, grief. In repeating the past he will update the script to include the shadings of subsequent experience. But whom he loves and how he loves will reflect that whining, pleading, raging boy.

For many men the denial of dependency on their mother is repeated in their subsequent relationships, sometimes by an absence of any sexual interest in women, sometimes by a pattern of loving and leaving them. For other men and women, however, dependency is the point of love relationships; and whomever they take to bed will always be (at least in their head) the ever-yearned-for, gratifying mother.

A lesbian relationship—like the one Karen Snow describes in her novel *Willo*—may also repeat love patterns of early childhood:

> Out of boredom, Pete takes a job welding in an aircraft plant. But the long hours of manual labor do not change her into the man. She is still the self-sacrificing one who will continue to cook and wash and iron and scrub floors. She will spend large chunks of her wages on Willo. . . .
>
> The masculine-feminine bond is frail compared with this mother-daughter bond. Each girl is merely moving in grooves that were carved deep into her early in childhood. Willo has always been the aloof princess served and scolded by a coarse, martyred woman; in fact, by two martyred women: her mother and her sister. Pete has

always been subservient to a glamorous mother, who was usually away from home, achieving. She has been housekeeper and cook, too, for a busy, burly father who had wanted a son.

In describing his taste in women, baby doctor/political activist Benjamin Spock also reveals a repetition compulsion, for, as he points out, "I have always been fascinated by rather severe women, women I then could charm despite their severity." The model for these women—as Dr. Spock is well aware—was his own demanding and highly critical mother. And if, in his early eighties, he is indeed a most exceptionally charming man, the wish to win over his mother may help explain why.

"I have always been amazed," he says, "at men who were able to love somewhat soft women." Such conquests, he suggests, are too easy to matter. "I always needed someone who thought I was special but who also offered a challenge." He says that both his first wife, Jane, and his second wife, Mary Morgan, are versions— although in quite different ways—of this type.

(Because Dr. Spock volunteered "to give permission for you and Mary to talk about me behind my back," let me note here that Mary Morgan disagrees. She maintains that she isn't this critical type of woman that Spock is describing. But, she adds, "He keeps trying to make me into that person"—which is also, of course, a compulsion to repeat.)

We repeat the past by reproducing earlier conditions, challenging as that can sometimes be, like the woman described by Freud who managed to find not one, not two, but three different husbands, all of whom fell fatally ill soon after they were married and subsequently had to be nursed by her on their deathbed.

We also repeat the past by superimposing parental images onto the present, myopic as that frequently can be, failing to recognize that being gentle doesn't have to mean being weak (daddy, alas, was gentle but he was weak), that silence may be companionable not punishing (mother's silences were always punishing) and that gentle, quiet people may be offering something new—if we could but see it.

We even repeat the past when we quite consciously are trying not to repeat it, hopeless as that may turn out to be, like the woman who disdained her parents' conventional and patriarchal marriage and decided that hers would have an entirely new format. Was her mother completely ruled by her bossy husband? Well, then, this lady's mate would be the ruled-over type. And furthermore she would be so unconventional, modern and free that she would openly bring her lovers into their house. But she then allowed her lovers to abuse her and humiliate her—I suppose her notion of modern was anything goes—and so, in her freewheeling life as an autonomous woman and wife she arranged to repeat her mother's despised submissiveness.

The repetition compulsion, writes Freud, explains why this one is always betrayed by his friends and why that one is always abandoned by his protégés and why each of a lover's love affairs may pass through similar stages and end the same way. For although there are people, writes Freud, who seem to be "pursued by a malignant fate, or possessed by some 'daemonic' power . . . their fate is for the most part arranged by themselves and determined by early infantile influences."

It seems reasonable to us to wish to transfer the pleasing past onto the present, to seek to repeat the delights of earlier days, to fall in love with those who resemble the first beloved objects of our affection, to do it again because we loved it the first time. If mom was truly wonderful, why shouldn't her son want to marry a girl like the girl who married dear old dad? Surely all normal love —it needn't be kinky, it needn't be blatantly incestuous—is bound to partake in part of transference love.

Repeating the good makes sense but we have trouble understanding the compulsion to repeat what causes pain. And while Freud has tried to explain this compulsion as part of a dubious concept called the death instinct, it can also be understood as our hopeless effort to undo—rewrite—the past. In other words, we do it and do it and do it and do it again in the hope that this time the ending will be different. We keep repeating the past—when we were helpless and acted upon—trying to master and change what has already happened.

In repeating painful experience we are refusing to lay to rest our childhood ghosts. We continue to clamor for something that cannot be. No matter how hard they clap for us now, she will never clap for us *then*. We have to relinquish that hope. We have to let go.

For we cannot climb into a time machine, become that long-gone child and get what we want when we oh so desperately wanted it. The days for that getting are over, finished, done. We have needs we can meet in different ways, in better ways, in ways that create new experience. But until we can mourn that past, until we can mourn and let go of that past, we are doomed to repeat it.

Weaving the past with the present, we can experience many kinds and stages of love. We can love, one way or another, throughout our life. "Only connect!" a character in E. M. Forster's *Howards End* exhorts us. And needy, tender, romantic, ecstatic, fearful, heedless, hopeful—how we do try!

We try through sexual love—the physical thrum and orgastic release; through eros—the urge for union and creation; through motherly love and brotherly love and neighborly love and friendship; through *caritas*—an altruistic loving. We try through human relationships that draw on one, or all, of the above. Shaped in whole or in part and for good or for ill by the instructors of our childhood, we try to love.

We try and we keep on trying because an unconnected life is not worth living. A life of solitude cannot be borne. In an eloquent passage, Erich Fromm writes:

> Man is gifted with reason; he is *life being aware of itself*. . . . This awareness of himself as a separate entity, the awareness of his own short life span, of the fact that without his will he is born and against his will he dies, that he will die before those whom he loves, or they before him, the awareness of his aloneness and separateness, of his helplessness before the forces of nature and of society, all this makes his separate, disunited existence an unbearable prison. He would become insane could he not liberate himself from this prison and reach out, unite. . . .

And so our noble achievement—the winning of separateness, of self—will also always be our grievous loss. That loss is necessary —there can be no human love without that loss. But through our love that loss may be transcended.

II The Forbidden and the Impossible

Psychic reality will always be structured around the poles of absence and difference; and ...human beings will always have to come to terms with that which is forbidden and that which is impossible.

—Joyce McDougall

6

When Are You Taking That New Kid Back to the Hospital?

For the error bred in the bone
Of each woman and each man
Craves what it cannot have,
Not universal love
But to be loved alone.

—W. H. Auden

Love may be the bridge from separate self to separate self, but the love that we initially have in mind is a love that is ours alone, a love that is all-encompassing and indivisible. It doesn't take long, however, to begin to realize that the love we receive is not exclusively ours, that there are other, rival claims upon our true love's love, that we crave what we cannot have—that we crave the impossible.

A little girl discovers, when she wakens on Christmas morning, the present she had longed for—a glorious doll's house, its tiny rooms neatly carpeted, wallpapered, hung with chandeliers and filled with furniture. She is gazing at it, enthralled, when her mother gives her a gentle nudge and asks a very simple, terrible question: Could she be grown up and generous enough to share her gift with her younger sister Bridget?

I thought. That question, Mother's simple question . . . was to me
the most complex question anyone had ever asked. I thought for a
whole minute while my heart stopped and my eyes blinked and my
face flushed with fury. It was a trick question, two-sided, flipping
back and forth, now-you-see-it-now-you-don't, the trick of a supreme magician who could—with cunning legerdemain under a silk
handkerchief—transform a few seconds of tranquility into an
eternity of chaos. The truth: no, I did not, under any circumstance
whatsoever, wish to share the doll's house with Bridget. . . . Or the
truth: yes, of course I wanted to share the doll's house with Bridget,
because not only would that please Mother and demonstrate how
generous and grown up I really was but because I knew that I loved
Bridget very deeply and identified with her yearning as she tentatively touched the miniature grandfather's clock in the miniature
hallway. (Get your nasty little fingers out of there, I wanted to
scream, until I give you permission.) Bridget was blissfully oblivious of my pain, my conflict. I had not, before that question, ever
been conscious of hating her or of loving her so absolutely. I never
felt, or had the ability to be unaware of feeling, the same way about
my sister again. And I could never bring myself to play with the
doll's house. Eventually it had to be given away.

Not many of us can recall with writer Brooke Hayward's piercing clarity such early childhood feelings of anguished hate. Nor
does our adult dignity permit us to recall the possessiveness and
greed which fueled that hate. But in the beginning we all want
exclusive possession of our treasures, including the first of our
treasures—our mother's love. And we don't want anyone else to
either be given, or to take, the goodies which belong to us alone.

For what will be left to us if we share with our rivals? Is anything less than everything enough? The wish to be loved alone
may very well be bred in the bone. Angrily and painfully, and with
more or less success, we learn to relinquish that wish—to let it go.

"A small child does not necessarily love his brothers and sisters," writes Sigmund Freud; "often he obviously does not. . . . He
hates them as his competitors, and it is a familiar fact that this
attitude often persists for long years, till maturity is reached or
even later, without interruption."

The discomfort we feel with hate may make us deny it in ourselves and in our children. It is easier to call it a Freudian myth. Yet the funny tales we all tell about the way our firstborn greeted the new baby—"You mean he's staying?" And, "When are you taking that new kid back to the hospital?" And, "Put him in the hamper and close the lid." And, "What do we need him for?"—acknowledges, in laundered form, the "intense dislike" which my dictionary calls hate.

Item: A few years ago my friend Harvey was baby-sitting with his three-year-old while his wife and newborn child were still in the hospital. Everything appeared to be smooth and serene. But at one point Harvey asked Josh, who was sitting beside him with his crayons and pad of paper, "How would you like to draw me a pretty picture?" To which Josh replied, looking coldly up at his father, "Not until you get rid of that other kid."

Item: The car-pool children were talking about the "worst thing in my life that ever happened." Like breaking an ankle. Or falling out of a tree. Or having an all-over case of poison ivy. And when it was Richard's turn he declared that "The worst and most terrible thing that happened to me was that my sister got born."

Item: "Well, here's the new baby you told me you wanted. What do you have to say?" I asked my son Tony when Nicky, his brother, was born. "What I have to say," Tony said without a moment's hesitation, "is, I've changed my mind."

Is sibling rivalry normal and universal? Ten out of ten psychoanalysts answer yes. And while it may be more intense in firstborn children, or between two children (or more) of the same sex, or when the children are fairly close in age, or when the families are smaller rather than larger, it is doubtful that any one of us is untouched by these rivalrous feelings, is wholly exempt. For all of us once experienced, in our early months of life, the illusion of completely possessing our mother. Symbiosis was strictly mama and me. The recognition that others have equal and even prior claims upon her love is our initiation into jealousy.

This is not to deny, of course, that there are also—or eventually—powerful bonds of loyalty and affection. Siblings can surely be allies and closest friends. But it is Genesis, not Freud, that says that the first act of murder on earth occurred between brothers. It is Genesis, not Freud, that attributes the first act of murder on earth to reasons which sound very much like sibling rivalry.

> And the Lord had respect unto Abel and to his offering; but unto Cain and to his offering He had not respect. And Cain was very wroth, and his countenance fell. . . . And it came to pass, when they were in the field, that Cain rose up against Abel his brother, and slew him.

We kill our brothers and sisters for having more, or even some, of our parents' love. But the killings are done, for the most part, inside our head. And eventually we will learn that the loss of indivisible love is another of our necessary losses, that loving extends beyond the mother-child pair, that most of the love we receive in this world is love we will have to share—and that sharing begins at home, with our sibling rivals.

We do not like it.

Indeed, Anna Freud includes among the normal characteristics of early childhood "extreme jealousy and competitiveness" and "impulses to kill rivals." But even though killing might strike us as a highly efficient method of retrieving our mother's undivided love, we quickly learn that hostile acts are destined not to win her love but to lose it.

The danger of losing our mother's love or our father's love—our loved one's love—terrifies us and threatens vast anxiety. And so if we have an impulse (smash that baby!) which might lead to such a loss, we want to make that impulse go away. Through one or more of our—mostly unconscious—mechanisms of defense, we can hold anxiety at bay by opposing, resisting, transforming, getting rid of—defending against—our dangerous and now unwanted impulse.

These defenses are not restricted to our problems with sibling rivalry. They serve us throughout our life, whenever a feared or actual loss begins arousing our anxiety. They serve us in what we unconsciously regard as emotionally dangerous situations. And although we will use every one of them at some time or another, the defenses that we favor regularly will become a central part of our style and character.

Here are the names and meanings of our common everyday mechanisms of defense.

And here is how we might use them to deal with our smash-that-baby impulse when it threatens us with the loss of our mother's love.

Repression means pushing the unwanted impulse (and any memories, emotions or desires associated with this impulse) out of consciousness. Thus, "I have no awareness of wanting to hurt this baby."

Reaction formation means keeping the unwanted impulse out of consciousness by overemphasizing the *opposite* impulse. Thus, "I don't want to hurt this baby; I *love* this baby."

Isolation means separating an idea from its emotional content so that, while the memory of the unwanted impulse remains, all of the feelings connected with it are pushed out of consciousness. Thus, "I have this recurring fantasy of boiling my brother in oil, but I don't have the slightest feeling of hatred toward him."

Denial means eliminating unwelcome facts, and the unwanted impulse connected with these facts, by revising them in our fantasies, words or behavior. Thus, "I don't have to hurt the baby because I continue to think of myself as an only child." (A gorgeous example of denial is the story about the little girl who was notified that a baby brother or sister was on the way. She listened in thoughtful silence, then raised her gaze from her mother's belly to her eyes and said, "Yes, but who will be the *new baby's* mommy?")

Regression means escaping from the unwanted impulse by moving back to an earlier stage of development. Thus, "Instead of hurting this baby who is taking my place with mother, *I'll* be the baby."

Projection means repudiating the unwanted impulse by attributing that impulse to somebody else. Thus, "I don't want to hurt this baby; he wants to hurt me."

Identification means replacing the unwanted impulse with more benign and positive feelings by becoming like somebody else—our mother, for instance. Thus, "Instead of hurting the baby, I'll mother him."

Turning Against the Self means directing our hostile impulse onto ourself, instead of hurting the person we want to hurt. Thus,

"Rather than hit the baby, I'll hit myself." Sometimes a person who turns against himself identifies with the person he is hating. Thus, "In hitting myself I'm really hitting the baby."

Undoing means expressing our hostile impulse either in fantasy or in fact, and then repairing the harm with an act of good will. Thus, "First I'll hit the baby (or imagine hitting the baby) and then I'll undo the harm I've done by kissing him."

Sublimation means substituting socially acceptable activities for the unwanted impulse. Thus, "Instead of hitting the baby I'll draw a picture."

Or maybe, like me (in response to my younger sister) grow up to write a chapter on sibling rivalry.

In addition to this list of formally designated "mechanisms of defense," almost anything can serve as a defense mechanism. And another important tactic used by many sibling rivals, including my younger sister Lois and me, is to distinguish ourselves from our siblings by allotting to them one set of characteristics, and allotting to ourselves another—an opposite—set. This defensive tactic goes by the name of "de-identification," which in practical terms means divvying up the turf. De-identification, I have come to understand, was crucial to my relationship with my sister.

For in dividing up the turf my sister and I became completely unlike each other. We ceased being rivals. We no longer ran the same races. By defining ourselves in opposing terms (outdoors/indoors, scientist/writer, extrovert/introvert, conventional/nonconformist) and by operating in drastically different places, my sister and I could deal with our competitiveness and jealousy by avoiding painful contests and comparisons.

De-identification begins around the age of six, most often between first and second same-sex children. It enables two brothers or sisters—it enabled Lois and me—to feel that you've got yours and I've got mine. Each could even feel superior. Nonconformists, I once believed, were inherently more interesting than conventional folks, while my sister just as smugly believed that people like her could be counted upon—in contrast, of course, to those flighty nonconformists. And I once believed it was nobler being an introvert. And Lois believed it was healthier being an extrovert. Everyone won.

Part of the turf that siblings divide may be their mother and father. So I took after our mother and Lois, our dad. By splitting up our parents and having exclusive rights to identification with one of them, each of us found her own noncompetitive niche.

But this polarization of roles—for my sister and me, for any two siblings—has severe limitations. Suppose we had both liked science or wanted to write? We might have shut off parts of our nature we would have been richer exploring. We might have turned out to be half of a whole human being. Furthermore, there are families in which the parents—not the siblings—are the ones who insist upon divvying up the turf, sticking their children with labels that may range from uncongenial to constricting, deciding: You're pretty. She's smart. And you are cheerful. And she is moody. And you have the common sense. And she has the talent. And even when their intention is to reduce the sibling rivalry by providing each child with a separate but equal identity, it may be a long, costly time before two brothers or sisters become unstuck from their labels and begin to figure out who they actually are.

(May, age twenty-five, says, "My mother used to characterize Margo as the 'smart twin' and May as the 'pretty twin.' As a result of this constant caricature of ourselves, I'm still trying to prove how smart I am and Margo how attractive she is.")

Nevertheless the staking out of a separate specific self, a self that is clearly different from our sibling's, can save us from coming in second or killing to win. At six or any age the defense of de-identification offers enormous relief from sibling rivalry.

Sarah, in her mid-thirties, says that she still finds herself dividing up the turf whenever she feels threatened by some other woman, telling herself what she has that this threatening woman does not have, and what she is that this woman cannot be, after which she is able to see and accept this other woman's positive qualities—just as she did with her sister three decades ago.

"If she's successful and gorgeous but she doesn't have any children, I tell myself," says Sarah, "that I have children."

"And if she's successful and gorgeous and she also has a child, I tell myself," says Sarah, "that I have four."

"And if she's successful and gorgeous and she also has four children, I tell myself," says Sarah—may the feminists forgive her—"that mine are all boys."

The ways we resolve, or fail to resolve, our feelings of sibling rivalry are often carried into adult life. And long after childhood's end, in other cities and other relationships, we may repeat our early sibling patterns.

Which are sometimes, like Sarah's, basically constructive. And which sometimes are not.

Psychologist Alfred Adler notes that if a child finds that he can fight and win against his sibling rival, "he will become a fighting child; if fighting does not pay, he may lose hope, become depressed and score a success by worrying and frightening the parents. . . ." Thus trouble with money, with health, with school, with social relationships or with the law may start in childhood and last into later life, and these troubles can serve the function of stealing parental attention away from successful siblings.

There are other self-damaging tactics for defending against sibling rivalry, tactics that may shape our adult life.

Calvin, for instance, twenty months younger than his brother Ted, was, from the start, the brighter, more competent child. But as he began to express himself, to assert himself, to display his capabilities, his mother apparently feared that Ted would be crushed. Her message to Calvin was: Don't beat your brother. Hold back. Slow down. Withdraw. If you want my approval you cannot compete with Ted. Her message, though largely unspoken, was exceedingly persuasive. Calvin complied.

And now he is in his forties and he still can't play for keeps: "In tennis I try to improve my strokes—not win. And in golf," he says, "I can be ahead all the way to the eighteenth hole, but at the eighteenth hole—I'll always blow it." In work as well as play Calvin's biggest problem, he says, is avoidance of competition. He dreams of success, he has grandiose schemes, he embarks, but . . .

"I get to the edge, to the crest, and then I can't do it," he says. "I can't take the risk of winning." For succeeding in the competitive world has the meaning, he has slowly come to perceive, "of killing my brother and losing my mother's love."

Psychologists Helgola Ross and Joel Milgram, who have done much interesting work on adult sibling rivalry, have found that this rivalry is rarely discussed between siblings or with parents or friends. It remains a secret, a shameful secret, a dirty little secret. And this secrecy, so Ross and Milgram believe, can help perpetuate the sibling rivalry.

Thus many brothers and sisters will remain ferocious rivals all their lives. They never let go of their jealousy and competitiveness. And in spite of everything else that may be happening to them elsewhere, they remain intensely embroiled with one another.

Anne, at eighty-nine, still feels resentful of her sister's popularity while her sister, eighty-six, still feels resentful of Anne's clearly superior intellect. (De-identification, we see, does not always work.)

And Richard and Diane are currently competing for who will attend to their aging mother (each of them wants to be the person in charge), a competition which seems to be nothing more than the final battle in the war over who will be crowned Most Dutiful Child.

And a pair of middle-aged sisters are still playing one-upmanship games, but now they compete through their children and their grandchildren.

And a pair of exceptional brothers—the novelist Henry and the philosopher William James—engaged in a lifelong struggle for power which started with Henry's birth and became for them "a prevailing mode of existence."

William used to snipe at Henry's much admired, highly nuanced literary style—"Say it *out*, for God's sake, and have done with it" —and Henry once complained to him that "I'm always sorry when I hear of your reading anything of mine, and always hope you won't—you seem to me so constitutionally unable to 'enjoy' it. . . ." And in a supreme gesture of sour grapes William declined election to the Academy of Arts and Letters because, he explained, his "younger and shallower and vainer brother is already in the Academy"—in other words, because Henry got there first.

Consider, too, the actresses/sisters Olivia de Havilland and Joan Fontaine, who from birth, writes Miss Fontaine, "were not encouraged by our parents or nurses to be anything but rivals . . . ," a rivalry inevitably heightened by their selection of the same career.

On the night Joan Fontaine won an Academy Award for best actress she sat at a table directly across from Olivia, thinking, as she looked at her big sister:

> Now what had I done! All the animus we'd felt toward each other as children, the hair-pullings, the savage wrestling matches, the time Olivia fractured my collarbone, all came rushing back in kaleidoscopic imagery. My paralysis was total. I felt Olivia would spring across the table and grab me by the hair. I felt age four, being confronted by my older sister. Damn it, I'd incurred her wrath again!

Billy Carter, in contrast, seemed unafraid of incurring the wrath of his big brother. And Jimmy Carter, blandly announcing that "I love Billy and Billy loves me," allowed his kid brother, throughout the Carter presidency, to make a public spectacle of himself. By drinking and shooting his mouth off and getting into financial scrapes, Billy competed with Jimmy for attention. And while he possessed no visible means of defeating his saintly, successful sibling rival, he could—through his "contemptuous and unrepentant conduct"—embarrass and damage him.

Psychologist Robert White, discussing sibling conflicts that have not been resolved during childhood, says that adult sibling rivals are still competing "for the favor of parents who might be aged, senile or even dead." And sometimes these "legacies of competition in the family circle," he says, spread into professional and social relationships, so that we respond to co-workers, friends, spouses, even our children, as if they were our brothers or our sisters.

A lab technician, for instance, complains about his three-years-older colleague who "is always breathing down my neck. He nags and finds fault with everything I do. I get so nervous that I make even more mistakes. It's just like it was with my older brother."

A magazine editor becomes so overwrought when Isabel, a younger and newer editor, is promoted before she is that she has to seek some psychological help. Why has her boss's preference for this attractive, ambitious editor left her so devastated? Why is she being tormented by feelings of jealousy, anger and rejection?

"I later discovered," she says, "that my rival, younger than I, had vaguely reminded me of my younger sister, Cynthia. Isabel's hair was curly like Cynthia's and she also had her winning ways —all of which I envied. I realized too that Cynthia had always been Dad's favorite daughter, and strangely, my boss's attitudes and mannerisms reminded me of my father. I could see now that, in a way, an early drama in my life was being replayed all over again. Here was my boss, pushing me aside to favor Isabel, just as my father had pushed me aside for Cynthia."

Marital sibling rivalry is something that Pam now finally understands, having replayed it for years with her husband, John, having been blindly caught up in it before she finally caught on that her *This is mine and this is yours and keep the hell off of mine* territoriality was a perfect repetition of her beleaguered relationship with her younger sister. Why was she so adamant—not merely annoyed but passionately adamant—in refusing to let John put his shirts in her suitcase? Why did it make her so furious when he wanted to join a lunch she was having with friends—her special friends? And why did she find it so hard to let him share these friends? Or a brush? Or a piece of cake? Or an area of knowledge? And why couldn't he, without her instantly bristling, hang up his jacket on "her" side of the closet?

Eventually Pam recognized that her rage at being encroached upon by her sister was being transferred onto her husband. And while she still tends toward a *This is mine and this is yours* territoriality, her response to her husband's trespasses are somewhat more mild than her old *Keep the hell off of mine.*

It seems clear that some of the patterns we repeat in later life are determined not only by parents but siblings too. Freud tells us that

The nature and quality of the human child's relations to people of his own and the opposite sex have already been laid down in the first six years of his life. He may afterwards develop and transform them in certain directions but he can no longer get rid of them. The people to whom he is in this way fixed are his parents and his brothers and sisters. All those whom he gets to know later become substitute figures for these first objects of his feelings . . . [and] are thus obliged to take over a kind of emotional heritage. . . .

This kind of emotional heritage is sometimes imposed on the following generation, which can happen when we view one of our children as "just exactly like me," while another of our children is viewed as the deeply resented sibling of our childhood. In one instance a mother who had been a put-upon younger sister came to adulthood still full of envy and rage, and managed, without even knowing it, to shape her oldest son into someone much like her older sister. In an interview with a psychiatrist the woman was asked about her wish to give her younger son the nicer bedroom, to which she replied emotionally that "she had been the younger, had always felt her older sister had the best of things and even now hated her very much."

As an older sister myself I will concede that firstborns tend to get the best of things, but they also, I'm certain, get the worst of them too. On the one hand, we experience—for months, maybe years beyond symbiotic union—an exclusive, special relationship with our mother. On the other hand, our loss—of this exclusive special relationship—is greater than that of our subsequent brothers and sisters. The birth of a new baby may evoke a sense of betrayal and bewilderment:

> My mom says I'm her sugarplum.
> My mom says I'm her lamb.
> My mom says I'm completely perfect
> Just the way I am.
> My mom says I'm a super-special wonderful terrific little guy.
> My mom just had another baby.
> Why?

Now it is generally agreed that parents tend to give their firstborn more attention than his siblings and to place more value upon him. It is also generally agreed that parents are less possessive, less anxious and less demanding with subsequent children. And so, if we are the younger, we may envy the older the rights of his premier position. And, if we are the older, we may feel that the younger is always being indulged. In other words, no matter what position we hold in the family order of birth, we can prove beyond a doubt that we're being gypped.

And sometimes we are.

For although parents are supposed to love their children more or less equally, sometimes—because one is smarter, prettier, easier, just like them, more successful, athletic, affectionate, or a boy—one child will receive preferential treatment.

In Max Frisch's intriguing novel, *I'm Not Stiller*, for instance, there is a striking exchange between two men, Wilfried and Anatol, who go to a cemetery to visit their dead mothers and then repair to a tavern and compare notes:

"Apparently his mother was extremely strict," writes Anatol, "mine not in the least. . . . I can remember listening at the keyhole as my mother told a group of friends all the witty and clever remarks I had made. . . . Nothing like that ever happened to Wilfried; his mother was worried that Wilfried would never achieve anything worthwhile. . . ."

Furthermore, notes Anatol, Wilfried's mother was a "practical woman who accustomed Wilfried at an early age to the idea that he would never be able to marry a proper woman if he didn't earn plenty of money." Anatol's mother, in contrast, was playful and indulgent and "attached more importance to my inner qualities, convinced that I could marry anyone I liked. . . ."

It is clear that Wilfried and Anatol had two very different mothers. Except . . . there was only one mother:

The men were brothers.

Sometimes the favored sibling arrogantly misuses his special position. And sometimes he feels guilty about it. And sometimes he feels trapped in his Best Kid role. But whatever his response, his brothers and sisters are likely to envy and resent him, and may carry their hostility well beyond childhood. The drunken Jamie of Eugene O'Neill's *Long Day's Journey Into Night*, raging bitterly at his younger brother, admits that he has been a "rotten bad influence on him." Why? Because, he says, "Never wanted you to succeed and make me look even worse by comparison. Wanted you to fail. Always jealous of you. Mama's baby, Papa's pet!"

But even when parents do not, in fact, play favorites, our sibling's presence means a gyp, a loss—a loss because that presence converts our mother's arms, eyes, lap, smile, peerless breasts from our own private turf into a jointly owned property.

How could a child not want to get rid of a brother or a sister?

How could a child not feel some sibling rivalry?

When three-year-old Josh saw his mother hugging his new baby brother he said, as plain as could be, "You can't love us both. And I want you to love only me."

To which his mother responded truthfully, "I love you very much. But . . . I don't love *only* you."

And this is a sorrowful fact of life that cannot be denied. We have to divide mother love with our brothers and sisters. Our parents can help us cope with the loss of our dream of absolute love. But they cannot make us believe that we haven't lost it.

We can, however, learn—if all goes well—that there is sufficient love to go around.

And we also can learn that sisters and brothers offer the possibility of another kind of loving family attachment.

For although sibling rivalry can cause great hardship and suffering, can follow us into adulthood, can become an emotional heritage that is transferred onto all kinds of other relationships, it can also become subordinate to continuing bonds of brotherly/sisterly love. Indeed, in recent years, there have been a growing number of studies on the lifelong involvement of siblings with each other, studies that focus not only on siblings as rivals but as comforters, caretakers, role models, spurs to achievement, faithful allies and best friends.

Sometimes, in fact, when there are no loving parents to sustain them, siblings may become what psychologists Michael Kahn and Stephen Bank call Hansels and Gretels, as intensely loyal and mutually protective as their fairy-tale counterparts. Hansels and Gretels often share a special language, become upset when they are separated from each other and regard the harmony of their relationship as far more important than individual advantage. They also grow up committed to sticking together at all costs, even the cost of excluding spouses and friends. Their loyalty to their siblings always comes first.

Four brothers—Eli, Larry, Jack and Nathan Jerome—became Hansels and Gretels in the face of their mother's death and their father's erratic and sometimes violent behavior. Grown men now, their loyalty endures. Listen to Nathan:

"I know as I sit right here, if I ever got in any trouble—the first ones I go to is my brothers. I don't call my father. I don't call my in-laws. I don't call my wife. I call my brothers."

And listen to Larry:

"If you [his brothers] came to me with any difficulty, you know, if it's financial, academic or whatever . . . I'd give you my last buck. And I *mean* that, sincerely, in *spite* of my responsibilities to my children and wife."

Hansels and Gretels are extremes of sibling closeness and the intensity of their relationship suggests that parental failure—or some tragedy—forced them to fend for themselves in the witchy woods. Hansels and Gretels are far less likely to develop in more benign family circles, which are able to give protection and love to their children. What may develop there is a not so intense but nonetheless caring support and connectedness.

For with time, and identification with a loving parent ("I'll be like you and learn to love this kid"), and reaction-formation ("Maybe I *do* love this kid"), and the pleasure of having a playmate, an admirer, a trailblazer or a sibling "us" against a parental "them," we can eventually moderate our rivalry. And this pest, intruder, competitor, this thief of our mother's love, can become our friend.

"We're brothers," I once heard my oldest, age eight, reply with utter disgust to a stranger's question.

I heard him speaking at age fifteen with pride and enthusiasm, with friendship and love. "We're brothers," he said.

But even when rivalries continue into adult life, change and reconciliation are possible. Old patterns persist but are not carved in stone. And sometimes the triumphs or troubles of a brother or a sister can alter the love-hate balance in favor of love. And sometimes a family crisis can bring siblings closer. Insight at any age into our hurtful repetitions may free us to do it differently at last. It need not always be the way it was.

Psychologist Victor Cicirelli, after more than a decade of sibling research, calls the sibling tie unique among human relationships in its duration, its egalitarianism and its sharing of a common heritage. Most siblings, he found, maintain some contact with each other until the end of their lives, with sisters playing the major role in preserving family relationships and providing emotional support. In one study of siblings over age sixty he found that 83 percent described their relationship with a brother or sister as "close." And since most of the evidence indicates that rivalry does diminish in old age, perhaps the repair and renewal of sibling relationships is one significant task of our final years.

Cicirelli, tipping his hat to the ambivalence of all human relationships, also notes that "one can conceive of rivalry as a feeling that is always latent, appearing strongly in certain circumstances while closeness is elicited in other circumstances." But while rivalry may be revived at any point in the course of our life, the hope is that growing up means making peace with our loss of indivisible love.

The great anthropologist Margaret Mead writes in her autobiographical *Blackberry Winter:*

> Sisters, while they are growing up, tend to be very rivalrous and as young mothers they are given to continual rivalrous comparisons of their several children. But once the children grow older, sisters draw closer together and often, in old age, they become each other's chosen and most happy companions.

Dr. Mead then goes on to speak of the value of sharing childhood memories. I know what she means.

For it was only with my sister Lois that I could reminisce about a springer spaniel named Corky, a house on Clark Street with a glorious apple tree in the back yard, our mother singing "The Two Grenadiers" as she drove us down to the seashore, our dad hitting golf balls on the living-room rug and a housekeeper named Catherine who taught us to say, when we said our prayers at night, "God bless my mother and father, and all my relations and friends, and—Bing Crosby." Sisters and brothers share what (no matter how close) no other contemporaries can share: the intimate, resonant details of family history.

This sharing, if we are able to get past the rivalry, can lay the foundation of a lifetime connection, a connection that can sustain us though parents die and children leave and marriages fail. For while brothers and sisters mean loss—the loss of our mother's exclusive love—that loss can yield immeasurable gain.

7

Passionate Triangles

As to your mother's marriage bed—don't fear it.
Before this, in dreams too, as well as oracles,
Many a man has lain with his own mother.

—Sophocles

Along with sharing parental love with our brothers and our sisters, we have to share it with another parent. New losses will be coming into view. For though Oedipus—the recipient of the comforting words above—hadn't only dreamed it but done it, too, he had done what we are told we all, at around the age of three, develop a most passionate longing to do: get rid of one parent and possess the other one sexually.

Such longings are forbidden and—persistent. They are relinquished and revived many times in our life. But the great renunciation—our first and fateful letting go—occurs when we withdraw from the contest in childhood, when we put an end to a love affair as intense as any we will ever know.

Yes, Virginia, there is an Oedipus complex.

And it speaks to us in our dreams and on the psychoanalyst's couch. And it speaks through the everyday wishes of everyday children. "When I grow up I'm going to marry—" the nearest and dearest person in our life. It surely makes good sense that in the world of a three-year-old child that nearest and dearest person will be a parent.

Well, okay, Virginia might say, I can accept romantic love: Boys *do* court their mommies; little girls flirt with their dads. It is the sexual aspect of Oedipus that (Virginia might say) seems so far-fetched—and offensive. Children, innocent children, do not have a sex life.

Yes, say the psychoanalysts, they do.

Indeed, dismaying as it may be to imagine lustful urges besetting a three-year-old, we must recognize that our sex life begins even earlier, starting with the oral delights (and they clearly are delights) of sucking at a bottle or mother's breast. It's true that this so-called "oral phase" bears very little resemblance to grown-up penis-in-vagina genitality. But from mouth to anus to genitals, certain portions of our body—our erogenous zones—are successively central sources of what can be viewed as *sexual* tension and *sexual* pleasure.

This classically Freudian view of our developing sexuality should, however, be seen as part of a broader picture which considers, along with sexual zones, our relationships with the people in our environment. Such relationships will produce what analyst Erik Erikson calls "decisive encounters," like the meeting of baby's mouth and mother's breast, with all that goes on between them to help or hinder his comfortable getting, her comfortable giving. In this partnership endeavor, which includes the erotic delights of seeing, of hearing, of being touched and held, there is a deep libidinal pleasure which—as Erikson observes—is barely conveyed by a term like "oral phase."

With a sex life that starts at birth, what makes the oedipal phase hold such fraught and special significance? Because our desires and yearnings run very deep. Because we are overwhelmed by the conflicts erupting out of this dangerous, passionate triangle. And because, though we have forgotten the wild wild fantasies which once ignited our mind, we are who we are because of what we have done with them.

It was Sigmund Freud who discovered and described the Oedipus complex. He said it was universal and inborn. And while, as we shall see, it involves both positive and negative feelings toward *both* of our parents, we will start with a look at his central, compelling thesis:

A boy falls in love with his mother. A girl falls in love with her father. The other loved/hated parent stands in the way. Lust, jealousy, competitiveness and the wish to dispose of our rival flourish in us long before we can spell d–a–d. These feelings, these unconscious urges toward incest and parricide, flood us with guilt and a terror of reprisals.

We remember little or none of this as adults. Nor, at the time, is this drama played out explicitly. What there may be instead is cuddling and hugging and nuzzling ("I love you, daddy"), and inexplicable blowups ("I hate you, mommy") and games in which the mommy doll is going to go away for a long, long time and nightmares in which a monster or tiger (as fearsome and mean as some of our own secret wishes) is chasing an utterly terrified little girl.

All this is the shadow play of the Oedipus complex. The raw uncensored emotions remain off stage. Nor do we consciously think that our rival will, like some monster or tiger, do us grave injury. But our unconscious fear of damage, and of the damage that *we* might inflict (for, remember, we not only hate our rival, we love her), and our fear that this hated rival (whom we also love and need) will stop loving us, engender insupportable inner conflicts.

Furthermore, we are small; they are big; we do not have what it takes either to defeat or to possess them. It becomes increasingly clear that we are doomed to be disappointed in our ambitions.

And so, at around age five, most girls and boys confront the necessity of giving up their forbidden oedipal wishes.

Which are never, however, completely given up.

And which, to greater and lesser degrees, and in sometimes quite troubled ways, continue to triangulate our life.

An obvious example is a woman's repeated compulsion to choose older men for marriage or love or sex, an arrangement designed (not always, but often) to gratify an unrelinquished fantasy of beating out mom and winning her daddy-lover. ("How old are you?" a young woman I know asked a man she had taken to bed. When he answered she gasped, "That's exactly my father's age." The man was rather nonplussed. "Is that good or bad?" he wanted to know. Her reply was a frankly unabashed "That's *fantastic!*")

My oedipal inclinations led me to fall in love repeatedly with twenty- to twenty-five-years-older men, whose wisdom, achievements and dedication to this or that noble cause echoed my childhood yearning for a hero to adoringly look up to. In order to marry a man my own age, as I eventually did, I had to give up my oedipal fantasies—learning, rather later than most, that being an equal partner in a relationship offered certain advantages unavailable to daddy's little girl.

But the longed-for oedipal daddy need not be an older man. He can simply be married or otherwise attached. When a young woman with a history of affairs with married men complains with a sigh that "the good ones are already taken," she might want to give some thought as to where that distressing notion came from in the first place.

The only man worth having, goes this version of the triangle, is a man who has been stolen from somebody else. But sometimes the stealing is valued more than the prize. Sometimes the beating-out-mother part is the most important part of the oedipal fantasy: If a man will leave his wife for you, it proves you're a better woman than his wife.

Except, once he leaves, you may no longer want him.

Mary Ann, age three when her father died, still seeks her dead father in man after married man. But her interest wanes if the man becomes available. Indeed, at heart, she is driven, not by her longing for her father, but by her rage at her mother and wish for revenge. Thus each of her love affairs is, in effect, a reproach to her lover's wife: "You're losing your husband because you're not taking good care of him." And each of her love affairs is, underneath, an angry attack on her mother, who "lost" her husband to death by not taking care of him.

Freud writes of a similar pattern in men whose precondition for loving is that there always must be "an injured third party." And so, when such a man falls in love, it is never with someone unmarried or disengaged. He repeats his childhood experience of loving a woman already possessed by another. And it is clear, says Freud, "that the injured third party" in such relationships "is none other than the father himself."

Analysts say that women whose lovers are, in their fantasies, father, may suffer, unaware, from feelings of guilt. With "sons" and "mothers" this may be even more true. Indeed, men may find themselves impotent if their wives too closely represent their mother; the impotence saves them from breaking the incest taboo. And, in the case of Arthur, who thought he had solved this problem by getting himself a mistress, as soon as she also began to take care of—to "mother"—him, he again became impotent.

Another man, white and middle-class, examined, in psychoanalysis, his preference for black or "exotic" women. Why would white and middle-class women not do? He learned that his choices were based on the fact that these "foreign" women, who clearly could not be blood relatives, stood for "not-mother" and therefore were safe to have sex with.

Passionate triangles may be played out at one or many steps removed from their source. They are also often played out in symbolic ways. Thus attitudes or actions that, on the face of it, "make no sense," may make psychological sense as versions of Oedipus.

(Analyst Ernest Jones, for instance, perceives Hamlet's famous procrastination as oedipal. He has sworn to kill his uncle, but he cannot. "Hamlet's vacillation," writes Jones, ". . . lies neither in his incapacity for action in general, nor in the inordinate difficulty of the particular task in question . . ." nor in his highly developed Christian conscience, nor in his legalistic view that the case for killing his uncle had not been proven. Jones argues that, in murdering Hamlet's father and wedding his mother, the uncle had done what Hamlet had longed to do. Thus Hamlet's "own 'evil' prevents him from completely denouncing his uncle's. . . . In reality his uncle incorporates the deepest and most buried part of his own personality, so that he cannot kill him without also killing himself.")

You don't have to buy Jones's *Hamlet* to buy the Oedipus complex. You can view it as one—not the only—key to the play. And indeed it is crucial to keep in mind that all human actions are products of many causes, that very rarely does A alone lead to B, and that earlier life experiences—illness or serious loss, our babe-in-arms relationship with our mother—will affect the way we deal with these passionate triangles. Or whether we're ready to deal with them at all.

Still, our sexual feelings and choices most likely express, in later years, our responses to oedipal conflicts. So too may the quality of our professional life. Lou, who has never stopped fearing the mighty father of his childhood, remains—at forty—submissive to authority figures, while Mike, still defiantly trying to topple his autocratic father, has become a political activist, fighting the "big guys" who push "little people" around. When such men examine their feelings they find themselves back in a five-year-old's world, where a little person loves/challenges/fears a big guy. And if help-less defeat or angry defiance remains the hallmark of the son-father relationship, defeat or defiance may color every subsequent relationship to authority.

Another oedipal problem, rather more common than one might guess, is fear of success—the so-called "success neurosis." This shows itself in women and men who say that they want to go upward in their careers, but who somehow manage to sabotage their ambitions—standing in the way of their own promotions, panicking if their ambitions are achieved. "The forces of con-science which induce illness in consequence of success," writes Sigmund Freud, ". . . are closely connected with the Oedipus com-plex. . . ."

Freud is referring to people whose childhood fears of competing with their same-sex parent continue to haunt them in their adult years and who—though unaware of it—equate success with the doing in of that parent. And so success is dangerous because there will be reprisals, or thus the unconscious mental scenario goes. If competition means kill or be killed and if all of a man's competi-tors stand for his father, he may stop competing, he may arrange not to succeed.

The revised scenario then might be:

I'll settle for second best.

I swear I'll never surpass you.

Please don't hurt me.

For certain women who fear success, the fear is that the assertive use of their powers would wipe out their mother rather than call down her wrath. Some of them also have the fear that making full use of their powers would risk doing harm to their father/husband too. Thus teen-age musician Emily, by changing her bowing technique, loses a competition she should have won. And the brilliant young lawyer Denise grows faint and has to leave the room because, in a talk with her boss, she suddenly sees that she can do what he does—only better.

These damage fears hook into early but still tenacious fears of being abandoned: Success means I'll perish because they'll all go away. Men also have these fears, but if we hear about them less, some analysts say, it is because what men fear even more is the *fear* of abandonment.

Now obviously there are good objective reasons to question success. There are pressures. There is the toll on family life. But when capable people who swear that they really want a better job are repeatedly late for job interviews or fall sick and cancel job interviews or manage to sound like idiots at job interviews, they may very well be avoiding, not wanting, success. And when people pursuing promotions become severely depressed or anxious when they are promoted, they may very well be suffering from a success neurosis.

The playing out of these triangles takes on another twist when we look at what analysts call the *negative* Oedipus complex, a passionate condition involving sexual yearnings for the same-sex parent and rivalrous feelings toward the other parent. In childhood we will grapple with both positive and negative oedipal feelings, and both sets of feelings will stay with us all of our life. Which means that while heterosexual impulses are, for most people, ascendant, all of us are to some degree bisexual.

(However, it has been said that the sexual development of a female is inevitably more difficult than a male's, because her positive Oedipus complex is always preceded by her negative Oedipus complex, because the first love of all human beings is the mother. At around age three we start linking this love to intense triangular fantasies that involve one happy pair, one odd man out. For girls as well as boys that happy pair is mother and child; the rival for both is a hairy intruder called daddy.

(Thus girls, in resolving their Oedipus complex, must suffer a double loss, giving up first their mother and then their father. Little boys can someday marry a new edition of their original passion. Little girls must submit their first love to a sex change.)

Homosexuality is one of the possible consequences of failing to work out these negative oedipal feelings. Another is pseudo-heterosexuality. A man, for instance, might choose a wife (and she needn't look or act "masculine") because she has certain qualities which make her, for him, a stand-in for a male lover. And a woman might choose a husband who is chronically unfaithful in order to (mentally) share the women he beds. Or else they may be more direct and seek, in passive or active homosexual roles, to get or to give what they sought from their same-sex parent.

We must recognize that our sexual intensities and propensities have a good deal to do with the nature we are born with. People differ from birth in the strength of their needs. But while these innate "givens" may account for certain tendencies, our sexual nature is surely both born *and* made. Indeed, our varied responses to all of the various aspects of our oedipal conflicts significantly reflect our human environment, which encompasses our brothers and sisters and perhaps other close relations, as well as the kind of parents we have and how they behave toward each other and toward us. Including sexually.

For remember that while King Oedipus desired to sleep with Jocasta, Jocasta also wanted to sleep with Oedipus. That passionate current flowed in both directions. And during the oedipal period, when children are feeling sexually drawn toward their parents, parents feel sexually drawn to their children too.

Yes, Virginia, normal parents—not perverts.

But the difference between the two are the restraints—both conscious and unconscious—put on those feelings. The difference is whether those feelings are acted upon. One psychoanalyst tells me that he has never yet seen, in his practice, "just a case of the kid with too strong impulses. The damage arises," he says, ". . . when the disturbed and disturbing parent interacts with the oedipally receptive child."

Seductive behavior from parents can excite and baffle and frighten their young children. An actual seduction, despite some recent claims that incest isn't all bad, is—in most experts' view—emotionally ravaging.

Psychoanalyst Robert Winer characterizes the human family as the provider throughout life of "transitional space," serving as a resting place between the individual and society, fantasy and reality, the internal and the external. Incest, he says, violates that space in two ways: An incestuous father assaults his daughter's separateness by in effect saying, "You are mine to do with as I will" while at the same time he forces a premature separateness on her by in effect saying, "You aren't my child; you're my lover." Dr. Winer says that incest "irreparably destroys the sacred innocence which binds the family." He also says that although family life may suffer from other forms of exploitation, incest "is the form, short of murder, with the most devastating consequences."

How could it happen?

"After her mother died when she was little she used to come into my bed every morning, sometimes she'd sleep in my bed. I was sorry for the little thing. Oh, after that, whenever we went places in an automobile or a train we used to hold hands. She used to sing to me. We used to say, 'Now let's not pay any attention to anybody else this afternoon—let's just have each other—for this morning you're mine.' People used to say what a wonderful father and daughter we were—they used to wipe their eyes. We were just like lovers—and then all at once we were lovers. . . ."

Similar stories of incest are not all that rarely revealed on the psychoanalyst's couch. This one, however, came not from the couch but from fiction. The daughter is the exquisite and very upper-class Nicole of F. Scott Fitzgerald's *Tender Is the Night*. The consequences for her? She becomes psychotic.

So does the hopeless, homely, poverty-stricken black child Pecola of Toni Morrison's novel *The Bluest Eye*, whose drunken father—excited by the "rigidness of her shocked body, the silence of her stunned throat . . . and the doing of a wild and forbidden thing"—untenderly rapes her.

The true-life versions of Pecola's story, when reported at all, appear in domestic courts or on police blotters. But many cases are not reported, because of the victim's fear of what such revelations will do to the family. In Suzanne Fields' valuable book about father-daughter relationships, *Like Father, Like Daughter*, a young social worker—called Sybil—describes her painfully nonfiction incest experiences:

"I have blotted out most of that period of my life but I do make a conscious effort to deal with it now. I think it started when I was eight. There would always be times at home and on trips when Daddy and I would be alone together for a few minutes. He started by having me touch him through his slacks. Later he exposed himself to me, and touched me with his hands. He always wanted me to kiss his penis but I never would."

Sybil says that when she was fifteen her father attempted intercourse but, by tensing her body, she prevented it. She then went to a counselor at a private agency and learned that she could go to court and have him arrested. But, she says, "it was horrible just trying to decide. If I went to court, my family would be destroyed. My brothers would never understand. How would we live? In the end I couldn't risk breaking up my family."

Although acts of incest are more common between fathers and daughters than they are between mothers and sons, mothers can also play dangerous games of seductiveness. Taking their sons to bed. Dressing in front of them. Handling their bodies when they should keep hands off. Dr. Winer describes a college student who was unable to date and who was still receiving backrubs from his mother. Backrubs? When parents fail to renounce their incestuous wishes, he observes, "incestuous fantasies may be realized in symbolic or displaced or partial forms."

Another analyst describes a more direct expression of motherly incest fantasies. His patient, the mother of a fourteen-year-old son, was worried about his sexual education. She didn't want him catching diseases from prostitutes; nor would a widow or divorcee quite do. She also rejected unmarried girls and wondered what would happen if she offered *herself* to her son as a transient sex partner. Her analyst, exercising psychoanalytic tact, helped her conclude that this was a poor idea.

Yes, parents have sexual feelings for their children, even for little children of three, four, five. And what they do with these feelings has a great deal to do with what children do with their oedipal conflicts. For acts of seduction aside, one extreme of parental behavior is overstimulation while the other extreme is a don't-touch pulling away. And somewhere between these poles are mothers and fathers who can confirm with loving discretion the value of physical pleasure in human relationships.

While making it perfectly clear that there is a special, private husband-and-wife relationship upon which sons and daughters cannot intrude.

While making it perfectly clear that no matter how powerful the wish, the child doesn't wind up walking away with the parent.

At dinner a four-year-old girl and her parents discuss the crowded conditions of their apartment. The daughter has a solution: "I'll move my bed into your room and then my room will have more space for my toys." When the father explains that the parents' bedroom is a private place, that a husband and wife need to have a room of their own, the little girl stops eating, starts to hit her father again and again and again, then falls into a crumpled heap at his feet. The third member of this triangle, the wife of the father, the mother of the girl, comments on this touchy, and touching, scene:

"I want to say to him, as I'm sure she does, Don't say that. I want to fudge the answer for her: It would be more crowded in our bedroom with two beds, or something like that. I don't want her to feel hurt, rejected. But I bite my tongue. She needs to understand, and more from her father than from me, that he loves both of us but in different ways."

But the scene is not yet played out. The mother, recalling her own old feelings of wanting to be her father's one and only, perceptively describes what happens next:

"He tells her he wants to give her a hug and that he's ready to play an after-dinner game with her. She slowly rises from the floor, regaining her dignity, smiling in anticipation of the hug and fun. I smile, too, for in both her pain and her graceful recovery, I see reflected my own jealousy, and a clue to my own growth from child to adult."

For in spite of the anguish we feel, the fact that we cannot steal our daddy from our mommy will lead us to growth and a place in the wider world. There will be consolations for our agonized but necessary loss. But to win an oedipal victory, to beat out our rival and get the parent we love, may do us more harm in the end than a defeat.

One woman, who lived with a man she loved, repeatedly turned him down when he asked her to marry him. She felt compelled to refuse, but didn't know why. She learned, in psychoanalysis, that she was equating marriage with having children and equating having children with having to die. Her mother had died when she was four and she had achieved a guilt-ridden oedipal victory, winning her father, taking her mother's place. And now she feared that marriage-meant-children-meant-that-she-too-would-die, as punishment for her wicked and longed-for triumph.

Damaging oedipal victories may occur through a parent's death —"I wanted my mother all to myself, and the next thing I knew my father had a heart attack." They may also occur when parents get divorced. Several recent studies indicate that boys are less able than girls to cope with their parents' marital breakup and that the effects on them—which include lowered scholastic achievement, depression, anger, diminished self-esteem, increased drug and alcohol use—are longer lasting and more intense. These studies also suggest that oedipal issues in part explain the greater problems that boys seem to have with divorce.

For according to Linda Bird Francke's "The Sons of Divorce," the mother still winds up with custody of the children—by agreement or by default—more than 90 percent of the time. Thus, when the child is a son, most mothers get the son—and the son gets the mother. "The oedipal conflict is supposed to be resolved in favor of the parent, not in favor of the child," says child psychiatrist Gordon Livingston of Columbia, Maryland, whose clinic annually sees as many as five hundred children of divorce. "Yet repeatedly, now, it's happening the other way." With the son (sometimes quite literally) replacing his father in bed, the ensuing sexual tension and guilt can lead to inner turmoil and troubled behavior.

Although boys between ages three and five seem especially affected by the oedipal implications of divorce, the phase of adolescence stirs up oedipal conflicts again, turning the teenage sons of divorce possessive and jealous. One sixteen-year-old, whose mother had gone on a date, deliberately locked her out of the house. "She had to wake me up to get back in," he later explained. "Just seeing me there turned the guy off." A fifteen-year-old was even more direct. "I want you home by eleven o'clock," he told his departing mother. "And alone."

One study found that boys between ages nine and fifteen are least willing to accept a stepfather. Younger boys, however, shaken by their oedipal anxieties, may be eager to bring a man into the house. "Who are we going to marry next?" one little boy insistently asked his mother. "We need to get a daddy around here."

But oedipal victories do not require either a death or divorce. They may be achieved when mothers (or fathers) favor their son (or daughter) over their spouse. In many a house lives a son whose mother pampers and adores him while she treats his father with undisguised contempt. Deprived of a man to identify with, guilty, fearing punishment for his success, oppressed by his mother's un-motherly demands, the successful young oedipal lover—if he could put it all into words—might very well wish he had lost the Oedipus contest.

So what would an analyst call a "healthy" resolution of the Oedipus complex? What is constructive renunciation at five? How do we give up passions that in our unconscious world are the stuff of Shakespeare and Sophocles? And what are the gains in this necessary loss of our forbidden, impossible dreams?

We are told that the Oedipus complex is never totally demolished, and that it will raise its head again and again. We will struggle with oedipal conflicts all our life. We will struggle to free our sexual love and vigorous self-assertion from childhood images of incest and parricide. We will sometimes succeed.

Our ability to deal with that love and that hate, that fear and guilt and renunciation, will—with luck—grow greater over time. But the patterns will take shape in those early years when we do what we must to resolve our Oedipus complex.

Which means we renounce our sexual love for our father (or

our mother). We identify with—strive to emulate—our mother (or our father). Indeed, believing that both of them would oppose our wicked wishes, we become like them in repudiating those wishes. We take in their moral standards and their rewards-and-punishment system. We acquire an inner law-enforcement agency.

There are losses and gains.

By identifying with our same-sex parent, we confront the nature and limits of gender identity, learning what we can and can't do as a female or a male, and letting go of our yearnings for the impossible.

By consolidating our own inner law enforcer—our superego—we confront the nature and limits of human freedom, learning what we can and can't do as a civilized human being, and letting go of our yearnings for the forbidden.

And by giving up our passionate entanglement with our parents, we travel the oneness-to-separateness road yet again, moving into a world that can only be ours if we forsake our oedipal dreams.

Margaret Mead notes that the Oedipus complex "has taken its name from failure—from the unfortunate Oedipus who failed to solve the conflict—and not from the successful, though often compromised, solutions that each civilization has worked out." She directs us to a mushy but relevant poem—"To a Usurper"—written before the age of Freudian consciousness, a poem in which a father identifies the ancient problem and describes how it will eventually be mastered.

> Aha! a traitor in the camp,
>   A rebel strangely bold—
> A lisping, laughing, toddling scamp,
>   Not more than four years old!
>
> To think that I, who've ruled alone
>   So proudly in the past,
> Should be ejected from my throne
>   By my own son at last!
>
> He trots his treason to and fro,
>   As only babies can,

And says he'll be his mamma's beau
   When he's a "gweat, big man"!

    . . . . . .

Renounce your treason, little son,
   Leave mamma's heart to me;
For there will be another one
   To claim your loyalty.

And when that other comes to you,
   God grant her love may shine
Through all your life as fair and true
   As mamma's does through mine!

8

Anatomy and Destiny

When you meet a human being, the first distinction you make is "male or female?"

—Sigmund Freud

Our infantile omnipotence—our dizzy, delicious, little-kid sense of power—crows that we can do and have and be anything. Sibling rivals and parents that we can never never possess notify us that no, this is not true. So does our discovery, at eighteen or so months of age, that girls and boys are different from each other. And whatever else this discovery of the anatomical differences may do, it will certainly instruct us in sex-linked limits.

For we cannot become both sexes although—it's been claimed —our wish to do so may be "one of the deepest tendencies in human nature." We cannot, like Virginia Woolf's transmutable hero/heroine Orlando, be a man and then a woman and sometimes both. Through our built-in bisexuality and our capacity for empathy we can experience some of the opposite sex's experiences. And through broader definitions of what it means to be a woman or a man we can expand our own sex's experience, too. But we also will have to recognize that neither sex is complete, that there are some limitations upon our potential, and that our gender identity, with all of its juices and joys, must shape itself to these limits—to this loss.

I am saying that the mere fact of our inhabiting a male or female body importantly defines—and confines—our experience.

I am saying that—close as we are—my husband and sons are

psychologically different from me in ways that women—any women—are not.

I am saying with Freud that no one can see us—nor can we see them—divorced from the "male" or "female" designation.

I am saying that sex-linked limits on our "anything's possible" omnipotentiality is yet another necessary loss.

It is argued that sex-linked limits have been culturally produced. It is argued that sex-linked limits are innate. What gender-identity studies seem to strongly suggest, however, is that—from the moment of birth—both boys and girls are so clearly treated as boys or as girls, that even very early displays of "masculine" or "feminine" behavior cannot be detached from environmental influences.

For parents make a distinction between boys and girls.

They have different ways of holding boys and girls.

They have different expectations for boys and girls.

And as their children imitate and identify with their attitudes and activities, they encourage or discourage them, depending on whether or not they are boys or girls.

Are there, in actual fact, *real* sex-linked limits? Is there an inborn male or female psychology? And is there any possible way of exploring such tricky questions unbiased by culture, upbringing or sexual politics?

Here are the answers, for instance, that I received from three feminist writers when I asked if they thought men and women differed innately.

Novelist Lois Gould replied: "Women menstruate, lactate and procreate; men inseminate. All our other differences come from trying to build civilizations around those primitive talents—as if they were the only ones we had."

And journalist Gloria Steinem replied: "For ninety-five per cent of life there are more differences between any two women or between any two men than there are between males and females as groups."

And novelist-poet Erica Jong replied: "The only difference between men and women is that women are able to create new little human beings in their bodies while simultaneously writing books, driving tractors, working in offices, planting crops—in general, doing everything men do."

Sigmund Freud would have answered the question differently.

Indeed, he went on record as saying that women are more masochistic, narcissistic, jealous and envious than men, and also less moral. He saw these qualities as the inevitable consequences of the anatomical differences between the sexes—the result of the fact (fact?) that the original sexuality of the little girl is masculine in character, that her clitoris is merely an undeveloped penis and that she correctly perceives herself as nothing more than a defective boy. It is the girl's perception of herself as a mutilated male that irrevocably damages her self-esteem, leading to resentments and attempts at reparation which produce all the subsequent defects in her character.

Well, as his friends say, who can be right about everything?

For in the years since this was written, science has established that while genetic sex is determined at fertilization by our chromosomes (XX for girls; XY for boys), all mammals, including humans, *regardless of their genetic sex*, start out female in nature and in structure. This female state persists until the production, some time later in fetal life, of male hormones. It is only with the appearance of these hormones, at the right time and in the right amount, that anatomical maleness and post-natal masculinity become possible.

While this may not tell us much about the psychology of femaleness and maleness, it does put a permanent crimp in Freud's phallocentricity. For, far from little girls starting out as incomplete little boys, in the beginning all human beings are female.

Despite his phallocentricity, however, Freud was smart enough to note at the time that his comments on the nature of women were "certainly incomplete and fragmentary."

He also said: "If you want to know more about femininity, enquire from your own experiences of life, or turn to the poets, or wait until science can give you deeper and more coherent information."

Two Stanford psychologists have tried to do just that in a highly regarded book called *The Psychology of Sex Differences*. Surveying and evaluating a broad range of psychological studies, authors Eleanor Maccoby and Carol Jacklin conclude that there are several widely held but dead-wrong beliefs regarding the ways in which males and females differ:

That girls are more "social" and more "suggestible" than boys. That girls have lower self-esteem. That girls are better at rote learning and simple repetitive tasks and boys more "analytic." That girls are more affected by heredity and boys by environment. That girls are auditory and boys are visual. And that girls lack achievement motivation.

Not true, say authors Maccoby and Jacklin. These are myths.

Some myths, however—or are they myths?—have not yet been dispelled. Some sexual mysteries remain unsolved:

Are girls more timid? Are they more fearful? More anxious?

Are boys more active, competitive and dominant?

And is it a female quality—in contrast to a male quality—to be nurturing and compliant and maternal?

The evidence, the authors say, is either too ambiguous or too thin. These tantalizing questions are still open.

There are, however, four differences which they believe to be fairly well established: That girls have greater verbal ability. That boys have greater math ability. That boys excel in visual-spatial ability. And that verbally and physically, boys are more aggressive.

Are these innate differences, or are they learned? Maccoby and Jacklin reject this distinction. They prefer to talk in terms of biological predispositions to learn a particular skill or kind of behavior. And talking in these terms, they designate only two sexual differences as clearly built upon biological factors.

One is boys' better visual-spatial ability, for which there is evidence of a recessive sex-linked gene.

The other is the relationship that exists between male hormones and the readiness of males to behave aggressively.

However, even that has been disputed. Endocrinologist Estelle Ramey, professor of physiology and biophysics at Georgetown Medical School, told me:

"I think hormones are great little things and that no home should be without them. But I also think that virtually all the differences in male and female behavior are culturally, not hormonally, determined. It's certainly true that *in utero* sex hormones play a vital role in distinguishing male from female babies. But soon after birth the human brain takes over and overrides *all* systems, including the endocrine system. It is said, for instance, that men are innately more aggressive than women. But conditioning, not sex hormones, makes them that way. Anyone seeing women at a bargain-basement sale—where aggression is viewed as appropriate, even endearing—sees aggression that would make Attila the Hun turn pale."

Although Maccoby and Jacklin's survey also concludes that little girls are no more dependent than boys, the female-dependency issue will not go away. A few years ago Colette Dowling's best-selling book *The Cinderella Complex* struck a responsive chord in women everywhere with its theme of a female fear of independence.

Here it was—the Cinderella Complex. It used to hit girls of sixteen or seventeen, preventing them, often, from going to college, hastening them into early marriages. Now it tends to hit women after college—after they've been out in the world a while. When the first thrill of freedom subsides and anxiety rises to take its place, they begin to be tugged by that old yearning for safety: the wish to be saved.

Dowling argues that women, in contrast to men, have a deep desire to be taken care of and that they are unwilling to accept the adult reality that they alone are responsible for their lives. This tendency toward dependency, Dowling maintains, is bred into them by the training of early childhood, which teaches boys that they're on their own in this difficult, challenging world and which teaches girls that they need and must seek protection.

Girls are trained *into* dependency, says Dowling.

Boys are trained *out* of it.

Even in the mid-1980s, at an Eastern liberal-elite private school where the mothers of students are doctors and lawyers and government officials and the students themselves are full of feminist rhetoric, there are echoes of the Cinderella Complex. One of the teachers, who gives a course in human behavior to the high school seniors, told me that he has asked them, for the last several years, where they expect to see themselves at age thirty. The answers, he said, are consistently the same. Both boys and girls expect that the girls will be bearing and rearing children, while also engaged in some interesting *part-time* work. And although the boys express a desire to have a great deal of freedom at that age, the girls routinely place the boys in successful *full-time* jobs, supporting their families.

Now it surely is true that a great many women live with a some-day-my-prince-will-take-care-of-me fantasy. It is true that the way girls are raised may help explain why. But we also need to consider that the source of female dependence may run deeper than the customs of early child care. And we also need to remember that dependence isn't always a dirty word.

For female dependence appears to be less a wish to be protected than a wish to be part of a web of human relationships, a wish not only to get—but to give—loving care. To need other people to help and console you, to share the good times and bad, to say "I understand," to be on your side—*and also to need the reverse, to need to be needed*—may lie at the heart of women's very identity. Dependence on such connections might be described as "mature dependence." It also means, however, that identity—for women—has more to do with intimacy than with separateness.

In a series of elegant studies, psychologist Carol Gilligan found that while male self-definitions emphasized individual achievement over attachment, women repeatedly defined themselves within a context of responsible caring relationships. Indeed, she notes that "male and female voices typically speak of the importance of different truths, the former of the role of separation as it defines and empowers the self, the latter of the ongoing process of attachment that creates and sustains the human community." It is only because we live in a world where maturity is equated with autonomy, argues Gilligan, that women's concern with relationships appears to be a weakness instead of a strength.

Perhaps it is both.

Claire, an aspiring physician, finds essential meaning in attachment. "By yourself, there is little sense to things," she says. "It is like the sound of one hand clapping. . . . You have to love someone else, because while you may not like them, you are inseparable from them. In a way, it is like loving your right hand. *They are part of you*; that other person is part of that giant collection of people that you are connected to."

But then there is Helen who, talking about the end of a relationship, reveals the risks inherent in intimacy. "What I had to learn . . . ," she says, "wasn't only that I had a Self that could survive it when Tony and I broke up; but that I had a Self *at all!* I wasn't honestly sure that, when we two were separate, there would be anything there that *was me*."

Freud once observed that "we are never so defenseless against suffering as when we love, never so helplessly unhappy as when we have lost our loved object or its love." Women will find these words particularly true. For women, far more often than men, succumb to that suffering known as depression when important love relationships are through. The logic thus seems to be that women's dependence on intimacy makes them, if not the weaker sex, the more vulnerable one.

It is important to keep in mind that what's being talked about is men and women in general. For of course there are women who cannot allow themselves intimacy, and men who open up with pleasure and ease. But it is argued—and I agree—that most women, when compared to most men, have a greater capacity for relatedness. And it is argued, and I agree, that this capacity makes for important male-female differences.

If women's nature is, in fact, more affiliative, more interdependent, more imbedded in personal relationships, why? Let us go back and ponder this question in light of how boys and girls establish their gender identity.

For, it is widely agreed, they *do* do it differently.

Consider, for instance, that both sexes—all of us—were originally symbiotically merged with mother, and that our first identification—everybody's first identification—was with her. It is true that boys and girls alike must escape symbiosis and set up mother-child boundaries. It is true that both boys and girls must break away. But an intense and prolonged symbiosis will threaten little boys' masculinity far more than it threatens little girls' femininity, because to be one with, the same as, or like the earliest caretaking figure is to be one with, the same as, or like (in most cases) a woman.

Thus girls, to be girls, can continue their initial identification with their mother. Boys, to be boys, emphatically cannot.

Girls, to be girls, can maintain their empathic tie and fluid connectedness with their mother. Boys, to be boys, emphatically cannot.

Girls, to be girls, can define themselves without repudiating their first attachment. Boys, to be boys, emphatically cannot. Indeed, they must develop what psychoanalyst Robert Stoller calls "symbiosis anxiety," a protective shield against their own strong yearnings to merge with mommy, a shield which preserves and extends their sense of maleness.

In their second and third years of life, then, boys decisively will turn away from their mother. They de-identify with what she is. But their pulling away, their protective shield, may involve a number of anti-female defenses. And so it may be that the price males pay for de-identification is a disdain, a contempt, sometimes even a hatred for women, a disowning of the "feminine" parts of themselves and an enduring fear of intimacy *because it undermines the separation upon which their male identity has been founded.*

This fear of intimacy, by the way, extends to male-male relationships as well. In a weird little novel called *The Men's Club* a group of middle-class men get together to share their life histories. This stripping away of the conventional barriers, this "feminine" step into intimacy, so undoes them that they wind up wrecking the house and howling—*ow-oo-ooo, ow-woo-oo-ooo*—like wild animals "until it seemed we were one in the rising howls, rising again and again, taking us up even as we sank toward primal dissolution. . . ."

While boys are threatened by intimacy, girls are more afraid of separation, for their feminine identity is founded upon their relationship with another. I think it might even be argued that we women are literally built for greater relatedness, for the female body is, after all, designed to make room for other human beings. Anatomically we can accommodate a penis in our vagina. We can shelter and nourish a fetus in our womb. And psychologically we seem to be far more willing and able than men to identify with, and adapt to, our love partner's needs.

It has been said that we women are brainwashed, that we have been raised to be so dependent on relationships that we will give up our soul, our self, to keep them intact. It has been argued that our adaptations are those of a slave. But could the widely acknowledged fact that women adapt more than men in private relationships be due to an innate capacity, a specifically female capacity to accommodate, a capacity that mirrors our developmental history and maybe even . . . our anatomy?

(And is such accommodation, which at its best embodies the value that imperfect attachments are better than perfect autonomy, really less "evolved" or less mature?)

Listen to Ella:

"I've added up the pros and cons and the pros come out ahead. I want the relationship. This means that I give up expecting to quit my job, because he's never going to make a whole lot of money. And it means I don't tell him he drank too much at the party, because he will always drink too much at the party. And it also means that I'm never indiscreet enough to ask who he sleeps with when he's out of town."

Why does Ella bother? Here is her answer.

"We've had thirty years of marriage. There is history. There is good sex, good times and grandchildren to share. I know I could live alone but we have something of value together that's worth preserving. So—I adapt."

One of the arguments offered for women's greater adaptability in relationships is based on what happens during the oedipal phase. For while little boys have had to relinquish a strong identification with their mother, she was, and can keep on being, their first love. Thus boys, to be heterosexual little boys, can continue to desire a woman, like mother. Girls, to be heterosexual girls, cannot. They have to renounce the original, and much beloved, object of their affections and shift their choice from a female to a male.

Analyst Leon Altman suggests that female flexibility derives from this sexual turning away from mother. "This renunciation," he writes, "prepares her for renunciation in the future in a way the boy is unable to match."

For a girl to give up her mother as her object of sensual longings is a difficult letting go, a radical loss. Indeed some analysts say that the notorious penis envy—from which, so Freud insisted, all females suffer—might be understood as a wish to avoid this loss.

If only I had what boys have—so the fantasy might go—I wouldn't have to renounce the first love of my life.

If only I had a penis—so the unconscious logic of early childhood might go—I wouldn't be required to give up my mother.

But early-childhood envy isn't restricted to penis envy; nor is penis, or other envy, restricted to girls. For as we come to know what bodies are and what they can do, we are bound to covet each other's parts and capacities. We want—of course we want!—that nourishing breast, that versatile penis, that magical, marvelous baby-making ability. Unlike the jealousy triangle, envy begins as a two-person drama: "You've got it; I want it."

To envy, the dictionary tells us, is "to be discontent at the possession by another of what one would like for oneself." Indeed, early origins of envy, some psychoanalysts speculate, may be traced to our envy of our mother's breast, an envy of that "source of all comforts, physical and mental," that reservoir of plentitude and power.

Later, when we learn about the anatomical differences, a boy might announce that he'd like to have babies too. Or he might deny that he cannot have babies by clinging to the poignant misapprehension that girls have baby girls and boys, baby boys. The defenses boys establish against their pregnancy, or womb, envy may lead to a lifelong lack of interest in babies. But it also has often been claimed that man's creative activities out there in the world are his paltry substitutes for—his externalized versions of —creating new life.

Some primitive tribes allow men to express their womb envy by means of couvade—the custom whereby the husband takes to his bed, as if for childbearing, when his wife is having a baby. And some puberty rites, so analyst Bruno Bettelheim has hypothesized, may in part be intended to help boys and girls to cope with their envy of each other's sexual specialties. Although this envy is equally distributed between the two sexes, Bettelheim notes, the envious female has always been far more focused upon. He therefore chooses to emphasize the pervasive envy of males for the female's productive vagina and milk-making breasts.

"I believe," writes Bettelheim, ". . . that the desire to possess . . . the characteristics of the other sex is a necessary consequence of the sex differences." But having the other's might mean we must lose our own. Through initiation rituals man attempts, he says, "to express and then free himself of his anxieties about his own sex and his wishes for experiences, organs and functions which are available only to persons of the other sex."

It has been observed that with changing social attitudes, a male's secret wish to bear babies need not be so buried. And so he shows up, along with his wife, at the natural childbirth classes and pants alongside her in the birthing room. A number of men (I'm not talking now of primitive men in primitive societies; I'm talking of middle-class modern American males) may so eagerly (though unconsciously) identify with their wife's baby-bearing capacity that, in the months she is pregnant, they—the men!—may become fatigued and sick to their stomach, and sometimes gain thirty pounds and grow a big belly.

More than fifty years ago Felix Boehm wrote of the male's intense envy of women's child-bearing capacity—his "parturition-envy"—and of his envy of women's breasts. Boehm observed "that it excites our envy when others have something *more* than we have ourselves. . . . The quality of the 'different' thing does not matter very much."

What matters is that bodily difference—for men as well as for women—is felt to be a diminution, a loss.

Envy of each other's sexual parts may begin as a literal wanting, but metaphorical meanings quickly accrete. Thus penis envy, for instance—which sounds so peculiar to our ears, which strikes many sensible people as sexist or silly—may start to make more sense as we move from the coveting of a nifty and versatile gadget to what possession of a penis might represent.

For the lack of a penis can be, for instance, a symbol around which are gathered earlier feelings of being deprived or gypped.

It can also be a symbol of fears that we aren't quite what the doctor, or mother, ordered:

> remember that every son had a mother
> whose beloved son he was,
> and every woman had a mother
> whose beloved son she wasn't.

And it can also be a symbol of being ill-equipped to do whatever it is in life that has to be done because—as one woman put it when she tried to describe her inferiority feelings—"there's nothing there."

Indeed, professional women will often speak of doubts about their capacities, of feeling that they do not have what it takes, of a certainty that they actually lack some feature that is crucial for success, of a belief—if they are successful—that their triumphs have been fraudulently obtained. Their conviction that men are "dressed for success" in a way that they are not is a working woman's version of penis envy.

Penis envy can also be a symbol of what it takes to acquire masculine power and prerogatives. For if penis means male and male means having all kinds of special advantages, then envy may form an unconscious link from advantage, to male advantage, to male anatomy.

In a recent study, some 2,000 children in grades three through twelve were asked a simple question: If you woke up tomorrow and discovered that you were a (boy) (girl), how would your life be different? And despite more than a decade of consciousness-raising on the subject of sex bias, the responses from both boys *and girls* reveal a distressing contempt for the female gender.

The elementary-school boys, in clear horror, often gave names to their answers like "The Disaster" or "The Fatal Dream." They then went on to say:

"If I were a girl, I'd be stupid and weak as a string." Or, "If I woke up and I was a girl, I would hope it was a bad dream and go back to sleep." Or, "If I were a girl, everybody would be better than me, because boys are better than girls." Or, "If I were a girl, I'd kill myself."

Boys felt that, as girls, they would have to be overly concerned about their physical appearance ("I couldn't be a slob any more—I'd have to smell pretty"); that their work would be trivial ("I would have to cook, be a mother and yucky stuff like that"); that their activities would be restricted ("I would have to hate snakes"); and that they would not be treated as well. The girls, alas, concurred in all these judgments.

"If I were a boy," wrote one third grader, "I could do stuff better than I do now." And, "If I were a boy, my whole life would be easier." And, "If I were a boy, I could run for President." And—heartbreakingly—"If I were a boy, my daddy might have loved me."

An occasional younger boy saw a few advantages in being female: "No one would make fun of me because I'm afraid of frogs." Beyond grade school, however, no boys envied girls, but girls continued to find man's lot most enviable.

Once upon a time little girls discovered that they lacked a bodily part. They wanted one. Some gave up the wish; some did not. Those who retain the wish seem to feel that they are lacking something that could make them good enough, better than, or complete. Their wish, then, is not for a penis, but for that "something" a penis has come to represent.

Penis envy may make women feel contempt for themselves or for other defectives—women. It may make some hate, and some overvalue, men. It may lead some to search for a husband who, as Evelyn said when she married, "is exactly the man I would be if I were a man." Or it may express itself as a demand for special treatment in payment for being mistreated, shortchanged, by fate.

Although little girls might see themselves as being "cut short of something," they aren't the only sex that suffers from penis envy. In the oedipal stage little boys—in their competition with daddy for mommy—want what he's got, and that means his penis too. This is not to say that children this young understand the role of a penis in intercourse; their notions of sexual acts are vague and bizarre. But like everything else that daddy has, his penis is strikingly bigger than what *they* have. And on the little-boy theory (which is often the grown-man theory) that bigger is better, they will envy it.

Thus the discovery of the sexes' anatomical distinctions may stir both boys and girls to feelings of envy. But the intensity of that envy, the importance of that envy, will vary in each unique, individual life. Another result of this preschool course in comparative anatomy may be a rather dramatic rise in anxiety, as we worry about the bodily parts that we might eventually lose, or have already lost.

For boys these fears will be linked to the fact that a whole group of people exist who appear to be penisless. Girls surely must have one! They don't? Then why is it gone? The value they place on this organ—it feels good; it looks good—and the seeming discovery that it can disappear, engenders the (come to think of it, quite reasonable) male fear called castration anxiety.

This anxiety is heightened by boys' oedipal ambitions: the presumptuous wish to take their father's place. And fears of paying a dreadful price for such how-dare-you! competitiveness may sometimes follow small boys into adult life. When a competent male keeps arranging to fail, or always puts himself down, or has trouble taking a woman he loves to bed, he may still be saying to the frightening father in his head: "You don't have to injure me—as you see, I'm no threat."

By the end of the oedipal phase we have acquired a richer, more complicated sense of what it means to be masculine or feminine. The resolution of our triangular conflicts helps shape what kind of woman or man we will be. Girls strengthen their feminine identification, hoping someday to marry a man like their father. Boys strengthen their masculine identification, hoping someday to marry a woman like mom. In the process, all of us more clearly learn what we cannot have or be. "Daddy, I love you!" a four-year-old says with a most erotic look. "I think I'll marry a man when I grow up." But that four-year-old is a boy and he will learn that the mommy he also dearly loves is the more standard model for objects of sexual longings.

While our gender identity shapes itself around our same-sex

parent, we identify with our other parent too. And in middle-class America here near the end of the twentieth century, the ways one can be male or female are wide, wide open. Nevertheless we have bodies whose parts will forevermore be different from each other. And, as we travel the road of psychosexual development, we will take different forks—one for girls and another for boys. As hetero-sexual humans we identify and love in accordance with gender patterns and possibilities. But it is how we perceive our limits that determines if our anatomy is our destiny.

For surely some sex-linked limits do exist. And surely we may perceive them as a loss. But a recognition of limits need not oppose —*indeed it may be a requirement for*—the creative development of our potentiality.

"The potter who works with clay recognizes the limitations of his material," writes Margaret Mead; "he must temper it with a given amount of sand, glaze it thus, keep it at such and such a temperature, fire it at such a heat. But by recognizing the limita-tions of his material he does not limit the beauty of the shape that his artist's hand, grown wise in a tradition, informed by his own special vision of the world, can impose upon that clay."

She is saying that freedom begins when we acknowledge what is possible—and what is not.

She is saying that if we come to know the nature of our clay, we can impose our destiny on anatomy.

9

Good as Guilt

Without guilt
What is man? An animal, isn't he?
A wolf forgiven at his meat,
A beetle innocent in his copulation.

—Archibald MacLeish

Anything *isn't* possible, the realities of love and our bodies persuade us. We aren't unbounded, and never will be free of the limits imposed upon us by the forbidden and the impossible —including the limits imposed upon us by guilt.

For whether or not we humans are the only creatures capable of guilt, we undoubtedly do it better than beetles or wolves. And although our guilty feelings haven't put an end to the Seven Deadly Sins or persuaded us to obey all Ten Commandments, they have without question slowed us down considerably.

Nevertheless we must recognize that while guilt deprives us of numerous gratifications, we and our world would be monstrous minus guilt. For the freedoms we lose, our constraints and taboos, are necessary losses—part of the price we pay for civilization.

Our guilt becomes our own when, at around the age of five, we begin to develop a superego, a conscience, when the "No, you can'ts" and the "Shame on you's" which used to be outside us regroup as our internal critical voice. Our guilt becomes our own when instead of feeling, "Better not do it; they will not like it," that "they" is no longer our mother and father but—us.

For we do not arrive in this world with a commitment to certain admirable moral precepts. We are not born intending to be good. We want, we want, we want, and only slowly relinquish reaching out and grabbing. But control cannot be called conscience until we are able to take it inside us and make it our own, until—in spite of the fact that the wrongs we have done or imagined will never be punished or known—we nonetheless feel that clutch in the stomach, that chill upon the soul, that self-inflicted misery called guilt.

True guilt, it can be argued, is not the fear of our parents' wrath or the loss of their love. True guilt, it can be argued, is the fear of our *conscience's* wrath, the loss of *its* love.

We resolve our oedipal conflicts by acquiring a conscience which—like our parents—limits and restrains. Our conscience is our parents installed in our mind. Later identifications, with teachers and preachers, with friends, with superstars and heroes, will modify what we value and what we forbid. And the emergence, over the years, of increasingly complex cognitive skills, will ready the ground for more complex moral ideas. Indeed, it is now believed that the stages of our moral reasoning (psychologist Lawrence Kohlberg says there are six) parallel the development of our thinking processes. But although our conscience is based on emotion *and* thought, and although it evolves and changes over time, and although it is built upon feelings from earlier stages, and although it expands beyond oedipal issues to take in all kinds of conflicts and concerns, this superego, this part of our self that contains our moral restraints and our ideals, is born of our primal struggles with lawless passions, is born of our *inner* submission to human law.

And if we breach those moral restraints or abandon those ideals, our conscience will observe, reproach, condemn.

And if we breach those moral restraints or abandon those ideals, our conscience will arrange to make us feel guilty.

There is, however, good and bad, appropriate and inappropriate guilt. There is deficient guilt and also excessive guilt. A few of us may know people who lack the capacity to have feelings of guilt about anything. But most of us know people (and a number of us *are* people) who are able to muster up guilt about virtually everything.

I am one of those people.

I feel guilty whenever my children are unhappy.

I feel guilty whenever one of my houseplants dies.

I feel guilty whenever I fail to floss after eating.

I feel guilty whenever I tell the whitest of lies.

I feel guilty whenever I step on a bug deliberately—all cockroaches excepted.

I feel guilty whenever I cook with a pat of butter that I have dropped on the kitchen floor.

And because, if there were room, I could easily list several hundred more of such genuinely guilt-provoking items, I would say that I am suffering from an excessive, indiscriminate sense of guilt.

Indiscriminate guilt is also the failure to distinguish between forbidden thoughts and forbidden deeds. Thus wicked wishes equal wicked acts. And although we adults believe that we have long ago learned to tell the two apart, our conscience may cruelly condemn us not just for the murder we carry out but for the murder that we harbor in our heart. And although we very well know that wishing does not make it so, it nevertheless may make us feel very guilty.

This lack of discrimination is one of the ways that we display excessive guilt. Disproportionate punitiveness is another. For guilty acts which require no more than a gentle "I'm sorry," a mental slap on the wrist, may inspire astonishing acts of self-flagellation: "I did it, how could I do it, only a low-down no-good moral monster could do it, and I hereby sentence this criminal—me—to death." This excessive punishing guilt is somewhat like pouring a whole cup of salt on an egg-salad sandwich. No one is disputing that perhaps the sandwich needs salt but—*not that much.*

Another form of excess might be called omnipotent guilt, which rests on the illusion of control—the illusion, for example, that we have absolute power over our loved ones' well-being. And so, if they suffer or fail or fall ill in body or in mind, we have no doubt that we alone are to blame, that had we done it differently, or had we done it better, we surely would have been able to prevent it.

A rabbi, for instance, tells of paying condolence calls—one winter afternoon—on two different families where elderly women had died.

At the first house, the bereaved son told the rabbi: "If only I had sent my mother to Florida and gotten her out of this cold and snow, she would be alive today. It's my fault that she died."

At the second house, the other bereaved son told the rabbi: "If only I hadn't insisted on my mother's going to Florida, she would be alive today. That long airplane ride, the abrupt change of climate, was more than she could take. It's my fault that she's dead."

The point here is this: By blaming ourself, we can believe in our life-controlling powers. By blaming ourself, we are saying that we would rather feel guilty than helpless, than not in control.

Others may have a need to believe that Someone Up There has control, that terrible things do not happen without a cause, that if they are struck by tragedy and devastating loss, they are struck because in some way they deserve it. There are those who cannot accept the thought that suffering is random or that evil men prosper and sorrows befall the good. And so they add to their suffering the conviction that they suffer because they should, that their pain is sufficient proof that they are guilty.

A woman whose child had been desperately ill once described to me an astonishing conversation she'd had with God, a God in whom, by the way, she had most earnestly proclaimed she did not believe. "You ought to be ashamed of yourself. You really should," she reproached Him. "What a bully you turned out to be. If you want to punish a disbeliever, punish the disbeliever—not her child. Stop picking on my daughter! Pick on me!"

Analyst Selma Fraiberg writes that a healthy conscience produces guilt feelings commensurate with the act and that guilt feelings serve to prevent our repeating such acts. "But the neurotic conscience," she writes, "behaves like a gestapo headquarters within the personality, mercilessly tracking down dangerous or potentially dangerous ideas and every remote relative of these ideas, accusing, threatening, tormenting in an interminable inquisition to establish guilt for trivial offenses or crimes committed in dreams. Such guilt feelings have the effect of putting the whole personality under arrest. . . ."

Such feelings are excessive, neurotic guilt.

Neurotic guilt may be fed by the events of pre-oedipal years— by the anxiety and anger evoked by early separations or struggles with parents. Thus, for instance, our conscience may exercise an I-was-left-because-I-was-bad-and-therefore-I-deserve-to-be-punished punitiveness. Or it may harshly condemn the parts of ourself that our parents—whose love we so deeply feared losing— condemned. Or it may carry a great load of anger once directed against our mother and our father and now vigorously redirected against ourself. As one psychoanalyst told me, "I think, in general, that anything that leaves the child on his own to grapple with anxiety and rage will predispose him to play it all out on a repetitive inner stage—to get stuck with inappropriate levels and kinds of guilt as an adult."

Such guilt may make us feel that if we ever kiss a fellow, we'll grow hair on our teeth. And if we ever talk back to our mother, we'll give her a heart attack. And if we decide to do what we are desperately longing to do—and it is wonderful—we shouldn't be doing it.

And sometimes, alas, like Dr. Spielvogel's frantic, fictional patient Alexander Portnoy—we *cannot* do it:

> Can't smoke, hardly drink, no drugs, don't borrow money or play cards, can't tell a lie without beginning to sweat as though I'm passing over the equator. Sure, I say *fuck* a lot, but I assure you, that's about the sum of my success with transgressing. . . . Why is a little turbulence so beyond my means? Why must the least deviation from respectable conventions cause me such inner hell? When I *hate* those fucking conventions! When I know *better* than the taboos! Doctor, my doctor, what do you say, LET'S PUT THE ID BACK IN YID! Liberate this nice Jewish boy's libido, will you please? Raise the prices if you have to—I'll pay anything! Only enough cowering in the face of the deep, dark pleasures!

Not everyone is as acutely aware as Portnoy, or his creator, Philip Roth, of the moral inhibitions with which we live. We may consciously feel we are freer than we are. For an important aspect of guilt is that it frequently works upon us without our knowing about it, that we can suffer the consequences of unconscious guilt.

Now we know what our conscious guilt feels like—we know the tension and the distress—but our unconscious guilt can only be known indirectly. And among the signs that may attest to the presence of unconscious guilt is a powerful need to injure ourself, a persistent need to get or to give ourself punishment.

Criminals leaving self-damaging clues (including Nixon, perhaps, and his Watergate tapes) are very often impelled by unconscious guilt. And so is the husband who, having spent the afternoon with a friend, comes home with her watch in the pocket of his shirt. And so is Dick who, having had a bitter fight with his father, smashes up his Chevy and gets himself hurt. And so is Rita who, watching her boss raise hell with his secretary, fleetingly thinks, "I'm glad it's her, not me"—and then promptly pays for her thought by accidentally spilling hot tea all over her lap.

And so are these erstwhile lovers, Ellie and Marvin.

Ellie and Marvin
Have been having secret meetings twice a week
For the past six months
But have thus far failed to consummate
Their passion
Because
While both of them agree
That marital fidelity
Is not only unrealistic but also
Irrelevant,
She has developed migraines, and
He has developed these sharp shooting pains
In his chest, and
She's got impetigo, and
He's got pinkeye.

Ellie and Marvin
Drive forty miles to sneaky luncheonettes
In separate cars
But have thus far done no more than

Heavy necking
Because
While both of them agree
That sexual exclusivity
Is not only adolescent but also
Retrograde,
She has developed colitis, and
He has developed these dull throbbing pains
In his back, and
She's started biting her nails, and
He's smoking again.

Ellie and Marvin
Yearn to have some love in the afternoon
At a motor hotel
But have thus far only had a lot of
Coffee
Because
He is convinced that his phone is being tapped, and
She is convinced that a man in a trench coat is following her, and
He says what if the motor hotel catches fire, and
She says what if she talks some night in her sleep, and
She thinks her husband is acting suspiciously hostile, and
He thinks his wife is acting suspiciously nice, and
He keeps cutting his face with his double-edge razor, and
She keeps closing her hand in the door of her car, so
While both of them agree
That guilt is not only neurotic but also
Obsolete,
They've also agreed
To give up
Secret meetings.

Unconscious guilt, however, may extract much higher prices than colitis, migraines, backaches or mild paranoia. It may insist on a lifetime of penance and pain. And this guilt may derive from any act or omission, from any thought, that our conscience in its infinite wisdom deems wicked. Thus our mother's ill health, our parents' divorce, our secret envies and hates, our solitary sexual gratifications—any and all can become our blame and our shame. And if the new brother or sister we didn't want and wish wish wish would disappear does in fact—by illness or accident—die, we may hold ourself responsible, we—not knowing we think it—might think: "Why did I kill him? Why didn't I save him? Why?"

And our lives may crash on the rocks of our unconscious guilt.

It was Freud who first observed that analysts sometimes work with patients who ferociously resist relief from their symptoms, who seem to hold on for dear life to emotional pain, and who cling to this pain because it gives them the punishment that they don't even know they want for crimes they don't even know that they have committed. He notes ruefully, however, that a neurosis which has defied an analyst's best efforts may suddenly vanish if the patient gets into an unhappy marriage, loses all his money or becomes dangerously ill. "In such instances," writes Freud, "one form of suffering has been replaced by another; and we see that all that mattered was that it should be possible to maintain a certain amount of suffering."

But sometimes people are guilty and people should suffer, including people like you and people like me. Sometimes guilt is appropriate and good. Not all guilt is neurotic—to be cured, to be analyzed away. We would be moral monsters if it could. But some of us exhibit certain deficiencies in our capacity for guilt.

I have a friend named Elizabeth who cannot acknowledge guilt because, in her mind, the guilty are shot at dawn. She has to be perfect, sinless, error-free. And so she will say, "The car was smacked up," because she would choke on the words "I smacked up the car." And she also will say, "His feelings got hurt," because she cannot accept that she hurt his feelings. At best she can say, "We forgot to buy tickets and now they're all sold out," when she was the only "we" in charge of tickets. And as for certain more drastic acts—she once had a love affair with her husband's best friend—she managed to persuade both herself and her husband that she was guiltless because he had driven her to it!

Elizabeth is quite capable of telling right from wrong. She is, however, incapable of believing that she could experience guilt—and survive.

Another kind of deficient guilt is displayed by people who punish themselves after they have committed some dreadful act, but who then go on to commit these dreadful acts again and again, again and again. For although their conscience acknowledges that what they did was wrong, and exacts quite brutal payments for their sins, their guilt never functions for them as a warning signal. It serves them only to punish, not to prevent.

It is known that certain criminals are actually seeking punishment in order to expiate unconscious guilt. It is known that certain criminals are suffering from distorted, not absent, guilt feelings. There are, however, the so-called psychopathic personalities who seem to display a genuine lack of guilt, whose antisocial and criminal acts, whose repetitive acts of destructiveness and depravity, occur with no restraint and no remorse. These psychopaths cheat and rob and lie and damage and destroy with remarkable emotional impunity. These psychopaths spell out for us, in letters ten feet high, what kind of world this world would be without guilt.

But we don't have to be a psychopath to allow some person or group to stand in the place of our individual conscience. And yet this too can lead to deficient guilt. For when we relinquish to others our sense of moral responsibility, we may become free of central moral constraints. This giving over of conscience can turn ordinary people into lynch mobs and operators of crematoria. And it may enable any of us to act in certain ways which on our own we would surely regard as unthinkable.

In a famous experiment testing conscience versus obedience to authority, experimental psychologist Stanley Milgram brought people into a Yale University psychology laboratory to engage— or so they were told—in a study of memory and learning. The experimenter explained that the issue to be explored was the impact of punishment on learning, and to that end the subject designated "teacher" was asked to administer a learning test to a "learner" strapped in a chair in another room—and to give him an electric shock whenever his answer was wrong. The shocks were executed by a series of thirty switches which ranged from slight (15 volts) to severe (450 volts), and the teacher was told that, with each wrong answer, he was to give the learner the next higher shock. Conflict began when the learner went from grunts to vehement protests to agonized screams, and the teacher became increasingly uneasy and wished to stop. But each time he hesitated, the person in authority urged him to continue, insisting that he must complete the experiment. And despite the concern for the level of shocking pain that was being inflicted, a large number of teachers continued to push the switches all the way up to the highest voltage.

The teachers did not know that the learners were actors, and that they were only simulating distress. The teachers believed that the shocks were painfully real. But some of them persuaded themselves that what they were doing was for a noble cause—the pursuit of truth. And some of them persuaded themselves that "He was so stupid and stubborn he deserved to get shocked." And some of them were simply unable, despite their conviction that what they were doing was wrong, to make an open break with the person running the experiment—to challenge authority.

Milgram notes that a "commonly offered explanation is that those who shocked the victim at the most severe level were monsters, the sadistic fringe of society. But if one considers that almost two-thirds of the participants fall into the category of 'obedient' subjects and that they represented ordinary people drawn from working, managerial and professional classes, the argument becomes very shaky."

It is tempting to read about that experiment and imagine ourselves walking out the door, able to know right from wrong and to act on that knowledge. It is tempting to think that our conscience would prevail. It is tempting to think that put to the test, we would be counted among the morally pure. And some of us would be. And some of us would fail. But all of us, in the course of our life, will engage in acts we know to be morally wrong. And when we do, the healthy response is guilt.

Healthy guilt is appropriate—in quantity and quality—to the deed. Healthy guilt leads to remorse but not self-hate. Healthy guilt discourages us from repeating our guilty act without shutting down a wide range of our passions and pleasures.

We need to be able to know when what we are doing is morally wrong.

We need to be able to know and acknowledge our guilt.

The philosopher Martin Buber, respectful of this need, tells us that "there exists real guilt," that there is value in the "paining

and admonishing heart" and that reparation, reconciliation, renewal require a conscience "that does not shy away from the
glance into the depths and that already in admonishing envisages
the way that leads across it. . . .

"Man," says Buber, "is the being who is capable of becoming
guilty and is capable of illuminating his guilt."

We seem to be more familiar with the prohibiting parts of our
conscience, the parts that limit our pleasures and water our joys,
the parts that are always watching us to judge, condemn and
mobilize our guilt. But our conscience also contains our ego ideal
—our values and higher aspirations, the parts that speak to our
"oughts" instead of our "don'ts." And another task of our conscience is to say in effect, "Good for you" and "You did well," to
encourage us and approve of us and praise and reward and love
us for meeting, or striving to meet, this ego ideal.

Our ego ideal is composed of our most wishful, hopeful visions
of our self. Our ego ideal is composed of our noblest goals. And
while it is an impossible dream that can never be fulfilled, our
reachings toward it provide a deep sense of well-being. Our ego
ideal is precious to us because it repairs a loss of our earlier childhood, the loss of our image of self as perfect and whole, the loss
of a major portion of our infantile, limitless, ain't-I-wonderful
narcissism which we had to give up in the face of compelling
reality. Modified and reshaped into ethical goals and moral standards and a vision of what at our finest we might be, our dream of
perfection lives on—our lost narcissism lives on—in our ego
ideal.

It is true that we will feel guilt when we fall short of our ego
ideal or when we override our moral restraints. It is true that guilt
will make us less happy, less free. If we could believe in "anything
goes," we could go merrily—guiltlessly—on our way. But without
ideals and restraints, what would we be? A wolf forgiven at his
meat. A beetle innocent in his copulation. Something beyond the
bounds of humanity.

We cannot be full human beings without the loss of some of our anything-goes moral freedom.

We cannot be full human beings without acquiring a capacity for guilt.

10

Childhood's End

To be a man is, precisely, to be responsible.

—Antoine de Saint-Exupéry

Moving from oneness to separateness, and from separate self to separate guilty self, we find that we are neither safe nor free. It becomes increasingly clear that the person in charge of us is . . . us, and we may resent the responsibility. Like the seven-year-old who, chastised by his parents for being naughty, replied to their rebukes indignantly, complaining to his mother and father, "I'm getting sick of this. Everything I do you blame on me."

Now perhaps it can be argued that this child was simply an early psychoanalyst representing the classically Freudian view that unknown unconscious forces determine our actions, that powerful wishes and needs and fears outside of our awareness impel us to want what we want and to do what we do.

How can we be responsible when our id—that modern-day devil—made us do it?

The answer is Saint-Exupéry's: To be a man, a woman, an adult, is to accept responsibility. And during those years that are bracketed by the dawning of conscience and end of adolescence we must —by slowly expanding the dominion of what we can be responsible for—become our own grownup.

We must start claiming as ours the welter of hungers and angers and conflicts that dwell inside us. We also must start learning to tie our own shoes. And as we extend the realm and the reign of our consciousness and competence we will find ourselves moving farther and farther from home. In the phase that Freud labeled "latency"—which is usually dated from ages seven to ten—we leave the benevolent fortress of family life. Our job as a latency kid is to acquire the social and psychological know-how without which we cannot manage this new separation, these new necessary losses.

Current research suggests that our latency phase may be linked to a biological clock, for greater psychic stability and important new cognitive skills converge at age seven and give us more control. We therefore, in theory, are better equipped to postpone and redirect our importunate urges. We can, with greater ease, be socialized. But unless we arrive at latency having established a separate self—and having relinquished our starring role in *Oedipus*—we will have trouble taking on these tasks.

For how can a girl leave for school when it is too dangerous and too sad without her mother? And how can a boy learn his ABCs with things like incest and parricide on his mind? And though most of us enter latency with the rigid and too-harsh conscience of an only recently converted sinner, we also must enter with trust enough—in others and ourselves—to allow that too-harsh conscience to be gentled. For how can we ever take chances, how can we ever risk and dare, if any error we make is a capital crime? How, if every path is blocked by self-imposed restrictions, can we move out to explore our latency world?

We are only seven years old, but it's time to move out.

In latency we will discover, with amazement and relief, that parents are fallible—"My dad says it was, but my teacher Miss March says that's wrong." In latency we will find a new set of people to admire, to be like, to love. With our oedipal tumult behind us and the storms of adolescence yet to come, we will turn our passions and energies toward learning. And through what we learn—through reading and riding and running some small portion of our universe—we will begin to acquire a feeling of mastery.

In an interview with Amy, my nine-and-half-year-old Washington neighbor, she talked about some of the things she has recently mastered:

"Crossing busy streets that don't have a stoplight.

"Making my own French toast and all kinds of sandwiches.

"Playing the violin.

"Doing cartwheels.

"Diving off a board without bending my knees.

"Understanding hard words—like the meaning of 'pastoral.'

"And knowing about the Republicans and the Democrats and Greece, knowing about the whole world and not just my neighborhood."

Analyst Erik Erikson, whose classic "Eight Ages of Man" describes the stages and challenges of the life cycle, sees latency as that stage when we develop what he calls a "sense of industry." The wish to do some kind of completed work. The capacity to handle the tasks and tools of our particular society. And a self-definition broadened to include—as we balance two-wheelers and learn words like 'pastoral'—new and enormously gratifying competencies. Erikson says that all children, "sooner or later, become dissatisfied and disgruntled without a sense of being able to make things and make them well and even perfectly. . . ." Work, even kids' work, offers us—as Joseph Conrad once said—a chance to find ourself, our own reality.

Along with learning to make things well, we deepen our self-definition by placing ourself in the context of a group, by seeing that we are members of something called "boys" or "girls" or "nine-year-olds" or "fifth-graders." Our sexual identity and our view of what a kid of our age can do are clarified and confirmed by this group membership, which enhances our sense of identity, our "*this* is who I am," at a physical and emotional distance from home.

For some of us there is also that flame-kindling grownup—mine was the leader of my Girl Scout troop, the first adult who believed that I could write—who can see us in special roles, in special self-defining roles, that our make-your-bed-and-stop-hitting-your-sister-and-don't-talk-fresh-to-your-mother parents cannot.

We also expand our world by our development of a sharper sense of reality, by a clearer distinguishing of fiction from fact, which allows us both to make practical plans and to play among our fantasies without the fear that they will take over our life.

Latency is another step in moving on and out. And at its ideal best it can give us that heady (though, as we shall see, ephemeral) feeling that we are finally getting it all together.

Some of us may recall this time of our childhood as hard and lonely and confusing. We were rotten at games; we were timid; we were left out. But many adults remember those years as full of ready friendships and triumphs and laughter. Indeed they are the gilded years that Dylan Thomas describes in his exquisite poem about youth and ease, "Fern Hill."

. . . .

And as I was green and carefree, famous among the barns
About the happy yard and singing as the farm was home,
In the sun that is young once only,
Time let me play and be
Golden in the mercy of his means,
And green and golden I was huntsman and herdsman, the calves
Sang to my horn, the foxes on the hills barked clear and cold,
And the sabbath rang slowly
In the pebbles of the holy streams.

. . . .

And honored among foxes and pheasants by the gay house
Under the new made clouds and happy as the heart was long,
In the sun born over and over,
I ran my heedless ways,
My wishes raced through the house high hay
And nothing I cared, at my sky blue trades, that time allows
In all his tuneful turning so few and such morning songs
Before the children green and golden
Follow him out of grace,

. . . .

In my interview with Amy I asked if her nine-and-a-half-year-old life was green and golden. Her answer was an "absolutely yes!" And her reasons why make her sound as if she has read—or written—the book on the latency child.

Amy explains that she feels "relaxed and comfortable, sort of grown-up but not old. I'm on my own but I don't have to earn my own living." The adults in her life, she says, no longer regard her as "a little person." However, she adds, she knows that "when I am out somewhere on my own, I can always come back and my mom and my dad will be waiting."

Amy belongs to a five-girl club called The Rainbow Fleet (because they all love rainbows). Amy has a best friend whose name is Anne (and whose secrets she'd never never tell). Amy likes board games and roller-skating and people who aren't bossy. And her current view of society is that "falling in love seems silly" and that "boys should play with boys and girls with girls."

What does she wish were different? Very little. She talks a lot, and thinks she should try to talk less. She would like to be kinder to her little brother. And she "desperately" longs for pierced ears but although she must wait for that great event until age thirteen, she isn't at all impatient to get older.

"I feel that when I am in high school it will all be so much harder," she explains. Then pauses. Then adds philosophically, "When I was six I thought *fourth grade* would be harder. But I found that when I got there I was ready for it."

Many latency kids do not feel ready for it.

Ten-year-old Nan tells her mother, "I will never wear lipstick— never. And you don't have to buy me stockings until I'm a hundred."

The fictional Peter Pan decides he won't become a man, opting instead to remain a permanent boy.

And sixth-grader Joy has daydreams of riding through woods— the leader of a Robin Hood band—but she first arranges, in fantasy, to indefinitely postpone the start of menstruation. She tells herself that a menstruating girl would not be comfortable leading a Robin Hood band. She does not tell herself that she is afraid to be led out of grace and into puberty.

In dividing up human development into characteristic stages, analysts differ slightly in how they slice it, with all of them agreeing that the ages for each of these stages cannot be precise. Still, many also agree that latency ends at about age ten; that next comes the phase of prepuberty, a time of "transition from barrenness to fertility"; that this is followed by puberty, defined for a girl by her first menstruation (called *menarche*) and for a boy by his first ejaculation; and that adolescence involves our nutty-desperate-ecstatic-rash psychological efforts to come to terms with new bodies and outrageous urges.

Unlike Peter Pan, and ten-year-old Nan, and Robin Hood Joy, there are many who embrace the first signs of adulthood. But even the most eager of grower-uppers has secret—often unconscious— yearnings to stay in the green and golden world of childhood.

Judy Blume's almost twelve-year-old heroine Margaret expresses both sides of her growing-up ambivalence.

On the one hand: "My mother's always talking about when I'm a teenager. Stand up straight, Margaret! Good posture now makes for a good figure later. Wash your face with soap, Margaret! Then you won't get pimples when you're a teenager. If you ask me, being a teenager is pretty rotten—between pimples and worrying about how you smell!"

On the other hand: "Are you there God? It's me, Margaret. I just told my mother I want a bra. Please help me grow God. You know where. I want to be like everyone else."

The moving-out process which starts with wriggling off our mother's lap, then onto our feet, then into other rooms, continuing as we go from the sights, sounds, smells of family life to the studies and tasks and games and rules of latency, deposits us—at puberty —on the shore of a turbulent sea where we plainly see that leaving could mean drowning.

Or maybe murder.

Alexander Portnoy, recalling "that extended period of rage that goes by the name of my adolescence," writes that "what terrified me most about my father was not the violence I expected him momentarily to unleash upon me, but the violence I wished every night at the dinner table to commit upon his ignorant, barbaric carcass. . . . And what was especially terrifying about the murderous wish was this: If I tried, chances were I'd succeed."

He also recalls, as he ran from his half-eaten dinner and slammed out the door, his mother warning, "Alex, keep this back talk up . . . continue with this disrespect and you will give that man a heart attack!"

Many sons and daughters, in the course of growing up, may fear that they will give their parents a heart attack.

Even when they don't show disrespect.

Indeed it has been proposed that asserting our right to a separate existence can unconsciously feel as if we are killing our parents and that therefore most—maybe all—of us (and especially those of us with clingy parents) have some degree of separation guilt. It has also been proposed that separation guilt is appropriate, that growing up is a form of homicide and "that the assumption of responsibility for one's own life and its conduct is in psychic reality tantamount to the murder of the parents. . . ." Thus, by becoming autonomous (instead of remaining dependent), by establishing inner restraints (instead of needing our parents to serve as our external conscience), by cutting emotional ties (instead of seeking our gratifications within the family), by taking care of our needs (instead of surrendering that care to our mother and father), we annihilate our parents' roles and take them unto ourself.

And, in that sense, are guilty of killing our parents.

But metaphorical murder is only one of the problems we deal with at adolescence, when our body and our psyche start coming unglued, when our normal teenage state is sometimes hard to distinguish from a state of insanity, when development—normal development—demands that we lose and leave and let go of . . . everything.

Zapped by hormones, our body undertakes a massive revision—enlarging our sexual parts and our hair supply, demonstrating (by menstrual flows and seminal emissions) that we are joining the race of the baby-makers, changing our height and our weight and our shape and our skin and our voice and our odors, till we hardly know what to expect when we wake up in the morning.

I remember a short teenage boy who had finally come to terms with his shortness and who in fact had developed a charming "short" personality, part of which consisted of listing the beauties who, at the time, were married to men—so he said—who were shorter than they were. He mentioned Jackie and Aristotle Onassis. He mentioned Sophia Loren and Carlo Ponti. He mentioned . . . And then (could it be overnight?) he awakened to find that he had belatedly grown several inches—and had to revise his entire "short" personality.

Yes, our body image—our inner picture of our outer state—undergoes dramatic changes at puberty, as beauty is lost, or found, or lost and then found again, as inches—and sometimes mere fractions of inches—of height, hips, width of ears or length of nose make the difference (it seems) between joy and despair, as power comes to reside in the development of a torso or the possession of just-like-Brooke-Shields' blue eyes and dark hair, as the question girls ask about boys—and boys more relentlessly ask about girls—is not "Are they smart? Are they nice?" but "What do they look like?"

In Delia Ephron's delightful book about adolescent angst called *Teenage Romance*, she offers a list of bodily things to worry about:

> If you are a girl, worry that your breasts are too round. Worry that your breasts are too pointed. Worry that your nipples are the wrong color. Worry that your breasts point in different directions.

> If you are a boy, worry that you will get breasts.

> Worry that your nose is too fat. Worry that your nose is too long. Worry that your neck is too fat. Worry that your lips are too fat. Worry that your ass is too fat. Worry that your ears stick out. Worry that your eyebrows are too close together.

> If you are a boy, worry that you'll never be able to grow a mustache.

> If you are a girl, worry that you have a mustache.

It has been said that for adolescents "to be different is to be inferior." Okay means being the same as everyone else. Thus any kind of physical deviation from the norm or a maturing that occurs too late or too soon can be a source of awkwardness, a source of shame and chagrin, and can form mental pictures that live with us ("I'll always feel bony and scrawny and too thin") long after the actual physical facts have altered.

But even when body changes occur on schedule, and even when they occur in standard ways, obsessions with diet and weight may develop into serious problems at adolescence. Perhaps the most drastic expression (primarily among girls) of a distorted and rejected body image is a mental/physical illness—anorexia nervosa—where severe food restrictions can cause emaciation, near-starvation, the end of menstruation and, not infrequently, death. While early emotional difficulties can play a major role in this disease, it is set into motion by the impact of puberty. Dr. Hilde Bruch, who has written extensively on the subject of anorexia, pictures the anorexic girl as a fearful fifteen-year-old Sleeping Beauty, escaping from adolescence, escaping from change.

But for most of us change is unstoppable at adolescence—changes in our body and in our head—and while we are making the trip from early to middle to late adolescence normality is defined as a state of disharmony. This disharmony need not be constant, and it need not even be visible; sometimes, indeed, it is quiet and covert. But the conflicts and mood swings and excesses are often flamboyant enough to provoke the following list from some teenagers' parents:

A normal adolescent is so restless and twitchy and awkward that he can manage to injure his knee—not playing soccer, not playing football—but by falling off his chair in the middle of French class.

A normal adolescent has sex on the brain—and very frequently in hand.

A normal adolescent describes as two major goals in life (1) putting an end to the threat of nuclear holocaust and (2) owning five knit shirts with a Ralph Lauren label.

A normal adolescent plunges from agony to ecstasy—and back again—in under thirty seconds.

A normal adolescent (who now is capable of abstract logical thinking) can use this new cognitive skill to contemplate deep philosophical issues but never to remember to take out the garbage.

A normal adolescent shifts from viewing her parents as merely fallible to regarding them as wrong about virtually everything.

A normal adolescent isn't a normal adolescent if he acts normal.

With that last poignant point Anna Freud fully agrees. Indeed she writes "that it is normal for an adolescent to behave for a considerable length of time in an inconsistent and unpredictable manner; to fight his impulses and to accept them; to ward them off successfully and to be overrun by them; to love his parents and to hate them; to revolt against them and to be dependent on them; to be deeply ashamed to acknowledge his mother before others and, unexpectedly, to desire heart-to-heart talks with her; to thrive on imitation of and identification with others while searching unceasingly for his own identity; to be more idealistic, artistic, generous and unselfish than he will ever be again, but also the opposite: self-centered, egoistic, calculating. Such fluctuations between extreme opposites would be deemed highly abnormal at any other time of life. At this time they may signify no more than that an adult structure of personality takes a long time to emerge. . . ."

At the end of this trip our psychic disruptions achieve some new kind of order as we learn to balance restraints and gratifications (without being either ascetics or hedonists). The sensual pleasures of childhood become the seasonings and garnishes of penis-in-vagina sexuality. In choosing someone to love we may typically start with ourself (in a rapture of teenage narcissism); then develop a same-sex crush (and maybe some am-I-homosexual anxieties); and eventually focus our interest on members of the opposite sex (after first renouncing—again!—our oedipal yearnings for mom or for dad which are renewed in the sexual stew of adolescence).

We may also start finding some answers to that universal question of adolescence: Who am I?

Now there was, in the course of those masterful years of our latency, the delusion that we had who-am-I all figured out. But under the onslaught of puberty, our sense of self, of selfsameness, of identity, liquefies into something confused and elusive. Among the seemingly endless tasks confronting adolescents is achieving a firm but still flexible sense of self, for as Erikson observes it is not until adolescence that we "develop the prerequisites in physiological growth, mental maturation and social responsibility to experience and pass through the crisis of identity."

Erikson sees this crisis as our struggle to become whole people in our own right, a wholeness we achieve by a unification—an inner synthesis—of what we have been and what we expect to be; of our sexual (which is broader than gender) identity; of the ethical, ethnic, occupational, private and societal parts of ourself; of new identifications with age mates and special adult figures beyond our family; of our choices and dreams. And although identifications and identity formation do not shut down at the end of adolescence, our continuing growth and development will rest on our adolescent reply to Who am I?

The point here is not that the self is born at adolescence—we know that it has already had a long history—but that it acquires a new quality, a new clarity, an organizing principle by which we stake out the boundaries of me and not-me. A state of what Erikson calls "identity confusion"—expressed through problems with work or intimacy, through over-identification with some peer hero, through the choice of a negative identity (I'd rather be totally awful than partly good), through feelings of vast isolation, through paralysis or breakdown—may occur if we fail to come through our identity crisis.

Along with, or maybe as part of, our adolescent identity crisis is the further toning down of our conscience's harshness, and an altering of our ego ideal from impossibly grandiose to something more realistic and . . . almost . . . attainable. For our ego ideal—our standards and expectations for ourself—is formed of the narcissistic dreams of our childhood. And those narcissistic dreams—those infantile visions of what human wholeness can be—have to grow up along with the rest of us. To hew to unrealizable goals and impossible dreams of perfection is to guarantee a perpetual sense of inadequacy, is to guarantee that whatever we do will never be good enough, is to guarantee failure time after time after time.

For if we must be the Smartest, a B-plus from our history teacher is a failure.

And if we must be Most Gorgeous, being runner-up for prom queen is a failure.

And if we must be Best Athlete, losing even a single tennis match is a failure.

Growing up means narrowing the distance between our dreams and our possibilities. A grownup has a grown-up ego ideal.

"When I was little," says thirteen-year-old Anita, "the gap between what I wanted and had was small. I think when I'm older the gap will be small again. But now between what I want and I have it's like this"—she makes a wide, wide space with her hands —"and everything"—she sighs—"is sort of bad."

Another reason why things may be "sort of bad" for Anita these days is that "I do not want to do," she says, "most of the things that my mother wants me to do." In her tug-of-war with her mom Anita's goal is perfectly clear: "What I'm trying to get out of this," she says, "is more freedom."

There is a course to adolescence which—from puberty to some-where over eighteen—is loosely marked by the following em-phases:

In early adolescence we are preoccupied with puberty's bodily changes.

In middle adolescence we are struggling with who-am-I and looking outside the house for sexual love.

In the late-adolescent phase we further mute our conscience's harshness and include—as a vital part of our ego ideal—values and commitments which are connected with our place in the wider world.

And through all these phases we have to work through, to swallow and chew and digest, an array of new and necessary losses, as we separate—really separate—from our parents.

This separation—this loss of the closest attachments of our life —is often frightening and always sad. The gates of Eden are clang-ing shut for good. And to this add the loss of our self-as-child and the loss of our former familiar body and the loss of our fuzzy innocence as we tune into the tough truths on the evening news. As with every important loss we need to mourn—we need to mourn our childhood's end—before we can be emotionally free to commit to love and to work in the human community.

It is said that adolescents, in this letting-go stage of life, experi-ence "an intensity of grief unknown in previous phases. . . ." It is then that we come to grasp the meaning of transience. And so we feel nostalgia for a past, a Golden Age, that never will return to us again. And, as we sigh over sunsets and summer's end and love gone astray and poems about "the land of lost content," we mourn

—without knowing we mourn—a far graver ending: the renunciation of childhood.

Mourning for our lost childhood is another—a central task—of adolescence. There are various ways to evade or accomplish that task.

College-bound Roger, for instance, snarls through his last few months at home, battling with his parents every day. He can't face his wish to stay, but if he arranges to leave feeling *mad* instead of *sad* he can avoid the pain of separation.

Brenda's promiscuity appears to be a statement of independence: I am a sexual woman, not a child. Except that the point of the sex is not the *during* but the cuddles before and after. She probably doesn't know that she is trying not to go away from mother.

Freshmen Shari and Kit pig out, indulging in eating binges: cake, cookies, a half-gallon of ice cream and such. In eating that much they are trying to offer themselves some mothering comfort for their loneliness. They are two little piggies who wish they could have stayed home.

"All though senior year [of high school]," says a college freshman at Yale, "I felt as though I were standing on the edge of a cliff, waving my arms to keep from falling off. Now I feel like a cartoon character in mid-flight across the canyon, wondering if I'm going to fall in or bridge the gap to the other side. . . ."

Going away to college is a time when many shaky selves will falter. Unbuttressed by family and friends, there are boys and girls who will turn to themselves and find . . . nothing there. The college counseling services are filled with students whose separation anxieties are being masked by desperate escapes from pain. And while most of these students are hardy enough to survive their struggles with separation anxiety, some of them may sink beneath their damaging and sometimes deadly solutions.

Drugs can blunt the mourning—why not get high instead of cry? Cults can replace the familial security. Dependent attachments or flights into marriage where mates are made into mommies can keep boys and girls adolescents all their life. And if these tactics fail—and separation pain cannot be held at bay—there may be crippling depression, breakdowns, suicide.

Compared to the age group of ten-to-fourteen-year-olds, the rate of suicide in 1982 rose about 800 percent among fifteen-to-nineteen-year-olds.

There are also thousands of kids like J. D. Salinger's teenage hero Holden Caulfield, unable to live in the present, pulled by the past. "Don't ever tell anybody anything," he writes, at age seventeen, from a psychiatric hospital. "If you do, you start missing everybody."

One way, of course, not to miss them is to stay at home, to not go, though you needn't always admit that you aren't going. For while some young people may openly cling, there are those who, under a show of great independence, nonetheless arrange to never depart.

The brilliant literary psychologist Leon Edel, for instance, reports that when Henry David Thoreau was about to graduate from Harvard, his mother suggested that he might "buckle on your knapsack and roam around abroad to seek your fortune." Henry burst into tears, thinking that his mother was sending him away from her. Later, as Thoreau the Transcendentalist, he did indeed go away—to a hut he built in the woods at Walden Pond, where he made much of the solitary, self-reliant life. However, Edel points out, his cabin was merely a mile away from his mother's house in Concord and there he returned for a visit—every day.

Thoreau once said, "Methinks I should be content to sit at the back door in Concord, under the poplar tree henceforth, forever." Edel says that that's what he in effect did—all his life. And although he created a myth of getting away from the world, of sturdy independence, "Thoreau, shut up in his childhood, could not leave home."

Adolescence is sometimes described (do you remember Margaret Mahler's stages of childhood?) as a second separation-individuation. It builds on the separate self we established back then. And if that self is too fragile, and if separation feels too much like death, we may be unwilling, unable to try it again.

"Adolescent individuation," writes analyst Peter Blos, "is accompanied by feelings of isolation, loneliness and confusion. . . . The realization of the finality of the end of childhood, of the binding nature of commitments, of the definite limitation to individual existence itself—this realization creates a sense of urgency, fear and panic. Consequently, many an adolescent tries to remain indefinitely in a transitional phase of development; this condition is called *prolonged adolescence*."

Fictional Holden Caulfield's plan for prolonging his adolescence is to figure out how to go on without growing up. The end of childhood seems like the end of all innocence. Rejecting becoming anything like the money-making hypocritical phonies of the adult world, he instead invents a fantasy—a glorious savior fantasy—in which . . .

> I keep picturing all these little kids playing some game in this big field of rye and all. Thousands of little kids, and nobody's around, nobody big, I mean—except me. And I'm standing on the edge of some crazy cliff. What I have to do, I have to catch everybody if they start to go over the cliff—I mean if they're running and they don't look where they're going I have to come out from somewhere and *catch* them. That's all I'd do all day. I'd just be the catcher in the rye. . . .

For many adolescents growing up means giving up and selling out. It means letting go of innocence and illusions. It means, explains twenty-one-year-old John, graduating from college in the tight job market of 1983 and being offered a position in the office of a conservative senator whose politics he deeply disapproves of and thinking that maybe he ought to play safe and take it. It also means relinquishing that sense of endless options—that feeling that he could (if he would just decide what he wanted) be a Soviet expert, marine biologist, journalist. What growing up also means, John says (although he hasn't yet done it), is: "Settling down with someone. Supporting myself. And owning life insurance."

Whether or not we agree that we need to own life insurance to qualify as grownups, to be a man (or a woman), as Saint-Exupéry observed, is to be responsible. Responsible means that we make and keep commitments. Responsible means, of course, that we tie our own shoes. But it also means that we are not allowed to blame our terrible childhood—or passion, temptation, ignorance or in-nocence—for acts that are ours, for deeds that we indeed do. For if, in fact, we do them, we are responsible.

It has often been argued that Oedipus, who killed his father, the king, and married his mother, cannot be held responsible because —poor ignorant fellow—he did not know. But analyst Bruno Bet-telheim suggests that the guilt of Oedipus derives precisely from his failure to know and that the point of the myth is to "warn of the utterly destructive consequences of acting *without knowing* what one is doing."

There comes a time when we aren't allowed not to know.

In the story of Job, as retold by the poet Archibald MacLeish in his play *J.B.*, the tormented hero is offered this cold comfort:

> There is no guilt, my man. We all are
> Victims of our guilt, not guilty.
> We kill the king in ignorance: the voice
> Reveals: we blind ourself.

J.B. will not accept this exculpation.

> I'd rather suffer
> Every unspeakable suffering God sends,
> Knowing it was I that suffered,
> I that earned the need to suffer,
> I that acted, I that chose,
> Than wash my hands with yours in that
> Defiling innocence. Can we be men
> And make an irresponsible ignorance
> Responsible for everything?

The answer to that question—the grownup's only answer to that question—has to be no.

And so, somewhere slightly before or after the close of our sec-ond decade, we reach a momentous milestone—childhood's end. We have left a safe place and can't go home again. We have moved into a world where life isn't fair, where life is rarely what it *should* be. Maybe we've even purchased some life insurance.

But it will not insure us against having to share love, against losing out to rivals, against the limits set by gender and guilt—against our many, necessary losses. There will always be the forbidden and the impossible. As Peter Blos writes: "The two Greek goddesses, Tyche and Ananke, the philosophical principles of Fortune and Necessity, replace the parental figures and become the forces to which man bows." It is tough to grow up.

But to acknowledge all this and nevertheless find our freedom, make our choices, recognize what we are and what we might be, is what a responsible adult is all about. Bowing to necessity, we must choose. This freedom to choose is the burden and the gift that we receive when we leave childhood, the burden and the gift that we take with us when we come to childhood's end.

III
Imperfect
Connections

We are all of us calling and calling across the
incalculable gulfs which separate us. . . .

—David Grayson

11

Dreams and Realities

... waking life is a dream controlled.

—George Santayana

Growing up means letting go of the dearest megalomaniacal dreams of our childhood. Growing up means knowing they can't be fulfilled. Growing up means gaining the wisdom and skills to get what we want within the limitations imposed by reality—a reality which consists of diminished powers, restricted freedoms and, with the people we love, imperfect connections.

A reality built, in part, upon the acceptance of our necessary losses.

And yet, though we repudiate our unfulfillable wishes, they press themselves upon us in sneaky ways. As symptoms and errors and mishaps and lapses of memory. As slips of the tongue and the pen ("Dear Dead—I mean Dad"). As accidents (for we wouldn't, on purpose, spill borscht on our rival's white dress—that would be *bad*). And as the dreams we dream—by night and by day.

Adults though we may be, the forbidden wishes, impossible wishes, of our childhood continue to insist on gratification.

And indeed our daydreams, our fantasies, are one of the ways we gratify these wishes. In fantasies our wishes can always come true. These conscious make-believings will express the changing concerns of our daily life. But they also are always connected to unconscious and unacknowledged early yearnings.

Fantasies can provide us with the magical solution, the fairy-tale ending. In fantasies we can do what we want to do. It is pleasing when our G-rated Hollywood happily-ever-afters drift through our consciousness—but they're not the only images that do. For our fantasies also traffic in unabashed glory, X-rated sex and bloody murder. And many of us, recoiling from these glimpses of disreputable desires, will sometimes feel guilty, ashamed and afraid of our fantasies.

Evelyn speaks with embarrassment of what, psychoanalysts say, is a common fantasy:

She dies, her funeral service is held and every pew in the church is packed with people and "one by one all the thousands of men and women whose lives I have touched step up to the altar to tell the assembled throng about the wonderful things I have done for them."

Such a good human being.

Such a generous person.

How grateful we are.

Now Evelyn, in the course of her life, has done many wonderful things for many people. Her life, in fact, has earned her fantasy. And yet she is deeply ashamed of it because, she says, "it nakedly reveals how hungry I am for attention and praise and acknowledgement."

Sexual fantasies also reveal some hungers that may stir up shame—and guilt.

Consider Helen, for instance, a quite happily married woman, who has written a whole scenario starring Ted that begins with an innocent movie date while her husband is out of town and ends, not so innocent, on his waterbed. And she wonders: Is this spiritual adultery? Is this any way for a young married woman to think? And how kinky can I get? Suppose there is Ted and his roommate on the waterbed? Or Ted and his sister? Or Ted and three ... Exactly what *are* you permitted to do in fantasy?

Many who accept quite far-out fantasies of sex may shudder at their hostile fantasies, wherein that brilliant woman they envy flunks law school, and their rich and arrogant brother-in-law goes bankrupt and the lovely flirtatious lady next door gets smallpox, and everyone else who makes them feel frightened, jealous, threatened, inferior or enraged suffers . . . reprisals.

The wife of a faithless husband put him to bed, in her head, with a long-term case of TB—"to take him out of the action," she said, "nothing fatal." But though it is hard to coax the admission from others, or from ourself, our hostile fantasies often *do* include fatal.

Take the gentle Amanda—self-effacing, afraid to compete— who, when someone upsets her, wishes him dead. She never complains or asserts herself but she is Murder Inc. inside her head, where her images of revenge are always merciless and swift and very permanent.

Take Barry, who, whenever his wife starts driving him up the wall, indulges in the pleasing fantasy of how sweet his life would be if, when his wife next rode a plane it . . . developed engine trouble.

And take a nice lady like me, the year that a twelve-year-old bully was picking on one of my children, sending him home from school in great distress. On many occasions, I have to confess, I solved the bully problem by mentally shoving him in front of a truck.

If ambitious fantasies make people blush, and sexual fantasies make people blush and feel guilty, fantasies of violence and death may make people blush and feel guilty—and frightened too.

This fear has to do with what psychoanalysts call "magical thinking"—the belief that we can control events with our mind, the belief that in primitive tribes is expressed by sticking pins in dolls and in modern times by sending forth "bad vibes," the belief that many sophisticated people are shocked to discover they hold: That thoughts can indeed do harm. That thoughts can kill.

I know a smart, sane woman who had been going through a terrible time with her mother. Bitter and angry, quarreling with her every day, she fantasized one evening as she drove there for a visit that her mother had suffered a fatal heart attack. Arriving at the street, she saw an ambulance roar past, stopping with a screech at her mother's front door; and paralyzed with fear, she watched a team of medics rushing in with a stretcher.

And out again with the body of the woman who lived in the flat upstairs from her mother.

"I was utterly convinced," she says, "when I saw that ambulance, that I had given a heart attack to my mother. And I have to confess that a part of me still believes, in some nutty way, that my 'magic' missed and got that poor lady instead."

(Before you smile with amusement at my friend's superstitious foolishness, perhaps you ought to ask yourself this question: If you had to swear on your children's life that something you said was the truth—and it was a lie—could you actually go ahead and swear it? I know I could not.)

This belief in wish fulfillment, in the omnipotence of thoughts, in the secret, injurious powers that thoughts can possess, belongs to a stage that we all pass through and that few of us ever totally outgrow. Given sufficient guilt about some terrible wish of ours, and seeing that terrible wish fulfilled in reality, we find all plausible explanations fleeing from our brain. "It is as though," writes Sigmund Freud, "we were making a judgment something like this: 'So, after all, it is *true* that one can kill a person by the mere wish!'"

Such judgments may leave us feeling afraid of our fantasies.

But even when we aren't afraid of what fantasies can do, we may be afraid of what our fantasies mean, appalled by those fleeting glimpses of our rage and eroticism and grandiosity. Do they represent our real reality? Do they tell the truth of what we are? In answering my question, one psychoanalyst related this lovely story:

There was once, in an ancient kingdom, a most famous holy man, renowned for his generous heart and his many good deeds. And the ruler of that kingdom, who esteemed the holy man, commissioned a great artist to paint his portrait. At a ceremonial banquet the artist presented the king with the painting, but when, with a flourish of trumpets, it was unveiled, the king was shocked to see that the face on the painting—the holy man's face—was brutish and cruel and morally depraved.

"This is an outrage!" thundered the king, ready to have the hapless artist's head.

"No, sire," the holy man said. "The portrait is true."

And then he explained: "Before you stands the picture of the man I have struggled all my life not to become."

What this analyst is saying is that all of us, including the very holiest, have impulses we struggle against every day. And while some of that struggle occurs outside our awareness, there are other urges and wishes—sometimes shaped into those little vignettes we call fantasies—that make us painfully conscious of the person we are trying not to become: the primitive and demanding and amoral and childish person that we sometimes find contained within our fantasies.

But psychoanalysts note that the crucial word in the preceding sentence is "contained." Fantasies are contained; they are not action. To acknowledge our primitive self is not to become our primitive self, for fantasies tend to express what, in actual life, we have civilized, harnessed, transformed and tamed.

They also point out that, whether we approve of it or not, anything in fact does go in our fantasies. Which doesn't mean, they add, that we should never feel any sense of concern about them.

For instance, they say, if our fantasies are persistently violent and cruel, or if our sexual fantasies are totally at odds with our sexual life, we may want to try to learn more about our angry feelings or our sexual conflicts. And they say that if our fantasies too completely serve as substitutes for life—if, in fact, there is *no* work and love, only fantasies—we may need to understand why we are living in our head instead of the world.

For the most part, however, they say that if we could feel less guilty, ashamed and afraid of our fantasies, we could find in them enormous release and relief. Recognizing them as essentially harmless. Recognizing them as substitutes for what we must, of necessity, lose. And using them to express and enjoy what we cannot or dare not live out in everyday life.

The conscious daydreams that drift through our mind, frequently uninvited, bring hints to us of a rogue subterranean world. In sleep, however, when normal restraints have been partially abandoned, we move—through dreams—much closer to that world. In dreams we regress in content and form—we tap into primitive wishes and into the primitive processes of our mind. For when we construct our dreams we draw on the vibrant, secret language of our unconscious.

In dreams we encounter a realm of the mind where contradictions abound, where the laws of objective reality do not apply, where images shift and merge, where the relationship between cause and effect is suspended and where time—past, present, future—are one and the same.

In dreams a host of feelings may be concentrated—condensed—on a single image, fusing and telescoping multiple meanings: "My mother was speaking but not with her own voice. It sounded just like my sister. And she had the red hair of my other sister. . . ."

Intense emotions appropriate to powerful but prohibited desires are shifted—displaced—onto something innocuous, safe: "I was standing in . . . the house we lived in when my brother was born. . . . I saw a ball lying in front of me and gave it [in lieu of her brother] a hard kick."

Basic preoccupations—with birth, death, sex, the body, members of the family—are represented by universal symbols, or by other visual metaphors that sometimes resemble outrageous, unseemly puns: A woman dreams of a German officer wearing the Nazi uniform of the SS. Her associations on waking are to her overbearing mother, urging her to eat with a Yiddish *"Ess! Ess!"*

The use of condensation, displacement and visual representation is called the dream work.

The logical part of our sleeping mind, like an editor revising a hard-to-read article, also plays a role in shaping our dreams. It tries to bring some order to the chaos. It takes the peculiar fragments that our dream work has produced and gives them a more-or-less coherent form. This is the form of the dream we recall on awakening.

This dream that we recall has been named by Freud the "manifest content" of the dream. The meaning of the dream is its "latent content." The interpretation of dreams requires the dreamer's associations—the ideas and feelings the manifest dream evokes—associations which sooner or later will lead from the dream we remember to the unconscious thoughts from which the dream derives.

Consider, for example, Hugo's dream.

"I was walking with a friend. We came to a butcher shop. Here the friend left me. I saw the butcher inside. He was blind. The shop was in shadow, brown-colored. The butcher called my name in a down-east Boston accent. I wanted meat for my cat. Though blind, he cuts up a kidney with a sharp knife."

Hugo, in psychoanalysis, has been starting to face his unhappiness with his marriage. Why, he asks, could he never see it before? Why has he conducted himself like an ostrich with his head stuck in the sand? What, exactly, has he been scared to look at?

The blindness in the dream makes Hugo associate to his own refusal to see: "No see, no hear, no know," he says; "that's me." The butcher, he says, "chops everything up so it's butchered." And then his associations bring him face to face with what he has feared to look at: "The butcher had an accent like an actor," he remembers, "whose name is . . . Kil[l]bride."

Not all of our dreams are so clear; they wear many disguises. But Freud says every dream contains a wish. He says that, no matter how scary or sad, our dreams seek wish fulfillment. And he says that our dreams are always linked to the forbidden, impossible wishes of our childhood.

Our daydreams—and our nighttime dreams as well—can allow impossible wishes to come true. And they can, in fact, make a difference in how we feel. For just as a dream about drinking a beer may quench our thirst sufficiently to keep us from waking to get a glass of water, so waking or sleeping fantasies that satisfy less permissible desires may reduce the urgency of those desires.

Gratification through fantasy is, to some degree, actually possible. Indeed our fantasies sometimes can seem almost real. But no matter how persuasive they seem or how gratified we may feel, we must be able to live in the grown-up world, we must be able to live with reality.

It isn't so bad.

For growing up is not the death of all that's swell and sweet. Growing up need not be the Big Chill. And as we become what I'll call by the awkward name of a "healthy adult," possessed of adult wisdoms, strengths and skills, few of us would choose to become a child again.

For as healthy adults we can leave and be left. We can safely survive on our own. But we're capable, too, of commitment and of intimacy. Able to merge and separate, to be both close and alone, we connect at varying levels of intensity, establishing loving bonds that may reflect the diverse pleasures of dependency, mutuality, generativity.

As healthy adults we feel our self to be lovable, valuable, genuine. We feel our self's "selfsameness." We feel unique. And instead of seeing our self as the passive victim of our inner and outer world, as acted upon, as helpless and as weak, we acknowledge our self to be the responsible agent and determining force of our life.

As healthy adults we can integrate the many dimensions of our human experience, forsaking the simplifications of callow youth. Tolerating ambivalence. Looking at life from more than one perspective. Discovering that the opposite of a very important truth may be another very important truth. And being able to transform separate fragments into wholeness by learning to see the unifying themes.

As healthy adults we possess, along with a conscience and, of course, guilt, a capacity for remorse and self-forgiveness. We are merely constrained—not crippled—by our morality. Thus we remain free to assert, to achieve, to win the competition, and to savor the complex delights of mature sexuality.

As healthy adults we are able to pursue and enjoy our pleasures but we also are able to look at and live through our pain. Our constructive adaptations and our flexible defenses allow us to achieve important aims. We have learned how to get what we want and we have repudiated the forbidden and the impossible, though we still—through our fantasies—tune into their claims.

But we know how to make a distinction between reality and fantasy.

And we're able—or able enough—to accept reality.

And we're willing—for the most part—to seek most of our gratifications in the real world.

What's called "reality testing" begins—through frustration—in early childhood, when we find that wishing doesn't make it so, when we find that we cannot long be warmed or comforted or fed by wishful fantasies. We acquire a sense of reality, which means that we can determine whether something is actually there or no, and which means that no matter how vividly we summon up an image of gratification, we can recognize that this image is a picture in our head and not a living presence in our bedroom.

A sense of reality also lets us assess ourself and the world with relative accuracy. Accepting reality means that we've come to terms with the world's—and our own—limitations and flaws. It also means establishing achievable goals for ourselves, compromises and substitutes that we put in the place of our infantile longings because . . .

Because as healthy adults we know that reality cannot offer us perfect safety or unconditional love.

Because as healthy adults we know that reality cannot provide us with special treatment or absolute control.

Because as healthy adults we know that reality cannot compensate us for past disappointments, sufferings and loss.

And because as healthy adults we eventually come to understand, as we play our friend spouse parent family roles, the limited nature of every human relationship.

But the trouble with healthy adulthood is that few of us are consistently adult. Furthermore, our conscious goals are often sabotaged unconsciously. For the infantile wishes we sometimes glimpse in dreams or fantasies exercise great power outside our awareness. And these infantile wishes may burden our work and our love with quite impossible expectations.

Asking too much of the people we love or asking too much of ourselves, we aren't—who is?—the "healthy adults" we should be. Growing up takes time and we may be a long time learning to balance our dreams and our realities.

We may be a long time learning that life is, at best, "a dream controlled"—that reality is built of imperfect connections.

12

Convenience Friends and Historical Friends and Crossroads and Cross-Generational Friends and Friends Who Come When You Call at Two in the Morning

Friendship is almost always the union of a part of one mind with a part of another; people are friends in spots.

—George Santayana

Moving into the world, we try to distinguish fiction from fact, our fantasies and dreams from what actually happens. Moving into the world, we try to accept the compromises of childhood's end. Moving into the world beyond the ties of flesh and blood, we try to form untainted ties of friendship. But these voluntary relationships, like all of our relationships, will have their disappointments as well as their joys.

For we once believed that our friends were our friends only when our love and trust were absolute, when we shared identical tastes and passions and goals, when we felt that we could bare the

darkest secrets of our souls with utter impunity, when we willingly would run—no questions asked—to help each other in times
of trouble. We once believed that our friends were our friends only
when they fit that mythic model. But growing up means giving up
that view. For even if we are lucky enough to have one or two or
three beloved "best friends," friendships, we learn, are at best an
imperfect connection.

Because friendships, like all our relationships, are hedged by
our ambivalence—we love and we envy; we love and we compete.

Because friendships—same-sex friendships—are our compromises, so it has been argued, with our normal (but mostly unconscious) bisexual tendencies.

Because friendships—cross-sex friendships—have to make their
peace with heterosexual lust.

Because even the best of friends are "friends in spots."

It has often been said that a friendship is judged by whether or
not we will stand by our friends in adversity. But there is an
opposing, more subtle, point of view which argues that it is relatively easy to come through in times of adversity and that the
tougher test of friendship is being wholeheartedly able to stand by
our friends in their joys. For intermingled with feelings of pride in
our friends and support for our friends are feelings of competitiveness and envy. We wish our friends well; we are conscious of only
good will. But sometimes there flits through our consciousness—
like a blip on a radar screen—the knowledge that part of us also
wishes them ill. And we fleetingly glimpse the truth that although
we would never, by word or by deed, do anything harmful to
them, we might not—if they failed to get that raise, that prize,
that good review—be quite as sorry about it as we will claim to
be.

Our contradictory feelings—our simultaneous love/hate feelings
—begin with the first major figures of our life, and later we transfer some of what we feel toward our mother and father and sisters
and brothers onto our spouses, our children and, yes, our friends.
Although our unfriendly emotions are, for the most part, kept from
awareness, and although, in friendship, the love outweighs the

hate, it is our human fate to suffer, to greater or lesser degrees, from the curse of ambivalence.

Dinah, wife and mother, receives a visit from Isobel, the beautiful beloved best friend of her childhood. She loves Isobel, but she wants to beat her too. She wants "to deal with the subtle threat of Isobel and any success she might have had in her life." She wants her, Dinah's, life—"even this moment as it was being played out in the boxlike kitchen—to be sincerely coveted by her good friend Isobel." And she is flooded with "that old instinct—like the one between two sisters—to protect Isobel from any criticism save [her] . . . own. . . ."

Love and competition, love and envy, Dinah knows, can coexist between the best of friends.

"The feeling I have," Marcy tells me, "and this isn't easy to talk about, is that no one should have it all—it isn't fair." And in order not to feel envy—"even with friends I dearly love, I need to know that they don't own all of life's goodies."

Embarrassed by her secret competitive feelings, Marcy notes, "I only want to be even—not superior." And so, when her friend Audrey—who is beautiful, rich, successful—"complains that her husband doesn't treat her well, I give her a lot of sympathy, I give her a lot of support, but I tell myself, 'Okay, so her husband doesn't treat her well—that's fair enough.' "

(And so, when I look at a friend of mine who—like Audrey—has it all, I am secretly glad that she is getting jowls.)

How uncomfortable it makes us merely to contemplate having such feelings towards our friends. How tempted we are to insist, *You* may feel them; *I* don't. But in my discussions with women—and men—about the mixed emotions present in friendships, most of them, after squirming a bit, could find some Dinah and Marcy in themselves.

If ambivalence makes us uneasy, how do we deal with the outrageous thought that we harbor sexual feelings toward our friends? Before rejecting that notion as an assault on our unalloyed heterosexuality, let us examine it:

Freud argued that all love relationships, not only lover-love but our love for our parents and children and friends and humanity, are always, at heart, a sexual love with the aim of some sort of sexual connection. In all but lover-love this aim is normally diverted, but the impulse remains in muted and altered form. And because we are all, to different degrees, bisexual human beings— because, as Freud put it, "no individual is limited to the modes of reaction of a single sex but always finds some room for those of the opposite one"—this muted and altered sexual wish will also be present in our same-sex relationships.

This means that male/male and female/female friendships contain unexpressed and unconscious erotic elements.

This doesn't mean, however, that we're dying to jump into bed with all of our friends.

Indeed, for most people, same-sex friendships simply would not be possible if sexual feelings were not cordoned off—partially repressed and partially given rechanneled expression as loving concern, as devotion, as affection. This friendly affection, however, most especially between men, is rarely conveyed through tender physical contact, for while women can kiss and embrace each other without stirring up homosexual anxieties, a punch on the shoulder or good-natured slap on the back is as far as most men (despite the current shift to less macho male stereotypes) can comfortably go.

Heterosexual Robert, on a camping trip with a friend, feels an urge, the first night out, to hug him. But afraid that an embrace will throw them both into a what-next sexual panic, he consciously refrains from this expression of affection until, at the end of the trip, he can hug him and leave. Robert sees his urge as a wish to express his love for his friend, and not as a wish for sexual conjunction. But his fear, a common male fear, is that "if we hug, the next thing you know, we'll take off our clothes and suck each other's cocks."

Was Robert's urge a homosexual urge? The psychiatrist who told me this story says yes. But only in the sense, he says, that in all such physical impulses there is always a repressed erotic element. Robert isn't aware of it, and even if he were, such sexual feelings don't make him a homosexual.

For even when there is consciousness of some erotic feelings, these feelings need not proclaim a sexual choice. As psychiatrists point out in a useful book, *Friends and Lovers in the College Years*, having "sexual feelings toward someone of the same sex"—or even having some homosexual experiences—"does not necessarily mean that individuals must define themselves as 'homosexual.' These feelings may be subordinate to heterosexual feelings, which represent the dominant sexual orientation."

On the other hand, these same psychiatrists also challenge the view that sexual restraint is a form of hypocrisy and that "honesty" and "openness" require us to play out all erotic urges. They also dispute the complaint that restricting sexual activities to one sex imposes undesirable and unnecessary constrictions on gratification.

Why not enjoy, instead of restrain, our normal bisexuality? Why not be friendly by making love to our friends? "There need not be a sharp distinction between sexual touching and friendship," argues researcher Shere Hite in her book *The Hite Report*. But it is, in fact, the sexual distinctions that we make in our roles as parent, as child, as lover, as friend, that provide us with a rich and mature and multifaceted emotional range. The insistent sexualizing of all our relationships would also impose undesirable constrictions.

To the extent that friendship requires the reining in of some of our sexual wishes, it is a less than complete, an imperfect, connection. But to take the view that friendship is a diluted version of love, "much as pink is regarded as a dilution of red," is surely to do it a serious disservice. Comparing the intimacy of friends and lovers, analyst James McMahon observes that friendships "differ from one's main relationship in that they generally do not involve the revelation of one's character and most basic needs in an often primitive and regressed way," meaning by this, I believe, that we can indulge ourselves, with a lover, in significant lapses of manners, control and dignity. Let us recall, for instance, the ratty robes that we have worn with our spouse at breakfast, our whining around the house when we have a bad cold, the boldness with which we help ourself to a forkful of food from his plate, the depths to which we sink when we are fighting with him. In addition to the regression—the ecstatic, exposed regression—of sexual love, we expose ourselves in other primitive ways, ways in which—no matter how many decades we have shared—we have never displayed with an intimate friend.

But in spite of what we reveal and expose within a love relationship, McMahon points out what all of us very well know: That no two people can hope to gratify all of each other's needs. That "no man or woman can be all things to another." Thus, even if lover-love is red and friendship is merely pink, pink saves us from a life of monotone. Our friendships can help to provide—in sometimes crucial and central ways—what lover-love lacks.

Listen to Faith, who describes herself as having a good, though surely not perfect, marriage: "Without my women friends I'd feel very lonely and very abandoned. They are essential. They are essential for the psychological talk, the introspective talk, the talk about fears and weaknesses and crazinesses. My husband doesn't have such conversations. My women friends do."

Listen to Lena, explaining her woman friend to her jealous husband in the shrewd and affecting French movie *Entre Nous:* "Madeleine helps me live. I'd suffocate without her."

Now listen to this husband: "If I told my wife I shot 986 in skeet, she would say, 'That's terrific.' She supports what I do, what I enjoy. But she really doesn't know what it means to shoot that high. Another man knows and appreciates what I'm talking about in a way a woman can't, at least one who doesn't shoot skeet."

Although men, like women, talk about the special importance of their same-sex friends, male friendships and female friendships are strikingly different. And considering what we have already learned about women's greater propensity for relatedness, we should not be surprised that studies show men friends to be less open and intimate. Here, for instance, is one man's not untypical description of his relationships with three "close friends":

> There are some things I wouldn't tell them. For example, I wouldn't tell them much about my work because we have always been highly competitive. I certainly wouldn't tell them about my feelings of any uncertainties with life or various things I do. And I wouldn't talk about any problems I have with my wife or in fact anything about my marriage and sex life. But other than that I would tell them

anything. [After a brief pause he laughed and said:] That doesn't leave a hell of a lot, does it?

Compare this cautious picture of "close" male friendships with Hilda's observation that "with women friends there is a soul feeling—something deep inside me can flow right up to the surface. Not much is held back; it's like talking to yourself." Compare it, too, with the friendships described below:

> I love my women friends for their warmth and compassion. I can share anything about my life with them and they never pass judgement or condemn. . . . There are no limitations on disclosure that I am aware of. The special quality of these female friendships is the openness. I have never been able to talk and share my feelings and experiences in the same way with any man.

I have heard these descriptions echoed by dozens of women of every age—and not by one man. Yet, ironically, all the celebrated friendships of myth and folklore are male friendships: Damon and Pythias, Achilles and Patroclus, David and Jonathan, Roland and Oliver, and—more recently—Butch Cassidy and the Sundance Kid. But what these friendships reflect, as sociologist Robert Bell notes, are acts of courage and sacrifice on behalf of each other. There are no celebrations, in these fabled male-male friendships, of emotional intimacy.

The conscious and unconscious links between admissions of weakness and male homosexuality, between admissions of vulnerability and male homosexuality, between admissions of loneliness, fear or sexual insecurities and male homosexuality, can help explain why men maintain more distance than women do in their same-sex friendships. With women, tender physical contact and emotional exposure are viewed with far less sexual alarm. Thus intimate female friendships, compared to intimate male friendship, do not pose as great a psychological danger.

The muted sexuality that is present in same-sex friendships is likely to be less muted with male-female friends, making it more difficult for women and men to be nonsexual buddies. In recent years, however, as more arenas have opened up to allow the two sexes to work and play as equals, friendships between men and women—friendships without an erotic agenda—have increased. There still remains the view, of course, as one man gracelessly puts it, that "men are for friendships and women are for fucking." But classmates, dorm mates, office mates and some married (though not to each other) husbands and wives are finding more social support for cross-sex friendships.

In one study, many of the men interviewed said that they felt emotionally closer to their women friends than to their men friends. "It is a real gut feeling I have," a male psychologist observed. "I feel that in general women care more about their friends than men do." And another man, a lawyer, said that "I am beginning to think that 'macho' threatens male friendship and that is not a threat with women friends. It gets down to the bottom line of there being trust with the woman that is often not there with the man."

Lucy, a married woman with four children, describes her friendship with a married man:

"We've found we have things to talk about that are different from what he talks about with my husband and different from what I talk about with his wife. So sometimes we call on the phone or meet for lunch. There are similar intellectual interests—we always pass on to each other the books that we love—but there's also something tender and caring too."

In a couple of crises, Lucy says, "he offered himself, for talking and for helping. And when someone died in his family, he wanted me there. The sexual, flirty part of our friendship is very small, but *some*—just enough to make it fun and different."

Nevertheless, she says, they have always managed to keep their friendship strictly friendship.

But because of the sexual pull, and the greater legitimacy given to heterosexual longings, male-female friendships are rarer than same-sex friendships. And when men and women achieve them, notes psychoanalyst Leo Rangell, they usually fit into one of the following categories:

Those that are, in effect, a same-sex relationship—"I think of her as myself or as I would another man."

Those that are, in effect, a family relationship—"I think of him as my father, my brother, my son."

And those that develop from a platonic palship to disguised—or perhaps quite undisguised—sexual love.

Rangell believes that a marriage bound by tenderness and affection is still "not quite a 'friendship' "—although it comes close. And while many couples would argue with him, insisting that they are both lovers and best friends, I too would distinguish lover-friendship from friendship—because of the intimate regressions McMahon discusses, and because of the far greater wish for exclusivity. On the other hand, there are many men and women who, like Lucy, have friendships which never progress to physical love, but who acknowledge the subtle presence of "a little bit of sex" in these relationships.

There is doubtless "a little bit of sex" in all of our relationships, but we learn to defer to conscience and social taboos. And in our unconscious, and sometimes conscious, letting go of erotic goals in our friendships, we lose—and we gain. Friendship, like civilization, is bought at the price, says Rangell, of restricting our sexual life. But friendship provides the setting for forms of pleasure and personal growth that may not be found on the wilder shores of love.

In adolescent friendships we use our friends, as we use our lovers, to discover, confirm and consolidate what we are. To some extent we always will use them that way. "There are strengths, there are facets of my personality," says May, a housewife and mother, "that, on my own, I might not see or acknowledge. My friends help me to see them. And they help me to aspire to other goals."

Friends broaden our horizons. They serve as new models with whom we can identify. They allow us to be ourself—and accept us that way. They enhance our self-esteem because they think we're okay, because we matter to them. And because they matter to us —for various reasons, at various levels of intensity—they enrich the quality of our emotional life.

Even though, with most of our friends, we form imperfect connections. Even though most of our friends are "friends in spots."

In my discussions with several people about the people we call our friends, we established the following categories of friendship:

1. Convenience friends. These are the neighbor or office mate or member of our car pool whose lives routinely intersect with ours. These are the people with whom we exchange small favors. They lend us their cups and silverware for a party. They drive our children to soccer when we are sick. They keep our cat for a week when we go on vacation. And, when we need a lift, they give us a ride to the garage to pick up the Honda. As we do for them.

But we don't, with convenience friends, ever come too close or tell too much: We maintain our public face and emotional distance. "Which means," says Elaine, "that I'll talk about being overweight but not about being depressed. Which means I'll admit being mad but not blind with rage. And which means I might say that we're pinched this month but never that I'm worried sick over money."

But which doesn't mean that there isn't sufficient value to be found in these friendships of mutual aid, in convenience friends.

2. Special-interest friends. These friendships depend on the sharing of some activity or concern. There are sports friends, work friends, yoga friends, nuclear-freeze friends. We meet to participate jointly in knocking a ball across a net, or saving the world.

"I'd say that what we're doing together is *doing* together, not being together," Suzanne says of her Tuesday-doubles friends. "It's mainly a tennis relationship but we play together well." And as with convenience friends, we can, with special-interest friends, be regularly involved without being intimate.

3. Historical friends. With luck we also have a friend who knew us, as Grace's friend Bunny did, way back when . . . when her family lived in that three-room flat in Brooklyn, when her father was out of work for seven months, when her brother Allie got in that fight where they had to call the police, when her sister married the endodontist from Yonkers, and when, the morning after she lost her virginity, Bunny was the person she ran to tell.

The years have gone by, they have gone separate ways, they have little in common now, but they still are an intimate part of each other's past. And so, whenever Grace goes to Detroit, she always goes to visit this friend of her girlhood. Who knows how she looked before her teeth were straightened. Who knows how she talked before her voice got un-Brooklyned. Who knows what she ate before she learned about artichokes. Who knew her when.

4. Crossroads friends. Like historical friends, our crossroads friends are important for what was—for the friendship we shared at a crucial, now past, time of life: a time, perhaps when we roomed in college together; or served a stint in the U.S. Air Force together; or worked as eager young singles in Manhattan together; or went through pregnancy, birth and those first difficult years of motherhood together.

With historical friends and crossroads friends we forge links strong enough to endure with not much more contact than once-a-year letters at Christmas, maintaining a special intimacy—dormant but always ready to be revived—on those rare but tender occasions when we meet.

5. Cross-generational friends. Another tender intimacy—tender but unequal—exists in the friendships that form across generations, the friendships that one woman calls her daughter-mother and her mother-daughter relationships. Across the generations the younger enlivens the older, the older instructs the younger. Each role, as mentor or quester, as adult or child, offers gratifications of its own. And because we are unconnected by blood, our words of advice are accepted as wise, not intrusive, our childish lapses don't summon up warnings and groans. Without the risks, and without the ferocious investment, which are always a part of a real parent-child connection, we enjoy the rich disparities to be found among our cross-generational friends.

6. Close friends. Emotionally and physically (by seeing each other, by mail, by talks on the phone) we maintain some ongoing friendships of deep intimacy. And although we may not expose as much—or the same kinds of things—to each of our closest friends, close friendships involve revealing aspects of our private self—of our private feelings and thoughts, of our private wishes and fears and fantasies and dreams.

We reveal ourself not only by telling but also by wordlessly showing what we are, by showing the unattractive—as well as the nice. And intimacy means trusting that our friends—although they don't, and should not, think we're perfect—will see our virtues as foreground, our vices as blur. "To be her friend," said a friend of the late political-activist and writer Jenny Moore, "was to be for a little while as good as you wish you were." And sometimes, with a little help—including some helpful don't-do-thats—from our friends, we can get there, and stay there.

Analyst McMahon writes that "growth demands relatedness" and that intimacy produces continuing growth throughout our life because being known affirms and strengthens the self. He quotes philosopher Martin Buber, who says that all real living is a meeting between I and Thou, and that "through the Thou"—through close encounters in which we open ourselves to each other—"a man becomes I."

Close friends contribute to our personal growth. They also contribute to our personal pleasure, making the music sound sweeter, the wine taste richer, the laughter ring louder because they are there. Friends furthermore take care—they come if we call them at two in the morning; they lend us their car, their bed, their money, their ear; and although no contracts are written, it is clear that intimate friendships involve important rights and obligations. Indeed, we will frequently turn—for reassurance, for comfort, for come-and-save-me help—not to our blood relations but to friends, to intimate friends like . . . Rosie and Michael.

Rosie is my friend.
She likes me when I'm dopey and not just when I'm smart.
I worry a lot about pythons, and she understands.
My toes point in, and my shoulders droop, and there's hair
    growing out of my ears.
But Rosie says I look good.
She is my friend.

Michael is my friend.
He likes me when I'm grouchy and not just when I'm nice.
I worry a lot about werewolves, and he understands.
There's freckles growing all over me, except on my eyeballs and
    teeth.
But Michael says I look good.
He is my friend.

.   .   .   .

When my parakeet died, I called Rosie.
When my bike got swiped, I called Rosie.
When I cut my head and the blood came gushing out, as soon as
    the blood stopped gushing, I called Rosie.
She is my friend.

When my dog ran away, I called Michael.
When my bike got swiped, I called Michael.
When I broke my wrist and the bone was sticking out, as soon as
    they stuck it back in, I called Michael.
He is my friend.

. . . .

Rosie would try to save me if there was a tidal wave.
She'd hunt for me if kidnappers stole me away.
And if I never was found again, she could have my Instamatic.
She is my friend.

Michael would try to save me if a lion attacked.
He'd catch me if I jumped from a burning house.
But if by mistake he missed the catch, he could have my stamp
    collection.
He is my friend.

In addition to helping us grow and giving us pleasure and providing aid and comfort, our intimate friendships shelter us from
loneliness. For although we are taught to strive for, and to value,
self-sufficiency, and although there is doubtless—in all of us—an
inner core of self we may never reveal, it matters to us enormously
that we matter to others and that we are not alone. "I need to
know," says Kim, "that there is someone besides myself who
really cares about whether I live or die." An old proverb puts it
another way: "One would not be alone, even in Paradise."

But the capacity for establishing intimate friendships varies
greatly, with some of us possessed of a natural gift and some of us
uncomfortable, inept or scared to death that closeness will lead to
rejection—or engulfment. Close friendships require a sense of self,
an interest in other people, empathy and loyalty and commitment.
They also require the letting go—the necessary loss—of some of
our fantasies of ideal friendship.

That distinguished old Roman, Cicero, in his much-cited essay

"On Friendship," asks "how can life be worth living . . . which lacks that repose which is to be found in the mutual good will of a friend?" So far so good. But he then goes on to impose upon friendship a burden no friendship could possibly sustain by defining it as a relationship between two "stainless" characters having *"a complete accord on all subjects human and divine. . . .* There must be complete harmony," proclaims the stringent Cicero, "of interests, purpose and aims, without exception."

Now it is true that when sociologists study adult friendships they find that similarities are the rule, that people choose friends who are like them in age and sex and marital status and religion, as well as in attitudes, interests and intelligence. It has even been suggested that, because friendship lacks the tumult of sexual love, it "may be more likely than love to connect the whole person with another total person." But while this may have been true in ancient times—in Cicero's time?—we moderns are too individualistic. Two people, two adults, will never match each other perfectly. Even the best of friends are friends in spots.

For among our close friends may be friends whom we should never ask for money—they're charming and bright but irredeemably cheap. Among our close friends may be friends with whom we cannot discuss a novel, or friends whose child-raising practices make us weep. We also may have close friends whose conscience strikes us as overindulgent; close friends whose compulsive tardiness we curse; close friends whose taste in food and clothes and dogs and politicians is incomprehensible—and whose taste in husbands or wives is even worse. We want our close friends to share our passions and values, our heroes and villains, our loves and our hates. But we may, in fact, have friends whom we will have to indulge and forgive for admiring Clint Eastwood movies and disdaining Yeats. And, sometimes, for failing us.

If Rosie told me a secret and people hit me and bit me,
I wouldn't tell what Rosie's secret was.
And then if people twisted my arm and kicked me in the shins,
I still wouldn't tell what Rosie's secret was.
And then if people said, "Speak up, or we'll throw you in this
    quicksand,"

Rosie would forgive me for telling her secret.

If Michael told me a secret and people clonked me and bopped me,
I wouldn't tell what Michael's secret was.
And then if people bent back my fingers and wrestled me to the
     ground,
I still wouldn't tell what Michael's secret was.
And then if people said, "Speak up, or we'll feed you to these
     piranhas,"
Michael would forgive me for telling his secret.

Cicero notwithstanding, intimate friendships will require that
we indulge and forgive, be indulged and forgiven. Stainless characters we are certainly not. And yet, despite the ambivalence, the
restricted sexuality and the fact that friends are friends only in
spots, the friendships we create may be as strong, and sometimes
stronger, than those we form through flesh and blood and law—
comforting and exuberant, "sacred and miraculous" connections.

13

Love and Hate in the Married State

The married state is . . . the compleatest image of heaven and hell we are capable of receiving in this life.

—Richard Steele

Our friends are less than perfect. We accept their imperfections and pride ourselves on our sense of reality. But when it comes to love we stubbornly cling to our illusions—to conscious and unconscious visions of how things should be. When it comes to love—to romantic love and sexual love and married love—we have to learn again, with difficulty, how to let go of all kinds of expectations.

These expectations flower in the steamy climate of our adolescence, when tenderness and sexual passion converge, when we fall in love with someone who embodies for us (with a little help from love's blindness) the perfect fulfillment of every human desire. Adolescent romantic love, says analyst Otto Kernberg, is the "normal, crucial beginning" of adult love. But many of us are done with adolescence before we are done with adolescent love.

And many of us recall a you-are-my-everything, I-can't-live-without-you passion. Our walks under stars. Our rides up to the moon. And whether or not we can make such love stay through the days and the years of our life, it may cast its shadow on everything that comes after:

Last night, ah, yesternight, betwixt her lips and mine
There fell thy shadow, Cynara! thy breath was shed
Upon my soul between the kisses and the wine;
And I was desolate and sick of an old passion,
    Yea, I was desolate and bowed my head:
I have been faithful to thee, Cynara! in my fashion.

In Freud's discussions of love he distinguishes sensual love, aimed at physical gratification, from love which is characterized by tenderness. There are both kinds of love in romantic sexual love. Freud also describes our overestimation—our idealization—of our beloved. This too is a part of romantic sexual love. Freud furthermore reminds us that even the deepest love relationship will not be proof against ambivalence and that even the happiest marriage will harbor some portion of hostile feelings.

Feelings of hate.

"The silken texture of the marriage tie," writes William Dean Howells, "bears a daily strain of wrong and insult to which no other human relation can be subjected without lesion." To which a modern sociologist adds: "One person, without any hostility, aggression or intent to hurt—merely through the expression of his existence—may be damaging for another."

The good news is that sometimes the bond between a husband and wife is stronger than any damage that can be done to it.

The bad news is that no two adults can do each other more damage than husband and wife.

Knowing my husband well, I know precisely which buttons to push to trigger his outrage. I also know how to soothe and smooth and make nice. And although you might think that such knowledge would keep my finger off the trouble-making buttons and allow me to fashion a marital paradise, that's not how my—or most—marriages tend to work.

Psychologist Israel Charny, in a provocative study of marriage, challenges "the myth that marital difficulties are largely the lot of 'sick' people or those who are not really 'mature.' " He argues that "empirically it cannot be denied . . . that the largest majority of marriages are riddled with profound destructive tensions, overtly or covertly." And he proposes to redefine our average, everyday, normal marriage as an inherently tense and conflict-ridden relationship whose success requires "a wise balancing of love and hate."

The tensions and conflicts of married life may begin with the death of romantic expectations, so beautifully described in the poem "Les Sylphides," where, dreaming of flowers and flowing rivers and satin and waltzing trees, two lovers marry.

> So they were married—to be the more together—
> And found they were never again so much together,
>   Divided by the morning tea,
>   By the evening paper,
>   By children and tradesmen's bills.
>
> Waking at times in the night she found assurance
> In his regular breathing but wondered whether
>   It was really worth it and where
>   The river had flowed away
>   And where were the white flowers.

Another foiled romantic is a doctor's wife named Emma, avid consumer of sentimental novels, novels which have tutored her to yearn for a "marvelous realm in which everything would be passion, ecstasy and rapture." Bitterly dissatisfied by her marriage, in which happiness has eluded her, lamenting "her too lofty dreams, her too narrow house," she makes her kindly but deadly dull and commonplace husband Charles "the sole object of the complex hatred engendered by her frustrations."

Emma is Flaubert's adulterous heroine Madame Bovary, a woman with a fevered romantic soul, a woman who expects from marriage "that marvelous passion which, until then, had been like a great rosy-plumaged bird soaring in the splendors of poetic skies." Not finding it in marriage, Emma does not let it go, or learn to temper romance with reality. Instead, recoiling from dailiness, she learns to hate her husband—and seeks romance elsewhere.

But we don't have to be adulterers to say, with Flaubert, "Madame Bovary, *c'est moi.*" We too have measured our dreams against our realities. We too may have strived for rosy-plumaged birds in poetic skies and found ourselves with a parakeet in a cage in the family room of a Silver Spring suburb.

"Marriage," writes anthropologist Bronislaw Malinowski, "presents one of the most difficult personal problems in human life; the most emotional as well as the most romantic of all human dreams has to be consolidated into an ordinary working relationship. . . ." And although, unlike doomed Emma, we adjust and adapt and compromise and make do, we sometimes may hate the married state for domesticating our dreams of romantic love.

We bring into our marriage a host of romantic expectations. We may also bring visions of mythic sexual thrills. And we may impose on our sex life many more expectations, more "shoulds," than the average everyday act of love can fulfill. The earth should move. Our bones should sing. Fireworks should explode. Consciousness —self—should burn on the pyre of love. We should achieve either paradise or a reasonable facsimile thereof. We will be disappointed.

In her book *Marriage Is Hell,* Kathrin Perutz describes the sexual mythology that lays such burdens on the marriage bed:

> The true man or woman must be deeply sexual; the only true intercourse between humans is sexual; levels of pleasure have almost become notches in the yardstick of goodness; and sexual variation is as necessary to marriage now as once social graces were. . . . Love must be made—or sex must be had—a prescribed number of times a week; otherwise one falls from grace and competition.

Such sexual shoulds transform the sex act into a test of performance and into proof of the state of our mental health, intimidating and shaming—and yes, disappointing—the husbands and wives who can't achieve apocalyptic orgasm. But even when passion is fever-pitch and all the systems are go, it is difficult to sustain such peaks of excitement. And couples may find that, after a time, sex is not so sexy anymore.

I bring the children one more glass of water.
I rub the hormone night cream on my face.
Then after I complete the isometrics,
I greet my husband with a warm embrace,

A vision in my long-sleeved flannel nightgown
And socks (because my feet are always freezing),
Gulping tranquilizers for my nerve ends,
And Triaminic tablets for my wheezing.

Our blue electric blanket's set for toasty.
Our red alarm clock's set at seven-thirty.
I tell him that we owe the grocer plenty.
He tells me that his two best suits are dirty.

Last year I bought him Centaur for his birthday.
(They promised he'd become half-man, half-beast.)
Last year he bought me something black and lacy.
(They promised I'd go mad with lust, at least.)

Instead my rollers clink upon the pillow
And his big toenail scrapes against my skin.
He rises to apply a little Chap Stick.
I ask him to bring back two Bufferin.

Oh somewhere there are lovely little boudoirs
With Porthault sheets and canopies and whips.
He lion-hunts in Africa on weekends.
She measures thirty-three around the hips.

Their eyes engage across the brandy snifters.
He runs his fingers through her Kenneth hair.
The kids are in the other wing with nanny.
The sound of violins is everywhere.

In our house there's the sound of dripping water.
It's raining and he never patched the leak.
He grabs the mop and I get out the bucket.
We both agree to try again next week.

Now to say all this is not to deny that we can have sexual moments as remarkable as any fantasist's dream, moments in which
the coming together—whether or not it involves perfectly syn-
chronized orgasms—involves a mutual wedding of passion and
love. Nor does an absence of storybook sex mean that we cannot

achieve what analyst Kernberg calls "multiple forms of transcendence," where—through acts of sexual love—we cross and erase the boundaries that separate self from other, woman from man, love from aggression and the present from the future and the past.

Testimony to such sublime moments is not restricted to Freudians or to fiction. Consider these poetic words from philosopher Bertrand Russell's autobiography:

> I have sought love, first, because it brings ecstasy—ecstasy so great that I would often have sacrificed all the rest of life for a few hours of this joy. I have sought it, next, because it relieves loneliness—that terrible loneliness in which one shivering consciousness looks over the rim of the world into the cold unfathomable lifeless abyss. I have sought it, finally, because in the union of love I have seen, in a mystic miniature, the prefiguring vision of the heaven that saints and poets have imagined.

Well, yes. But for many—perhaps most—couples such moments are extraordinary and rare. Or they succumb to custom, and custom stales. For although in sexual love we may strive to continue with our body the connections we have made with our heart and our mind, there are times when the leap from love to ecstasy fails. There are times—there are plenty of times—when what we will have to settle for are imperfect connections.

But the contrast between the marriage we wanted and the marriage we got spans more than romantic and sexual disappointments. For even when we marry with an earthier vision of what a good marriage should be, the married state—and the person with whom we are sharing it—must fail to meet some, sometimes all, of our expectations: That we will always be there for each other. That we will always be faithful and loyal to each other. That we will accept each other's imperfections. That we will never consciously hurt each other. That although we expect to disagree on many minor matters, we surely will be in agreement on major matters. That we will be open and honest with each other. That we will always go to bat for each other. That our marriage will be our sanctuary, our refuge, our "haven in a heartless world."

Not necessarily. Certainly, not all the time.

For along with these expectations I have collected marital tales of promises broken, harm deliberately done, disloyalty, infidelity, zero tolerance of each other's limits and flaws, and teeth-and-claws disagreements on such not so minor matters as money, having children, religion and sex. "If I rated my husband," says Meg, "on pain inflicted and trust betrayed, I guess I'd have to call him my worst enemy." Echoing her perception, a psychologist suggests that husbands and wives are each other's "intimate enemies."

Enmities arise because our unmet expectations become metaphors for all that our marriage lacks. She didn't take his side in his fight with his brother. The day she lost the baby he was out in L.A. on business and wouldn't come back. The inevitable daily insults and wrongs of marriage will also attack the silken texture of the marriage tie, making him think, "She'll never understand me," making her think, "I've married the wrong guy."

Listen to Millie:

"Sometimes when I talk to him about problems—mine or the kids'—or I say something searching and deep, or I say something desperate, I get, from the way he is answering me, that he hasn't heard me at all, and that furthermore he didn't hear me yesterday; and then, if I'm feeling a special need for understanding or admiration or *something*, I'll use the fact that he isn't giving it now as evidence that he doesn't give it ever, that he doesn't ever, ever really listen to me, or see me, or know who the hell I am, or care to know. And then the downward spiral starts and everything he says I'll use against him as further proof that he tunes me out, that he's utterly insensitive to my needs."

The words above are approximately what Millie has said to me, not only recently but over the years. For even though she has, she says, a steadfast, solid marriage, she comes to times when all her love goes dead, when the gap between what she has to have and what he has to give cannot be bridged. And what is left as she looks at this man, who is stable and cheerful and kind, and handy around the house and devotedly faithful, is a feeling, she says, like "You want to give a big sigh," is a feeling of "Oh, God, what am I doing here?" is a feeling that "I've got the wrong guy—there must be someone more attuned to my needs," is the feeling that she says is, "Yes, it's hate."

• • •

Our early lessons in love and our developmental history shape the expectations we bring into marriage. We are often aware of disappointed hopes. But we also bring into marriage the unconscious longings and the unfinished business of childhood, and prompted by the past, we make demands on our marriage, unaware that we do.

For in married love we will seek to reclaim the loves of our early yearning, to find in the present beloved figures of yore: The unattainable parent of oedipal passion. The unconditionally loving mother of childhood. And the symbiotic unit where self and other meld, as we once did before. In the arms of our own true love we strive to unite the aims and objects of past desire. And sometimes we hate our mate for failing to satisfy these ancient, impossible longings.

We hate him because he hasn't ended our separateness.

We hate him because he hasn't filled up our emptiness.

We hate him because he hasn't fulfilled our save-me, complete-me, mirror-me, mother-me yearnings.

And we hate him because we waited all these years to marry daddy—and he isn't daddy.

We do not, of course, enter marriage with the conscious intention of marrying daddy—or mommy. Our hidden agenda is also hidden from us. But subterranean hopes make for seismic disturbances. And until people learn "to distinguish between their conscious and attainable goals and . . . their unconscious and unattainable goals," writes analyst Kubie, "the problem of human happiness, whether in marriage or otherwise, will remain unsolved."

There are, of course, unconscious goals which marriages do indeed meet—normal goals, and also deeply neurotic ones. There are "complementary marriages" where the husband's and wife's requirements dovetail so well that even when they look very much like marriages made in hell, they satisfy both partners' psychic needs.

The doormat-bully relationship, the worshiper-idol relationship, the helpless-helper relationship, the baby-mommy relationship are examples of neurotic complementarity. And although these polarized roles can be the source of great conflict between a husband and wife, they are also the expression of a profoundly shared assumption about their marriage.

The doormat and bully agree that married love is about authority, bondage, control.

The worshiper and idol agree that married love is about ego confirmation.

The helpess and helper agree that married love is about security through dependency.

And the baby and mother agree that married love is about unconditional caring and nurturing.

These shared assumptions explain the passionate bonds that link a couple even when their marriage appears catastrophic. Together they get the marriage they want to get. They are "couples in collusion," but any inner or outer change can pose a threat to the delicate balance of their collusive relationship.

Consider, for instance, the marriage between a man who wants a mommy and a woman who nurtures and nourishes just like mom, a woman who—responding to his helplessness and charm —provides maternal care and admiration. This arrangement has something to offer both baby-husband and earth-mother wife, until she wants some taking care of too, until she grows weary to death of providing nonstop admiration, until—in some cases—she wearies of his adulteries. Her husband, however, will find her less than total devotion absolutely intolerable. My wife, he'll complain, is selfish, unloving, unfair. He'll keep crying for his mother, but the perfect mother he needs is no longer there. What there is is an upsurge of tension in the marriage.

A more complicated version of the complementary marriage involves what is called projective identification, an unconscious and subtle two-way exchange in which one partner makes use of the other partner to contain and experience some aspect of him- or herself.

For instance, there's Kevin, a macho man who unconsciously hates and repudiates all his anxiety and who "puts" his anxiety into his wife, Lynne, ridding himself of these feelings by attributing them to—projecting them onto—his wife and then psychologically pressuring her to actually *feel* his cast-off, disavowed feelings. And so, when their son is two hours late, Lynne is tearing her hair out and Kevin is scornfully saying, "You worry too much." He doesn't worry at all because he is getting Lynne to do the worrying for him—and despising her anxiety rather than his.

And then there's the wife who hates pushy people and gets her husband to do the screaming and pushing. And the wife with the spendthrift husband who expresses, for her, the indulgent part of herself. A projective identification is always received by a person with tendencies in that direction, but it is "put" there by a partner who has a need to have it played out—by somebody else.

"If a woman has been taught to deny her own ambitious and competitive strivings for competence and mastery," says psychologist Harriet Lerner, "she may choose a man who will express these for her. If it is a weakness or dependency that is intolerable for her to acknowledge, she can find a partner who will play out the role of the incompetent and helpless person that she fears herself to be. If she has learned to please and protect others, she may just happen to find herself married to a man who is tactless and provocative. Women often choose a spouse who will express just those traits and qualities they most need to deny within themselves, or those qualities they wish they could express themselves but can't. A woman may then rage against her spouse as he expresses the very qualities she chose him for."

By arranging for our partner to contain some parts of ourself, our marriage may be troubled but intact. But here is what can happen when a projective identification is disrupted:

A mid-thirties wife starts therapy because she can't run her house or take care of her children. She has felt helpless and anxious her whole married life. Her husband, who not only works full time but also takes care of the household, earnestly speaks of his willingness "to spare no efforts or money to help his wife."

But as she gets into the treatment and starts showing signs of improvement, her husband becomes increasingly dissatisfied, first denigrating the treatment, then refusing to pay for the treatment and then, in a fit of rage, assaulting his wife. Eventually this "gregarious, affable, flexible, mature person with genuine concern for his wife's welfare" becomes so distraught that he signs himself into a hospital. With his wife no longer expressing his anxiety and helplessness, this "healthy" man has become, in effect, his "sick" wife.

There are marriages where projective identification and complementarity are quite constructive. But whenever essential needs unmesh, there is risk. And ironically, two partners locked in a pathological marriage may stick together neurotically ever after, while wholer and healthier couples who are able to change and grow may rupture the arrangements that hold them together.

Ironically, the thrust of human development may also contribute to tensions in a marriage.

Impossible expectations, unmet needs and unmeshed needs are continuing sources of marital tension and strife. They produce the hellish parts of the married state. But it also has been argued that the fact that marriage involves a husband and wife is sufficient to explain the presence of hate. It has been argued that the fact that men are men and women are women—two different species?—is a fundamental cause of conflict in marriage.

It is furthermore argued that conflicts in marriage arising from sexual differences run deeper than simple changing sex-role concerns. Here is how Dorothy Dinnerstein, an audacious and brilliant psychologist, explains the origins of our sexual warfare:

Dinnerstein makes the argument that women, as our first caretakers, "introduce[d] us to the human situation and . . . at the beginning seem[ed] to us responsible for every drawback of that situation. . . ." Thus they become the recipients—as men, as fathers, do not—of our most primitive emotions and expectations. Our demand for nurturance from the all-giving mother, our infantile rage at the disappointing mother, our rebellion against the all-controlling mother, distort our adult visions of women—and men. And these early distortions, she says, have impaired not only our personal growth but also our capacity to love each other.

Dinnerstein says that our gender arrangements—our division of opportunities and privileges—proceed from the central role of women in child care. And "while much of our pleasure in living has been woven into these arrangements," she observes, "they have apparently never felt wholly comfortable or beneficial to either of the sexes. Indeed, they have always been a major source of human pain, fear and hate: a sense of deep strain between women and men has been permeating our species' life as far back into time as the study of myth and ritual permits us to trace human feeling."

That pain and fear and hate, she says, will prevail until women are freed from their scapegoat-idol-provider-devourer role. That pain and fear and hate, she says, will continue to permeate male-female relationships until men and women raise their children together.

So long as the first parent is a woman, then, woman will inevitably be pressed into the dual role of indispensable quasi-human supporter and deadly quasi-human enemy of the human self. She will be seen as naturally fit to nurture other people's individuality; as the born audience in whose awareness other people's subjective existence can be mirrored; as the being so peculiarly needed to confirm other people's worth, power, significance that if she fails to render them this service she is a monster, anomalous and useless. And at the same time she will also be seen as the one who will not let other people be, the one who beckons her loved ones back from selfhood, who wants to engulf, dissolve, drown, suffocate them as autonomous persons.

In adult life . . . we lean over backward in our heterosexual arrangements to keep this original threat at bay. We will have to continue to do so, in some way, until we reorganize child care to make the realm of the early non-self as much a male as a female domain.

Does the sex war derive from the fact that women raise children? Psychology shows some support for this point of view. For the divergent paths of development taken by boys and girls—but, I would argue, some inborn differences too—result in vastly dissimilar sets of experiences and assumptions, particularly in the realm of human relationships. Remember that little boys, in the process of forming their gender identity, must break—more sharply than girls—from the mother tie, for girls can be girls while intimately identifying with mother but little boys, if they want to be boys, cannot. Thus intimate relatedness becomes a comfortable, valued condition for women, while too much closeness poses a threat to men. And this sexual difference leads to so great a gender gap, writes therapist Lillian Rubin, that husbands and wives often live as "intimate strangers."

"I want him to talk to me." "I want him to tell me how he really feels." "I want him to put off his I'm-okay mask and be vulnerable." Wives often complain that they're beating their fists against a shut-tight door. And husbands, as Dr. Rubin's patient illustrates, often feel bewildered and beleaguered:

> The whole goddam business of what you're calling intimacy bugs the hell out of me. I never know what you women mean when you talk about it. Karen complains that I don't talk to her, but it's not talk she wants, it's some other damn thing, only I don't know what the hell it is. Feelings, she keeps asking for. So what am I supposed to do if I don't have any to give her or to talk about just because she decides it's time to talk about feelings? Tell me, will you; maybe we can get some peace around here.

The female need to share feelings—to hear about his, to talk about hers—collides with the male's reluctance to get *that* involved. In the case of Wally and Nan, this communications chasm opened up so wide that it came very close to swallowing their marriage.

Wally had never been, says Nan, "a big talker or tuner-inner," but there was enough between them to make it work. And then they moved to Washington, where Wally began an important job at the White House.

"For the first three months," Nan says, "it was okay; I was having fun." Then Wally's work took over inexorably. "Communication between us completely broke down," Nan recollects. "He was absolutely not talking to me." He left the house before she was up in the morning. As he walked through the door at night, both phones would ring. And whenever she tried to talk to him about . . . anything, he would tap his fingers impatiently on the table and ask, with annoyance, "What's the bottom line?"

Nan says, "He wouldn't listen to my feelings. And so I gave up trying to tell him my feelings."

In the middle of this desolate time, their son was involved in an accident and died. Wally ran from grief by working late. Nan expressed her sorrow and rage by "yelling and screaming and ranting and raving," she says. When Wally ignored her, she turned to barbiturates. And after a couple of years of popping pills, she was inches away from dying of them.

Later a psychiatrist asked Wally how he had felt about the pills. When he said it had helped the marriage, Nan wanted to scream. "What he meant," says Nan, "is with pills I wasn't hysterical, wasn't critical, wasn't a person. I'd turned into what he'd become for me—a machine."

She says she hated him.

"When I came out of the pills," says Nan, "I started getting very, very angry." I don't want this marriage, she said; this marriage is done. She found a lover and moved with him to Europe, walking out on her husband and other son. Nine months later, reaching across the wreckage of their lives, Nan and Wally returned to each other.

This happened years ago. They soon will celebrate their twenty-fifth anniversary. What has helped this marriage to come through? He has, with outside help, grown somewhat better—not good, but better—at tuning in to her. She has, with help, grown better at making do. But she also says, "I know that if I need him now, he's going to be there for me." There are many shared pleasures, she says. And the sex is still great.

The bad news is that no two adults can do each other more damage than husband and wife.

The good news is that love can survive the hate.

Men pursue autonomy; women yearn for intimacy. This sexual difference makes for marital strains. And while it may not lead to the explosive tensions that blew Nan and Wally apart, it may help explain why women tend to have more complaints to make about marriage than men do.

For studies consistently show that "more wives than husbands report marital frustration and dissatisfaction; more report negative feelings; more wives than husbands report marital problems; more wives than husbands consider their marriages unhappy, have considered separation or divorce, have regretted their marriage; and fewer report positive companionship."

To these studies add the following findings: That wives "conform more to husbands' expectations than husbands do to wives'." That wives make more concessions and adaptations. And that wives suffer more than husbands do from depression, phobias and other emotional problems.

Sociologist Jessie Bernard concludes that the cost of marriage is higher for wives than for husbands. She says the same marriage is different for women and men. She writes: "There are two marriages, then, in every marital union, his and hers." And in terms of good mental health, of psychological well-being, all the studies show that his marriage is better.

And yet, despite psychological problems and negative responses, more women than men find marriage a source of happiness. Having a greater need than men for love and companionship in a lasting relationship, they "demonstrate this need," says Jessie Bernard, "by clinging to marriage regardless of the cost."

Contemplating the future of marriage, Jessie Bernard predicts that in some form or another it will survive, although "the demands men and women make on marriage will never be fully met; they cannot be. . . ." She says that men and women, no matter what their arrangements are, "will continue to disappoint as well as to delight one another. . . ." And marriage, she says, will continue to be an "intrinsically tragic" relationship—"tragic in the sense of embodying the insoluble conflict . . . between incompatible human desires. . . ."

Our incompatible human desires, our conflicts, our disappointments assure us all of hate in the married state. But the use of that brutal word hate, of that unloving, unlovable word, may make us wince. And if we are genial, mild-mannered types we might find it hard to convince ourself that we could possibly feel such a violent emotion. Particularly in marriage. Particularly in relation to someone we love.

But hate can be unconscious as well as conscious. Hate can be transient as well as entrenched and sustained. Hate can be a blip as well as a constant drumbeat of bitter anger and pain. Hate isn't always a bang; it is sometimes a whimper.

It is easy enough to recognize hate in what have been described as "cat and dog" marriages, where a husband and wife—though deeply bound to each other—are engaged in continual warfare day and night. But there also are "sunshine" marriages which present a facade of happiness and "deny and keep inner realities out of sight." The envy of neighbors and friends, these couples may pay a mental-health price for denying all conflict. They may suffer from physical symptoms much of the time. Or perhaps they'll do just fine and their children—picking up the hidden strains of strife—will pay the price for them.

Between these two extremes are husbands and wives who go through seasons in their marriage when all the connections are broken and darkness prevails, when the tolerance that allows them to accept their unmet expectations fails, when they feel—if they can be honest about it—hate. And sometimes they express that hate through physical acts of abuse and *Who's Afraid of Virginia Woolf?* verbal savagings. But sometimes they choose to deliver far more disguised and indirect I-hate-you messages.

There are, for instance, no shouting matches in Wendy and Edward's house. For twenty-plus years their style has been low-key. An example: Tensions arise and Edward, by way of apology, buys Wendy an enormous bouquet of roses. Wendy arranges the flowers in a vase and then they go out for the evening together. When they return, they find the roses dead. "She somehow forgot to put water in the vase and she killed off the roses," Edward said. "I think that she was trying to tell me something."

Wendy may not even know when she feels hostile toward her husband. Rachel's feelings are at her fingertips. "I'll find myself on the tennis court, the two of us partners in doubles, and I'll start to play against him," she admits. Whenever she hates her husband, she says, "I play for the other side. I don't want him to win."

Fantasies are another way of expressing marital hatred without an open exchange of hostilities. Connie, a gentle woman I know, allows herself to imagine that her husband's plane has dropped into the sea. She also enjoys the fantasy of disposing of him with the aid of a Mafia hit man.

"I don't think I really mean it," she says, "but I don't completely not mean it. And simply thinking about it cheers me up."

When I mention Connie's fantasies to married men and women, many are sincerely horrified. "Never. I've never had such thoughts," they say. But perhaps, after all, that is not such a terrible way to deal with feelings of hatred in marriage. Perhaps, says psychoanalyst Leon Altman, we could love better if we could hate more cheerfully.

And perhaps we could hate more cheerfully if we could keep in mind the compelling finding that animal studies reveal: That there are no personal bonds without aggression. That animals devoid of aggression band without bonding, unite anonymously. Nobel scientist Konrad Lorenz concludes unequivocally: No aggression, no love. And Otto Kernberg writes that it is often our failure to acknowledge our aggression which "transforms a deep love relation into . . . one that lacks the very essence of love."

Erikson calls adolescent love "an attempt to arrive at a definition of one's identity" by trying out our self-image on somebody else. Sex at adolescence, he says, is also largely an act of "identity searching." In other words, this sexual love belongs to the identity crisis that Erikson says is part of the normal life cycle, when the love we feel is self-involved, is less about loving our lover than finding our self.

Our adolescent love is also self-involved—narcissistic—in the extent to which we idealize our beloved. For while it is probably true that being in love requires us, as George Bernard Shaw once observed, to greatly exaggerate the difference between one person and another, adolescent love often goes to extremes. These excessive idealizations are sometimes a way of acquiring attributes by attributing them to the person we acquire. The deal goes like this: I'm not perfect, so I'm going to make you perfect, and by loving you I'll make that perfection mine.

In the course of normal development toward adult forms of love, the narcissistic elements diminish. We begin to see that actual person out there. We bring into the relationship a capacity to empathize and care, to feel guilt if we cause pain, to feel a wish to repair the damage and offer comfort. Insofar as the person we love embodies certain ideals that we value, we continue to view our beloved as ideal, but our idealizations exist side by side with a realistic knowledge of whom we are loving. And if our love is to grow into lasting love, into adult love, into a mature and enduring —and loving—marriage, that knowledge will bring us face to face with our disappointments, our bitter, bad feelings, our hate. But that knowledge will also open us to gratitude.

Gratitude for finding—in our present love relationship—some of the longed-for loved ones of our past.

Gratitude for receiving—in our present love relationship—some of what we never had in the past.

Gratitude for retrieving—through our sexual acts of love—some of the symbiotic bliss of the past.

And gratitude for the feeling of being known, being understood, by our beloved.

Freed from love's blindness, however, we will have to face the reality that other mates could also inspire such gratitude, that other marriage relationships could gratify our needs—perhaps even better. And indeed, from time to time, we may have yearnings for other relationships, yearnings which—if our love is to last —we renounce. But longing and renunciation may actually add further richness to mature love.

"All human relationships must end," Kernberg reminds us in discussing the characteristics of mature love, "and the threat of loss, abandonment and, in the last resort, of death is greatest where love has most depth." But awareness of this offers something more than a glimpse into grim reality; "awareness of this," he writes, "also deepens love."

In a poem about illusion and reality, W. H. Auden offers two pictures of love. And in the romantic version he sardonically captures all of love's young dreams:

> And down by the brimming river
>   I heard a lover sing
> Under an arch of the railway:
>   "Love has no ending.

I'll love you, dear, I'll love you
    Till China and Africa meet,
And the river jumps over the mountain
    And the salmon sing in the street.

I'll love you till the ocean
    Is folded and hung up to dry,
And the seven stars go squawking
    Like geese about the sky.

The years shall run like rabbits,
    For in my arms I hold
The Flower of the Ages,
    And the first love of the world."

Against this blissful vision Auden starkly summons up the chilling and inescapable inroads of time, time "which watches from the shadow and coughs when you would kiss," time which erodes adolescent dreams of wholeness, happiness, salvation, transcendence, passion, time which eventually teaches us the nature of the choices we have made. He ends with this:

O stand, stand at the window
    As the tears scald and start;
You shall love your crooked neighbor
    With your crooked heart.

Auden's cynical song about perfect love, about endless love, about love that lasts until China and Africa meet, may correctly portray the hazards of romanticism. And surely we long-term lovers will learn about sorrow and the crookedness of hearts. And surely in time we will start to confront the failures of understanding and the disenchantments familiarity brings. In time we will face the knowledge of what we can never, never expect from one another.

These lost expectations are necessary losses.

But on these lost expectations we can build our adult love. We can strive to love to the best of our crooked abilities. We can, though far less frequently, walk under stars and ride up to the moon, while bowing to love's limits and fragilities. And we can, through love and through hate, preserve that highly imperfect connection known as marriage, where beloved mates are beloved enemies too.

Remembering anew that there can be no human love without ambivalence.

And learning that what we must do with our "love forever; hate never" dreams is—let them go.

14
Saving the Children

If Garp could have been granted one vast and naive wish, it would have been that he could make the world *safe*. For children and for grownups. The world struck Garp as unnecessarily perilous for both.

—John Irving

The lives of children are
Dangerous to their parents
With fire, water, air,
And other accidents;
And some, for a child's sake,
Anticipating doom,
Empty the world to make
The world safe as a room.

—Louis Simpson

A new dream will arise when we begin to have our babies—the dream of keeping them safe from every harm. But even the loftiest schemes for our children's happiness and well-being may be less than ideal from our children's point of view. And although we yearn to save them from the perils and pains of life, there are limits to what we can and ought to do. We will have to let go of so much of what we hoped we could do for our children. And, of course, we will have to let go of our children too.

For just as children, step by step, must separate from their parents, we will have to separate from them. And we will probably suffer, as most mothers (and fathers) suffer, from some degree of separation anxiety.

Because separation ends sweet symbiosis. Because separation reduces our power and control. Because separation makes us feel less needed, less important. And because separation exposes our children to danger.

Mrs. Ramsay, mother of eight, admits to herself that "she felt this thing that she called life terrible, hostile and quick to pounce on you if you gave it a chance. . . . And yet she had said to all these children, You shall go through it all. . . . For that reason, knowing what was before them—love and ambition and being wretched alone in dreary places—she had often the feeling, Why must they grow up and lose it all? And then she said to herself, brandishing her sword at life, Nonsense. They will be perfectly happy."

But powerful and protective as the heroine of *To the Lighthouse* might be, the sword she brandishes cannot keep life from pouncing. Her beautiful daughter Prue, grown up and married, dies tragically of some illness connected with childbirth, while Andrew, the son with the wonderful gift for mathematics, is blown up in France in the war, when a shell explodes. In *The World According to Garp*, a child's mishearing of the word *undertow* evokes an image of the Under Toad—a slimy and bloated creature, a vile and wicked and watchful creature, waiting to suck us under and drag us to sea. In the perilous world of the Under Toad it is difficult and frightening to see our children leave the safety of our arms.

For many mothers do believe that their actual bodily presence stands between their children and all harm. It is, I confess, a belief that I used to share. I once (I know this sounds ludicrous) was positive that as long as I was right there, my sons couldn't choke to death on a piece of meat. Why? Because I knew that I would keep nagging them to take smaller bites and chew carefully. And because I also knew that if worse really came to worst, I would seize a knife and perform a tracheotomy. Like many mothers, I saw myself—and in some ways see myself still—as their guardian angel, their shield of invulnerability. And although I have had to let my sons explore more and more of this perilous world alone, I am haunted by the anxiety that they always will be at far greater risk without me.

It isn't only mothers who are concerned about the hazards of separation. Fathers link separation and danger too. One father says that what he used to do when his son first learned to crawl was to get down on the floor and crawl behind him, "so that," he explains, "if an overhead light fixture suddenly fell from the ceiling, I could catch it before it landed on his head."

In the poem at the start of this chapter a father, saying goodnight to his daughter, muses upon the dangers beyond her room. He then goes on to contemplate the dangers of attempting to keep her there:

> A man who cannot stand
> Children's perilous play,
> With lifted voice and hand
> Drives the children away.
> Out of sight, out of reach,
> The tumbling children pass;
> He sits on an empty beach,
> Holding an empty glass.

He concludes that, danger or no, we must let them go.

We fear separation because it poses a threat not just to our children's life and limb but also to their—as we see it—fragile psyches. Several mothers confessed to me that in any new situation, when leaving their child at camp or a friend's house or school, they spend an absurd amount of time attempting to describe to the surrogate parent every nuance and need of their child's personality. They want this person to understand that he's quiet but profound, or gets upset if hurried through his meals, or may appear tough but is basically terribly sensitive, or must not ever be asked to remove his baseball cap from his head, even during dinner or in the bathtub.

"It only recently dawned on me that I wasn't letting go," one mother told me. "Wherever my kid went, I'd always be there first, trying my best to orchestrate his environment."

We sometimes may not be aware that it is hard for us to separate from our children, and that we are holding on to them too tightly.

And this absence of awareness can sometimes make our separation problem their problem. Consider this mother, who drops off her four-year-old child at nursery school, where he's quickly engrossed in putting pegs in a pegboard.

"Goodbye, I'm leaving now," his mother tells him.

The boy looks up and says a cheerful goodbye.

"But I'll be back very soon," his mother tells him.

The boy, without looking up this time, says, " 'Bye."

"Yes, I'll be back at twelve o'clock," the mother assures her son, and adds—when this doesn't rattle him—"Don't worry." At which point, having at last been convinced that his mother's departure is something to worry about, he bursts into tears.

Painful separations in our own early-childhood history can color our separations from our children. Through them we relive the past and may try to repair it. Selena who, as a child, had been traumatically abandoned, thought leaving was hell and thought that her sons couldn't bear it. And she felt compelled to make— whenever she and her husband went away on vacation—a reassuring Travel Book for her children.

"It had pictures of me and my husband pasted in it," Selena explained. "It also had pictures of where we were going to be. It had drawings and it had messages saying, 'We love you. Don't be afraid. We'll soon be together.' " It was, I suspect, the kind of comfort that Selena once had needed desperately.

However, her younger son, Billy, a much sturdier person than she, told her one day when she spoke of a forthcoming trip that he hoped that she and his father would have a very, very good time, "and you don't have to make us one of those dumb Travel Books."

Our problem with separation is not just a matter of physical distance; it involves our children's emotional separateness too. We may rush in too eagerly with assistance and advice, with "Do it like this" or "Wait, I'll do it for you." We may have trouble allowing them to be what they wish to be and, within reason, to do what they wish to do. We may even give them too much understanding.

For, believe it or not, there is a creature called the "too-good mother," the mother who insistently gives too much, the mother who stunts development by not allowing her child to feel any frustration. Furthermore such mothers may hasten to empathize so totally and immediately that their children can't tell if their feelings are really their own. One young woman who had difficulty feeling separate from her mother made a statement, then followed it with this: "Now that I've said that, I'm not sure if I thought it or my mother thought it, or if I only thought that my mother would have wanted me to think it."

Her mother had held her, but could not let her go.

Psychoanalyst Heinz Kohut describes the troubled—often emotionally deadened—children of certain psychologically savvy parents, parents who "had from early on communicated to them, frequently and in great detail, what they (the children) thought, wished and felt." These parents were, for the most part, neither cold nor rejecting people. Furthermore, their claims about knowing their children's own feelings better than their children did actually turned out to be, for the most part, correct. But from their children's point of view, these eager parental insights became an intrusion, a threat against their self. And they walled themselves off emotionally to protect the core of that self from the danger— the *danger*—of being understood.

Parents often have trouble seeing their children as separate people who are moving, psychologically, away. I am told of a mother who, while walking her daughter to school one day, encountered another mother and started to chatter: "We're on our way to school, and we really love the school, and we have a good time, and we've got a wonderful teacher," until she was interrupted by her child, who quite angrily said, "No, Mommy, *we're* not going to school—*I* am."

Part of letting our children go is also letting them be, and that means letting go of our expectations for them. For consciously and unconsciously, even before they are born, we dream many dreams about what kind of children we want. Indeed, some experts say that our image of our newborn may be so compelling that "a mother might need to give up the fantasy of the very different baby she had hoped to have, and to mourn the loss of that idealized baby, before she can mobilize her resources to interact with the baby she actually has."

There are, at birth and thereafter, many fantasies and many expectations.

As extensions of ourself we expect our children to make us look good to the outside world—to be attractive, accomplished, courteous, mentally healthy. "Stop biting your nails," Dale hisses to her nine-year-old, only partly in jest. "You'll ruin my good name."

As improvements on ourself we expect our children not to possess any of our less appealing qualities. "I was a whiner, loud-mouth and klutz when I was her age," Rhoda says; "I can't stand her to be."

As our second chance in life we expect our children gratefully to make use of the opportunities we offer them—the theater, the music, the travel, the money for college, as well as the loving understanding—that "I wish to hell," says Scott, "had been lavished on me."

And because we believe ourselves to be better parents than our parents, we expect to produce "better" children than they produced.

At every step of the way and on almost every conceivable issue —the shape of their ears at birth, the smoothness of their toilet training, how far and how fast they can throw a ball at eleven, their scores on their SATs, their voting choice in their first election, whom they are sleeping with at age twenty-seven, what kind of clothes they are wearing and what kind of car they are driving when they are thirty—we will have expectations.

Some of our expectations will be realized. But there will be plenty of disappointments as well. She isn't a reader. He didn't make the basketball team. She likes Ronald Reagan. He only likes fellows. Growing up under our roof, our children, directly and obliquely, will be exposed to our values, our styles, our views. But letting them go eventually means respecting their right to choose the shape of their life.

Letting our children go, and letting our dreams for our children go, must be counted among our necessary losses.

Examining the character of erotic and motherly love, Erich Fromm suggests this nice distinction: "In erotic love, two people who were separate become one. In motherly love, two people who were one become separate." And then he adds, "The mother must not only tolerate, she must wish and support the child's separation."

For in the beginning mother and baby do something akin to a dance, a dance in which neither partner is wholly the leader, a dance in which the rhythms of rest and activity, distance and contact, clatter and calm, are regulated by both the dancing partners. Together this one specific mother and one specific child fit into each other's back-and-forth cues and responses, and this synchrony—this "goodness of fit"—facilitates both the infant's inner harmony and his first relationships with the outside world.

"The mother's love and her close identification with her infant," writes psychoanalyst D. W. Winnicott, "make her aware of the infant's needs to the extent that she provides something more or less in the right place and at the right time."

But later, if he is to grow, she must selectively and gradually stop being that all-accommodating mother.

Winnicott, who has written approvingly about what he calls "primary maternal preoccupation"—a mother's consuming investment in her new child—also describes the importance of her readiness "to let go . . . as the infant needs to become separate." He concedes that it is "a difficult thing for a mother to separate from her infant at the same speed at which the infant needs to become separate from her," but, as he so frequently notes in his writings, it is the good-enough mother's carefully calibrated *failure* of adaptation, her failure to give him everything he needs, that permits her child slowly . . . slowly to learn to tolerate frustration, to acquire a sense of reality and to learn to get some of what he needs for himself.

Analyst Margaret Mahler, in her seminal separation-individuation studies, has found that "the emotional growth of the mother in her parenthood, her emotional willingness to let go of the toddler—to give him, as the mother bird does, a gentle push, an encouragement toward independence—is enormously helpful. It may even be," she writes, "a sine qua non of normal (healthy) individuation."

All of them are telling us that when it is time to let go, we have to let go.

The ability to hold and let go when it's time to hold and let go is the natural, unlearned gift of the "good-enough mother," who doesn't have to be Mother Earth—or even psychoanalyzed—to do whatever she needs to do just fine. The good-enough mother, Winnicott writes, is the mother who is there. She loves in a physical way. She provides continuity. She is ready to respond. She gradually introduces her baby to the world. And she believes that her baby exists from the very start as a human being in his own right.

Later, when it is time to let go, this good-enough mother will help by . . .

But let's let the Danish philosopher Søren Kierkegaard offer his own shimmering perception:

> The loving mother teaches her child to walk alone. She is far enough from him so that she cannot actually support him, but she holds out her arms to him. She imitates his movements, and if he totters, she swiftly bends as if to seize him, so that the child might believe he is not walking alone. . . . And yet, she does more. Her face beckons like a reward, an encouragement. Thus, the child walks alone with his eyes fixed on his mother's face, *not* on the difficulties in his way. He supports himself by the arms that do not hold him, and constantly strives towards the refuge in his mother's embrace, little suspecting *that in the very same moment that he is emphasizing his need of her, he is proving that he can do without her*, because he is walking alone.

But the need for a mother—and father—to emotionally let go isn't a one-time event that occurs in infancy. In the course of defining themselves and expanding the realm of their autonomy, our children will tug at the ties again and again. And we will renegotiate our relationship with our children not only as boys and girls but as women and men, passing through many stages of separation.

"Each transition from one phase to the next," writes psychoanalyst Judith Kestenberg, "presents a challenge to both parents and children to give up outdated forms of interaction and to adopt a new system of coexistence. The ability of a parent to meet his side of this challenge depends on his inner preparedness to accept the new image the child forms of him and to erect a new image of his child."

An image of a separate, sturdy child who is probably going to make it without his mother.

But will he?

Some notes from my hometown:

Three of the four Bromfeld children are heavy drug users.

The Blakes' twenty-three-year-old son committed suicide.

The eighteen-year-old daughter of the O'Reillys has been hospitalized for depression.

The Chapmans' seventeen-year-old son committed suicide.

The Rosenzweigs' fifteen-year-old daughter is anorectic.

The Mitchells' oldest son was indicted for pushing.

The Kahns' youngest son had a breakdown and had to be hospitalized.

The Daleys' nineteen-year-old daughter is a Moonie.

The Farnsworths' sixteen-year-old daughter attempted suicide.

The Millers' seventeen-year-old son ran away.

Question: Are the parents of these children the ones responsible for all of this pain and this damage?

A letter from a mother to child psychologist Haim Ginott suggests that many mothers think they are:

Not one of us willingly would do anything to cripple our children spiritually, morally or emotionally and yet we do just that. I cry often inside for things I have done and said thoughtlessly and I pray not to repeat these transgressions. Maybe they aren't repeated but something else just as bad is substituted, until I am frantic for fear that I have injured my child for life.

The fear that this woman is speaking of is distressingly familiar. It is a fear that almost all mothers share: that our flaws as a person and parent will do permanent harm to our children and that even our best intentions will not protect them.

Listen to Ellen:

"I'd vowed to be rational, reasonable, sensible and fair with them in a way my mother had never been with me. I found myself being totally unreasonable and unfair more times than I care to recall. I remember thinking how stupid it was of her to buy me off —how demeaning, almost. And then I'd find myself buying my children off. I remember how, before I had kids, I'd see mothers in supermarkets shame their kids into tears, scream at them, behave in an absolutely vulgar, disgusting and altogether unreasonable way. I remember thinking how I'd absolutely never, ever, ever, do anything like that. But I did."

Despite our resolutions, we will sometimes catch ourselves mistreating our children the way that we were mistreated. And in various other guises, using our daughters and sons as the characters in our drama, we may re-enact hurtful parts of our own early history. For, as we have learned, there is a compulsion to repeat the significant relationships of our past, including the deprivations and hurts, the buried resentment and rage, that we experienced back when we were children. Psychiatrists inform us that the "tendency of adults to replay old fears and conflicts with new characters, though this is often unwitting, disrupts the peace of family life with bewildering frequency." And sometimes, casting our children as our mother or father or bitterly envied sister, we repeat with them what we did—or wanted to do.

Catching ourselves repeating the painful patterns of early relationships, we fear we are causing long-term harm to our children. We also may fear that we are the source of enduring emotional injury because of the violent anger we sometimes feel toward them.

In her book *The Mother Knot*, writer Jane Lazarre observes that although women differ vastly from one another, "still there is only one image in this culture of the 'good mother.' At her worst, this mother image is a tyrannical goddess of stupefying love and murderous masochism which none of us can or should hope to emulate. But even at her best, she is . . . quietly receptive and intelligent in only a moderate, concrete way; she is of even temperament, almost always in control of her emotions. She loves her children completely and unambivalently.

"Most of us," Jane Lazarre concludes, "are not like her."

And we fear that our imperfect love will harm our children.

For unambivalent love, no-strings-attached love, so we believe, will foster our children's emotional well-being, saving them from drugs, depression, wretched relationships, injured self-esteem in spite of our almost uncountable failures and flaws. We trust that a mother's perfect love, no matter what else we may do, will send them armored into the cold hard world. They will thrive because we love them, but what hope do they have if we sometimes feel anger, feel . . . hate?

Winnicott, in his list of some of the reasons why a mother could hate her baby, displays a rich understanding both of motherhood and ambivalence when he notes that

> The baby is an interference with her private life. . . .
> He is ruthless, treats her as scum, an unpaid servant, a slave.
> His excited love is cupboard love, so that having got what he wants
>   he throws her away like orange peel.
> He is suspicious, refuses her good food and makes her doubt
>   herself, but eats well with his aunt.
> After an awful morning with him she goes out, and he smiles at a
>   stranger, who says: "Isn't he sweet?"
> If she fails him at the start she knows he will pay her out forever.

It made perfect sense to this pediatrician-turned-analyst that a mother who loved her baby could also feel hate. But most of us, confronted with such emotions, are going to feel anxiety, are going to feel guilt, are going to fear that we have become the Under Toad.

"I am angry with my baby . . . " Jane Lazarre confesses, describing the end of a long hard mothering day. "I yell into his little face for his endless crying and throw him roughly into his crib. Then I quickly sweep him into my arms, protecting him from his insane mother, fearing that I will . . . drive my child crazy. For, if I interpret the experts correctly, that is not a hard thing to do."

Not true.

What is true, however, is that we can glut ourselves with how-to-raise-children information and that we can strive to become more mature and aware but that none of this will spare us from the—yes—inevitability that some of the time we are going to fail our children. Because there is a big gap between knowing and doing. Because mature, aware people are imperfect too. Or because some current event in our life may so absorb or depress us that when our children need us we cannot come through. Our mother dies, our husband is unfaithful, there are troubles with our health, troubles with work, and although we aren't inclined to shirk our obligations to our sons and daughters, we are pulled away by a host of distracting emotions.

We will have to give up the hope that, if we try hard, we somehow will always do right by our children. The connection is imperfect. We will sometimes do wrong.

Facing our fallibility as mothers and as fathers is another of our necessary losses.

But human beings have always been raised by fallible human beings. All we need to be is good enough. And letting our children go, we good-enough mothers can assume that we have provided the right—emotional—stuff. Yet we also need to remember that we can be the best kind of parent a person could be—loving, protective, patient, dependable, tender, supportive, empathic and self-sacrificing—and nevertheless our children, like those Bromfeld and Chapman and Miller and other children, might not make it out there.

There is what some psychiatrists call the True Dilemma Theory of Parenthood: that no matter how much of our life we devote to our children, the result is not entirely within our control. For what happens to them will also depend on the world beyond the family. It will also depend on the world inside their head. It will also depend on the nature they have been born with. And from the very beginning, it will depend on how badly or well each individual baby and mother connect with each other.

For the old view of a baby as a blank tablet—a tabula rasa—or an infinitely malleable blob of clay has in recent years given way to the recognition that babies are born with specific temperaments and coping capacities. The growing field of infant research has established that what babies know is greater, and present much earlier, than once was suspected. It also has established that every baby, right from birth, is—like a snowflake—different from every other baby.

There are "juicy" full-of-life babies, ready for maximum engagement with the world. There are passive babies, who tend to tune out rather quickly. There are babies so hypersensitive that a mother's touch or voice can become an assault. Freud long ago took note of "the importance of innate (constitutional) factors," observing that endowment and chance together determine "man's fate —rarely or never one of these powers alone." Current research confirms that babies are born with certain qualities that we, as parents, can neither confer nor withhold. And in the earliest stages, a baby's sense of well-being importantly depends on how he and (mainly) his mother "fit" together.

Fit, as we saw earlier, is the way that a mother and child tune in to each other, a progressive emotional dialogue of back-and-forth cues and responses which, when all goes well, fosters development. But sometimes the fit is "bad"—not because either mother or baby is "bad" but because their styles and rhythms are out of sync. And sometimes a bad fit—a passive baby, for instance, with a high-energy mother—can make a baby feel constantly intruded upon, can make a mother feel constantly rejected, can make for spiraling patterns of discomfort and disappointment and can make for trouble later on in life.

Psychoanalyst Stanley Greenspan, Director of the Clinical Infant Development Program at the National Institute of Mental Health and one of the major figures in infant research, offers this example of a bad fit:

Mrs. Jones gives birth to a vigorous baby. She finds his eager activity "scary as hell." Perhaps she herself has been born, Greenspan says, with a nervous system easily swamped by stimuli. Loving her baby and meaning very well, she may nonetheless withdraw from his—as she perceives it—frightening aggressiveness, a withdrawal which could lead to a severe impairment of his normal development. She isn't a bad mother. He isn't a bad baby. But they've got a bad fit.

There are also bad fits that begin with a caring and very hard-trying mother—and a baby who is temperamentally difficult. No, the mother didn't make the baby difficult. No, it isn't her fault— he was born that way. Yet these colicky, fussy, constantly crying, body-stiffening, inconsolable babies—who display these reactions from the very first day—may persuade a quite competent mother (and *her* mother, and some of her friends) that she is a failure. Such mothers, convinced that their babies were perfect babies until they wrecked them, may suffer terribly from guilt and shame. And often such mothers cannot be helped to find better styles of relating to their babies until they are helped to give up taking the blame.

There is a burgeoning awareness of the importance of this subtle issue of fit. There are clinics which, studying mothers and babies in action, offer instruction in how to improve a fit. Dr. Greenspan, for instance, would help Mrs. Jones to see her baby as active, not aggressive. She would still get frightened, he says, but she'd be less withdrawn. With this change, Greenspan says, "we could get the baby through the stages of early ego development." But "there will still be tensions between Mrs. Jones and her baby," Greenspan concedes. "And we can't predict what he'll do with these tensions later."

We have talked about what mothers and fathers bring to their roles as parents. The point here is that our newborns bring something too. When a baby boy resists the cuddles of his affectionate mother because he's so active her cuddles feel like constraint, when a baby girl cries and grows rigid in response to her mother's voice because she is hypersensitive to sound, when a baby backs away whenever his mother presents new experiences because he is, by nature, "slow to warm up," we are forcefully reminded that mothers do not create their babies out of nothing. With relief—or is it regret?—we must accept this limitation on parent power.

Although we can't claim full credit or blame for the child we bring into the world, we are—after birth—the prime fashioners of his environment. And even if we and our baby are temperamentally out of sync we can, with help, with growth, with an understanding of what's going on, better adapt to his needs and improve the fit. Believing, as we do, that what happens in childhood matters a lot, we surely will try to make what happens benign. But "what happens" in childhood includes both external events—what actually happens to children *out there*—and internal events—what happens to them *in there*.

There are limits to what we can do about the dramas being played out in either location.

For we cannot protect our son from being the shortest boy in the class, and we cannot protect our daughter from being funny-looking, and we cannot protect them from being picked last because they can't hit a ball, and we cannot protect them from learning disabilities. We cannot protect them from "fire, water, air and other accidents," or from losing a parent to death or to divorce. And no matter how much we love them our love may not be enough to protect them from feelings of inadequacy or abandonment.

Now there are ways of rearing children which read like recipes for psychotics, and ways which seem to support their soundness and strengths. There are positive experiences that we surely can offer our children and potentially harmful out-in-the-world events from which all children surely should be shielded. On the other hand, because every child is born with certain qualities, with certain styles and tendencies, certain "givens," his nature is going to interact with the nurture he receives in unique and sometimes unpredictable ways. This interaction occurs not merely in the outside world but in that inner world between his ears. Thus it's not just a person's experience, but the way in which he experiences his experience, which confers its psychological meaning upon him.

Looking at Shelley Farnsworth, who at sixteen had attempted suicide, her parents poke through the past for explanations:

Shelley was an undersized and fragile little baby. Mrs. Farnsworth was terrified that she might die. Did she transmit her anxiety to Shelley?

The Farnsworths went away for a long vacation when Shelley was only one year old. Perhaps she feared that they were never coming home again.

The Farnsworths had a second child when Shelley was eighteen months old. In retrospect, it doubtless was too soon.

The Farnsworths moved when Shelley was nine years old. Moving, as everyone knows, can be very disrupting.

When Shelley was twelve the Farnsworths' marriage went through a terrible time. How did the tension and bitter fighting affect her?

Shelley began smoking pot at thirteen. The Farnsworths disapproved, but they really didn't take it all that seriously.

In Shelley's sophomore year the Farnsworths began putting pressure on her to make good grades and get into a good college. Was it too much pressure?

In her junior year the Farnsworths' beautiful, bright and beloved daughter took an overdose of sleeping pills.

Did one or all of these factors on the Farnsworths' list of guilts bring Shelley to the point where she wanted to die? Or did one or all of these factors weigh too heavily on her inborn vulnerabilities? We cannot know if anything they had or had not done would have made the story come out differently.

We cannot know.

Freud originally believed that a traumatic external event—a sexual seduction during childhood—was the cause of neurotic problems in adult life. He later came to believe that most of the sexual stories recounted on the couch were fantasies and not external reality. Building on this, Freud concluded that the wishful imaginings of a person's unconscious (and the conflicts and guilt and anxieties they evoke) have the impact on his life of "real" events. The converse of this would be that the way his unconscious mind responds to a "real" event can determine the kind of impact it has on his life.

On the one hand, then, there are times when, although a child's outer world, his "real" world, is quite benign, his inner world may flood him with anxiety.

For instance, the oedipal boy, if his cravings for mom are especially strong and his dreams of doing dad in are especially bloody, may—in spite of a loving and unintimidating father—imagine him to be dangerously punitive. In subsequent years, if this boy elaborates on his frightening lust-and-punishment fantasies, he may grow up to be a troubled man, a man who suffers from fear of success in work or in love or in both—not because his youthful oedipal urges were cruelly squelched but because they were so intense and he was so scared of them.

On the other hand, there are children who, confronted with the most brutal real events, have emerged with health and abilities intact.

For research reveals that not everyone who suffers a damaging childhood grows up to be a damaged human being. And some boys and girls display, in the face of assault and deprivation, such abilities to adjust and survive and triumphantly prevail that they have been actually labeled "the invulnerables." There are children whose later achievements in life, despite a nightmarish past, despite a background of "soul-destroying" experiences, teach us a vast respect, writes psychoanalyst Leonard Shengold, "for the enigmatic, contradictory workings of the soul." He observes:

> Human beings are mysteriously resourceful, and some do survive such childhoods with their . . . souls not unscarred or unwarped but at least in some part intact. . . . Why this should be so *is* mysterious; part of the explanation is innate endowment. What was it that enabled one of my patients with two psychotic parents to become, from age four on, the real parent in the family—a sane caring person who was able to help her siblings and even take care of her psychotic parents? I have no adequate answer.

But the psychic survival of these few is no evidence at all against the destructive potential of bad early child care. Nor does the psychic damage of children in positive environments prove that good early care is a waste of time. For although Freud once observed "that as far as the neurosis was concerned, psychical reality was of more importance than material reality," it is clear that material acts of deprivation, intrusion and cruelty in childhood would pose a threat to most children's psychic reality. It is clear that the constant interplay of inner and outer reality together shapes the human personality.

It is true that emotional injury can occur at any age. It is true that all through life a person may alter and repair his past experience. It also is true that the link between early experience and future emotional health is currently being challenged by some well-credentialed child-development experts. Obviously, this book stands with those—the majority, I believe—who maintain that what happens in childhood matters enormously, who maintain that the early years are our children's most crucial and vulnerable years because their psyche—their "soul"—is first taking form. But we also must understand that, though we might rather feel guilty than helpless, there are limits to the power parents possess. We also must understand that in both their outside world and the world inside their head, there are dangers in the lives of these children we desperately—so desperately—long to protect over which we may have no control.

In Vladimir Nabokov's elegant memoir, *Speak, Memory*, he describes the experience of looking into his newborn son's eyes and seeing the shadows "of ancient, fabulous forests where there were more birds than tigers and more fruit than thorns. . . ." Our fantasy is that we can keep it that way. Our fantasy is that if we are good and loving parents, we can hold the tigers and thorns at bay. Our fantasy is that we can save our children.

Reality will find us late at night, when our children are out and the telephone rings. Reality will remind us—in that heart-stopping moment before we pick up the phone—that anything, that any horror, is possible. Yet although the world is perilous and the lives of children are dangerous to their parents, they still must leave, we still must let them go. Hoping that we have equipped them for their journey. Hoping that they will wear their boots in the snow. Hoping that when they fall down, they can get up again. Hoping.

> Who said that tenderness
> Will turn the heart to stone?
> May I endure her weakness
> As I endure my own.
> Better to say goodnight
> To breathing flesh and blood
> Each night as though the night
> Were always only good.

15

Family Feelings

Daughter am I in my mother's house,
But mistress in my own.

—Rudyard Kipling

In our twenties and early thirties, we acquire this second family in which we are the responsible adults. We may even imagine we're starting a family from scratch. But although we may move to Australia—or even the moon—we cannot detach ourselves so easily from our first, our original family, from that intricate web of relationships which connects us, albeit imperfectly, to each other.

In our twenties and early thirties, we are lovers and workers and friends. We are partners in a marriage, our children's parents. But we also continue to be, in ways that may no longer suit us, our parents' children.

For our family, our first family, was the setting in which we became a separate self. It was also the first social unit in which we lived. And when we walked away we carried along its many central, shaping lessons. We are bound to that family inwardly, no matter how hard we may strive to be self-created. And most of us —if only in distant, dutiful, cursory ways—are bound to that family outwardly as well.

But although we maintain the connection—the inner connection, the outer connection—we continue to struggle to sort ourselves out from our family. Learning to look at the world through our own instead of our parents' eyes. Reassessing the roles our parents consciously and unconsciously assigned to us. And examining family myths—unspoken or spoken themes and beliefs which characterized our family as a group.

Although we maintain the connection there are things we must give up to be the mistress (or master) of our own house.

There are, once again, some necessary losses.

A family's collective character may be clear to the outside world and discernible as a "corporate characteristic." It sometimes seems easy to label a family. The Bachs were a musical family. The Kennedys an ambitious, athletic family. And our first family, perhaps, was a genteel, outdoorsy or intellectual family. A corporate characteristic is a family's public face; its myth is its inner image of itself. And while they may converge, there are unconscious family myths which neither the outside world—nor the family—may recognize.

Family myths help stabilize the organizational structure of a family. They preserve a certain emotional unity. And they are passionately defended from disruption by all members of the family. But many family myths distort reality, in sometimes quite grotesque and harmful ways. And to maintain a given myth, says family-dynamics expert Antonio Ferreira, may require "a certain amount of insightlessness."

With which of these common family myths did we, for instance, grow up with? With which, as a matter of fact, do we still go along? That ours is a united, harmonious family. That our men are always weak, our women strong. That ours is a hard-luck family. That ours is a special, superior family. That we never give up, or fall apart, or do wrong. Or that we must count on each other and must count on no one else because the outside world is hostile and dangerous.

"Our house was a cave," my friend Geraldine says, "and our mother was the dragon who stood guard, and unless you were related you didn't get in." She confesses that it was not until both she and her brother had married that they learned that friends could be as trustworthy as kin, that they learned that you didn't have to be a member of the family to be trusted.

One of the more troublesome of these family myths, or themes, is the myth of the united, harmonious family, which may require a desperate denial of all dissension and distance among the members of the family unit. Listen to the tone of this mother insisting (with her husband's full agreement) on the harmonious happiness of their home:

> We are all peaceful. I like peace even if I have to kill someone to get it. . . . A more normal, happy kid would be hard to find. I was pleased with my child! I was pleased with my husband! I was pleased with my life! I have *always* been pleased! We have had 25 years of the happiest married life and of being a father and mother.

You wonder whom she had to kill to get peace.

This family quest to fit together absolutely perfectly, this quest for "pseudo-mutuality," treats any assertion of difference as such a threat to the relationship that no one involved can separate, change or grow. And although it has been argued that the families of schizophrenics show an "intense and enduring" pseudo-mutuality, less drastic variations of this theme of desperate harmony can also be found in many "normal" households.

Producing adult children who may feel bereft and abandoned every time their husband or wife disagrees with them.

Or producing adult children too afraid of their assertiveness to compete.

Or producing adult children who are repeating with their own young sons and daughters the life-constricting lesson that difference is damaging and separation fatal.

Now obviously a family myth will not have a uniform impact on all of its members. We each will respond in our own individual way. Nevertheless, these myths, if they are powerful and insistent, are going to have to be reckoned with someday. And we will need to examine them and, if we must, to escape from them and, if we choose, to make them truly our own.

Along with exploring these myths, we also may need to explore the roles that our family's mythological system imposes on us, or the roles unconsciously fashioned for us by one or both of our parents, sometimes even before we were actually born. Dr. Ferreira discusses a man whose allotted role, as a boy, was to be "like mother, dumb and stupid." The man recalls that "I was trying so hard to be what my mother wanted me to be that I actually felt very proud of my dumbness and inability to spell . . . for then she [mother] would laugh at my dumbness, pleased with me, and say that 'I was her son all right,' since, like her, I didn't seem to be able to accomplish much in school or about anything else. . . . [And] even today, when in the presence of my parents, I've caught myself trying to behave as if I were dumb!"

There are all kinds of roles that parents may lay on their children. A clingy, dependent mother, for instance, might reverse roles and make her child the mother. An unhappily married father might assign his daughter the role of substitute wife. Some parents might impose on a child the role of ideal self, pressing him to be what they wished to be. And other parents, in sometimes blatant and sometimes subtle ways, might lay on their child the role of family scapegoat.

"It is often assumed," writes analyst Peter Lomas, "that a sense of identity derives precisely from . . . the allocation of a definite role in the family system. But the important difference is that which exists between the recognition of the other person as a unique human being and the recognition of him merely in his role." A parent's demand that a child fulfill a role that ignores who he is can be disastrous.

Consider Biff Loman, son of the poignant, doomed Willy of *Death of a Salesman*. Biff "can't take hold," he says, "of some kind of a life." And he can't take hold because he can neither escape, nor can he fill, the go-getter role that his father has imposed on him. At age thirty-four—furious and heartsick—Biff finally explodes:

"I am not a leader of men, Willy, and neither are you. . . . I'm one dollar an hour, Willy! I tried seven states and couldn't raise it. A buck an hour! Do you gather my meaning? I'm not bringing home any prizes any more, and you're going to stop waiting for me to bring them home!"

Willy will not hear it and Biff rages on: "Pop, I'm nothing! I'm nothing, Pop. Can't you understand that? . . . I'm just what I am, that's all."

Willy still will not hear. And Biff, his fury spent, is sobbing as he tries to communicate with his dreamer-father: "Will you let me go, for Christ's sake? Will you take that phony dream and burn it before something happens?"

But Willy would rather destroy his son—Willy would rather die —than burn that dream.

The allotment of roles, however, isn't restricted to families in trouble. Wholesome families have roles for their children too. And sometimes they are spelled out—Joe Kennedy wanted his oldest, his namesake, to be President. And sometimes, without a word, the message comes through. But although studies show that children know exactly which role the parental unconscious assigns to them, perhaps we can measure a family's health by the freedom it gives us *not* to accept the assignment.

In building a life of our own, we challenge our family's myths and roles—and, of course, we challenge the rigid rules of childhood. For leaving home will not become an emotional reality until we stop seeing the world through our parents' eyes.

"Our subjective experience of life and our behaviors," writes psychoanalyst Roger Gould, "are governed by literally thousands of beliefs (ideas) that compose the map used for interpreting the events of our life (including our own mental events). When we grow, we correct a belief that has restricted and restrained us unnecessarily. For example, when we learn as young people that there is no universal law requiring us to be what our parents wanted us to be, we are released to explore and experiment. A door to a new level of consciousness is opened. . . ."

But opening up these doors is often frightening.

For if safety means staying close to our parents (first, to their actual bodies; later, to their rules and moral codes), we are likely to feel endangered if we distance ourselves through the choices that we make: If we fail to become, or even to marry, a doctor. If our spouse is a whole other race and color and creed. If we choose to quit the synagogue, the cousins' club, the Democratic party. Or if, although they know better, we refuse to heed their advice on health insurance.

There are agonizing moments when our parents are angry, insulted, bitter, in pain, as we tell them—yet again—that we're doing it *our* way. And there are agonizing moments when we wonder if, in response to our show of autonomy, our parents will say, "In that case, to hell with you." "I assert myself," says Vicky, age twenty-three, "with tears in my eyes and fear in my heart, because I'm always scared that I'll lose my mother." But in spite of that fear, she says, and in spite of her very deep love for her mother, "I guess I have to do what I have to do."

Not everyone does. Not everybody can.

Carter practices law only fifteen or twenty minutes away from the deluxe apartment of his widowed mother, driving her to her card games and doctor's appointments and dentist's appointments, dining with her on Tuesdays and on Sundays. A good boy does what his father would do if he were still alive, is the value agreed upon by mother and son. And although, unlike his late daddy, Carter sleeps with other women now and then, he has remained, through his twenties and thirties, emotionally faithful to his mother—and unwed.

And then there is Gus, who always wanted to be a veterinarian but who joined the family food-supply business instead. There is Jill, who having moved out of state and acquired a job, an apartment and several lovers, was coaxed back home to Boston—"Your father really isn't too well"—and into a proper marriage with an accountant. And there also is Rhoda who, having broken her mother and father's heart by marrying "wrong" and moving to New York City, routinely returned to New Jersey where, her mother at her side, she continued to buy her clothing and her cold cuts. (And where, her mother still at her side, she eventually got her then-illegal abortion.)

Mother knows best. Father knows best. And secretly we may fear that they indeed do. And rightly or wrongly, we also may fear that they will not love, approve of, respect or rescue us if we pick our own path.

"Parents continue to monitor us during the twenties," writes Roger Gould. "When we do it their way, we're afraid we're capitulating. When we violate their rules and are successful, we feel free but also triumphant and somewhat guilty. When we're faced by a failure, we wonder if they weren't right all along."

The point here is not that freedom lies in aggravating our parents and that, if our choices please them, we have sold out. Our options aren't defiance or compliance. A person could actually want to be a dentist just like her dad and live in Wilkes-Barre just like her parents and grandparents. A person could also marry a person he doesn't really love because she is black and his family is white, right and Southern. We stay in thrall to our parents as long as *our* way is simply whatever *their* way isn't. Our separation from them does not require repudiation. It requires free choices.

In our twenties we establish a life that is independent, or so we believe, of our parents. We harbor the illusion that, having made our rational choices, we are not like them in ways that we don't wish to be. But as we enter our thirties we discover our many resemblances to our parents, acquired in spite of ourselves, unconsciously. We discover, as one woman put it, "that this person who's being vindictive just like my mother, isn't my mother *out there* but my mother *in me*."

We begin to recognize our identifications.

To recognize that even though we are sneakier about it, we are every bit as controlling as our father. To recognize that even though we may travel to Europe alone, we are every bit as cautious as our mother. To recognize a tone of voice, a facial expression, an attitude, a compulsion, which belong to our mother or father and which we hate in our mother or father and which—are ours.

Acknowledging these disquieting parental identifications, we may begin to free ourselves from repeating them. We also, however, may find that we can summon up more tolerance for that mother and father "in me" and the real folks "out there." For if, in our twenties, we focused on the ways that we were nothing at all like our parents, we are now tuning in to the qualities we share. And as we recapitulate our mother's and father's experiences—in marriage and, especially, in parenthood—we may grow less judgmental.

Indeed, it has often been said, that in becoming parents ourselves, we now understand what our mother and father went through and thus can no longer blame and denounce them, as once we could easily do, for all that we have suffered at their hands. Parenthood can be a constructive developmental phase in which we heal some of the wounds of our own childhood. It also may allow us to recast our old perceptions of that childhood in less alienated, more reconciling ways.

But parenthood—our parenthood—can also serve a reconciling function by giving our parents better parts to play, by freeing them to be—as grandma and grandpa—more loving, indulgent, tender, patient, generous, you name it, than they had ever been as mother and father. No longer concerned with instilling moral values, no longer in charge of discipline and rules, no longer dedicated to building character, they become their best selves, and we —in our pleasure at all they can offer our children—begin to forgive them their sins, both real and imagined.

Here is how this played out between one woman—my mother, Ruth Stahl—and her daughter Judith:

I remember always wanting an enormous amount from my mother, though no more than my mother wanted from me, and entangled in disappointment and hurt and anger and frustration and passionate love, we—my mother and I—grew up together. And struggled together. And enjoyed some measure of happiness together. But it wasn't until I had children that we finally found the roles that allowed us to suit each other perfectly: I as the mother of her glorious grandsons; she as terrific as any grandma could be.

Within this special relationship I first began, I think, to know my mother; to understand something of her history; to note that she could be brave and that she could be funny and that she could recite every word of "Annabel Lee." To love her for instructing me in the pleasures of lilacs and books and female friendships. To love her for loving her grandsons better than me.

Not deeper, perhaps. Not necessarily more. But certainly . . . better.

For to me my mother had always been the most alluring and most vexatious of women. For me the cost of loving had always come high. With all of my children, however, my mother had only one face and that face always smiled upon them. To them she gave free love till the day she died. "Grandma says I'm completely great," reported my oldest son, who viewed her just as unambivalently. But between my mother and me ambivalence was, for many years, the name of the game.

I had lived with my mother in anger and love—I suppose most daughters do—but my children only knew her in one way: As the lady who thought they were smarter than Albert Einstein. As the lady who thought they wrote better than William Shakespeare. As the lady who thought every picture they drew was a Rembrandt. As the lady who thought that whatever they were and whatever they wanted to be was . . . completely great.

My mother asked nothing more of my sons than the pleasure of their company. My mother had had a more stringent agenda for me.

"Be better," she said. "Try harder," she said. "Do it," she said, "my way. Or else you'll get hurt, you'll get sick, you'll fall in a hole." "Don't do anything bad," she said, "or you'll break your mother's heart. Be a good girl."

And I yearned for her love and approval and I yearned to be her good girl, but I yearned for freedom and autonomy. And the pain of growing up was recognizing that I could not have it all. And so when my mother pleaded, "Why don't you listen to me? I only want what's good for you," her rebel daughter, shaking her head and drawing the battle lines, replied, "Let *me* decide what's good for me."

But my mother had no dreams to lay on my children. She had tried . . . and succeeded . . . and failed with my sister and me. She was done with that now and her grandsons couldn't defeat her. Or disappoint her. Or prove anything—anything good or anything bad—about her. And I saw her free of ambition, free of the need to control, free of anxiety. Free—as she liked to put it—to enjoy.

"Grandparenthood," writes psychoanalyst Therese Benedek, "is parenthood one step removed. Relieved from the immediate stresses . . . grandparents appear to enjoy their grandchildren more than they enjoyed their own children."

And enjoy them my mother certainly did.

For she had at last come to a place in her life where happiness wasn't yesterday or tomorrow, where happiness wasn't elusive or remote, where happiness wasn't what should have been or might still be someday, but now—in her kitchen—eating lunch with her grandsons. Or on the living-room couch, reading books to her grandsons. Or buying double-dip ice-cream cones for her grandsons. Or trying to catch a pigeon with her grandsons.

How lucky for them. How lucky for her. And how lucky for me. For with the children between us we had found our optimal distance, not too close and not too far apart. Linked by Anthony-Nicholas-Alexander, my mother and I had made a new connection.

But do not let me glorify the reconciliations of family life. These connections, like all our connections, remain imperfect. And not every mother and daughter can use the new generation to heal the wounds of the past.

There are mothers living out of reach of their daughters. There are mothers living in smothering intimacy. There are those who want nothing more to do with diapers ("I won't let her make a sitter out of me"). There are busy, independent, career-women mothers who don't have time for playgrounds or trips to the zoo. There are mothers who are jealous of the love and attention their daughters give to their children ("Can't I have some time alone with you?").

There also are daughters jealous of the love and attention their mothers give to their children. There are daughters engaged in run-from-mother flight. There are daughters who'll always be four years old with their mothers. There are daughters who, having read some child-psychology books in college, have decided that mother never did anything right.

There are distances that are too vast, that are unbridgeable. But many of us, as we reach our middle years, may find ourselves more willing to try to bridge them.

Writing about "Family Matters" in the *Harvard Educational Review*, Joseph Featherstone observes that in midlife

> my friends are much more interested in their own family history. We were always reluctant to think historically about our lives and the lives of our parents; we read about the past, but somehow we never thought of our own lives as part of the same grand tapestry that included the nineteenth-century Irish farmers, *shtetl* peasants, Renaissance cardinals, seventeenth-century Puritans, African warriors and London mechanics. We were struggling toward a future, trying to live in the present. This is a matter of age, partly—the young have the twin duties of escaping history and family life. That often meant cutting ourselves off from the past and our families, a break that was seldom as final as it seemed at the time.

In our middle years we may seek to reconnect ourselves with what now is known as our "roots." We may seek, instead of shun, identifications. For although we know very well that we alone are fully responsible for our lives, we also recognize that we can use all the help we can get, including the good stuff—the talent, the moral consciousness, the enterprise, the whatever—which may be ours (we hope) simply by virtue of our membership in our family.

So we are pleased to learn that our Great-grandma Evalyne sang with a light opera company or that our father's father was a Wobbly or that our mother's Uncle Nate—like Willy Loman's brother Ben—went into the jungle and came out a millionaire. We like to think that the qualities which produced these admired achievements are part of our heritage. We find comfort in telling ourselves —as a woman I know once actually did in a moment of crisis— that "the blood of Charlemagne runs through my veins."

In turning to the past we also begin to see our parents in a new light, to see how they were fashioned by their history. And we often discover secrets—virtually every family has secrets—which can have great impact on our family feelings.

Like discovering that a parent had been married before. Like discovering that a parent's death was a suicide. Like discovering, as Claire did, that her mother had borne an illegitimate child and had given him up for adoption when Claire was two. Like discovering, beneath the sometimes elaborate revisions and deceptions, what kind of people our parents actually are.

But not completely.

In Herbert Gold's memoir-novel, *Fathers*, the hero, now middle-aged, takes his daughters to a skating rink, just as his father had taken him years ago. "I remember why skating with my father gave me such joy," he writes. "It was the hope of intimacy, waiting to be redeemed. . . . I believed the abyss between my father and me, between others and me, could be crossed. . . . Like a gangster I sought to penetrate my father's secret soul. The limits remained, unredeemed."

In midlife, in those years from ages thirty-five to forty-five or fifty, we learn that many hopes remain unredeemed. There is plenty that we wanted, and did not receive, from our parents. It is time to know, and accept, that we never will.

In studying families, Featherstone observes that he is "struck again and again by the mysterious capacity of people to give and withhold themselves on their own terms." But in our middle years, as our mothers and fathers begin to age and sicken and die, we may begin rewriting these . . . terms of endearment. For now that the world belongs to our generation—not to theirs—we see how little power they ever had: To love us perfectly. To understand us perfectly. To save us from sorrow and solitude—and from death.

We see how little power they had, and how little we have now, to build sturdy bridges across the gulfs which separate us. Letting go of our vain expectations as parents and children and spouses and friends, we learn to give thanks for even imperfect connections.

IV Loving, Losing, Leaving, Letting Go

This is what youth must figure out:
Girls, love, and living.
The having, the not having,
The spending and giving,
And the melancholy time of not knowing.

This is what age must learn about:
The ABC of dying.
The going, yet not going,
The loving and leaving.
And the unbearable knowing and knowing.

—E. B. White

16

Love and Mourning

Did someone say that there would be an end,
An end, Oh, an end, to love and mourning?

—May Sarton

This is the Hour of Lead—
Remembered, if outlived,
As Freezing persons recollect the Snow—
First—Chill—then Stupor—then the letting go—

—Emily Dickinson

We are separate people constrained by the forbidden and the impossible, fashioning our highly imperfect connections. We live by losing and leaving and letting go. And sooner or later, with more or less pain, we all must come to know that loss is indeed "a lifelong human condition."

Mourning is the process of adapting to the losses of our life.

"In what, now," asks Freud in "Mourning and Melancholia," "does the work which mourning performs consist?" He replies that it is difficult and slow, involving an extremely painful, bit-by-bit inner process of letting go. He is talking, as I will be here, about the mourning we do at the death of people we love. But we may mourn in a similar fashion the end of a marriage, the coming apart of a special friendship, the losses of what we'd once had . . . been . . . hoped might be. For, as we shall see, there is an end, an end to much that we have loved. But there can be an end to mourning, too.

· · ·

How we mourn and how, or if, our mourning is going to end, will depend on what we perceive our losses to be, will depend on our age and their age, will depend on how ready all of us were, will depend on the way they succumbed to mortality, will depend on our inner strengths and our outer supports, and will surely depend on our prior history—on our history with the people who died and our own separate history of love and loss. Nevertheless, there does seem to be a typical pattern to normal adult mourning, despite individual idiosyncrasies. And it seems generally agreed that we pass through changing, though overlapping, phases of mourning and that after about a year, sometimes less but often far longer indeed, we "complete" a major part of the mourning process.

Now many of us find it difficult to hear about phases of mourning without bristling, without the sense that some Julia Child of sorrow is trying to provide us with a step-by-step recipe for the perfect grief. But if we can hear about phases not as something that we—or others—*must* go through, but as something that may illuminate what we—or others—have gone or are going through, perhaps we can come to understand why "sorrow . . . turns out to be not a state but a process."

And the first phase of this process, whether the loss has been anticipated or not, is "shock, numbness and a sense of disbelief." This can't be happening! No, it cannot be! Perhaps we will weep and wail; perhaps we will sit there silently; perhaps waves of grief will alternate with periods of stunned incomprehension. Our shock may be mild if we've lived long and hard with the dead's impending death. Our shock may be less (let's face it) than our relief. But the fact that someone we love no longer exists in time and space is not yet entirely real, is beyond our belief.

Mark Twain, whose daughter Susy—"our wonder and our worship"—died suddenly at the age of twenty-four, writes in his autobiography of that initial state of benumbed disbelief:

> It is one of the mysteries of our nature that a man, all unprepared, can receive a thunder-stroke like that and live. There is but one reasonable explanation of it. The intellect is stunned by the shock and but gropingly gathers the meaning of the words. The power to

realize their full import is mercifully wanting. The mind has a dumb sense of vast loss—that is all. It will take mind and memory months and possibly years to gather the details and thus learn and know the whole extent of the loss.

Although an expected death will usually stun us less than one we are unprepared for, although with a fatal illness our major shock may come when that illness is diagnosed and although in the time preceding the death we may sometimes engage in "anticipatory mourning," we will initially find it difficult—despite such preparation—to assimilate the death of a person we love. Death is one of those facts of life we acknowledge more with our brain than we do with our heart. And often, although our intellect acknowledges the loss, the rest of us will be trying hard to deny it.

A man whose wife, Ruth, had died was found frantically waxing the floors of their house on the day of her funeral; family and friends would be coming and "if the house is a mess, Ruth will kill me," he earnestly said. When Tina died, her younger brother Andrew inquired, "Why must we say that she's dead? Why can't we just pretend she's in California?" I, when told of the sudden death of a dearly loved young girl, grotesquely replied to her weeping father, "You're kidding!" And sometimes, as in the shared delusion of the family below, the denial of death defies the clinical facts.

An elderly woman was rushed to the hospital by her family following the sudden onset of a stroke. Within a few hours she died, and the attending intern immediately informed the several grown children who had remained at the hospital. Their immediate reaction was disbelief, and together they went in to see their mother. After several minutes they came from her room insisting that she was not dead, and they requested that the family physician be called. Only after the diagnosis was confirmed by a second physician did they accept the obvious reality. . . .

Some disbelief, some denial, may continue well beyond the initial shock. Indeed, it may take the entire mourning process to make of the impossible—death—a reality.

· · ·

After the first phase of mourning, which is relatively short, we move to a longer phase of intense psychic pain. Of weeping and lamentation. Of emotional swings and physical complaints. Of lethargy, hyperactivity, regression (to a needier, "Help me!" stage). Of separation anxiety and helpless, hopeless despair. And of anger too.

Annie, age twenty-nine when her husband and daughter were killed by a truck, recalls how angry she was, "how I hated the world. I hated that man in the truck. I hated all trucks. I hated God for making them. I hated everyone, even John [her four-year-old son] sometimes because I had to stay alive for him and if he hadn't been there I could have died too. . . ."

We are angry at the doctors for not saving them. We are angry at God for taking them away. Like Job, or the man in the following poem, we are angry at our comforters—what right have they to say that time will heal, God is good, it is all for the best, we'll get over it?

> Your logic, my friend, is perfect,
> Your moral most drearily true;
> But, since the earth closed on *her* coffin,
> I keep hearing that, and not you.
>
> Console if you will, I can bear it,
> 'Tis a well-meant alms of breath;
> But not all the preaching since Adam
> Has made Death other than Death.

There are those who insist that anger—toward others, and also toward the dead—is invariably a part of the mourning process.

Indeed, a great deal of the anger that we focus on those around us is the anger we feel, but won't let ourselves feel, toward the dead. Sometimes, however, we do express it directly. "God damn you! God damn you for dying on me!" a widow recalls having said to her dead husband's picture. Like her, we love the dead, we miss and need and pine for our dead, but we also are angry at them for having abandoned us.

We are angry at, hate, the dead the way an infant hates the mommy who goes away. And like that infant we fear that it is our anger, our hatred, our badness that drove them away. We have guilt about our bad feelings and we also may have great guilt for what we have done—and what we didn't do.

Guilty feelings too—irrational guilt and justified guilt—are very often a part of the mourning process.

For the ambivalence that is present in even our deepest love relationships tainted our love for the dead while they were alive. We saw them as less than perfect and we loved them less than perfectly; we may even have fleetingly wished that they would die. But now that they are dead we are ashamed of our negative feelings and we start berating ourselves for being so bad: "I should have been kinder." "I should have been more understanding." "I should have been more grateful for what I had." "I should have tried to call my mother more often." "I should have gone down to Florida to visit my dad." "He always wanted a dog, but I would never let him have one, and now it's too late."

Of course there are times when we ought to feel guilt for the way that we treated the dead, appropriate guilt for harm done, unmet needs. But even when we loved them very, very well indeed, we still may find grounds for self-recrimination.

Here are a mother's musings on the death of her son at the age of seventeen:

> Missing him now, I am haunted by my own shortcomings, how often I failed him. I think every parent must have a sense of failure, even of sin, merely in remaining alive after the death of a child. One feels that it is not right to live when one's child has died, that one should somehow have found the way to give one's life to save his life. Failing there, one's failures during his too brief life seem all the harder to bear and forgive. . . .
>
> I wish we had loved Johnny more when he was alive. Of course we loved Johnny very much. Johnny knew that. Everybody knew it. Loving Johnny more. What does it mean? What can it mean, now?

We feel guilt about our failures toward someone we love when he or she dies. We feel guilt about our negative feelings, too. And what we may do to defend against, or alleviate, our guilt is to

loudly insist that the person who died was perfect. Idealization—
"My wife was a saint," "My father was wiser than Solomon"—
allows us to keep our thoughts pure and to keep guilt at bay. It is
also a way of repaying the dead, of making restitution, for all of
the bad we have done—or imagined we've done—to them.

Canonizing—idealizing—the dead is frequently a part of the
mourning process.

Discussing idealization in her excellent book *The Anatomy
of Bereavement*, psychiatrist Beverley Raphael gives us Jack, a
forty-nine-year-old widower who described his dead wife
Mabel in terms of unremitting adulation. She was, he declared,
"the greatest little woman ever . . . the best cook, the best wife
in the world. She did everything for me." Dr. Raphael then goes
on to observe:

> He could say nothing negative of her and insisted their life together
> had been perfect in every way. The intensity of his insistence on this
> was harsh and aggressive, as though he dared anyone to prove oth-
> erwise. It was only after careful exploration that he revealed his
> resentment toward her for her coddling and intrusive control of his
> life, and how much he had longed for his freedom. He then became
> able to talk in a more realistic way, cheerfully, yet sadly, talking of
> the good and the bad. . . .

Anger, guilt, idealization—and attempts at reparation—seem to
suggest that we do in fact know the dead died. Yet alternately, or
even simultaneously, their death may still continue to be denied.
John Bowlby, in his book *Loss*, describes this paradox:

"On the one hand is belief that death has occurred with the pain
and hopeless yearning that that entails. On the other is disbelief
that it has occurred, accompanied both by hope that all may yet
be well and by an urge to search for and to recover the lost person." A child whose mother leaves him will deny the departure,
will search for her, Bowlby says. It is in a similar spirit that we—
as left, bereft adults—search for our dead.

This searching may express itself unconsciously—as restless
random activity. But some of us consciously seek the dead as well.
Beth looks for her husband by going again and again to all of the

places they'd gone to together. Jeffrey stands in the closet among the clothes his wife used to wear, smelling her smell. Anne, the widow of the French movie actor Gérard Philipe, describes her search for her husband at the cemetery:

> ...I went to find you. A mad rendezvous.... I remained outside reality, without being able to go in. The tomb was there, I could touch the earth that covered you and without being able to help it, I began to believe that you would come, a little late as usual; that soon I would feel you approach me....
>
> There was no point in telling myself that you were dead.... You weren't coming, no, you were waiting for me in the car. A mad hope, that I knew to be mad, and still it overtook me.
>
> "Yes, he's waiting in the car." And, when I found it empty, I protected myself once more, as though trying to give myself respite: "He's taking a walk on the hill." I went down to the house, talking to friends the while, looking for you on the road. Without believing in it, of course.

Searching for the dead we sometimes even summon them up: We "hear" their step in the driveway, their key in the lock. We "see" them on the street and eagerly follow them for a block; they turn and we confront . . . a stranger's face. Some of us may bring our dead back to life with hallucinations. Many of us bring our dead back to life in our dreams.

A father dreams of his son—"I dreamed one night that dear More was alive again and that after throwing my arms round his neck and finding beyond all doubt that I had my living son in my embrace—we went thoroughly into the subject, and found that the death and funeral at Abinger had been fictitious. For a second after waking the joy remained—then came the knell that wakes me every morning—More is dead! More is dead!"

A mother dreams of her daughter—"It's very ordinary, my dream. She's just there—and not dead."

A woman dreams of her sister—". . . She often comes to me, you know; we have a laugh. . . ."

A daughter (Simone de Beauvoir) dreams of her mother—"She blended with Sartre, and we were happy together. And then the dream would turn into a nightmare: Why was I living with her once more? How had I come to be in her power again? So our former relationship lived on in me in its double aspect—a subjection that I loved and hated."

A son dreams of his father—"I carried him to the ocean. He was dying. He died peacefully in my arms."

A son dreams of his mother (his first dream about her since her death)—"She was laughing at me sadistically because I couldn't get off a moving train. She was baring her teeth with a really sadistic laugh. I was shocked when I woke up but I told myself that, in the midst of all of my wonderful memories, I shouldn't forget about this part of her too."

This same son dreams of his mother some months later—"I was walking somewhere alone; ahead of me were three women in floor-length nightgowns. One of the figures turned; it was my mother, and clear as can be she said, 'Forgive me.' "

A daughter dreams of her father—"I dreamt he was running away and I wanted to catch him, it was terrible."

A widow dreams of her husband one month after his suicide—"There are two spiral staircases set side by side. I'm going up one and he's going down the other. I reach out my hand to make contact but he pretends he doesn't know me and keeps going down."

And the writer Edmund Wilson repeatedly dreams longing dreams of Margaret, his dead wife:

Dream. There she was alive—what was the catch?—that she was supposed not to exist any more—but there she was, and what was to prevent our living together again?

Dream. Thought in dim grayish dream I could tell her how silly I'd been about making mistake about not being able to see her again.

Dream. I was getting into bed with her—there was no reason after all that we shouldn't be together.

Dream. She was ill and supposed not to have long to live, lying on a bed somewhere we had gone to see a woman doctor—as we were talking, it occurred to me that she might get well, and if I could make her believe that I loved her and wanted her to get well, the trouble might disappear. . . .

In fantasies and dreams, in all of our searchings for the dead, we try to deny the finality of the loss. For the death of someone we love revives our childhood fears of abandonment, the ancient anguish of being little and left. By summoning up the dead we can sometimes manage to persuade ourselves that the person we lost is still here, that we aren't bereft. But sometimes, as in this chilling story told to me by a sensible, down-to-earth friend, summoning up the dead may persuade us they're dead.

Two years to the day after Jordan's young wife had committed suicide, he lay in bed with Myra, a new ladylove. A woman who'd been a friend of his late wife Arlene. A woman he viewed as a stand-in for Arlene. A woman he had been pressing to be like Arlene. A perfectly lovely woman he wasn't quite prepared to marry because she wasn't, after all, Arlene.

That night in bed, however, when he awoke and glanced at Myra's sleeping body, "I didn't see Myra; I saw the corpse of Arlene. I couldn't make it turn back," he said, "I couldn't get back to the reality of Myra. I was laying there, in panic, with this corpse."

He finally got out of bed and fled the apartment.

Now happily married to Myra, Jordan says that his experience was terrifying, but liberating too. It allowed him, at last, to get on with the rest of his life. It made him understand that he couldn't resurrect his wife, that "I couldn't replace Arlene with another Arlene." He says, "After that, I was able to let her die."

In this acute phase of grief some of us will mourn quietly, some vocally—though it isn't our style to rend garments and tear our hair. But in our own different ways we will have to pass through the terror and tears, the anger and guilt, the anxiety and despair. And in our own different ways, having managed somehow to work our way through our confrontations with unacceptable losses, we can begin to come to the end of mourning.

Starting with shock and making our way through this phase of acute psychic pain, we move toward what is called the "completion" of mourning. And although there still will be times when we weep for, long for, miss our dead, completion means some important degree of recovery and acceptance and adaptation.

We recover our stability, our energy, our hopefulness, our capacity to enjoy and invest in life.

We accept, despite dreams and fantasies, that the dead will not return to us in this life.

We adapt, with enormous difficulty, to the altered circumstances of our life, modifying—in order to survive—our behavior, our expectations, our self-definitions. Psychoanalyst George Pollock, who has written extensively on the subject of mourning, has called the mourning process "one of the more universal forms of adaptation and growth . . ." Successful mourning, he argues, is far far more than making the best of a bad situation. Mourning, he says, can lead to creative change.

But he and his colleagues warn us that mourning is rarely a straightforward, linear process. So does Linda Pastan in a powerful poem that begins with "the night I lost you" and traces the long hard ascent through the stages of grief until the final stage is approached and . . .

> . . . now I see what I am climbing
> towards: *Acceptance*
> written in capital letters,
> a special headline:
> *Acceptance,*
> its name is in lights.
> I struggle on,
> waving and shouting.
> Below, my whole life spreads its surf,
> all the landscapes I've ever known
> or dreamed of. Below
> a fish jumps: the pulse
> in your neck.
> *Acceptance.* I finally
> reach it.
> But something is wrong.
> Grief is a circular staircase.
> I have lost you.

Going through stages of grief, Pastan says, is like climbing a circular staircase—and like learning to climb it "after the amputation." In his record of mourning following the death of his cherished wife, C. S. Lewis uses identical imagery:

> How often—will it be for always?—how often will the vast emptiness astonish me like a complete novelty and make me say, "I never realized my loss till this moment"? The same leg is cut off time after time. The first plunge of the knife into the flesh is felt again and again.

In another section he writes:

> One keeps on emerging from a phase, but it always recurs. Round and round. Everything repeats. Am I going in circles . . . ?

It sometimes seems that way. And sometimes we do.

And even when, eventually, we accept and adapt and recover, we may suffer from "anniversary reactions"—recurringly mourning our dead, with feelings of pining and sadness and loneliness and despair, on the day in the calendar year that marks their birth or their death or some special shared occasion. But in spite of setbacks, recurrences and the sense that our sorrow keeps doubling back on itself, there is an end to mourning, to even the seemingly most inconsolable mourning, as this record of a daughter's grieving testifies:

> I awake in the middle of the night and tell myself, She's gone. My mother is dead. Never will I see her again. How to grasp this?

> Oh, Mama, I don't want to eat, to walk, to get out of bed. Reading, working, cooking, listening, mothering. Nothing matters. I do not want to be distracted from my grief. I wouldn't mind dying. I wouldn't mind it at all. I wake from sleep in the middle of every night and say to myself, "My mother is dead!" . . .

> Mourning. . . . You seem to be filled with it. Always. In a sense, like a pregnancy. But . . . pregnancy imparts a sense of doing something even while inactive, [whereas] mourning bequeaths a sense of futility and meaninglessness in the midst of activity. . . . Her death is the only thing on my mind. . . .

> My everydayness has snapped and I am in quarantine from the world. Want nothing from it, have nothing to give to it. When things

get too bad, the whole world is lost to you, the world and the people in it.

It's all a rotten hoax, this life of ours. You go from zero to zero. Why attach yourself to love only to have your beloved ripped from you? The upshot of love is pain. Life is a death sentence. Better not to give yourself to anything. . . .

I have to begin from the beginning and repeat: She's dead. As if it's just struck me. And I find myself drowning, engulfed by the disorder of the current, wanting to seize her hand to bring me to shore. Missing her so. . . .

Some days I can look at her photograph and the image revives me, reinforces her for me. On other days, I gaze at her and am blinded with tears. Newly bereft. . . .

This outpouring of feeling, of self-pity, is . . . a crying on Mama's shoulder, a wailing into the wind, a hiccuping amid sobs against an irrevocable crashing surf. A lament. A dirge. You come. And you go. I had her once, and now she's gone. So, what's new? What's the point?

Am I healing? I'm able to gaze at her photograph without that tourniquet tightening round my throat, clamping memory. . . . I'm beginning to see her in *her* life, and not only myself bereft of her life. . . .

Piece by piece, I reenter the world. A new phase. A new body, a new voice. Birds console me by flying, trees by growing, dogs by the warm patch they leave on the sofa. Unknown people merely by performing their motions. It's like a slow recovery from a sickness, this recovery of one's self. . . . My mother was at peace. She was ready. A free woman. "Let me go," she said. Okay, Mama, I'm letting you go.

In another passage this daughter talks about being weaned from her mother's material presence, but "filled with her as never before." She is describing, in her own words, the process that psychoanalysts call "internalization." It is by internalizing the dead, by making them part of our inner world, that we can at last complete the mourning process.

Remember that, as children, we could let our mother go, or leave our mother, by establishing a permanent mother within us.

In a similar way we internalize—we take into ourselves—the people we have loved and lost to death. The "loved object is not gone," psychoanalyst Karl Abraham writes, "for now I carry it within myself. . . ." And while surely he overstates—the touch is gone, the laugh is gone, the promise and possibilities are gone, the sharing of music and bread and bed is gone, the comforting joy-giving flesh-and-blood presence is gone—it is true nonetheless that by making the dead a part of our inner world, we will in some important ways never lose them.

One form of internalization—I've discussed this earlier—is identification. It is through identifications that we can develop and enrich our emerging self. And through identifications we can take into our self aspects of those we have loved and who are now dead—aspects that are often abstract but are on occasion startlingly concrete.

Therapist Lily Pincus describes one woman who took up gardening after her brother, a passionate gardener, had died, and another, rather dull, woman who acquired a gift for repartee after her husband, the witty one, had died. We can identify, as well, with some of our dead's less lovable aspects, and identifications can be pathological too. But by taking in the dead—by making them part of what we think, feel, love, want, do—we can both keep them with us and let them go.

Mourning, we are told, can end in constructive identifications. But the process of mourning will often go awry. For when those we love die we may deal with their death by failing to deal with their death or by remaining "stuck" in the mourning process.

In prolonged or chronic mourning we do not move past the second phase. We are mired in a state of intense, unremitting grief, clinging without relief to our sorrow, anger, guilt, self-hatred or depression, unable to get on with the rest of our life. It is difficult to give anyone a timetable for mourning; not one year but two years or more may be normal for some. But a time will have to come when we become willing to let go of the lost relationship. Our mourning is pathological when we cannot, and we will not, let it go.

Beverley Raphael describes one version of chronic mourning:

There is continued crying, preoccupation with the lost person, angry protest, and the bereaved goes over and over the memories of the lost relationship which is often intensely idealized. Mourning does not draw to its natural conclusion, and it almost seems that the bereaved has taken on a new and special role, that of the grief-stricken one.

She adds that by such grieving "it is as though the lost person lives on in the grief." The poets understood this long ago. When Shakespeare's King Philip chides Constance: "You are as fond of your grief as of your child," she offers him this desperate explanation:

> Grief fills the room up of my absent child,
> Lies in his bed, walks up and down with me;
> Puts on his pretty looks, repeats his words,
> Remembers me of all his gracious parts,
> Stuffs out his vacant garments with his form;
> Then, have I reason to be fond of grief.

Another version of chronic grief is the so-called "mummification" of the dead, the keeping of every object that the dead one once possessed exactly where and how he or she had kept them. Queen Victoria, for instance, when her beloved Prince Albert died, had his shaving equipment and clothes laid out every day, and all of his possessions remained the way that he had arranged them in his lifetime. But whether chronic grief is expressed by creating domestic shrines or by hopelessness and sorrow and ready tears, the message is the same: "This will not be healed by the passage of years. I'll never get over it."

Mourning is also disordered when it is absent or delayed in an effort to avoid the pain of loss. And although an absence of mourning can, if and when the barriers drop, flip over into its opposite— chronic mourning—the avoidance of painful feelings can be maintained, sometimes, for years or even a lifetime.

Remember that I am talking about the loss of people we've loved, not people from whom we're emotionally disengaged. I am talking of losses that give us good cause to grieve. And if instead of feeling bereaved, we are coping magnificently, shedding no tears and carrying on as if nothing disruptive has happened, we are only deceiving ourselves into thinking we're "taking it very well" for, in actual fact, we cannot take it.

We may, for instance, unconsciously fear that if once we started weeping, we'd never stop, or that we would have a breakdown or go insane, or that the weight of our grief would crush or drive away those around us, or that all of our earlier losses would swamp us again. How do we know we are fending off mourning and not just untouched by the loss? Bowlby says there are many different clues: We may be tense and short-tempered, or wooden and formal, or forcedly cheerful, or withdrawn, or drawn excessively to booze. We may have physical symptoms, trading in psychic for bodily pain. We also may have insomnia and bad dreams. And we may not be able to tolerate any discussions of, or references to, the dead.

Psychoanalysts, and Shakespeare, say that failure to mourn can be hazardous to health and that mourning is a way to relieve the ache:

> Give sorrow words; the grief that does not speak
> Whispers the oe'r fraught heart, and bids it break.

But whether or not sorrow speaks, death may have long-term harmful effects on the mental and physical health of the survivors, who—at a higher rate than those who have not lost someone to death—die, or kill themselves, or contract diseases, or have accidents, or overindulge in smoking, drinking, drugs, or suffer from depression and various other psychological disturbances. A woman whose husband's death left her seeing the future as bleak and empty—"a big black hole"—told me that she consciously had to decide that she would keep going, "that I would live." She believes that after such losses we all have some choice between living and dying and she says she has watched a friend "choose the other way." And while some who decide not to stay may have a fantasy of after-death reunion, others—like Hans Castorp's father in Mann's novel *The Magic Mountain*—simply seem unable to go on.

> The father, Hermann Castorp, could not grasp his loss. He had been deeply attached to his wife, and not being of the strongest himself, never quite recovered from her death. His spirit was troubled; he shrank within himself; his benumbed brain made him blunder in his business . . . ; and the next spring, while inspecting warehouses on the windy landing-stage, he got inflammation of the lungs. The fever was too much for his shaken heart, and in five days, notwithstanding all Dr. Heidekind's care, he died.

Studies of stress consistently identify the loss of a close family member as the most stressful event of everyday life. It is a "life stressor" that most of us will bear. The statistics are these: Some eight million Americans, every year, experience death in their immediate family. There are, every year, 800,000 new widowers and widows. And approximately 400,000 children, every year, die before they reach age twenty-five.

Loss through death is a major life stressor, and every life stressor, hundreds of studies show, increases the risk of mental and physical ills. But not everyone who suffers such loss is equally susceptible to these ills. The intriguing question, of course, is what makes the difference, what increases vulnerability?

Here are some answers the Institute of Medicine finds wide agreement on: Those with a poor prior history of mental or physical health are at greater risk. So are those dealing with death by suicide. So are those spouses whose relationship with the husband or wife who died was especially ambivalent or dependent. Those who experience loss without the support of a social network tend to find the trauma more intense. And the younger do worse than the older—studies find that one frequent consequence of childhood loss is a higher risk of adult-life mental illness.

This book began with a look at the toll that is taken by early loss and separation. We saw that the earliest losses feel much like death. We saw that in our young years we may misunderstand our experience of being left—we may see it as an abandonment because we are unlovable and bad. Our response can be feelings of helplessness and/or guilt and/or absolute terror and/or fury. We also may feel unendurably sad. And we may not have the resources, either the inner or outer resources, to deal with these feelings.

Thus children may mourn a death but may not be able to mourn in a way that lets them work through the enormity of their loss. They may fail to fully resolve childhood losses in childhood. They also may acquire certain tactics for dealing with loss that do them damage then—and later on. In a family of caring adults, children often may find the support and encouragement to express the full gamut of feelings, to mourn till it's done. But, as I noted above and as we saw in detail in Chapter One, the losses of early childhood may continue to dwell within us all of our life.

The Danish writer Tove Ditlevsen, who lost both parents when she was very young, offers this autobiographical portrait:

> When you have
> once had
> a great joy
> it lasts always
> quivers gently
> on the edge of all the
> insecure adult days
> subdues inherited dread
> makes sleep deeper.
>
> The bedroom was
> an island of light
> my father and mother
> were painted
> on the morning's wall.
> They handed a shining
> picture book toward me
> they smiled to see
> my immense joy.
>
> I saw they were young
> and happy for
> each other
> saw it for the first
> saw it for the last time.

> The world became eternally
> divided into a before
> and after.
>
> I was five years old
> since then everything
> has changed.

Perhaps it was that "great joy" which allowed Tove Ditlevsen to produce thirty-two books of poetry and fiction and memoirs and children's stories and essays. Perhaps that great joy helped, but it didn't save her. There were three failed marriages. There also was drug addiction. And in 1976 she committed suicide.

Is everyone who loses a mother or father in early childhood doomed to despair thereafter, wrecked for life? Do all major childhood losses produce pathology? The answer is certainly no, in spite of the many studies that show that the risk is higher. Children who are by nature constitutionally sturdy will also be sturdy in the face of loss. But even more fragile children may be helped by empathic adults to adapt to loss by means of constructive mourning.

Some analysts have argued that no young child has the ego strength to mourn to completion. Bowlby and others have strongly disagreed, insisting that what children need (although these conditions, they concede, are often not met) are: A good relationship with the family before the death. A reliable, comforting caretaker after the death. Prompt, accurate information about the death. And encouragement to join in the family grieving.

Surely these outer conditions can make a great difference. But let us not forget that children live both out in the world and inside their head. Not all well-loved children, invited to mourn, can do what must be done to let go of the dead, and it may not be done until adulthood, and it may not be done without professional help.

But sometimes it is. In this scene below, Dr. Raphael suggests the kind of response that can help a child mourn and come to the end of mourning.

Jessica was five. She showed her mother the picture she had painted. There were black clouds, dark trees and large red splashes.

"My," said her mother. "Tell me about this, Jess." Jessica pointed to the red splashes. "That's blood," she said. "And these are clouds." "Oh," said her mother. "See," said Jessica, "the trees are very sad. The clouds are black. They are sad too." "Why are they sad?" asked her mother. "They are sad because their Daddy has died," said Jessica, the tears slowly running down her cheeks. "Sad like us since Daddy died," said her mother, and held her closely, and they wept.

Loss at an early age can make it harder for us to negotiate future encounters with separation and loss. But even those who are spared major losses in their growing-up years may never really get over the death of a child. Middle-class parents living today in this modern industrial world expect their sons and daughters to survive them. The death of a child is perceived as a death out of season, a monstrosity, an outrage against the natural order of things.

Yet among my own middle-class friends I can count eleven— eleven!—children, between the ages of three and twenty-nine, children who have been lost to death by accident and suicide and disease. How do mothers and fathers mourn such deaths? How do they—do they?—come to the end of mourning?

It seems from what I have read and from the tears that I have seen shed over daughters and sons dead many years ago, that parents—including women and men with loving, productive lives —may never give up grieving for their lost child.

Indeed, holding on to grief may feel like fealty to the dead, while giving it up may seem like a betrayal. "I'm proud of myself," says Vera, whose twenty-nine-year-old daughter June died seven years ago, "when I can say her name without a tremor." But, she quickly adds, "I'm *horrified* when I can say it without a tremor."

During the months between her daughter's cancer diagnosis and her death, Vera lived in "suspended unreality." She protected her four younger children by muting the truth. She took care of June, who had moved back home, and "tried to make it as good for her as possible." And she "play-acted" hope and good cheer—they never never wept together, she and June, except the day they sat

and watched a drama on TV and heard two characters exchange
these lines:

"Am I going to die?"

"Yes."

"I don't want to die."

After June's death, Vera says that she became "the walking
dead." In private she wept, but in public her play-act continued.
"I felt that my grief was too great," she explains, "that it was a
potent poison, that it would sink everyone. And I thought that it
was my job to show my children that you could live through it, to
protect them from being scared to death of life."

When Vera's last child left home, however, five and a half years
later, she started developing pains "that felt like a heart condition.
I was very depressed. I wept all the time." She sought help.

Today she says she feels better, but she says that she still feels
diminished, though to us who are her friends she offers wisdom,
comfort, strength and, yes, delight. But her losses are powerful
losses, for she says that what she has lost is not only June, her
much-loved firstborn child. She has lost her sense of herself—her
central definition of self—as her children's protector.

"I had this fantasy that I could make my children safe. My role
in life was to be their great protector. June's death was a defeat
for me; it taught me I was helpless, helpless, helpless. I could save
nobody. I could fix it for nobody."

She mourns for her daughter. She mourns for that part of herself.

Anthropologist Geoffrey Gorer, in his pioneering book *Death,
Grief, and Mourning*, concludes that the most distressing and enduring of all griefs is a mother's and father's grief for a dead grown
child. But mourning the loss of a child, or the hopes of the child-
who-was-to-be, may begin at any stage of the parenting process
and may need to be acknowledged and understood by the outside
world as well as by those who experience the loss. A miscarriage
—"They said it was nothing . . . but it was my baby, and it
counted"—may be mourned as a loss. An abortion—no matter
how sensible and necessary it seems—may have to be done, but
may have to be mourned as a loss. A stillborn's cruelly compressed
life and death certainly will have to be mourned as a loss. And so

must the death of a baby who, attached to tubes and machines, survives for only a handful of days or weeks.

Margaret was twenty-two when she lost her baby, born too early. He lived a little while and then he died. And "then there was the empty room at home, and it came all over me like a great tidal wave of grief. I was so sad, so empty, I thought I'd never feel whole again."

With the death of a child who has lived in a family, has become a person, little or big, has become known, the loss that is mourned includes not only the future expectations but the shared past. The response to this most untimely of deaths—the anger, guilt, idealization, the pining, ambivalence, sorrow and despair—"may alter, forever," writes Raphael, "the course of the parents' life and even of the parents' relationship to one another."

Among my friends, the parents of the eleven children who died do not stand out as monuments to grief. They laugh, make love, make plans, do what they must. I know that one of them trusts that she will meet her child again in some Hereafter. But most of them, I suspect, make do without such consolations. And most of them, I suspect, will never be able to fully assimilate their loss.

On the day that his dead daughter Sophie would have been thirty-six years old, Sigmund Freud wrote in a letter to a friend:

> Although we know that after such a loss the acute state of mourning will subside, we also know that we shall remain inconsolable and will never find a substitute. No matter what may fill the gap, even if it be filled completely, it nevertheless remains something else.

It is traumatic for a child to lose a parent. It is traumatic for a parent to lose a child. But the loss of a husband or wife is a compendium of many different losses.

For we may mourn—in the death of a spouse—our companion, our lover, our intimate friend, our protector, our provider, our partner in parenthood. We may mourn no longer being a part of a pair. And in marriages where our life was lived entirely through our spouse, and the spouse through whom we lived is no longer there, we may mourn the shattering loss of a whole way of life.

Some of us—whose role was to cook for, to care for, to be with our mate—may mourn the loss of the purpose of our existence. And some of us—whose sense of self was built upon our spouse's approving presence—may find that we also are mourning the loss of that self.

"Our society is set up," writes Lynn Caine in her painfully frank autobiographical *Widow*, "so that most women lose their identities when their husbands die." She says that after her husband's death, "I felt like one of those spiraled shells washed up on the beach. Poke a straw through the twisting tunnel, around and around, and there is nothing there. No flesh. No life. Whatever lived there is dried up and gone."

Vicky, the wife of an actor who died at the height of his career, led a glorious life as The Wife of the Star, with famous and interesting people and travel and parties and glamorous evenings and . . . and suddenly she is spending her evenings alone. "I liked what I had," she tells me, completely unreconciled almost eighteen months after his death. "I don't want anything else. I want what I had."

Elaine was forty-five when her husband died—she had tenderly nursed him for several years. Her existence revolved entirely around his care. Her feeling when he died was that "her own life had no meaning now without him, that she had no other role or use in life."

Fern, despite a career and grown-up children who love and enjoy her, enjoys very little since the death of Dan. She says only he could make her feel like a valued, desirable woman, that she cannot love herself except through a man. She is frantically, frantically, frantically trying to find one.

Does having a famous name and an independent, separate identity safeguard widows from extremes of grief? It doesn't necessarily work that way. Actress Helen Hayes, describing the two years following her husband's death, has these devastating words to say: "I was just as crazy as you can be and still be at large. I didn't have any really normal minutes during those two years. It wasn't just grief. It was total confusion. I was nutty. . . ."

And even widows who aren't "nutty" may feel an aching sense of disorientation. "God has moved me up into a more advanced class," said one woman after the death of her husband. "The desks are still a little too big for me."

The death of a spouse destroys a social unit, imposes new roles and confronts us—the living—with a terrible loneliness. The future may seem worthless while the past is often suffused in a rosy glow. We may want to hold on to the past but bit by bit, feeling every tender—and ugly—emotion, we must mourn the death in our marriage and let it go.

Although my focus here is on mourning the death of those we love, I should mention that other marital death called divorce. For the breakup of a marriage is a loss like the death of a spouse, and will often be mourned in closely parallel ways. There are some important distinctions: Divorce evokes more anger than death, and it is, of course, considerably more optional. But the sorrow and pining and yearning can be as intense. The denial and despair can be as intense. The guilt and self-reproach can be as intense. And the feeling of abandonment can be even more intense—"He didn't *have* to leave me; he *chose* to leave me."

Divorce can also, like widowhood, strip those who have been left of their sense of self. Listen to Monique:

"There was once a man who lost his shadow. I forget what happened to him, but it was dreadful. As for me, I've lost my own image. I did not look at it often; but it was there, in the background, just as Maurice had drawn it for me. A straightforward, genuine, 'authentic' woman, without mean-mindedness, uncompromising, but at the same time understanding, indulgent, sensitive, deeply feeling, intensely aware of things and of people. . . . It is dark: I cannot see myself any more. And what do the others see? Maybe something hideous."

Monique is someone all of us know, *The Woman Destroyed* of Simone de Beauvoir's short story. Maurice is her husband, who leaves after twenty-two years. In losing him, Monique also loses a life-sustaining image of herself. What is left, as the book-cover photo suggests, is a naked figure in the fetal position, huddled on the bare floor of an empty apartment.

According to recent studies, the costs of divorce—both the physical costs and the emotional ones—can be higher than those imposed by a spouse's death. The completion of mourning may be harder, too. For the problem with divorce is that we both are alive although the marriage is through and that, as psychiatrist Raphael notes, "the 'bereaved' must mourn someone who has not died. . . ."

I have heard many women say—I've heard a few men say it too —that they would have rather been widowed than divorced, that death would have not entangled them in continuing fights over property and children, in feelings of jealousy, in feelings of failure. In either case, the loss of a mate with whom we have shared a history shatters the former conditions of our life. "The world breaks everyone," Hemingway writes, "and afterward many are strong at the broken places." Some are. Some aren't.

Some of us, losing our spouse, may suffer a permanent impairment.

Some—like Hermann Castorp—may not survive.

Some—like the widow who chose not to die—will say, "I have plenty to do, and I'm glad I'm alive, but nothing that I do is as good without him."

Some—but widowers at a much, much higher rate than widows —will remarry.

Some widows will get their first job and relearn how to date.

And some, no longer half of a whole in a complementary marriage, will take on some of the qualities of their dead mate, will find in themselves certain talents and strengths that they had chosen to delegate to that mate, and—feeling rather astonished and maybe even rather disloyal—they may burst into bloom.

The list of the mourned must also include the loss of a brother or sister, a sorrow—in childhood particularly—that may be heavily laced with triumph and guilt. Triumph at getting rid of the rival at last. Guilt about the wish to get rid of that rival. Sorrow at being bereft of a playmate, a roommate, a companion. The pain of having lost—and having won.

Memory: Our family is taking a trip on an ocean liner. My little sister Lois disappears. The ship is searched. No Lois. The ship is searched again. No sign of Lois. My mother, completely convinced that her two-and-a-half-year-old has drowned, is frozen with grief.

But I, her very rivalrous four-and-a-half-year-old, am feeling some extremely mixed emotions:

Have my most ardent (and wicked) dreams come true? Has my dearest (and darkest) wish been granted? Have I, thanks to the terrible magical powers of my mind, succeeded at last in getting rid of my sister? Oh, what horror! Oh, what guilt! And oh, what joy!

After a couple of hours, however, my sister—who hasn't drowned, after all—is found. My mother, released from her terror, faints dead away. I too am swept with relief, having labored under the belief that I am a murderer. I am swept with relief and . . . disappointment.

But now we are middle-aged, and we have become beloved friends, my sister and I. And now she has cancer in breast and bone and lung. Looking through old family photographs, we laugh and cry and share memories together. And I want her to take the whole trip with me; I do not want my sister to fall off the boat.

When brothers and sisters grow up and leave home they find that their sibling relationships are optional. Some establish a powerful tie that lasts into adult life; others maintain the most minimal connections. Still others, like me, become free as adults to see our siblings as people who could be our friends. And as time goes on and parents die and our siblings are all that remain of our first family, we may begin to value them both as comrades and co-custodians of our past. And when they die, we mourn them, as this poet mourns the death of her big brother.

When we found out what the disease would do,
lying, like any council's stalwarts,
all of us swore to play our parts
in the final act at your command.

The first was easy. You gave up your left hand
and the right grew wiser, a juggler for its king.
When the poor dumb leg began to falter
you took up an alpenstick for walking
once flourished Sundays by our dead father.
Month by month the battleground grew thinner.
When you could no longer swallow meat

we steamed and mashed your dinner
and bent your straw to chocolate soda treats.

And when you could not talk, still you could write
questions and answers on a magic slate,
then lift the page, like laundry to the wind.
I plucked the memory splinter from your spine
as we played at being normal, who
had eased each other in the cold zoo
of childhood. Three months before
you died I wheeled you through the streets
of placid Palo Alto to catch
spring in its flamboyant tracks.
You wrote the name of every idiot flower
I did not know. Yucca rained.
Mimosa shone. The bottlebrush took fire
as you fought to hold your great head on its stem.
Lillac, you wrote, *Magnollia, Lilly,*
And further, *olleander. Dellphinium.*

O man of many L's, brother, my wily
resident ghost, may I never spell
these crowfoot dogbane words again
these showy florid words again
except I name them under your spell.

The deaths that we, presumably, are supposed to best take in
our stride, are the deaths in the fullness of time of our mothers
and fathers. But when I said to a friend whose mother was eighty-
nine when she died, "Well, she certainly had a chance to live a full
life," my friend responded angrily with, "I hate it when people say
that she lived a full life, as if I therefore shouldn't feel sad that
she's dead. Because I'm feeling very sad that she's dead. I'm going
to miss her."

My friend Jerome, whose father—after a rich and vigorous life
—had died at the age of seventy-eight, at home, told me, "I had
prepared myself for his death for some little time, but when the
time finally came I wasn't ready." Even though he knew that death
had come to his father in the proper season, "I still didn't want to
let go. I wasn't ready."

Jerome said Kaddish, the Jewish prayer for the dead, every

morning and night for eleven months, "to reaffirm my father's faith in the deity. I found it comforting in that it gave me a time every day to think about my father." He says he still thinks of him often and "every year, at Passover, I miss him terribly."

Sometimes our mourning is eased by the thought that our parents died an accepting, peaceful, "good" death. For although we will miss them terribly, it may hurt us even more if we've watched them vainly struggle against that death. Sitting at their bedside, we may feel impelled to say, "Don't fight so hard. Give up the fight. Go gentle."

> You have grown wings of pain
> and flap around the bed like a wounded gull
> calling for water, calling for tea, for grapes
> whose skins you cannot penetrate.
> Remember when you taught me
> how to swim? Let go, you said,
> the lake will hold you up.
> I long to say, Father let go
> and death will hold you up. . . .

In mourning a parent we also may seek consolation in the thought that we have had a chance to say goodbye—to express our love and gratitude, to finish unfinished business, to achieve some sort of reconciliation. "I had grown very fond of this dying woman," Simone de Beauvoir writes of the death of her mother. "As we talked in the half-darkness I assuaged an old unhappiness; I was renewing the dialogue that had been broken off during my adolescence and that our differences and our likenesses had never allowed us to take up again. And the early tenderness that I had thought dead for ever came to life again. . . ."

It is said that the loss of parents in the course of adult life can serve as a developmental spur, pushing sons and daughters into becoming full grownups at last, imposing a new maturity on those who—as long as they remained So-and-so's child—could not achieve it. Indeed, many students of mourning maintain that in any kind of death "there is no loss which cannot lead to gain."

And while like the rest of us, they would gladly forgo the gain if they could forgo the loss, life doesn't offer anyone such sweet options.

Rabbi Harold Kushner was told when his firstborn, Aaron, was three that the boy had a rare disease which produced rapid aging, that his child would be hairless, stunted in growth, look like a little old man—and die in his teens. Writing about this most unjust, most unacceptable death, Kushner addresses the question of losses and gains:

> I am a more sensitive person, a more effective pastor, a more sympathetic counselor because of Aaron's life and death than I would ever have been without it. And I would give up all of those gains in a second if I could have my son back. If I could choose, I would forego all the spiritual growth and depth which has come my way because of our experiences, and be what I was fifteen years ago, an average rabbi, an indifferent counselor, helping some people and unable to help others, and the father of a bright, happy boy. But I cannot choose.

So perhaps the only choice we have is to choose what to do with our dead: To die when they die. To live crippled. Or to forge, out of pain and memory, new adaptations. Through mourning we acknowledge that pain, feel that pain, live past it. Through mourning we let the dead go and take them in. Through mourning we come to accept the difficult changes that loss must bring—and then we begin to come to the end of mourning.

17

Shifting Images

> ...I have found a mourning process for oneself as one gets older and must come to terms with change resulting from this unavoidable progression. One might describe this process as mourning for former states of the self, as if these states represented lost objects.
>
> —Dr. George Pollock

We will mourn the loss of others. But we are also going to mourn the loss of our selves—of earlier definitions that our images of self depend upon. For the changes in our body redefine us. The events of our personal history redefine us. The ways that others perceive us redefine us. And at several points in our life we will have to relinquish a former self-image and move on.

The ages and phases of man—the tasks and character of successive stages of life—have been annotated by (and this surely does not exhaust the list) Confucius, Solon, the Talmud, Shakespeare, Erikson, Sheehy, Jaques, Gould and Levinson. The modern research suggests that there are normal predictable stages of adult development—though people go through them in drastically different ways. And it proposes that—in the general framework within which our separate destinies are worked out—periods of stability alternate with periods of transition.

In periods of stability, we are putting together a structure for our life—making key choices, pursuing certain goals. In periods of transition we are challenging the premises of that structure—raising questions, exploring new possibilities. Each transition leads to

termination of a previous life structure, and each termination—
writes the research psychologist Daniel Levinson—"is an ending,
a process of separation or loss." He goes on to say:

> The task of a developmental transition is to terminate a time in
> one's life; to accept the losses the termination entails; to review and
> evaluate the past; to decide which aspects of the past to keep and
> which to reject; and to consider one's wishes and possibilities for
> the future. One is suspended between past and future, and strug-
> gling to overcome the gap that separates them. Much from the past
> must be given up—separated from, cut out of one's life, rejected in
> anger, renounced in sadness or grief. And there is much that can be
> used as a basis for the future. Changes must be attempted in both
> self and world.

In the course of these changes we move from baby to kid to
adolescent and then into the stages of adult life: Breaking away
from the pre-adult world—the Early Adult Transition—between
ages seventeen and twenty-two. Making, during our twenties, our
first commitments to a job, a life-style, a marriage. Revising our
selections in our late twenties and early thirties—the Age Thirty
Transition—to add what is missing, to modify and exclude. Settling down and investing ourselves, during most of our thirties, in
work, friends, family, community, whatever. And reaching, at
about forty, those bridging years which take us from early to middle adulthood. Levinson calls this time the Mid-life Transition. For
most of us it's a crisis—a mid-life crisis. I have had one of my own:

> What am I doing with a mid-life crisis?
> This morning I was seventeen.
> I have barely begun the beguine and it's
> Good-night ladies
> Already.

> While I've been wondering who to be
> When I grow up someday,
> My acne has vanished away and it's
> Sagging kneecaps
> Already.

> Why do I seem to remember Pearl Harbor?
> Surely I must be too young.

When did the boys I once clung to
Start losing their hair?
Why can't I take barefoot walks in the park
Without giving my kidneys a chill?
There's poetry left in me still and it
Doesn't seem fair.

While I was thinking I was just a girl
My future turned into my past.
The time for wild kisses goes fast and it's
Time for Sanka.
Already?

There are those who insist on speaking in a doggedly upbeat way of this time of our life when our skin and our marriage are fading, when a number of youthful dreams have gone down the drain and when—although in our heart of hearts, we're only seventeen—the rest of us is slowly sagging southward. Life begins at forty, we're told; we're getting better, not older; if Sophia Loren is what middle-aged is, it ain't bad. But before we can come to some positive view of the other side of the mountain, we need to acknowledge that middle age is sad, because—not all at once, but bit by bit and day by day—we lose and leave and let go of our young self.

Now we may attempt to tell ourselves that we haven't changed since college, but this is rather difficult to do. For the fact is that in college we did not have drooping eyelids, or laugh lines that remained when our laughing was through. We also may try to tell ourselves that we're only as young as we feel, but that silly slogan merely begs the question. For if we drink coffee at bedtime, we will be up until 2 A.M. with a case of insomnia. And if we eat pizza at bedtime, we will be up at 2 A.M. with indigestion. How young can we feel? Finally, we may tell ourselves that we are, in mid-life, sexier than ever. Indeed, this very well may be the case. But another fact to face is that, as we move about in the world, we inspire far less lust than we do respect. We're not quite prepared to settle for only respect.

When I was young and miserable and pretty
And poor, I'd wish

What all girls wish: to have a husband,
A house and children. Now that I'm old, my wish
Is womanish;
That the boy putting groceries in my car
See me. It bewilders me that he doesn't see me.

Quoting that poem in a wistful essay entitled "The Age of Maturity," the author, Charles Simmons, goes on to say, "Me too." The checkout girl at the market, he notes, doesn't continue to flirt with a man forever. There comes a time when she no longer flirts with you. There comes a time, too, he complains, when you are "screened out" as a sexual person, when the girl who stops you on the street to ask you for directions "does it because you are safe, not because you are beautiful."

But despite Charles Simmons' pangs, the mid-life decline of youthful good looks is far more wounding for women than for men, for men can be wrinkled and balding and in other ways battered by time and still be viewed as sexually attractive. A man who is heading toward fifty can find himself many responsive thirty-year-olds; he has money and power he did not have in his youth; and although he is long in the tooth, he even may look more attractive these days with his confident air, crinkled eyes and graying sideburns.

It is different, Susan Sontag argues, for a woman.

"Being physically attractive counts much more in a woman's life than in a man's," she writes, "but beauty, identified as it is for women, with youthfulness, does not stand up well to age.... Women become sexually ineligible much earlier than men."

Thus a woman may fear aging because age will steal her power —her sexual power to attract a man—a loss I heard one woman, no longer a knockout at forty-five, actually, bitterly, liken to castration. But neither power nor fierce competitiveness—I want to be the prettiest girl in the room—explains the sense of doom with which many women see their girlhood beauty fading. For if youth is linked to beauty, and beauty is linked to a woman's sexual attractiveness, and her sexual attractiveness is important to her winning and holding a man, then age's assaults on beauty can catapult her into a terror of abandonment.

"My husband is going to trade me in for a younger and prettier model," goes her nightmare. "And no other man will want me and I'll have to spend the rest of my life alone."

It is one of those mid-life nightmares that often comes true.

"Most men experience getting older with regret, apprehension," writes Sontag. "But most women experience it even more painfully: with shame. Aging is a man's destiny, something that must happen because he is a human being. For a woman, aging is not only her destiny . . . it is also her vulnerability."

But even without abandonment, the fading of youthful beauty is experienced as—and is, in fact—a loss. A loss of power. A loss of possibilities. Once we could harbor the fantasy that, from across a crowded room, a stranger would rush to our side and make us his own. But this fantasy belongs to Romeo's Juliet, not to Juliet's mother. We must let it go.

And we may start to feel that this is a time of always letting go, of one thing after another after another: Our waistlines. Our vigor. Our sense of adventure. Our 20/20 vision. Our trust in justice. Our earnestness. Our playfulness. Our dream of being a tennis star, or a TV star, or a senator, or the woman for whom Paul Newman finally leaves Joanne. We give up hoping to read all the books we once had vowed to read, and to go to all of the places we'd once vowed to visit. We give up hoping we'll save the world from cancer or from war. We even give up hoping that we will succeed in becoming underweight—or immortal.

We feel shaken. We feel scared. We do not feel safe. The center's not holding, and things are falling apart. All of a sudden our friends, if not us, are having affairs, divorces, heart attacks, cancer. Some of our friends—men and women our age!—have died. And as we acquire new aches and new pains, our health care is, of necessity, being supplied by internists, cardiologists, dermatologists, podiatrists, urologists, periodontists, gynecologists and psychiatrists, from all of whom we want a second opinion.

We want a second opinion that says, Don't worry, you are going to live forever.

(A man in his forties confesses to me that, struck with a moderate case of tennis elbow, he found himself worried, sleepless, sorely vexed. "What was bothering me," he explains, "was the fear that my body was deteriorating. First my arm goes—what will go on me next?" He worried so much, he says, "that I actually took the time to review my life insurance, though I know that tennis elbow is rarely fatal." But he also has started to know that although tennis elbow isn't, life is.)

We find in every ache and bodily change and diminished capacity intimations of our own mortality. And looking at the subtle, or maybe not so subtle, decline of our mothers and fathers, we recognize that we're soon to lose our shield between us and death, and that after they are gone, it will be *our* turn.

Furthermore, as our parents succumb to the frailties of the flesh, their needs encroach on our time and our equanimity. We're caught up again in their lives and there is much talk of money and health on the telephone. Our children, now grown, can take care of themselves, but can a widowed mother or father live alone? With impatience, resentment, sorrow and guilt accompanying, and at times outweighing, our love, we physically and emotionally accommodate to our parents' growing dependencies.

In mid-life we discover that we are destined to become our parents' parents. Few of us factored this into our life's plan. As responsible adults we try to do the best we can, though we liked it better being our *children's* parents. But, as we are finding—with exceedingly mixed emotions—that's ending too. For our children are gradually leaving, leaving for other houses and cities, for other countries. They are living beyond our control and beyond our care. And although empty nests have advantages, we will need to adapt to being just part of a pair, to no longer being the heads of a throbbing, blooming, sneakers-all-over-the-living-room household, to no longer being—and never again to be—that unique and special mom of "I'll ask my mom."

As our past realities start to collapse, we challenge the self-definitions that have sustained us, finding that everything seems up for grabs, questioning who we are and what it is we are trying to be, and whether, in this life of ours, the only life we have, our achievements and our goals hold any value. Does our marriage make sense? Is our work worth doing? Have we matured—or have we simply sold out? Do our connections with family and friends rest on a loving exchange or on desperate dependencies? How free and how strong do we wish—do we dare—to be?

And if we are going to dare, we see that we'd better begin daring now, for we've started measuring time as time left to live. We know that the meter is running and that our choices are steadily narrowing and that, although there is still much to want and to give, some precious parts of our life are over forever. Our childhood and youth are gone and we must pause to mourn our losses before we move on.

We may not move on easily. Although Dorothy Dinnerstein argues that "renunciation of what has been inexorably outlived is by definition affirmative," and that "we let go of youth's acute, hopeful excitement for the richness of sensibility, the easy exercise of nurturant strength, that middle age carries," we rarely let go without some sort of a struggle. Faced with the losses that midlife has already brought, or is soon to bring, faced with a sense of finiteness and mortality, few of us will renounce our youth with anticipation of gain. And many of us will fight it all the way.

And so we may dig in our heels and respond with rigidity, maintaining the status quo, resisting all change. Or we may make desperate attempts to be young again. Or we may fall prey to psychosomatic ailments. Or we maniacally may distract ourselves with causes and courses and self-improvement projects.

The change-resisters defy the realities of time by hanging on to their power and to their non-negotiable ways of doing things. They insist that their children remain obedient to their wishes, that their younger business associates—"little pip squeaks," one man calls them—"know their place," that their spouses not go off—as another man put it—in "cockamamie new directions." Like the unbending oak tree in a storm, they are broken by any changes in their health, their marital status, their careers. They cannot, they will not, they fiercely refuse to adapt.

The youth-seekers do not want to stand pat; they want to go back in time. They liked what they had and want to have it again. And so a number of long-married men, and a growing number of women, are seeking newer, younger marriage partners. Or love/ sex affairs which, at least for a while, help them forget sagging penises or breasts. Or restoration through surgeons and spas and colorists and cosmetics and exercise classes. We're not talking here of doing, as most of us try to do in mid-life, whatever we can to keep ourselves pasted together. We are talking of something more—for the youth-seekers want the looks, and the life, of twenty years ago.

The psychosomatic sufferers trade off psychic distress for physical ills, including heart attacks and perhaps even cancer. Indeed, David Gutmann argues in an excellent paper on psychoanalysis and aging, that the mid-life man, uncomfortable with the emergence at this time of certain passive, dependent needs, can externalize them in the form of bodily ailments and bring them to "the one major institution in our society that recognizes and even insists on a dependent stance—the hospital. By becoming a patient, the middle-aged man says, 'It is not *I*, but my diseased organs, that asks for help. My spirit is still willing; but my heart, liver or stomach is weak.' "

The self-improvers distract themselves by filling up their time; they are running too fast to notice what they have lost. And while learning new skills and returning to school can be positive experiences, frantic activity also has its costs. It can serve as a way of avoiding confrontation with middle age by engaging in outer, rather than inner, development. It can also, as we will see, be very exhausting.

> I've finished six pillows in Needlepoint,
> And I'm reading Jane Austen and Kant,
> And I'm up to the pork with black beans in Advanced Chinese
> Cooking.
> I don't have to struggle to find myself
> For I already know what I want.
> I want to be healthy and wise and extremely good-looking.
>
> I'm learning new glazes in Pottery Class,
> And I'm playing new chords in Guitar,
> And in Yoga I'm starting to master the lotus position.
> I don't have to ponder priorities

For I already know what they are:
To be good-looking, healthy, and wise,
And adored in addition.

I'm improving my serve with a tennis pro,
And I'm practicing verb forms in Greek,
And in Primal Scream Therapy all my frustrations are vented.
I don't have to ask what I'm searching for
Since I already know that I seek
To be good-looking, healthy, and wise,
And adored.
And contented.

I've bloomed in Organic Gardening,
And in Dance I have tightened my thighs,
And in Consciousness Raising there's no one around who can top
  me.
And I'm working all day and I'm working all night
To be good-looking, healthy, and wise.
And adored.
And contented.
And brave.
And well-read.
And a marvelous hostess,
Fantastic in bed,
And bilingual,
Athletic,
Artistic . . .
Won't someone please stop me?

There are other, less frenetic mid-life reactions which reflect the
chaos and anguish of this stage, when, although we may be at our
prime, we know that we're in the grip of time, that "our ground
time here," as a poet and many airline hostesses warn us, "will be
brief." Thus we may—many do—become severely depressed. Or
embittered—"Is this all there really is?" Or achingly disappointed
at having failed to meet our ideals, to achieve our goals. Or bored
and restless—"So *now* what?"—if we've achieved them. Or self-
destructive—drinking, pill-popping, driving too fast or directly
attempting suicide. Or envious of the young—even our own young
flourishing sexual sons and daughters. Or guilt-stricken at the bad
we have done and the good we have left undone. Or despairing—

wanderers in "a dark wood . . . wild, rugged and harsh," wondering if we will ever again find the path.

Psychoanalysts concede that they cannot predict with certainty how any of us will react to a mid-life crisis. We all have unknown weaknesses—and strengths. But if we reach this turning point with major unresolved conflicts or an earlier phase of development incomplete, we are more likely than not, they say, to repeat in our present experiences our past anxieties and flawed solutions. For instance:

The loss of sons and daughters as they grow and go away, or the loss—through death or divorce—of a marriage partner, may serve to revive old separation anxieties.

The loss, or impending loss, in mid-life of beauty, vigor, potency, whatever, may feel near-fatal to the pathological narcissist.

The loss, or modification, of external definitions—Perfect Parent, Youngest Dean of a University—may throw into panicked confusion those who never established an inner core of identity.

But even we sturdier souls (with work and love and a sense of self and a history of only minimal damage) will not traverse the mid-life passage unscathed.

"God ordains," George Bernard Shaw once wrote, "that every genius shall have an illness at forty." Non-geniuses have an illness at forty too. Some will wither and fail, but even those who do eventually prevail may first inflict great pain on both themselves and those they love before they can begin to change and grow.

Randy shattered his marriage after both of his parents had died and he recognized, "That's it; I'm gonna die too." And after almost four decades of being a very, very good boy and doing whatever he was expected to do, he found that with his parents' death "my ties to responsibility were severed. I was cut loose from the past and from my need to continue to be good."

He decided then and there that "there has got to be something better than this continual schlep of work and duty." He decided that if there weren't a change, he would die. He was ready to fall in love with another woman. And soon, very soon, without really having to try, he met a fascinating and unstable charmer—Marina —and fell in love, "life-shatteringly" in love, with her.

Randy, looking back, says that he still perceives Marina as "the great passion of my life. She was brilliant, enchanting, witty, charming, cleverly seductive and"—he recalls with proud delight —"she wanted me. It was like suddenly being led into a room illuminated by a thousand sparklers. I was . . . obsessed with her."

Telling himself that at age thirty-seven "this was my last chance for sexual happiness," this highly respected lawyer with two daughters and a wife "I never stopped loving," left his family to live with this . . . this "gypsy."

It was, he still believes, "in spite of the pain, in spite of the cost, in spite of the buckets and buckets of tears that were shed, the most life-enhancing experience of my life. . . . It taught me about life, living, pain, pleasure, loneliness. . . . It taught me to grasp the full measure of my sexuality. . . . It taught me to find new dimensions in myself." And it finally taught him, after a year away, that where he belonged was home with his own wife and children.

For what he learned, he says, was that he wasn't made for a rapture-and-torment relationship. That in fact he preferred the calm, loving wife he had left. That, cutting himself off from the daily routine of steady-state warmth and generous sharing, he was —oh, yes!—turned on, but so bereft. He had shucked off the role of responsible, you-always-can-count-on-me husband only to learn that that's who he wanted to be. "I acquired," he says, "a painful and very difficult clarity. I discovered I couldn't be happy without my wife. I discovered I loved her unconditionally. I discovered that life without her really sucked."

He told her that if she'd let him come home, he'd stay with her forever. She let him come home.

Of his marriage today Randy says, "Oh, sure, I'd like it if in some ways she were better. But, of course, in some ways I could be better too. And I haven't forgotten the past; I remember some of those nights—and some of those days—with the sparklers." But, he adds, "I live with a sharper knowing of what my wife and I have. And I live with a wish to treasure and preserve it."

Like Randy's, the important change that results from a mid-life upheaval may be in the way that our previous life is perceived. Clearer on who we are and what it is that we really want, we may re-commit ourselves to our earlier choices. But sometimes we can only continue to live with our old choices on new and quite dramatically different terms. And sometimes, we give up our old choices entirely.

Many marriages fail in mid-life because someone feels, like Randy, a "do or die" urgency. Speak now, leave now, or forever hold your peace. And since divorce has almost completely ceased to disqualify anyone from society's approval and awards, there are no social sanctions, there are only our inner—assailed by mid-life—sanctions. Thus, if we find that our marriage meets too few of our expectations, or if it is good enough and we want great, or if—although we recognize that marriage means ambivalence—we are feeling far less love than hate, we may start raising the question of Why not seek a new relationship before we get too faded and juiceless and scared? And our answer, as the spate of mid-life divorces seems to suggest, may be—why not?

Why not end a marriage—now that the children are almost all grown—which lacks shared interests, passion, excitement, pleasure? Why not try for a marriage with more emotional gratification? Time's running out.

The sense of time running out may also serve to unravel some of those couples' collusions that we looked at earlier, in Chapter Thirteen, those I'll-be-the-baby-and-you'll-be-the-parent and I'll-be-the-doormat-and-you'll-be-the-bully and I'll-be-the-sick-one-and-you'll-be-the-well-one marriage arrangements. When these collusions collapse, when one of the partners ceases to play the agreed-upon role, the other partner may leave to seek a new mate. But sometimes marriages can survive the end of these marriage conspiracies. Sometimes couples can—in the pressure cooker of mid-life—renegotiate the terms of their marriage.

Roger Gould describes the great rewards—for certain fortunate husbands and wives—of the mid-life reworking of a marriage:

> The old conspiracies are abandoned. In their place is a relationship based on empathic acceptance of our authentic partner, who is not a myth, not a god, not a mother, not a father, not a protector, not a censor. Instead there is just another human with a full range of passions, rational ability, strengths and weaknesses, trying to figure

out how to conduct a meaningful life with real friendship and companionship. From this new dynamic, many different forms of marriage may follow: two very separate lives, in which husband and wife come together only periodically, as their rhythm of relating dictates; total sharing of one life in work and leisure; or variations between these two extremes. In any case it is a relationship of equals, without rank, position or self-abrogation.

Growth and change in mid-life may mean reworking, making peace with or putting an end to previous arrangements. But whichever approach we choose, life won't be the same. Outwardly or inwardly, the years of our middle age will express the losses and gains of our mid-life crisis.

In work, for instance, a man may begin to ruefully accept the limits and disappointments of his achievements. Or, wishing for more occupational satisfaction, he may leave his job and embark on a new career. Or he may give a smaller place to work in his schedule and in his heart, and a larger place to his private concerns or community. Or, having toned down his competitive strivings for power and success, he may become free to foster the careers of younger people—to be, in mid-life, a generous, generative mentor.

Perhaps the women who've always worked, who worked while raising a family, will revise their careers in mid-life in a similar way. But researchers haven't much yet to say on this subject. For with most married middle-class women, paid work—until very, very recently—was something that they shouldn't have to do. The women's movement, however, drastically altered this point of view so that, by the mid-1970s, every mid-life woman I knew was making plans to try to re-enter the job market. There were negative reasons for doing so—"I have to have a job, or who will I say that I am when I go to a party?" But there also were positive reasons—women felt socially sanctioned, maybe even urged—to give fuller rein to their talents and their competencies.

Many of their husbands, however, didn't—and some still don't —regard this return to work as an unmixed blessing.

Indeed, many mid-life husbands whose wives have recently started a job are feeling abandoned, untaken-care-of, shut out. "I might as well have a roommate," some husbands complain. HER OUTSIDE PREOCCUPATION CAN LEAVE HIM ISOLATED AT TIME OF MORE LEISURE, a headline in *The Wall Street Journal* proclaims. For just as these husbands are slowing down and turning inward toward home, their wives are turning outward toward a career.

Psychologists call this problem the "out of phase" or the "career trajectory" problem.

This male-female shift is linked to the fact that, as researchers inform us, women become more "masculine" at mid-life, while mid-life men may become less aggressive, less driven to succeed and, in various other ways, more "feminine." This change in the sexual balance, whether or not wives take up careers, can lead to disruptive tensions in a marriage. But there also are great advantages to ourselves and to our relationships in unifying the poles of our sexual nature.

This doesn't mean that men become women, that women become men or that both of the sexes become the same—unisexual. It simply means that at mid-life we can amend our self-definition to include what psychologist Gilligan calls both "voices."

In Chapter Eight we looked at the difference in male and female development and at the fact that women are more invested than men in intimate relatedness and men more invested than women in autonomy. Gilligan found that even highly successful professional women describe themselves in the context of a relationship, while men, in describing themselves, perceive their identity in terms of power and separateness. Gilligan says that we live in a world where masculine autonomy is far more valued than feminine connection. But she argues that both of these voices—the voice of relatedness as well as the voice of separateness—are needed to define adult maturity.

Women and men, says Gilligan, have different modes of experiencing. In mid-life, some psychological thinkers believe, these two opposing modes begin to converge.

David Gutmann proposes that this convergence is abetted by the decline of our parenting functions in mid-life, by the ending of what he colorfully calls "the chronic emergency of parenthood."

As young parents, he notes, we raise children whose requirements for two kinds of care—physical and emotional—tend to be handled by a division of labor. Typically, the husband gives over the nurturing role to his wife (and she then expresses his softer, more passive yearnings). And typically, the wife gives over the aggressive role to her husband (and he then becomes the expresser of her aggression). "During the active and critical period of young parenthood," Gutmann writes, "each sex concedes to the other that aspect of their sexual bimodality that could interfere with their special responsibility in parenting." Thus the demands of parenthood press us into a polarization of sex roles.

But, Gutmann says, this isn't, or doesn't have to be, a permanent arrangement.

For as parents enter mid-life and their sons and daughters take command of their own safety, the restraints imposed by parenthood phase out. At mid-life there is less demand to repress a man's femininity, a woman's masculinity. The direct expression, says Gutmann, of the other-sex part of ourself is one of the positive consequences of mid-life. He writes:

> Thus, men begin to live out directly, to own as part of themselves, some of the qualities of sensuality and tenderness—in effect, the "femininity"—that were previously repressed. . . . They become particularly engaged by warm, supportive human contacts. . . . By the same token, women discover in themselves an executive and "political" capacity that had hitherto lain fallow and unrecognized. . . . Even in determinedly patriarchal cultures, older women become more intrusive, more domineering, more "political" and less sentimental. Like men, they begin to live out the hitherto closeted duality of their own nature.

Another central duality that we will confront at mid-life is the creativeness/destructiveness duality. We confront it out in the world, and inside ourselves too. Our struggle to reconcile these two poles is one of the final tasks that we must do in our step-by-step movement away from what Roger Gould has given the name of "childhood consciousness."

The essence of childhood consciousness is our illusion, argues

Gould, that we can live in a state of absolute safety. And living forever and ever in a state of absolute safety is an irresistible, hard-to-relinquish illusion.

We sustain this illusion as children, he says, by believing in four assumptions, which we learn, by the end of high school, are untrue. But until we can repudiate them emotionally as well as intellectually, they will flourish in our unconscious and exert great power over our adult lives.

The first false assumption, which surfaces and must be emotionally challenged between our late teens and around age twenty-two, is: "I will always belong to my parents and believe in their version of reality."

The next false assumption (challenged between twenty-two and twenty-eight) is: "Doing it their way with will power and perseverance will bring results, but when [I'm] frustrated, confused, tired, or unable, they will step in and show me the way."

The third false assumption (challenged in our late twenties and into our thirties) is: "Life is simple, not complicated. There are no significant unknown inner forces within me; there are no multiple coexisting contradictory realities present in my life."

The fourth false assumption (challenged in mid-life) is: "There is no evil in me or death in the world; the demonic has been expelled."

Gould means that we finally learn in mid-life that no matter how well-behaved we are, we will die. We finally learn that there is no safety out there. We give up our childhood belief that if we'll only be good boys and girls, we'll be forever protectively taken care of. Disaster and death, we discover, fall on sinners and saints, on black hats and white hats alike. And while we may not choose to live out our lives as sinners and black hats, this discovery can free us to confront what Freud calls our id and what Gould describes as "our darker, mysterious center"—and to use some of the energies and passions that we find there to open up and revitalize our life.

The point here is this: As children we bury our anger and greed and competitiveness because we fear they will sweep us—and safety—away. Who'd love and protect such a nasty, voracious child? And as we grow up we may fear that we will go out of control—run wild—unless we keep these uncivilized feelings at bay. And who'd love us, who would keep us from danger, then? But in mid-life, having learned that no one is going to keep us from danger, we're less constrained from exploring our center, our id. And once we have embarked on our so risky, so exciting explorations, we are likely to make some self-transforming discoveries:

We will find, for instance, that we can let ourselves know how we feel without automatically acting upon those feelings.

We also will find that acknowledged feelings are easier to control than those we deny.

And we also will find that if we can acknowledge, reclaim and harness some of the untamed feelings of our childhood, we can become, in mid-life, more empathic, more lusty, more daring, more nuanced, more honest and more creative.

In a beautiful essay on the vitalizing aspects of our "mysterious center," or id, or dynamic unconscious, Hans Loewald warns against "the madness of unbridled rationality," expressing his conviction that "we would lose ourselves in a chaos . . . if we were to lose our moorings in the unconscious. . . ." Gould adds his voice to this theme when he speaks of connecting "with the insane in us before we can go on to an enlarged sanity." He says that by tapping into our original, primitive passions we begin, at mid-life, to be whole and wholly alive.

This theme of connecting constructively with our own inner heart of darkness has been echoed by other students of mid-life. Analyst Elliott Jaques, studying the development of creative artists, sees—in the work of those whose careers continue beyond their youth—a mid-life crisis and a mid-life transformation. He describes a shift from a hot-from-the-fire, "precipitate" creativity to a worked-over, modified, "sculpted" creativity. And he sees the mid-life emergence of "a tragic and philosophical content," in contrast to the young artist's more lyrical outpourings.

This sculpted creativity and this tragic and philosophical content, writes Jaques, derive from the recognition of mortality and of "the existence of hate and destructive impulses inside each person." Jaques says that such recognition can produce so much anxiety that the response is a recoil away from further development. And he says that mature creative work, or, for non-artists, mature creative living, depends on the "constructive resignation" to hate and death in the midst of life.

Levinson also addresses man's awareness in mid-life of the destructive forces in nature and in himself. He writes:

> The Mid-Life Transition activates a man's concerns with death and destruction. He experiences more fully his own mortality and the actual or impending death of others. He becomes more aware of the many ways in which other persons, even his loved ones, have acted destructively toward him (with malice or, often, with good intentions). What is perhaps worse, he realizes that he has done irrevocably hurtful things to his parents, lovers, wife, children, friends, rivals (again, with what may have been the worst or the best of intentions). At the same time he has a strong desire to become more creative; to create products that have value for himself and others, to participate in collective enterprises that advance human welfare, to contribute more fully to the coming generations in society. In middle adulthood a man can come to know, more than ever before, that powerful forces of destructiveness and of creativity coexist in the human soul—in my soul!—and can integrate them in new ways.

Integration—the unifying of seemingly opposite tendencies—is seen as the grand achievement of mid-life. But of course it's a process we've met with previously. It began with our childhood struggle to heal the split between good and bad mother, to heal the split between devil and angel me, to balance our wish for attachment with our wish to be separate and free. The struggle—now on a higher level—continues.

And so we strive to integrate our feminine self with our masculine self.

We strive to integrate our creative self with the self that knows inner and outer destructiveness.

We strive to integrate a separate self that must die alone with a self that craves connection and—yes—immortality.

And we strive to integrate a wiser, more seasoned middle-aged self with the youthful zest of the self we are leaving behind.

But in spite of our youthful zest, we will have to let go—at mid-life—of our earlier self-image. Our season is autumn; our springtime and summer are done. And in spite of the calendar imagery, we won't—when we reach the end—get to run through the seasons all over again.

Nor can we stop time.

"I've managed, with plenty of tears, to accept the losses of middle age," I recently heard a fiftyish friend of mine say. "In fact, I'm mature and adjusted enough to really like where I am. I just wish The Powers That Be would let me *stay* here."

All of us who've managed to survive our mid-life crisis would be grateful just to "stay here" too—here with our seasoned sense of things, with passion and perspective, with people we love and work we want to do. Having relinquished our former self, unwrinkled and immortal, we feel we have done enough—we would like to be through with the letting go and the losing and the leaving.

We aren't through.

18

I Grow Old . . . I Grow Old

I grow old . . . I grow old . . .
I shall wear the bottoms of my trousers rolled.

—T. S. Eliot

An aged man is but a paltry thing,
A tattered coat upon a stick, unless
Soul clap its hands and sing, and louder sing
For every tatter in its mortal dress.

—W. B. Yeats

It's hard for the soul to sing as it gets older. The angst of mid-life seems, in retrospect, a breeze. Shoved or eased into age, we ruefully learn that fifty was nifty and that those who died at sixty died too young. And we learn that even though we have a song or two to be sung before all the lights go out, the coming of age has brought us to the final scenes of the play—and death waits in the wings.

Old age brings many losses; we shall hear from those who rail against these losses. But there is another, more hopeful point of view. It argues that if we truly mourn the losses of old age, mourning can liberate us, can lead us through to "creative freedoms, further development, joy and the ability to embrace life."

But first the bad news—exhaustively, and sometimes exhaustingly, documented in Simone de Beauvoir's book *The Coming of Age*, where she traces the sorrows of aging from the first recorded lament all the way to the present. The earliest text on the subject, she tells us, was produced by the Egyptian philosopher-poet Ptah-hotep, who voiced back in 2500 B.C. a theme that has resounded through the centuries:

> How hard and painful are the last days of an aged man! He grows weaker every day; his eyes become dim, his ears deaf; his strength fades; his heart knows peace no longer; his mouth falls silent and he speaks no word. The power of his mind lessens and today he cannot remember what yesterday was like. All his bones hurt. Those things which not long ago were done with pleasure are painful now; and taste vanishes. Old age is the worst of misfortunes that can afflict a man.

Old age is the worst of misfortunes, worse even than death, de Beauvoir argues, because it mutilates what we have been. To support her bitter contention, she presents a most distinguished array of witnesses:

From Ovid: "Time, O great destroyer, and envious old age, together you bring all things to ruin. . . ."

From Montaigne: "Never a soul is to be seen, or very few, who in growing old does not take on a sour and mouldy smell."

From Chateaubriand: "Old age is a shipwreck."

From Gide: "It is a long time now since I ceased to exist. I merely fill the place of someone they take for me."

"Old age," says de Beauvoir, summing up the evidence, "is life's parody."

Now no one would deny that age can burden us with profound and plentiful losses—of health, of people we love, of a home that has been our haven and pride, of a place within a familiar community, of work and status and purposefulness and financial security, of control and choices. Our bodies notify us of declining strength and beauty. Our senses become less acute; our reflexes slow. We have poorer concentration, less efficiency in processing new information and lapses . . . What's her name again? I know it's a name I know . . . in short-term memory.

Old age, a number of people point out, is what you're stuck with if you want a long life. And, as an eighty-plus friend observes, "more of us are limping through it than dancing through it."

Yet we cannot discuss old age as if it were a single entity, a sickness, a termination, a wait for The End. For although mandatory retirement and Medicare and Social Security payments and senior-citizen discounts at the movies may technically mark the onset of old age, experiences of significant loss related to our aging may not occur until many many years later. Indeed, students of aging now tend to subdivide old age into the "young old" (sixty-five to seventy-five), the "middle old" (seventy-five to eighty-five or ninety) and the "old old" (eighty-five or ninety to whatever), recognizing that each of these groups has different problems and needs and capabilities. They also recognize that while good health and good friends and good luck—and a good income—certainly make aging easier to take, it is our attitude toward our losses as much as the nature of our losses which will determine the quality of our old age.

There are elderly men and women, for instance, who regard every ache and pain, every physical decline or limitation, as an outrage, an assault, a humiliation, an intolerable loss. But there also are those who manage to take a more positive view of the matter and who can say, like the French writer Paul Claudel: "Eighty years old: No eyes left, no ears, no teeth, no legs, no wind! And when all is said and done, how astonishingly well one does without them!"

The difference between these two attitudes is the difference, writes social scientist Robert Peck, between "body preoccupation" and "body transcendence," between treating physical aging as our enemy or our master—and making some sort of reasonable peace with it. It has also been observed that, given the very same bodily ravages Paul Claudel describes, one kind of person (a health pessimist) would perceive himself as half dead and capable of nothing, another kind of person (a health optimist) would perceive himself as in the pink of condition and capable of everything, and a third kind of person (a health realist) would clearly perceive his deficits and also what he still could do in spite of them.

In her book *Sister Age,* that elegant transcender and realist M. F. K. Fisher argues for dealing sensibly with old age—for acknowledging and attending to "all the boring physical symptoms of our ultimate disintegration." But, she quickly urges, what's important "is that our dispassionate acceptance of attrition be matched by a full use of everything that has ever happened in all the long wonderful-ghastly years to free a person's mind from his body . . . to use the experience, both great and evil, so that physical annoyances are surmountable in an alert and even mirthful appreciation of life itself."

She offers her apologies for sounding "mawkish and banal" but adds, "I believe it."

Another magnificent woman, actress/writer/psychologist Florida Scott-Maxwell, speaks thusly of the ills that beset her eighties. *"We who are old* know that age is more than a disability. It is an intense and varied experience, almost beyond our capacity at times, but something to be carried high. If it is a long defeat it is also a victory. . . ."

She adds: *"When a new disability arrives* I look about me to see if death has come, and I call quietly, 'Death, is that you? Are you there?' So far the disability has answered, 'Don't be silly, it's me.' "

Although aging is not an illness, there is a slowdown of physical functions and an increase in physical vulnerabilities which may bring a zesty, full-of-life sixty-five-year old to his knees by the time he hits eighty. There are physical impairments that can render us, against our will, dependent. There are organic and irreversible diseases of the brain over which neither courage nor character can prevail. And even if we aren't assailed by arthritis, Alzheimer's, cataracts, heart disease, cancer, stroke and all the rest, the body has multifarious ways of reminding the octogenarian, "You are old."

Such messages are delivered, Malcolm Cowley writes in his book *The View from 80:*

—when it becomes an achievement to do thoughtfully, step by step, what he once did instinctively
—when his bones ache

—when there are more and more little bottles in the medicine cabinet . . .

—when he fumbles and drops his toothbrush (butterfingers) . . .

—when he hesitates on the landing before walking down a flight of stairs

—when he spends more time looking for things misplaced than he spends using them after he (or more often his wife) has found them

—when he falls asleep in the afternoon

—when it becomes harder to bear in mind two things at once . . .

—when he forgets names . . .

—when he decides not to drive at night anymore

—when everything takes longer to do—bathing, shaving, getting dressed or undressed—but when time passes quickly, as if he were gathering speed while coasting downhill. . . .

A gerontologist adds this: "Put cotton in your ears and pebbles in your shoes. Pull on rubber gloves. Smear Vaseline over your glasses, and there you have it: instant aging."

It is a fact of life that the majority of the aging have chronic health problems and that they do not respond to treatment as fast as the young. But healthy as well as ill, some people at sixty-five will sink into old age, self-sentenced to a kind of living death. And ill as well as healthy, some people at eighty—or until they take their last breath—will live to the hilt.

But even if we greet old age with health and hope intact, we must struggle against society's view of aging. For although in today's America almost 27 million people are currently over the age of sixty-five, and although life expectancy rose from an average of 47 years in 1900 to 74.2 years in 1981, these elderly are—for the most part—perceived as sexless, useless, powerless, out of the game.

"Old age in America is often a tragedy . . ." writes the noted gerontologist Robert Butler. "We pay lip service to the idealized images of beloved and tranquil grandparents, wise elders, white-haired patriarchs and matriarchs. But the opposite image disparages the elderly, seeing age as decay, decrepitude, a disgusting and undignified dependency."

Exemptions may be granted to selected politicians and artists and movie stars. But most of the old are pitied or patronized. Malcolm Cowley notes ruefully, "We start by growing old in other people's eyes, then slowly we come to share their judgment."

It is hard not to.

For sexually we are neutered by the silent message that lust in old age is unseemly, that the fires of passion should either burn out or be screened. Everyone knows—or should know—that not only "dirty" but "clean" old men and women can want and can have a sex life in their last decades. But the image of aging flesh enmeshed in lustful sexual acts remains, for many—most—people a repellent one.

In a sensitive study of age an eloquent Englishman, Ronald Blythe, describes how society unsexes the old, noting that "should an old person not seem to be in full repressive control of these urges, he or she is seen as either dangerous or pathetic, though nastily so in both instances. The old often live half lives, because they know that they would arouse disgust and fear if they attempted to live whole ones. All passion is not necessarily spent at seventy and eighty, but it pays the old to behave as though it were."

(My favorite exception to this view of sexuality came from a seventy-five-year-old lady I knew, who told me that she continued to do what her mother, long ago, had told her to do: "Be a cook in the kitchen, a lady in the parlor and *tahka*"—that's Yiddish for also—"a whore in the bedroom.")

When we give up our sexuality we give up the riches it brings us —sensual pleasure, physical intimacy, heightened self-worth. And when in many other ways we get the word from the world that the old are diminished, we may find it harder and harder to fight diminution.

Retirement from work, which is often forced upon women and men in young old age, can contribute to that feeling of diminution.

"I was depressed at the thought of retiring," says a doctor, now seventy-nine, "because I wasn't quite sure what would happen to me. You see, I had had my position for so long—my specialist work, my hospital staff, my professional travels, my teaching. All these things which I had were what I *was*, and to have to give them up at sixty-five left me with something quite unrecognizable."

Work shores up our identity; it anchors both the private and social self; it defines that self to itself and to the world. And lacking a workplace to go to, a circle of colleagues to connect with, a task to confirm our competence, a salary that puts a value on that competence, a job description that serves as a shorthand way of telling strangers who we are, we may—when we have retired—start to ask, with growing anxiety, "Who am I?"

This is still a bigger problem for men than for women.

For the meaning of work has been psychologically different for men and for women in the past, with the work a man did defining him more comprehensively than work defined a woman. And although the psychological difference may be narrowing very fast as increasing numbers of women enter the job market, men's work remains less optional because—let me stick my neck out—they can't have babies.

Stripped of his work definition and stripped of his social justification, the retiree will often lose status and self-esteem. And while some people use retirement to travel, pursue new projects, enjoy more time with their family, fulfill old dreams, many—including those engaged in fulltime volunteer work—can feel, by society's standards, socially useless.

For those people who've had a long history of losses which they have never absorbed and resolved, retirement may revive old fears and sorrows. But even without such a history, the loss of income and status, the isolation and boredom, may lead to despair. The end of work is an exile if there is nothing out there to absorb our interest and energies. And the old live in a society in which there very often is nothing out there.

Perhaps the ultimate retiree is that monumentally tragic hero King Lear, who gives up his lands and his powers to two of his daughters, trusting them to take care of him with the love and respect due a father—and a king—"while we unburden'd crawl toward death." But divested, as he is, "of rule, interest of territory, cares of state," Lear is disdained and mistreated by these daughters. For he has become a helpless old man who cannot make good the threat that "I'll resume the shape which thou dost think I have cast off for ever."

There have been, in the past, societies which granted their elderly power, honor, respect. And moralists, through the centuries, have eulogized the nobility of old age. But frequently heard is a subtext which describes the coming of age as powerless, pleasureless, lonely and full of bitterness. And Homer has Aphrodite declaim, in no uncertain terms, that even the gods themselves despise old age.

Our modern perception of age is that the elderly are a burden. That they're people who take and have nothing left to give. That their wisdom isn't especially wise, and can't show us how to live. That their conversations are mired in boring irrelevancies. Often the old evoke what Ronald Blythe calls a "mounting distaste"— and "a spiritual and physical drawing-back." And to further attack their self-image is the "profound, underlying problem," an expert tells us, ". . . that the old are not loved."

Unloved and condescended to and not listened to and viewed as a separate species, the old are set apart and often ignored. For we live in a society where youthfulness is worshiped and the old are (not so secretly) abhorred. And as we grow old and society counts us out of the game of life, it can teach us to share in its rejecting perceptions. It can teach us—unless we beware—to abhor ourselves.

Without optimism and energy to resist society's view, we too may think at sixty-five that we're done, that at this point in our history the best is behind and the worst is yet to come, that we are trapped in "this absurdity . . . this caricature,/Decrepit age that has been tied to me/As to a dog's tail."

It is a vision of age which we can acquire long before we're sixty-five.

Indeed, I used to share the view that growing old could only bring me losses. I once thought the best role in life was Pretty Young Thing. I thought that time must lead me from sunshine to darkness. I never wanted any season but spring. I still find it hard to imagine that if I stay around long enough I will be an old woman. But that no longer seems like all bad news to me. For the people I've talked with and read about—some public, some private people—have shown me how rich a human life can be. At the end of our sixties. And into our eighties. And even past ninety.

My friend Irene is the youngest of these—she is only sixty-eight —and she tells me it isn't too late to take up tennis. But then nothing is ever too late for Irene, who recently began to write a novel. And a few years ago embarked on singing lessons. And prior to that took science courses at Harvard. And still dreams of learning to paint, play a musical instrument, pay a visit to Iceland and tap-dance.

"My problem," says Irene, "is that I'm greedy—I want to do everything." I sometimes think that maybe she already has. She has picketed all her life on behalf of causes that she has hoped would make the world better. She has raised a family, been married for forty-three years. She has read more books and gone to more movies and plays and poetry readings than any ten women. She is a traveler and a feminist and a bike rider and a poet and a staunch and loving friend to women and men of every conceivable age and experience.

She is also thoroughly, unabashedly sexual.

"Now that you're older," I once asked Irene, "don't you miss the men who used to look at you so lustfully?" She stared at me for a moment, then responded indignantly with "*Used* to? What are you saying—*used* to?"

But doesn't she get a lump in her throat when she sees a pair of young lovers and knows that *that* she'll never have again? Doesn't she ever wish she could still bear a child? The answer is yes, she sometimes does, "but most of the time I feel full—I don't feel deprived." And although she is too realistic these days to indulge herself in wild, romantic daydreams, she feels no sharp sense of loss because "reality," she says, "has wonders in it."

And then there's the English professor, who is eightyish and retired and living alone, and whose pleasures involve friends, books, good meals at the Faculty Club, and who calls herself—in a cheerful letter to a former student—a "lucky old gal." In the midst of her shrewd observations about her readings and her companions, she has this to say about her time of life:

"Don't ever let anyone tell you that age is all loss. It's damn lonely at times, a bit loveless, too. But the perspective upon a long personal past with experience to season and focus that perspective —that is a positive and unique gift of being *old*."

The gifts of youth, however, can remain with us in age. And we can continue to learn and to create. For as Longfellow's poem "Morituri Salutamus" nicely reminds us, "nothing is too late/Till the tired heart shall cease to palpitate." He then goes on to cite some stirring examples:

> Cato learned Greek at eighty; Sophocles
> Wrote his grand Oedipus, and Simonides
> Bore off the prize of verse from his compeers,
> When each had numbered more than four-score years. . . .
> Chaucer, at Woodstock with the nightingales,
> At sixty wrote the Canterbury Tales;
> Goethe at Weimar, toiling to the last,
> Completed Faust when eighty years were past.

There are other elderly people, some still living, some now dead, who offer up bountiful visions of tomorrow, affirming—amid their losses and limits and multiplying infirmities—that existence is good.

Hear the miner's mother, at eighty-two still scrubbing the doorstep and tending her son, who says, "Life is so very sweet . . . I still find it sweet."

Hear the artist Goya, whose drawing of an old, old man— painted at eighty with desperately failing eyesight—bore the triumphant inscription "I am still learning."

Hear the Montessori teacher—vivacious, amused, alert—who says, "I'm nearly ninety-one and I'm arthritic from the top of my head to my toes . . ." but "I see well, so I read. Thankfully, I read. Oh, books, how I love you!"

Hear the student, age seventy-two, who is busy getting his Ph.D. in psychology and who says, "I have more projects than I can do in the next fifty years. I don't have time to die."

Hear the writer Colette who, though she spent her last years in pain on her divan-bed, set out—and lived out—these plans for her seventh decade:

"I am planning to live a little longer, to go on suffering in an honorable fashion, which is to say without noisy protest and without rancor . . . to laugh all to myself about things in secret, and also to laugh openly when I have reason to, [and] to love whoever loves me. . . ."

And hear Lady Thelma, ninety, who awakens every morning full of plans and who says that, although she's "terrifically old . . . there are still things that I have to do—a lot more things. Are you listening up there?"

I must mention one more woman, a memorable woman, a psychoanalyst and teacher, a lover of movies and books and museums and good laughs, who kept throughout her life that very sweetest of all hungers—her curiosity—and whose overriding interest in life was people.

The feeling was mutual.

Indeed, on her eightieth birthday, an Eightieth Birthday Committee was formed to accommodate all who wished to honor her day, and it took five separate parties—as it might for some queen of the Orient—to celebrate.

But she never queened it over anyone—she was always the active listener, perched at the edge of her chair with encouraging "ahs," and in her wise and benign and utterly unsentimental presence people grew bigger.

"She didn't praise my work—she helped me tell myself I'd done well," said one of her students. And a former patient recalled that "instead of being my comforting mother, she tried to teach me how to mother myself." A friend of hers, attempting to describe the special magic that I and others instantly sensed in her presence, explained, "She always made you feel that you were being given something. No one ever left her empty-handed."

I met her only once—a small, fragile lady, attending a lecture in a wheelchair. She was struggling to breathe, and vividly alive. Within the brief time that we talked, I fell under her spell, I fell in love, I needed to know her. And I thought, I'll drive to her house tomorrow and leave a rose at her door, and maybe she'll like that, maybe she'll let me know her.

She died before I had a chance to know her.

But among the many legacies this lady left behind is a dream she told to a friend, who shared it with me. And much like poetry, it captures her essence in a few compelling images.

In the dream she sits at a table. She is dining with some friends. She is eating, eating with pleasure, from her plate and theirs. But before she has finished her dinner, a waiter starts clearing the dishes away. She protestingly raises her hand. She wants to stop him.

But then she reconsiders. And she slowly drops her hand. She'll let him clear—she will not tell him no. Her meal isn't finished, the food still tastes good and she'd certainly like to have more. But she's had enough, and she's ready to let the rest go.

This is the dream of a woman wholly in life until she died, the dream I would like to dream at the end of my days. This is a dream that tells me life can gently be set aside when it's lived to the full —not only in spring but in winter.

There is not, however, one "right" way of living old age to the full. People age well in many different modes. And sometimes quite opposite roads can lead to what sociologists call high life satisfaction.

Good aging is seen, for instance, among the so-called "reorganizers," who continue to fight the shrinkage of their world, maintaining a highly active life by replacing—with new relationships and new projects—whatever it is that the coming of age has taken from them.

But good aging can also be seen among the so-called "focused" types, who display only medium levels of activity, replacing a broader spectrum of involvements and concerns with one or two special interests such as gardening or homemaking or grandchildren.

And good aging can also be seen among the so-called "disengaged"—inner-directed but certainly not self-absorbed—who accept and adapt to their shrinking world and who find great satisfaction in contemplative, withdrawn, low-activity lives.

There are those whose good old age consists of gazing with serenity at the troubled, imperfect world which they inhabit, in contrast to, say, the Gray Panthers, who are enjoying their old age by fighting "for social initiative, for freedom, justice and peace for all persons everywhere." There also are those who pride themselves on maintaining their manners and morals in the face of some of age's cruelest blows, and those who in their last decades give up the poses and deceptions of a lifetime.

Old age can be active or disengaged, feisty or serene, a keeping up of our front or a dropping of masks, a consolidation of what we know and what we've done before, or a new—even unconventional —exploration. Consider, for instance, Jenny Joseph's "Warning":

> When I am an old woman I shall wear purple
> With a red hat which doesn't go, and doesn't suit me,
> And I shall spend my pension on brandy and summer gloves
> And satin sandals, and say we've no money for butter.
> I shall sit down on the pavement when I'm tired
> And gobble up samples in shops and press alarm bells
> And run my stick along the public railings
> And make up for the sobriety of my youth.
> I shall go out in my slippers in the rain
> And pick the flowers in other people's gardens
> And learn to spit.

Less rebellious old ladies may prefer to rock in their rocking chairs. That too, of course, can make for a good old age.

It is easier to grow old if we are neither bored nor boring, if we have people and projects we care about, if we are open and flexible and mature enough to submit—when we need to submit—to immutable losses. The process, begun in infancy, of loving and letting go can help prepare us for these final losses. But stripped—as age does strip us—of some of what we love in ourselves, we may find that a good old age demands a capacity for what is called "ego transcendence."

A capacity to feel pleasure in the pleasures of other people.

A capacity for concern about events not directly related to our self-interest.

A capacity to invest ourselves (though we won't be around to see it) in tomorrow's world.

Ego transcendence allows us, while perceiving ourselves as finite, to connect to the future through people or through ideas, surpassing our personal limits by means of some legacy we can leave to the next generation. As grandparents, teachers, mentors, social reformers, collectors of art—or creators of art—we can touch those who will be there when we are gone. This endeavor to leave a trace—intellectual, spiritual, material, even physical—is a constructive way of dealing with the grief we are feeling over the loss of ourself.

An investment in the future through the leaving of a legacy can help enhance the quality of old age. But so does a stronger emphasis on the pleasures of the moment and a capacity to live in the here and now. In a good growing old we can stop obsessing about time running out and learn to fully inhabit the time we are in, acquiring what Butler calls "a sense of presentness or elementality," and what Fisher calls that reward of age "when the sound of a child's laugh, or the catch of sunlight on a flower petal is as poignant as ever was a girl's voice to an adolescent ear, or the tap of a golf-ball into its cup to a balding banker's."

When the present and future have value to us, old age can be enhanced. But of course the past is of vast importance too. Through memory we can be sustained by the "great sights" of our own history, by a "vanished geography" we can always walk through. We also can engage in what Butler terms "the life review"—a taking stock, a summing up, a final integration of our past.

In examining the past we are engaged in the central task which Erikson assigns to the eighth age of man. And if this examination is not to lead to disgust and despair but to "integrity," we will have to accept our "one and only life cycle," call it our own and—imperfections and all—find meaning and value in it.

We will have to accept, says Erikson, "the fact that one's life is one's own responsibility."

Old age is our responsibility too.

Indeed, it has been argued that healthy-enough older people should not be exempt from the judgments of the world, and that if they are boring, garrulous, self-centered, vapid, querulous or obsessed with the state of their belly and their bowels, we sometimes ought to say to them, "Shape up!"—or as Ronald Blythe rather coolly puts it, "How can you expect us to be interested in this minimal you, with your mean days and little grumbles?"

Butler adds that the old should not be treated as if age made them moral eunuchs. He says that they still can do harm, and still atone. He says that the old remain capable of cruelty and greed and assorted misdeeds and that it "denigrates their humanness" to exempt them from responsibility and guilt.

He also says that the old "have made—and continue to make—their own contribution to their own fate." These contributions to the specific character of an old age may begin in childhood.

For in our daily experience we see evidence of the elderly becoming ever more clearly what they have been. And the way we too may age—be it self-pityingly or bitterly or gallantly—has been in large measure prepared for earlier on. All of us have met those types whom Fisher calls "bright souls"—merry, lively, serene both in youth and old age. But because the greatest stresses of life are likely to occur in our later years, and because disturbing traits are very likely to be accentuated by stress, the mean may get meaner, the fearful may get more afraid and the apathetic may sink into near-paralysis.

Many students of aging agree that the core of our personality tends to remain rather constant through our life, concluding that we are, in old age, the person we've always been . . . except maybe more so. In a study of *Personality and Patterns of Aging*, the authors found that, confronted with "a wide range of social and biological changes," the aging person

> continues to exercise choice and to select from the environment in accordance with his own long-established needs. He ages according to a pattern that has a long history and that maintains itself, with adaptation, to the end of life. . . . There is considerable evidence that, in normal men and women, there is no sharp discontinuity of personality with age, but instead an increasing consistency. Those characteristics that have been central to the personality seem to become even more clearly delineated. . . .

But although our present is shaped by our past, personality changes are possible, even unto the seventh, eighth, ninth decade. We are never a "finished product"—we refine and we rearrange and we revise. Normal development doesn't end, and over the course of our life, important new tasks—or crises—will arise. We can change in old age because every stage of our life, including our last one, affords new opportunities for change.

"All is uncharted and uncertain," writes octogenarian Florida Scott-Maxwell; "we seem to lead the way into the unknown. It can feel as though all our lives we have been caught in absurdly small personalities and circumstances and beliefs. Our accustomed shell cracks here, cracks there, and that tiresomely rigid person we supposed to be ourselves stretches, expands. . . ."

Among the great expanders of our time is the world-famous baby doctor Benjamin Spock, a vigorous octogenarian who has traveled quite a way from his conservative WASP New England Republican origins. Furthermore, although he probably ceased to believe early on that Calvin Coolidge was our greatest President, all of Spock's astonishing life changes have taken place in his sixties and seventies.

For during those years the highly respected author of *Baby and Child Care*, a book whose sales figures are currently over 30 million and whose reassuring good sense had won him the affection and gratitude of mothers all over the world, put his reputation, repose, comfort and income on the line because his conscience told him that he had to. Morally outraged by the Vietnam war, Spock became increasingly involved in the antiwar movement of the 1960s, marching in demonstrations, being arrested for civil disobedience and, in 1968, indicted, tried and convicted for conspiracy to aid and abet draft resistance. (Subsequently, however, a higher court not only overturned the conviction but directed an order of acquittal.)

The consequences of his political activism, Spock tells me, were sometimes painful, for many of those who had formerly been so admiring reviled him as a commie, a traitor and worse. But once he became convinced of the moral correctness of his position, there was no turning back, he explains, because "You can't say to people, 'Well, I think I've done enough,' or 'I'm getting scared,' or 'I might lose some sales on *Baby and Child Care.*' "

Not turning back, Spock ran for President on the People's Party ticket in 1972, and for Vice President in 1976. He also became a feminist, his consciousness raised by critics like Gloria Steinem, who admonished him for being "a major oppressor of women, in the same category as Sigmund Freud." Spock jokes that "I tried to get what satisfaction I could from being linked that closely with Sigmund Freud," but he took her and other criticisms of his sexism to heart and is now a staunch defender of women's rights.

Another major change in the 1970s was ending his marriage to his wife, Jane, a marriage which had lasted for almost half a century. And yet, when I ask Spock if he ever feels guilty about leaving his wife, he answers without hesitation that he does not, explaining that the divorce had been preceded by five years of therapy in an effort to resolve their marital differences.

"I'm a fantastically guilt-ridden person, a person who feels guilty about . . . everything," Spock says. But it was precisely because of his gift for guilt that he was compelled to try particularly hard and long—too long, he now believes—to repair the marriage. Like his political activism, his decision to divorce was well thought out—intellectual, not emotional—and once made, not subject to second thoughts and agonizing. Divorcing Jane, he felt then and he feels now, was "the right thing."

In 1976 Benjamin Spock took a new wife, a feisty woman—forty years younger than he—named Mary Morgan, who introduced him to his first body massage and his first Jacuzzi and his first (initially "very difficult") experience as stepfather to a teenaged girl. Spock says he fell for Mary because she was "energetic, vivacious, determined and beautiful—and I liked her enthusiasm for me, I ate it up." With her heavy Arkansas drawl (she calls him "Bin"), sassy ways and insistent physicality, she isn't much like the sixty-five-year-old lady with the Vassar in her voice whom, he suspects, his sons expected him to marry. But Mary is—in addition to cuddly—a shrewd, highly competent woman who now arranges the details of Spock's professional life, who worries about him and takes care of him—and who gives him the adoration he adores. The differences between them are the normal tensions of marriage; they aren't due, Spock says, to the difference in age. And in response to my question he describes himself, judiciously, as "a happily married man—with reservations."

The Spocks live part of the time in Arkansas and part of the time on two sailboats—one in the Virgin Islands, one in Maine—with Spock continuing to speak out on political issues and to engage in an occasional act of civil disobedience, while writing a column on child care for *Redbook* magazine. In addition, he is currently receiving individual therapy, couples therapy and group therapy because, he ruefully tells me, two wives, two sons and several therapists have informed him over the years that he is a man who is out of touch with his feelings.

Meanwhile, however, he doesn't seem all that worried about it. Indeed, he seems like a man who is feeling pretty damn good about himself. He says that there is a photograph taken of him at age one which may help explain why.

In this photo he is sitting in a little-boy-sized chair, elegantly turned out in a hat, a dress, a fancy coat with scalloped collar, neat white socks and sparkling Mary Jane shoes. His feet don't quite touch the ground but his hands are firmly planted on the arms of his chair. And on his handsome and amiable face is a smile, a smile of confident expectation, the smile of a child who knows, Spock says, "that the world is his oyster."

It is clear that he still believes that the world is his oyster. And why not? He has come to his eighties with his intelligence, passions, health and good looks intact. In any room he enters he is more than likely to be the most noticeable (six feet four and slim, with perfect posture), the most charming (great hugger, great kisser, great storyteller), the most cheerful (twinkling blue eyes, ready laughter) and the most sheerly attractive person present. He is an ardent sailor, an enthusiastic early-morning rower, an accomplished late-into-the-night dancer. He is also, he says, the beneficiary of good genes ("I think that the fact that I'm spry at eighty is partly that my mother lived to be ninety-three") and of a lifelong optimism which derives from the fact that his mother—harsh and critical though she could be—"gave me a feeling of being very well loved."

Spock describes himself as a man who has grown "younger in spirit as the decades have gone on," as well as less judgmental, less hard-driving, less reserved and far more demonstrative. He says, "I can recognize that I'm old, and I'm not embarrassed that I'm old, but I don't—I never do—*feel* old." He concedes, however, that he "can't expect to have the same perkiness and vigor at ninety that I've managed to maintain at eighty. You're got to begin sliding sooner or later." His concern when the slide starts, he says, is to not be pathetic, is to remain dignified, is—and he is kidding but also not kidding—"to be particularly careful to look at my suits to make sure there's no spots on them, and to be particularly concerned when I come out of the bathroom in public that I've zipped up my zipper."

As for death, he says it doesn't worry him—"probably," he adds with a grin, "because I'm not in touch with my feelings." But, he hastens to promise, he'll keep trying to get in touch with them— "I'm going to keep trying, right up until the end."

Our earlier life history is important in determining our capacity to change and grow in old age. But age itself may also call forth new strengths and new capabilities that weren't available at previous stages. There may be more wisdom, more freedom, more perspective and more toughness. There may be more candor with others, more self-honesty. There also may be a shift in the way we perceive the hard times in our life—a shift from "tragedy" to "irony."

By tragedy I mean a perception that leaves no room for other possibilities. Tragedy is all-encompassing and all black. There is no yesterday. There is no tomorrow. There is no hope. There is no consolation. There is only absolutely rotten, totally irreparable now. Irony sees the same event written a little smaller. Its blackness doesn't fill the entire screen. Irony offers a context in which we are able to tell ourselves that things could be worse. It also offers a context in which we even might imagine that things could get better. This shift in perception from tragedy to irony may be the special gift of our late years, helping us to deal with our accumulating losses and sometimes also helping us to grow.

With flexibility and perhaps a touch of irony, we can continue to change and grow in old age. But we also can change and grow in old age—though Sigmund Freud said otherwise—through psychoanalysis and psychotherapy.

Certainly psychotherapy can ease the emotional problems that the coming of age may initiate or intensify: anxiety, hypochondria, paranoia and—most prevalent—depression. But in addition to the relief that psychotherapy can provide, psychological work with the old can effect sweeping change, bringing vital transformations through a process Pollack calls "mourning-liberation." He writes:

> The basic insight is that parts of self that once were, or that one hoped might be, are no longer possible. With the working out of the mourning for a changed self, lost others, unfulfilled hopes and aspirations, as well as feelings about other reality losses and changes, there is an increasing ability to face reality as it is and as it can be. "Liberation" from the past and the unattainable occurs. New sublimations, interests and activities appear. There can be new relationships. . . . Past truly can become past, distinguished from present and future. Affects of serenity, joy, pleasure and excitement come into being.

Psychoanalysts report that psychoanalysis with the elderly has helped their patients retrieve their sense of self-worth; has helped them to forgive others—and themselves; has helped them find new adaptations when old age has rendered their past adaptations unworkable; has even helped a woman in her mid-seventies to become orgastic for the first time! In this same report we encounter a woman who—sixty years after the fact—was able to get over the anger she felt at the death of her mother, becoming free thereafter to write, to stabilize her marriage and to accept the prospect of her own mortality. We also encounter a man who, ending a six-year analysis at age sixty-five, experienced a vital new sense of aliveness. And although he died at age seventy, he felt that in his final eleven years he was happier than he had ever been in his life.

Why, a seventy-six-year-old woman was asked, are you seeking therapy at *your* age? Reflecting both her losses and hopes, she answered, unforgettably, "Doctor, all I've got left is my future."

Some of the old sit waiting, Blythe tells us, for Meals on Wheels or death—whichever comes first. Some of the old, like my friend the seventy-two-year-old Ph.D. candidate, have so many projects they'll never have time to die. Some speak of death, some think of death, some suffer enough to long for death, and others will deny and deny and deny, successfully persuading themselves that death will make an exception in their case.

But there seems to be no evidence that the old are especially haunted by fears of death. Indeed, they may be less frightened of it than the young. Furthermore, the conditions of their dying—it often is said—are of greater concern to them than is death itself.

Nevertheless, it is true, as Sophocles poignantly observes in a play he wrote at the age of eighty-nine, that

> Though he has watched a decent age pass by,
> A man will sometimes still desire the world.

And it also is true that in dying and death—whatever the dying is like, whatever the death means—we come face to face with the ultimate separation.

19

The ABC of Dying

A person spends years coming into his own, developing his talent, his unique gifts, perfecting his discriminations about the world, broadening and sharpening his appetite, learning to bear the disappointments of life, becoming mature, seasoned—finally a unique creature in nature, standing with some dignity and nobility and transcending the animal condition; no longer driven, no longer a complete reflex, not stamped out of any mold. And then the real tragedy . . . : that it takes sixty years of incredible suffering and effort to make such an individual, and then he is good only for dying.

—Ernest Becker

When I was a little girl I used to close my eyes at night and imagine the world going on and on forever. I'd imagine, with absolute terror, the world going on and on forever—and me not there. Freud writes that we are incapable of imagining our own death, but I am here to tell you that's not true. Please God, I used to pray, I know you can't take death away. But couldn't you just arrange for me to stop thinking about it?

Whether or not fear of death is, in fact, a universal fear, it is surely a feeling that most of us cannot abide. Consciously or unconsciously, we push death thoughts away. We live a life in which death is denied. This doesn't mean we deny the fact that all men and women, including ourselves, are mortal. Nor does this mean we avoid the articles, seminars, TV programs which feature the now chic subject of Dying and Death. What it means is that, despite all the talk, we go about our lives with the fact of our finitude held at emotional bay. Denial of death means never allowing ourselves to confront the anxiety summoned by visions of this last separation.

You may be asking, What's so bad about that?

For how can we live as fully conscious animals, the only creatures on earth that *know* they will die? How can we, in the chilling words of Ernest Becker's great book *The Denial of Death*, endure the awareness that we are "food for worms"? Our denial of death makes it easier to walk through our days and our nights unmindful of the abyss beneath our feet. But denial of death will also, as Freud and others convincingly argue, impoverish our lives.

Because we consume too much psychological energy fending off our thoughts—and fears—of death.

Because we replace death fears with other anxieties.

Because death is so interwoven with life that we close off parts of life when we shun thoughts of death.

And because the emotional knowledge that we surely will die someday can heighten and fine-tune our sense of the present moment.

"Death is the mother of beauty," writes the poet Wallace Stevens.

"Life without death is meaningless . . . a picture without a frame," says the "black holes" physicist John A. Wheeler.

"And if one is not able to die, is he really able to live?" asks the famed theologian Paul Tillich.

And novelist Muriel Spark, in her disturbing-the-peace book on death—*Memento Mori*—has one of her characters speak the following lines:

"If I had my life over again, I should form the habit of nightly composing myself to thoughts of death. I would practice, as it were, the remembrance of death. There is no other practice which so intensifies life. Death . . . should be part of the full expectancy of life. Without an ever-present sense of death life is insipid. You might as well live on the whites of eggs."

. . .

In the spring of 1970, within six shocking weeks, my good friend's teen-age daughter died of an embolism, my husband's best friend died of cancer at age thirty-nine and my mother's heart failed just short of her sixty-third birthday. I lost my fear of flying that spring—I'll fly on anything now—for I had become re-acquainted with mortality and I recognized that even if I stayed grounded all of my life I still would die. And as Jodi's death and Gersh's death and my mother's death and the death that would someday be mine suffused me with anxiety and confusion, what I wanted was someone to teach me what to do with it all.

To teach me how to know death and go on with life.

To teach me how to love life and not fear death.

To teach me, before it was time for me to take the final exam, the ABC of dying.

For awareness of our mortality may heighten our love of life without making death—our personal death—acceptable. Looking death straight in the eye, we may hate it a lot. And although our sense of finitude may be the mother of beauty, the frame of the picture and even the yolk of the egg, it may make a mockery of our works and our days.

By assaulting our feelings of personal significance.

By rendering all of our enterprises meaningless.

By tainting our deepest and dearest attachments with transience.

By taunting us with the question Why were we born if it wasn't forever? By taunting us with the question Why is there death?

Some philosophers tell us that there can be no birth without death, that procreation must preclude immortality, that the earth could not sustain both reproduction and eternally living beings, that we need to clear out and make room for the new generations. Some theologians tell us that Adam and Eve could only be capable of seeing, and of choosing between, good and evil by eating of the forbidden fruit and thus giving up immortality for knowledge, for moral choice, for becoming human. Ecclesiastes tells us that "to every thing there is a season," including a "time to be born, and a time to die." And, pursuing a rather less speculative response to the question Why death? some scientists have theorized that our cells have a maximum life span, that human beings are genetically programmed to die.

There are various other responses, but to those who find death unacceptable, all justifications are unacceptable too. They view death as an evil, as a curse laid on their lives. And some of them—rejecting the scientists' view—maintain that death is not "natural" but an ill that will eventually be cured. Indeed, there are people who actually do arrange with cryonics companies to be deep-frozen at death and later thawed, while others are persuaded that through megadoses of nutrients they can extend their lives . . . perhaps to eternity. It is possible that some of those striving for physical immortality are spurred by their love of life and their vast faith in science. But I suspect that most of them are spurred by their vast terror—their terror of death.

Indeed, it is hard for most of us to contemplate our death without being scared of it.

We are scared of annihilation and of non-being. We are scared of going into the unknown. We are scared of an afterlife where we may have to pay for our sins. We are scared of being helplessly alone. There are many, it is said, who fear the agonies of a last illness, whose fear is of dying—not of being dead. But it also has been said that we carry within us, all of our life, a dread of abandonment.

Our earliest separations, it is argued, have given us all our first, bitter foretaste of death.

And our later encounters with death—with death down the road or with death knocking at our door—revive the terrors of those first separations.

There is no more rending account of one man's anguished confrontation with his mortality than Leo Tolstoy's "The Death of Ivan Ilych," where an ailing man comes to realize that "something terrible, new and more important than anything before in his life was taking place. . . ."

He comes to realize that he is dying.

"My God! My God! . . . . I'm dying . . . it may happen this moment. There was light and now there is darkness. I was here and now I'm going there! . . . There will be nothing. . . . Can this be dying? No, I don't want to!"

A chill comes over Ivan Ilych, his hands tremble, his breathing ceases and he feels only the throbbing of his heart. Choked with anger and misery, he thinks, "It is impossible that all men have been doomed to suffer this awful horror!"

More specifically, he thinks that it is impossible for *him* to suffer this horror.

> The syllogism he had learnt from Kiesewetter's Logic: "Caius is a man, men are mortal, therefore Caius is mortal," had always seemed to him correct as applied to Caius, but certainly not as applied to himself. That Caius—man in the abstract—was mortal, was perfectly correct, but he was not Caius, not an abstract man, but a creature quite separate from all others. He had been little Vanya, with a mamma and a papa . . . and with all the joys, griefs and delights of childhood, boyhood and youth. What did Caius know of the smell of that striped leather ball Vanya had been so fond of? Had Caius kissed his mother's hand like that, and did the silk of her dress rustle so for Caius? . . . Had Caius been in love like that? Could Caius preside at a session as he did? "Caius really was mortal, and it was right for him to die; but for me, little Vanya, Ivan Ilych, with all my thoughts and emotions, it's altogether a different matter."

Although Ivan Ilych says, "It cannot be that I ought to die. That would be too terrible," he also understands that death is near. *It* arrives in the midst of his working day, to "stand before him and look at him." He is petrified. It joins him in his study, where he is "alone with *It*: face to face with *It*." He shudders with fear.

He ponders the question "Why, and for what purpose, is there all this horror?"

"Agony, death . . ." he asks himself. "What for?"

Ivan Ilych's family and friends cannot relieve his anguished aloneness, for none of them speak—or will let him speak—of his dying. Indeed, they not only avoid all mention of this gruesome subject; they pretend to his face that he isn't dying at all.

This deception tortured him—their not wishing to admit what they all knew and what he knew, but wanting to lie to him concerning his terrible condition, and wishing and forcing him to participate in that lie. Those lies—lies enacted over him on the eve of his death and destined to degrade this awful, solemn act . . .—were a terrible agony for Ivan Ilych. And strangely enough, many times . . . he had been within a hairbreadth of calling out to them: "Stop lying! You know and I know that I am dying. Then at least stop lying about it!"

Such taboos against speaking of death, such lies and deceptions surrounding death, have been vigorously challenged in recent years, with books like Elisabeth Kübler-Ross's highly influential *On Death and Dying* urging us to open up a dialogue with those who are terminally ill. Psychiatrist Kübler-Ross describes the enormous relief provided to dying patients when they are invited to share their fears and their needs. And she argues that such dialogues can ease their journey toward death, a journey she sees divided into five stages:

Denial, she says, is the first response to the news of a fatal illness: "There must be some mistake! This cannot be!"

Anger (at the doctors, at fate) and envy (of the undying) come next—the classic question here is, "Why me?"

Bargaining is the third response, an attempt to postpone the inevitable, promises made in exchange for a longer run—though the woman who swears she'll be willing to die if she can just live long enough to see her son married, may then renege on the bargain with: "Now don't forget I have *another* son."

Depression, the fourth of these stages, is a sorrowing over past losses and a sorrowing over the great loss yet to come. And the need of the dying engaged in a preparatory mourning of their own death is for someone to sit with their sadness and let them be sad.

Acceptance, the final stage, "should not be mistaken," says Kübler-Ross, "for a happy phase." It is "almost void of feelings"; it seems to be, she says, a time when the struggle is done. She concludes that when the dying have been given some assistance in working their way through all of the previous stages, they will no longer be depressed or scared or envious or angry or unreconciled, but will contemplate their coming end "with a certain degree of quiet expectation."

Does everyone pass—should everyone pass—through these five stages of dying? Critics of Kübler-Ross say no, and no. Not everyone wants to look at his death; some people do best if they cling, till the end, to denial. Some people, raging and raging "against the dying of the light," will go out the way Dylan Thomas said we should go—and what he said was, "Do not go gentle. . . ." Nor do all of those who arrive at an acceptance of their death arrive there via the stages that she describes. And some critics fear that a "right" way to die, a Kübler-Ross right way to die, may be mindlessly imposed upon the dying.

Dr. Edwin Shneidman, who has also worked extensively with the dying, writes that "my own experiences have led me to radically different conclusions" from those of Kübler-Ross. He continues:

> . . . I reject the notion that human beings, as they die, are somehow marched in lock step through a series of stages of the dying process. On the contrary . . . the emotional states, the psychological mechanisms of defense, the needs and drives, are as variegated in the dying as they are in the nondying. . . . They include such reactions as stoicism, rage, guilt, terror, cringing, fear, surrender, heroism, dependency, ennui, need for control, fight for autonomy and dignity, and denial.

He also, challenging Kübler-Ross's view that acceptance occurs in the last stage of dying, argues that this is not necessarily so. He writes that there is no "natural law . . . that an individual has to achieve a state of psychoanalytic grace or any other kind of closure before death sets its seal. The cold fact is that most people die too soon or too late, with loose threads and fragments of life's agenda uncompleted."

But however correct the criticism of Kübler-Ross's five stages, her critics seem to agree with her central theme: that only by drawing close to the dying, only by not fleeing death, can we discover what each Ivan Ilych needs. That need may be for silence, for talk, for the freedom to weep or rage, for the touching of hands in wordless communication. That need may be, and often is, to be allowed to be a baby again. We can make ourselves available to be used as they wish to use us, but we cannot teach the dying how to die. If we are there, however, and if we are paying careful attention, they will teach us.

In 1984, I watched three women I loved very dearly die of cancer. All of them in their fifties, all of them vitally in life, they—all of them in cruel prematurity—died. One faced her fate straight on —she knew she was dying, she talked about death, she calmly accepted it. One, knowing death was near and wishing to choose her moment of dying, hoarded her pills and committed suicide. And one, the blond-haired, blue-eyed interloper I'd known since birth—my sister Lois—fought against her death, until the moment she closed her eyes, with awesome ferocity.

Lois—the great rival of my childhood, the tagalong pest I had come so deeply to love—has died of cancer in the autumn of this awful year, just as I sit down to write this chapter. She died in her bed at home, and, watching her during those last hours, I believe that she died free of pain and free of fear. But as long as she was conscious, she maintained her defiance of death—she was out to beat it.

For although Lois knew very well indeed that she had a fatal illness, she didn't intend to let it push her around. So she wrote her will, settled her affairs, held some discussions with her husband and children and then—having thoroughly dealt with the administrative details—she turned from death and concentrated on life. Furthermore, she concentrated not on mere survival but on enjoying whatever there was to be enjoyed, refusing to let the limits imposed by her steadily failing body intrude upon her pleasures or her relationships.

When tennis—her great passion—was no longer possible, she bit her lip and put her racquet away, directing her athlete's body toward more sedentary activities, becoming a vigorous knitter, reader, writer. In the last few months of her illness, with her energies further depleted, her weight at ninety-five pounds, her eyesight dim, she planned new adaptations—could she, perhaps, learn a foreign language on cassettes? In the last week of her life she sent me her recipe for Chinese spicy noodles (a dried noodle in the envelope, to make sure that I purchased the right kind), and through the blur of her heavy-duty pain killers still remembered to ask about *my* health. She never became obsessed with herself— even in that last week—obsessed with her sickness, her suffering, her fate. And she never, until the coma of her final day of life, broke her connections with the people she loved.

Nor did she say goodbye, because she wasn't planning to leave; she was planning—or at least trying her damnedest—to live. "Some of us do survive," she once told me, "and why not focus on hope instead of despair?" And for most of the hard four years during which she battled her spreading cancer, she focused on hope.

Now make no mistake: My sister was neither a martyr nor a saint. She had her times of terror and despair, times when she couldn't do anything because her body was wracked with nausea and pain, times when she bitched and wept and moaned and asked —only part in jest—"What did I do? What did I do to deserve this?" But most of the time she didn't cry, and she didn't brood about dying. She was fighting to live, and she was fighting to win. She believed until the end that if a person really tried, the human spirit could triumph over biology. And although she didn't beat death, we watched her play—she really did play—a championship game.

There are people like Lois at every age and with all kinds of fatal ailments who hang on to hope, who fight to stay alive, trusting in will, in spirit, in remissions, in brand-new miracle drugs or—in miracles. "Don't they know they can't make it?" we may wonder, having heard the grim statistics. But they have heard them too, and what they do is tell us, and themselves, "I'm not a statistic."

In videotapes about a thirty-nine-year-old doctor painfully dying of cancer, he—and his wife and a brother and doctors and clergymen—describe his harrowing struggle to stay alive. In his final weeks, refusing to quit, he insisted on being fed through a vein in his neck and as the pains worsened he grew so dependent upon narcotic drugs that he underwent—observers agreed—a personality change. Some doctors have said that by his insistence on taking command of his case, this man prolonged his life "unnecessarily." But just before he died, when asked by his wife if his fight for survival had been worth it, he answered with an unequivocal "Yes."

My friend Ruth did it differently. Knowing the game was lost, knowing that only pain and death lay ahead, she arranged a last, perfect evening for her and her loving, beloved husband and then —when he left for work the next day—took an overdose. With her artist's esthetic sense and her lifelong need to maintain control, Ruth wouldn't permit the cancer to have its way with her—to ravage her further (she was a beautiful woman), to impose further suffering (she had suffered enormously), to strip her (as she feared she'd be stripped) of herself.

In all the endeavors of her hard and sometimes tragic life, Ruth had been feisty and brave, she had been a fighter. Red hair streaming and green eyes ablaze, she had stood up against brutal losses —and prevailed. But faced with this illness after the last chemotherapy treatments had failed and she'd been sent home to wait for a difficult death, she preferred to select the time and place of the meeting. And although I know that suicide may be viewed as a crime or a sin, or cowardly, or weak, or pathological, I believe that Ruthie's suicide—the suicide of my sorrowing, suffering friend—was an act of courage and consummate rationality.

Perhaps Ruth's suicide is what psychoanalyst K. R. Eissler has called a revolt against death, a way that "the condemned cheats the executioner." But it also is a suicide which strikes me as healthy, not sick, as right, not wrong. Let me hasten to declare that I believe that most suicides are, indeed, pathological and that most of the would-be suicides need to be helped to live, not permitted to die. I also believe, however, that under certain special conditions, self-murder can be a sane and legitimate option—the best response available to the horrors of terminal illness, or to the dependencies and deteriorations of age.

But whatever we think of such suicides, people are committing them. In 1982, for instance, for every 100,000 men the suicide rates were 28.3 for ages sixty-five to sixty-nine, 43.7 for ages seventy-five to seventy-nine and 50.2 for eighty-five plus. In these—and indeed in every age category—the suicide rates per 100,000 *women* were lower, sometimes astoundingly lower: 7.3 for ages sixty-five to sixty-nine, 6.3 for ages seventy-five to seventy-nine and 3.9 for eighty-five plus!

Sometimes very old couples, their competencies failing, may make the poignant decision to die together rather than be separated or rendered helpless by their growing infirmities. Thus Cecil and Julia Saunders—ages eighty-five and eighty-one respectively —ate hot dogs and beans for lunch, drove their Chevy to a quiet place, rolled up the windows, put cotton in their ears, after which Cecil fired twice into his waiting wife's heart, then aimed the gun at his own heart and fired. The suicide note which they left was addressed to their children:

> This we know will be a terrible shock & embarrassment. But as we see it, it is one solution to the problem of growing old. We greatly appreciate your willingness to try to take care of us.
>
> After being married for 60 years it only makes sense for us to leave this world together because we loved each other so much.
>
> Don't grieve, because we had a very good life and saw our two children turn out to be such fine persons.
>
> Love Moth & Fath

As for the terminally ill, there is a growing interest in self-arranged termination. The wish to not suffer, to stay in charge, to be remembered by loved ones the way they were motivates some to choose the hour of their death. And while our instincts may prompt us to hasten to reach out a rescuing hand and cry, "Don't do it," while we are aware that many who wish to die today may want to live if they'll but wait a week, while we are concerned with the often traumatic effects on the family of a suicide, we also —like one writer—must ponder: "Who knows how he may be tempted? It is his case; it may be thine."

Now certainly there are people who would never opt for suicide but who nonetheless greet death with open arms, who look upon their death as a release, as a relief, as deliverance, surcease. Death is not their enemy. Death becomes a friend. It offers the chance to lay their burden down, whether the burden they yearn to lay down is the agony of a last illness; the helplessness, uselessness, loneliness of old age; the sufferings, at any age, attendant upon an unendurable loss; or the struggle of trying to live in a world which assails us, as Mark Twain writes, with "care, grief [and] perplexity." The reason, Twain explains in an autobiography which recounts many terrible losses, that "annihilation has no terrors for me" is

> because I have already tried it before I was born—a hundred million years—and I have suffered more in an hour, in this life, than I remember to have suffered in the whole hundred million years put together. There was a peace, a serenity, an absence of all sense of responsibility, an absence of worry, an absence of care, grief, perplexity; and the presence of a deep content and unbroken satisfaction in that hundred million years of holiday which I look back upon with a tender longing and with a grateful desire to resume, when the opportunity comes.

This "tender longing" for death, this grateful welcoming of death is one of many versions of acceptance. For there is also resigned acceptance ("Men must endure their going hence, even as their coming hither"), practical acceptance ("When I catch myself resenting not being immortal, I pull myself up short by asking whether I should really like the prospect of having to make out an annual income tax return for an infinite number of years ahead"), joyful acceptance ("Without regret for father, mother, sister,/Or any memory of this world below,/My soul in joy embraces her redeemer"), democratic acceptance ("Thou shalt lie down/With patriarchs of the infant world—with kings,/The powerful of the earth—the wise, the good,/Fair forms, and hoary seers of ages past,/All in one mighty sepulchre") and what I think might be called creative acceptance.

This is the kind of acceptance that my friend Carol displayed toward her death. An acceptance, without bitterness, of her fate. An acceptance of herself as a highly valued, uniquely valuable human being. An acceptance which permitted her, during the autumn afternoons of her dying, to speak with equal interest about the music that she wished to have played at her funeral and how to cook a terrific ratatouille.

With no belief in an afterlife and zero expectations of a reprieve, and with—like Ruth and Lois—some terrible times, some of the time, with physical pain, she spent her last weeks in her bedroom saying goodbye to her family and friends, and waiting—with astonishing calm—to die. She invited all of us to engage with her in some no-nonsense talk of her mortality, but death wasn't the only subject she had on her mind. She wanted to talk about us, about the coming election, about the latest gossip, and she continued to offer her funny and wise and utterly irreverent comments on . . . everything. No, she wasn't relentlessly gallant; there were times when she needed to cry about all the sweetness that she was leaving behind. And once she summed up her feelings about her premature departure by quoting this verse of Robert Louis Stevenson:

> And does it not seem hard to you,
> When all the sky is clear and blue,
> And I should like so much to play,
> To have to go to bed by day?

It did seem hard, but as Carol became increasingly acquainted with her death, she also accepted going to bed by day.

During one of our visits Carol said to me, "I've never died before," then added, "so I don't know how to do it."

But having watched the dying of this serene, undespairing, most remarkable woman, I want to tell you all, Oh, yes, she did.

What do we know about who dies how? Not an enormous amount, though it often is said that accomplishment makes it easier, that those who have achieved what they set out to do in life die more contentedly than those who have not. Philosopher Walter Kaufmann, in maintaining that satisfaction with our accomplishments "makes all the difference in facing death," illustrates his argument with the following poem by Friedrich Holderlin:

A single summer grant me, great powers, and
A single autumn for fully ripened song
   That, sated with the sweetness of my
      Playing, my heart may more willingly die.
The soul that, living, did not attain its divine
Right cannot repose in the nether world.
   But once what I am bent on, what is
   Holy, my poetry, is accomplished,
Be welcome then, stillness of the shadows' world!
I shall be satisfied though my lyre will not
   Accompany me down there. Once I
   Lived like the gods, and more is not needed.

Kaufmann argues that if we achieve—"in the face of death, in the race with death"—a project that is truly, uniquely our own, our "heart may more willingly die" because we have, in some sense, triumphed over death. In a similar vein Hattie Rosenthal observes in her "Psychotherapy for the Dying" that it "is the person who is convinced that he has lived a full life who is ready to die, and who develops comparatively little anxiety."

In many discussions of who dies how it also is maintained that we die in character, die the way we live: That the spunky die with spunk. That the stoics submit unprotestingly to this final necessity. That those who deny reality will continue, till their death day, to deny it. That those who overzealously guard their desperately won independence will feel shamed and shattered by their dying's dependencies. That those for whom separation has always been a terror-filled walk into the darkness will find this last separation the ultimate terror.

But there is also the observation that our dying may sometimes provide a new opportunity, that dying may sometimes permit— yes!—growth and change, that dying may precipitate a further stage of emotional development that had—until now—been well beyond our capacities. Eissler writes that "the knowledge or the vague feeling that the end is approaching may enable some persons to step aside, so to speak, and view themselves and significant sectors of their lives with humility and also with insight into the futility of so much that is taken too seriously so long as the world is near and man is passionately living *in* it." He says that this final stage can dissolve certain deeply entrenched ways of being, permitting what he calls "a last step forward."

This concept of a "last step forward" helps me understand how Lois, who had always been viewed as the "weak one" in our family, became, in her dying, so brave and so strong—such a fighter. It also helps explain the "perfect death" that is described by Lily Pincus, the death of her up to that moment very dependent, anxiety-ridden mother-in-law:

Who after a stroke, awoke, sat up and asked to see all the people in the house, then serenely bid each one a loving goodbye. Who then calmly closed her eyes, saying, "Now let me sleep." And who, when a doctor arrived to jolt her out of her final sleep with an injection, roused herself just long enough to persuade him to let her be, to let her die peacefully.

"What hidden strengths," asks Pincus, "in this delicate, frightened woman, who throughout her life had avoided facing anything difficult and who had never been able to make a decision, had enabled her not only to die in this way, but to ensure that her final sleep remained undisturbed?" Her answer, like Eissler's, is that approaching death may bring about remarkable, utterly unforeseen transformations.

Eissler goes so far as to argue that the experiencing of our dying can be the "crowning" achievement of our life. He writes:

The full awareness of each step that leads closer to death, the unconscious experience of one's own death up to the last second which permits awareness and consciousness, would be the crowning triumph of an individually lived life. It would be taken as the only way man ought to die if individuality were really accepted as the only adequate form of living and if life in all its manifestations were integrated, which would of course include death and the sorrows of the terminal pathway.

But not all of us are going to have the chance to reflect on our dying while we are dying. Accidents and ailments will take some of us instantaneously, unaware. Nor, in fact, do all of us have the *wish* to reflect on our dying while we are dying. Many of us, indeed, would psychologically rather not be there when it happens. According to Philippe Ariès, in his study of death throughout history, the concept of the "good death" has been redefined, so that instead of its being a conscious, expected, ritualized departure, as once it was, a good death today "corresponds exactly to what used to be the accursed death": Sudden death. The death that strikes without warning. The death that takes us quietly in our sleep.

Contrasted with a slow dying, often alone, in a hospital bed— plugged into tubes and machines and subject to bureaucratic failures and sometimes worse—sudden death may strike us as a great blessing, as a very good death indeed. But perhaps new approaches to the dying process—I am thinking, in particular, of the growing hospice movement, which provides compassionate care and relief from pain without artificial extension of life—may again redefine the good death as one in which there is time to experience our dying.

But whether or not we have the chance to experience our dying, whether or not our dying becomes a "last step forward," an instrument of growth, we can—long before we arrive at the month, the week, the day, the hour of our death—enrich our life by remembering that we will die. Now many believe, like La Rochefoucauld, that even the brave and clever should always "avoid looking it [death] straight in the face." Perhaps we can only do so if death does not mean the end of everything that we are. Perhaps we can only do so if we are able to set our own death within some context of after-death continuity.

Indeed, it has been argued that there is—in all of us—a need for connections that last beyond our own lifetime, a need to feel that our finite self is part of a larger something that endures. There are various contexts in which we may experience, or struggle toward, this connection. And each of these contexts can offer us an image of what it seems fair to call . . . immortality.

Our most familiar image of immortality is religious, with an indestructible soul and a life after death, with the promise that our last separation will lead to eternal reunion, with the assurance that all will not be lost, but found. However, as Robert J. Lifton points out in his brilliant discussion of modes of immortality, not every religion rests its case on a literal afterlife or an immortal soul. Rather, he writes, what is more universal to the religious experience is a sense of connection with a spiritual *power:* A power "derived from a more-than-natural source." A power in which we share and which protects us. A power through which we may be reborn—spiritually, symbolically—into a realm of "death-transcending truths."

Freud argues that such religious beliefs are illusions built up by man to make his helplessness in this world endurable. He writes that just as children depend on their parents to protect them, so anxious adults depend on gods and God. He says we create religion to "exorcise the terrors" of nature and to make up for the sufferings civilization imposes. And he says that we use religion to reconcile ourselves to fate's cruelty, "particularly as it is shown in death."

But religion isn't the only context in which we can summon up for ourselves images of after-death continuity. We can agree with Robert Lifton that death brings about "biological and psychic annihilation," while also agreeing with him that death does not therefore have to mean the absolute end. There are other ways of imagining how some part of us might endure—beyond our death, beyond annihilation. There are other ways of imagining immortalizing connections and continuities.

Living on through nature, for instance—through oceans, mountains, trees, recurring seasons—serves some of us as an image of immortality. We die, but the earth goes on and on and on. Furthermore, in returning to earth, as the poem "Thanatopsis" describes, we are literally part of that endless continuity:

> . . . Earth, that nourished thee, shall claim
> Thy growth, to be resolved to earth again,
> And, lost each human trace, surrendering up
> Thine individual being, shalt thou go
> To mix forever with the elements . . .

For others among us, immortality resides in those works and acts which have some impact on future generations—in the causes we fight (sometimes die) for, in the discoveries we make, in what we construct or teach or invent or create. Here the Emperor Hadrian, vividly drawn in Marguerite Yourcenar's novel, ponders—as he approaches death—the relation between his endeavors and immortality:

> Life is atrocious, we know. But precisely because I expect little of the human condition, man's periods of felicity, his partial progress, his efforts to begin over again and continue, all seem to me like so many prodigies which nearly compensate for the monstrous mass of ills and defeats, of indifference and error. Catastrophe and ruin will come; disorder will triumph, but order will too, from time to time. . . . Not all our books will perish, nor our statues, if broken, lie unrepaired; other domes and other pediments will arise from our domes and pediments; some few men will think and work and feel as we have done, and I venture to count upon such continuators, placed irregularly throughout the centuries, and upon this kind of intermittent immortality.

There are people who surely can count on living on through their civilization-changing works—the Hadrians and Homers, the Michelangelos and Voltaires and Einsteins (and Hitlers). But we need not appear in the history books nor engage in world-shaking enterprises to view what we do as having continuing impact. Our everyday works and our private acts may yield significant consequences that ripple and ripple and ripple down through time.

And then there is the image of biological continuity, the image of living on through our children and theirs, or a broader—"biosocial"—image of living on through our nation, our race or mankind. Some of us do perceive ourselves as a link in a chain of life which stretches, unbroken, from the past to the future, connecting us never-endingly to the lives that have been and will come, offering us—as long as man lasts—immortality.

But beyond the four images thus far described of after-death continuity are direct, intense experiences of transcendence—experiences that re-echo our old ecstatic merger with mother, experiences of oneness in which boundaries and time and death itself disappear. These unbounded oneness experiences may occur, as we have seen, through sexual passion, drugs, art, nature,

God. They give us a sense of "an indissoluble bond . . . with the external world as a whole," a sense that "we cannot fall out of this world."

Not every adult, however, can experience this oneness. "I cannot discover," Freud writes, "this 'oceanic' feeling in myself." Nor will everyone find—in religion or nature or man's works or the bio-(social or logical) connection—visions of immortality that make it easier to look on death. Simone de Beauvoir says, "Whether you think of it as heavenly or as earthly, if you love life immortality is no consolation for death." Woody Allen makes the same point: "I don't want to gain immortality through my work. I want to gain immortality by not dying." And the fatally ill young man who is asked if he can take comfort in knowing that his friend will weep for him when he is gone, gives his friend an answer that clearly rejects such abstract versions of immortality: "Not unless I be aware and hear you weeping."

Some people insist that any hope of after-death continuity—even without other worlds or immortal souls—is always denial of death, is nothing more than a defense against anxiety. Lifton, however, argues that a sense of immortality is "a corollary of the knowledge of death . . .," of the knowledge that, despite our connections to the future and past, our existence is finite.

Our existence is finite. The self that we have created through so many years of effort and suffering will die. And sustained though we may be by the idea, the hope, the certainty that some portion of us will eternally endure, we also must acknowledge that this "I" who breathes and loves and works and knows itself will be forever and ever and ever . . . obliterated.

So whether or not we live with images of continuity—of immortality—we also will have to live with a sense of transience, aware that no matter how passionately we love whatever we love, we don't have the power to make either it, or us, stay. Centuries of poets have addressed themselves to the brevity of existence and what their exquisite images have to say is that all is vanity, that we have but an hour to strut upon the stage, that the days of wine and roses vanish swiftly, that we must die. The poets have also offered us—in every voice, in every emotional tone—the words in which the dying say goodbye. And as I consider my finitude, and plan what I ardently hope is well ahead, I turn to this poem by Louis MacNeice for the words I would most wish to say at my last leaving:

> The sunlight on the garden
> Hardens and grows cold,
> We cannot cage the minute
> Within its nets of gold,
> When all is told
> We cannot beg for pardon.
>
> Our freedom as free lances
> Advances towards its end;
> The earth compels, upon it
> Sonnets and birds descend;
> And soon, my friend,
> We shall have no time for dances.
>
> The sky was good for flying
> Defying the church bells
> And every evil iron
> Siren and what it tells:
> The earth compels,
> We are dying, Egypt, dying.
>
> And not expecting pardon,
> Hardened in heart anew,
> But glad to have sat under
> Thunder and rain with you,
> And grateful too
> For sunlight on the garden.

20

Reconnections

But as she has grown, her smile has widened with a touch of fear and her glance has taken on depth. Now she is aware of some of the losses you incur by being here—the extraordinary rent you have to pay as long as you stay.

—Annie Dillard

My youngest son is waiting to hear from the college of his choice. He'll be leaving home. My mother, my sister, too many dear friends are dead. I'm taking calcium pills to save my middle-aged bones from osteoporosis. I'm living on Lean Cuisine in a last-ditch effort to defeat my middle-aged spread. And although my husband and I have maintained our imperfect connection for twenty-five rich full years, the bombs of divorce and widowhood are falling all around us. We live with loss.

Both in my life and this book I have tried to talk about loss in a number of different languages: The scholarly and the vernacular. The subjective and the objective. The private and the public. The funny and the sad. I have found illumination and consolation in the theories of psychoanalysis, in the vivid, compressed intensities of poems, in the fictional realities of Emma Bovary, Alex Portnoy, Ivan Ilych and in the as-told-to-me secrets of strangers and friends. I have found them, too, in the subterranean exploration of my own experience. Here's what I've learned:

I've learned that in the course of our life we leave and are left and let go of much that we love. Losing is the price we pay for living. It is also the source of much of our growth and gain. Making our way from birth to death, we also have to make our way through the pain of giving up and giving up and giving up some portion of what we cherish.

We have to deal with our necessary losses.

We should understand how these losses are linked to our gains.

For in leaving the blurred-boundary bliss of mother-child oneness, we become a conscious, unique and separate self, exchanging the illusion of absolute shelter and absolute safety for the triumphant anxieties of standing alone.

And in bowing to the forbidden and the impossible, we become a moral, responsible, adult self, discovering—within the limitations imposed by necessity—our freedoms and choices.

And in giving up our impossible expectations, we become a lovingly connected self, renouncing ideal visions of perfect friendship, marriage, children, family life for the sweet imperfections of all-too-human relationships.

And in confronting the many losses that are brought by time and death, we become a mourning and adapting self, finding at every stage—until we draw our final breath—opportunities for creative transformations.

In thinking about development as a lifelong series of necessary losses—of necessary losses and subsequent gains—I am constantly struck by the fact that in human experience opposites frequently converge. I have found that little can be understood in terms of "eithers" and "ors." I have found that the answer to the question "Is it *this* or *that?*" is often "Both."

That we love and we hate the same person.

That the same person—us, for instance—is both good and bad.

That although we are driven by forces that are beyond our control and awareness, we are also the active authors of our fate.

And that, although the course of our life is marked with repetition and continuity, it also is remarkably open to change.

For yes, it is true that as long as we live we may keep repeating the patterns established in childhood. It is true that the present is powerfully shaped by the past. But it also is true that the circumstances of every stage of development can shake up and revise the old arrangements. And it's true that insight at any age can free us from singing the same sad songs again.

Thus, although our early experiences are decisive, some of these decisions can be reversed. We can't understand our history in terms of continuity *or* change. We must include both.

And we can't understand our history unless we recognize that it is comprised of both outer and inner realities. For what we call our "experiences" include not only what happens to us out there, but how we interpret what happens to us out there. A kiss is *not* just a kiss—it may feel like sweet intimacy; it may feel like outrageous intrusion. It may even be only a fantasy in our mind. Each of us has an inner response to the outer events of our life. We must include both.

Another set of paired opposites which tend to merge in real life are nature and nurture. For what we come into the world with— our innate qualities, our "constitutional givens"—interacts with the nurture we receive. We cannot view development in terms of either environment or heredity. We must include both.

As for our losses and gains, we have seen how often they are inextricably mixed. There is plenty we have to give up in order to grow. For we cannot deeply love anything without becoming vulnerable to loss. And we cannot become separate people, responsible people, connected people, reflective people without some losing and leaving and letting go.

Notes and Elaborations

CHAPTER ONE   THE HIGH COST OF SEPARATION

page 22
Separation from mother:
Anna Freud, the noted child psychoanalyst and her colleague Dorothy Burlingham directed three nurseries, the Hamstead Nurseries, in England during World War II, recording with exquisite and poignant detail the reactions of young children separated from their families. In *War and Children* Miss Freud writes: "The war acquires comparatively little significance for children so long as it only threatens their lives, disturbs their material comfort or cuts their food rations. It becomes enormously significant the moment it breaks up family life and uproots the first emotional attachments of the child within the family group. London children, therefore, were on the whole much less upset by bombing than by evacuation to the country as a protection against it" (p. 37). She also notes that separation is painful even when the mothers concerned "are not 'good mothers' in the ordinary sense of the word. . . . It is a known fact that children will cling even to mothers who are continually cross and sometimes cruel to them. The attachment of the small child to its mother seems to a large degree independent of her personal qualities . . ." (p. 45).

page 22
"There is no such thing":
Winnicott, *Collected Papers*, "Anxiety Associated with Insecurity," p. 99.

page 23
may be permanent:
British psychoanalyst John Bowlby's three-volume work on attachment and loss (see note below) is a pioneering study of the nature of human attachment and the effects on young children of temporary and permanent separation. In *Loss* he presents material supporting the view that "there is a tendency to underestimate how distressing and disabling loss usually is and for how long the distress, and often the disablement, commonly last." He lays emphasis "on the long duration of grief, on the difficulties of recovering from its effects, and on the adverse consequences for personality functioning that loss so often brings" (p. 8).

page 24
separation anxiety:
Studies of separation reactions can be found in Bowlby's three volumes—*Attachment, Separation, Loss*—and in Heinicke and Westheimer's *Brief Separations*. My usage of separation anxiety comes from the discussion of its two meanings in *Brief Separations*, pp. 327–328.

page 25
time accelerates with the years:

See Goldstein, Freud, Solnit, *Beyond the Best Interests of the Child*, for a discussion of the child's sense of time (pp. 40–42).

page 25

"the frustration and longing":

See Bowlby, *Loss*, p. 10. He is quoting James Robertson, who worked with Bowlby on studies of children and separation.

page 25

a typical sequence of responses:

Discussions of protest, despair and detachment can be found in Bowlby, *Separation*, pp. 26–27 and *Loss*, pp. 19–22.

page 26

"assured himself and anybody":

A. Freud and Burlingham, *War and Children*, pp. 99–100.

page 26

This response is called detachment:

In *Loss*, Bowlby writes that detachment—which sometimes alternates with tenacious clinging—is "regularly seen whenever a child between the ages of about six months and three years has spent a week or more out of his mother's care and without being cared for by a specially assigned substitute" (p. 20).

page 27

"it's like a scar on your brain":

Fraiberg, *Every Child's Birthright*, p. 160.

page 29

"stomach love":

The phrase is from A. Freud and Burlingham's *War and Children*, p. 190. The Freudian view of love's origins must be understood within the context of Sigmund Freud's dual-instinct theory, which proposes that human beings are impelled by two basic instinctual drives: the sexual and the aggressive. In Freud's usage, sex encompasses many component instincts which only at puberty are organized into the genital sexuality we usually think of as sex. Component instincts, however, are present from birth and are first manifested as oral drives for which the infant seeks gratification through sucking and eating. Thus it is the sexual drive, in its oral form, which initially impels the infant toward his mother. The gratification of this instinct becomes the basis, in Freud's view, for love. In *Standard Edition*, Vol. 23, "An Outline of Psychoanalysis," Freud writes: "A child's first erotic object is the mother's breast that nourishes it; love has its origin in attachment to the satisfied need for nourishment" (p. 188). For further discussion, see Freud's *Standard Edition*, Vol. 7, "Three Essays on the Theory of Sexuality." A. Freud and Burlingham's *Infants Without Families* provides a brief summary of this view of the origins of love (p. 23).

page 30

"The love of others":

Suttie, *The Origins of Love and Hate*, p. 30. Suttie, anticipating Bowlby, relates love to the animal instinct of self-preservation. But he says that what distinguishes man from other animals is the "extreme degree to which the definite, stereotyped, specific instincts of 'self-preservation' of his pre-human ancestors are 'melted down' . . . into a dependent love-for-mother . . ." (p. 20).

In recent years, many "object relations" theorists have also challenged the stomach-love point of view. Pointing to the importance of the early mother-child relationship, they have argued that Freud's dual-instinct theory doesn't give that relationship the centrality it deserves. Thus British analyst W. R. D. Fairbairn, for instance, in his book *An Object Relations Theory of the Personality*, rejects the dual-instinct theory and argues instead that the baby's primary need is not to gratify oral sexual drives but to seek relationships. In psychoanalytic parlance the blood-less word "object" actually means *human* object. And so, when Fairbairn proposes that the infant is object-seeking from the start, he simply is saying that first comes the need for attachment, that babies are seeking a mother, not a meal. (He also holds the view that aggression is not a basic instinct but a reaction to experiences of frustration in the pursuit of that attachment.)

There are some interesting efforts at reconciliation between object-relations theory and Freud's dual-instinct theory in Modell's "The Ego and the Id: Fifty Years Later," *The International Journal of Psycho-Analysis*, Vol. 26, Part 1, pp. 57–68, and Loewald's "Instinct Theory, Object Relations and Psychic Structure Formation," *Journal of the American Psychoanalytic Association*, Vol. 26, No. 3, pp. 493–506. And for more on the British object-relations theorists, see Sutherland's review in the *Journal of the American Psychoanalytic Association*, Vol. 28, No. 4, pp. 829–860.

page 30
"attachment behavior":
Bowlby's *Attachment* presents this view of the mother-infant bond, using extensive material from animal studies.

page 30
breaking that crucial bond:
There is much compelling evidence, for instance, in studies of the institution-raised child, about the dangers of nonconnection. A classic work on this subject is Rene Spitz's "Hospitalism," *The Psychoanalytic Study of the Child*, Vol. 1. Dr. Spitz, an internationally famous psychoanalyst, spent many years conducting analytic research in child development. His hospitalism study found severe developmental retardation in infants reared in an institution with no mother and no mother substitute, but only "one-eighth" of a nurse. Spitz concludes that we must "take into consideration in our institutions, in our charitable activities, in our social legislation, the overwhelming and unique importance of an adequate and satisfactory mother-child relationship during the first year . . ." (p. 72).

page 30
foster home:
If a reliable mother-child bond is essential for healthy human development, we must be appalled by those current adoption procedures where a child is shunted from foster home to foster home—interminably—before the hearings and paperwork are complete. According to *Foster Care 1984: A Report on the Implementation of the Recommendations of the Mayor's Task Force on Foster Care*, p. 58, the average waiting time from foster care to final adoption in New York City is now an unbelievable six years—six years of tenuous and frequently broken connections.

page 30
hospital stay:
See James Robertson's "A Two Year Old Goes to Hospital," a documentary film which movingly demonstrates the impact of separation on a hospitalized child. See also my article on the emotional implications of hospitalization for children and the changes in hospital policy that are helping to allay separation fears: Viorst, "The Hospital That Has Patience for Its Patients: A Look at Children's Hospital in Washington, D.C.," *Redbook*, February 1977, pp. 48–54.

page 30

working mothers:

The Division of Employment and Unemployment Analysis of the Bureau of Labor Statistics says that as of March 1983, 50.5 percent of women with children under six were in the labor force. This is a total of 7.6 million women.

page 31

"In the years":

Fraiberg, *Every Child's Birthright*, p. 111. This view has been challenged by Harvard psychologist Jerome Kagan, who offers evidence that infants in full-time day care can in fact flourish, developing with neither intellectual nor emotional impairment, and with no harm done to the mother-child attachment. His is the kind of study which women who must, or wish to, work will find consoling. But it cannot be embraced without taking note of a number of highly significant ifs:

—if the caretaker is sensitive, warm, responsive and constant—not one of several interchangeable caretakers.

—if the infant-caretaker ratio is small—three to one.

—if the mother is reliably present, before and after day care, in the child's life.

—and if the day care begins before or after the age of maximum separation anxiety.

This material is presented in *Infancy*, by Kagan, Richard B. Kearsley and Philip R. Zelazo. The authors studied 33 Chinese and Caucasian children from working- and middle-class families in the Boston area who were enrolled in an experimental full-time day-care center starting at age three and a half months to five and a half months and continuing until age 29 months. Comparing these children to a home-reared control group, the authors conclude that responsible day care does not hold hidden psychological or intellectual dangers. They remind the reader, however, that "we are evaluating how children grow under surrogate care conditions that are, according to current theoretical views, similar to home rearing" (p. 176).

page 32

early childhood losses make us sensitive:

With some modifications and additions, Bowlby's *Separation* and *Loss* form the basis of my discussion in this chapter of anxiety, depression and defense in adult functioning.

page 32

"a rock . . . feels no pain":

From the Simon and Garfunkel song "I Am a Rock."

page 33

"when my mother left me":

Marilynne Robinson, *Housekeeping*, p. 214.

page 33

"gigantic and multiple":

Ibid., p. 195.

CHAPTER TWO   THE ULTIMATE CONNECTION

page 34

"harmonious interpenetrating mix-up":

Balint, *The Basic Fault*, p. 66.

page 34
"I'm in the milk":
Maurice Sendak, *In the Night Kitchen*, unpaged.
page 34
Our original bliss connection:
Analyst Otto Rank offers us the concept of the womb as paradise, the "blessed primal condition," in *The Trauma of Birth*, p. 113. He argues that every anxiety can be traced to the anxiety of birth and that "every pleasure has as its final aim the reestablishment of the intrauterine primal pleasure" (p. 17). Although we cannot bear our separation from paradise, says Rank, the memory of primal anxiety—the anxiety of birth—prevents us from turning back to a womblike state. Rather we are "urged forward to seek for Paradise in the world formed in the image of the mother, instead of seeking it in the past, and, in so far as this fails, to look for it in the sublime wish compensations of religion, art and philosophy" (p. 190). Indeed Rank seems to ascribe all human activity, both normal and pathological, to our reactions to the primal birth situation, though in his later writings he shifts the emphasis from physical to psychological birth.
page 34
"for which deep down":
Mahler, Pine, Bergman, *The Psychological Birth of the Human Infant*, p. 227. Analyst Margaret Mahler postulates two developmental stages which occur between our literal birth and our "psychological birth," some five months later. She calls the earliest stage of extrauterine life the *normal autistic phase*, during which we are utterly unaware, according to Mahler, of the existence of any other human presence. This normal autistic phase is followed by the *normal symbiotic phase*, which begins in the second month when our shut-tight universe expands and we merge with our mother to form "a dual unity within one common boundary" (p. 44). Symbiosis is brought to an end by the "psychological birth of the human infant," a step-by-step process of separation-individuation which will be discussed in the next chapter.

Mahler's formulation and description of a universal symbiotic phase during the second to fifth months of life are based on studies begun in the late 1950s of normal infant-mother pairs. Mahler concedes that she and her colleagues are relying on their carefully observant "psychoanalytic eye" but cannot ultimately prove the correctness of the inferences they have made about the inner world of preverbal infants. But the book's conclusions about symbiosis and separation-individuation, and the wealth of clinical vignettes that accompany them, support her contention that her formulations are plausible and useful.

Further clues to the nonverbal workings of the mind can be obtained through patients who have regressed to the symbiotic phase or who have continued to function symbiotically at later stages of development. See Mahler's book *On Human Symbiosis and the Vicissitudes of Individuation*, Vol. I.
page 35
"Afterwards, the compromise":
Kumin, *Our Ground Time Here Will Be Brief*, "After Love," p. 182.
page 36
"the perfect compromise":
Bak, "Being in Love and Object Loss," *The International Journal of Psycho-Analysis*, Vol. 54, Part 1, p. 7. In a similar vein, analyst Jacobson writes in *The Self and the Object World* that the desire "to re-establish the lost unit . . . probably never ceases

to play a part in our emotional life. Even normally, the experience of physical merging and of an 'identity' of pleasure in the sexual act may harbor elements of happiness derived from the feeling of return to the lost, original union with the mother" (p. 39).

page 36
"further and further":
Lawrence, *Lady Chatterley's Lover*, p. 208.

page 36
"as if the opposites":
W. James, *The Varieties of Religious Experience*, p. 306.

page 36
"to return from the solitude":
Ibid., p. 311. James is quoting the German idealist Malwida von Meysenburg.

page 36
"I am two":
Mr. Allen confirms having made this statement but neither I nor his office have been able to establish where it originally appeared.

page 36
"one vast world-encircling harmony":
James, *The Varieties of Religious Experience*, p. 311. James is quoting the German idealist Malwida von Meysenburg.

page 37
"pure moments":
Dillard, *Pilgrim at Tinker Creek*, p. 82. A friend of mine described a similar experience of oneness upon viewing Rembrandt's painting "The Night Watch," when "time stopped, the museum I was standing in disappeared, I was inside the painting."

page 37
"when she [the soul]":
James, *The Varieties of Religious Experience*, p. 321. James is quoting Saint Teresa.

page 37
"the *me*, and the *we*":
Ibid., p. 329. James is quoting Sufi Gulshan-Raz.

page 37
"Ecstatically, I merged":
Silverman, Lachmann, Milich, *The Search for Oneness*, p. 247.

page 38
"thinking crazily":
This case is cited in Silverman, Lachmann, Milich, *The Search for Oneness*, p. 5.

page 38
"I am not I":
Rank, *The Trauma of Birth*, p. 177. Rank, by the way, is quoting an ecstatic Islamic mystic, not a psychotic child. Clearly there are striking similarities between the psychotic and the spiritual union.

page 38
Consider Mrs. C:
The case of Mrs. A.C. is discussed by analyst George Pollock in "On Symbiosis and Symbiotic Neurosis," *The International Journal of Psycho-Analysis*, Vol. 45, Part 1, pp. 1–30.

page 39
"Probably the greatest reason":
Searles, *Countertransference*, p. 42.

page 39
"I have always felt":
Smith, "The Golden Fantasy: A Regressive Reaction to Separation Anxiety," *The International Journal of Psycho-Analysis*, Vol. 58, Part 3, p. 314. Smith's paper, pp. 311–324, provides examples of the golden fantasy, including the vignette of the spoon-fed lady.

page 40
"regression in the service of the ego":
The term was coined by analyst Ernst Kris. See his *Selected Papers of Ernst Kris*, "Some Problems of War Propaganda," where he writes: "The antithesis of regression and ego control, of irrational and rational behavior, is a dangerous simplification. No such exclusion exists. To put it in the negative: He who cannot *pro tempore* relax, let loose the reins and indulge in regression, is according to generally accepted clinical standards ill. Regression is not always opposed to ego control; it can take place, as it were, in the service of the ego" (p. 448).

page 40
"To merge in order":
Rose's statement is quoted in Silverman, Lachmann, Milich's *The Search for One-ness*, p. 6. Rose argues that there is great growth-promoting value in our ability, throughout life, to "temporarily suspend the distinction between self and others and thus momentarily experience a state of mind similar to the early unity with mother" (pp. 5–6).

page 40
The Search for Oneness:
The next several paragraphs are summaries of material drawn from Silverman, Lachmann, Milich, *The Search for Oneness*. See the book for further details on experiments with subliminal *Mommy and I Are One* messages.

page 41
"No one":
Searles, *Countertransference*, p. 176.

page 42
"an incurable wound":
Nacht and Viderman, "The Pre-Object Universe in the Transference Situation," *The International Journal of Psycho-Analysis*, Vol. 41, Parts 4–5, p. 387.

page 42
"The force behind":
Robinson, *Housekeeping*, p. 192.

CHAPTER THREE   STANDING ALONE

page 43
"something at the root":
This line and the verse that begins the chapter are from Richard Wilbur's poem "Seed Leaves," *The Norton Anthology of Poetry*, Allison et al., eds., pp. 1201–1202.

page 44
"psychological birth":
The Psychological Birth of the Human Infant by Mahler, Pine and Bergman is the basis for the separation-individuation material in this chapter. Additional information is provided by two papers: "The Separation-Individuation Process and Identity Formation," pp. 395–406, and "Object Constancy, Individuality, and Internalization," pp. 407–423, both by Mahler and John B. McDevitt, found in *The Course of Life*, Vol. 1, Greenspan and Pollock, eds. In these groundbreaking studies, separation and individuation are presented as two different but intertwined lines of development, with separation meaning the child's achievement of an inner— intrapsychic—sense of separateness from his mother, and individuation meaning the child's acquisition of the specific qualities that make him an individual. Mahler's four subphases of separation-individuation are differentiation (from five to nine months), practicing (from nine to fifteen months), rapprochement (from fifteen to twenty-four months) and consolidation of individuality and the beginning of emotional object constancy (from twenty-four to thirty-six months).

page 44
"hatched":
Mahler writes that "we came to recognize at some point during the differentiation subphase a certain new look of alertness, persistence and goal-directedness. We have taken this look to be a behavioral manifestation of hatching and have loosely said that an infant with this look 'has hatched' " (p. 54). This and all further notes for this chapter referring to Mahler are from *The Psychological Birth of the Human Infant*.

page 44
"emotional refueling":
Mahler credits Furer with the term "emotional refueling" and notes: "It is easy to observe how the wilting and fatigued infant 'perks up' in the shortest time following such contact; then he quickly goes on with his explorations and once again becomes absorbed in his pleasure in functioning" (p. 69).

page 45
a love affair with the world:
Mahler credits analyst Phyllis Greenacre with the phrase "love affair with the world" (p. 70).

page 45
"I celebrate myself":
Walt Whitman, "Song of Myself," *The Norton Anthology of Poetry*, Allison et al., eds., pp. 816–820.

page 45
At eighteen or so months:
At this stage our mind becomes capable of creating symbols and manipulating images. We can picture a separate me and a separate mother, a mother who therefore isn't the ever available appendage that we had thought her to be. The concept of a mother who is separate from oneself and who, when absent from view, possesses an independent existence elsewhere, is what Piaget calls "object permanence."

page 48
split in two:
This discussion of splitting is derived from Kernberg's *Object Relations Theory and*

Clinical Psychoanalysis. He postulates that our early interpersonal relationships are reproduced internally as images—as an inner image of ourself (a self-image) and of our mother (an object-image) along with the emotional atmosphere (good or bad) under which a particular experience (feeding, playing, whatever) occurs. In taking in these experiences we split the good and bad. Loving, pleasing baby-mother contacts are grouped together as good internal images, while painful rejecting contacts become bad internal images. Splitting, he writes, begins as a normal inability of the immature mind to integrate, but by three or four months it becomes an active defense mechanism. The defense is against the danger that our aggression (either strong innate aggression or intense aggression produced by early frustration) will spoil or destroy what we love. Splitting gradually disappears in the third year but if we continue to have great anxiety about our aggression, we may perpetuate splitting into adult life.

page 49

object constancy:

Our earliest mother memory is "recognition memory"—confronted with her face, we know her face. Later, when we have physical or psychological need of her, we can summon up her image in her absence. At fifteen to eighteen months we can evoke our mother's image—"evocative memory"—without any special stimulus or need, with evocative memory linked to our grasp of the concept "object permanence"—the independent existence of absent others. However, writes Mahler, the concept of "emotional object constancy" implies something more than all of the above. "It also implies the unifying of the 'good' and 'bad' object into one whole representation" so that " . . . the love object will not be rejected or exchanged for another if it can no longer provide satisfactions; and in that state, the object is still longed for, and not rejected (hated) as unsatisfactory simply because it is absent" (p. 110). Selma Fraiberg, though putting object constancy at an earlier age, offers a full and fascinating discussion of the subject in a paper entitled "Libidinal Object Constancy and Mental Representation," found in *The Psychoanalytic Study of the Child*, Vol. 24.

page 50

holding environment:

Winnicott has written a great deal about the maternal "holding environment," a concept he has named and discusses in eloquent and highly accessible language. See his *Collected Papers*, "The Depressive Position in Normal Emotional Development," and *The Maturational Processes and the Facilitating Environment*, "The Capacity to be Alone."

CHAPTER FOUR   THE PRIVATE "I"

page 52

a model of the mind:

Freud's three-part division of the mind, his structural theory of the mind, is first set forth in the *Standard Edition*, Vol. 19, "The Ego and the Id." Heinz Hartmann later used "self" to refer to the entire person—body and mind—and located the representation of that self in the system ego.

page 52

an image of "psychic self":

The formation of a self involves, among other achievements: Knowing where our body ends and the world begins. Being able to organize memories, establish inner images of outer reality and have some sense of what that reality is. Tolerating our mixed emotions. Acquiring a healthy and stable narcissism. And forming identifications with our parents. See McDevitt and Mahler's "Object Constancy, Individuality and Internalization," *The Course of Life*, Vol. 1, Greenspan and Pollock, eds., pp. 407–423.

page 52

identification is one of the central processes:

My material on identification was drawn from Edith Jacobson's *The Self and the Object World*, Roy Schafer's *Aspects of Internalization*, Otto Kernberg's *Object Relations Theory and Clinical Psychoanalysis*, and John McDevitt's "The Role of Internalization in the Development of Object Relations during the Separation-Individuation Phase," from the *Journal of the American Psychoanalytic Association*, Vol. 27, No. 2, pp. 327–343.

page 52

"I am a part":

The line is from Tennyson's poem "Ulysses," *The Norton Anthology of Poetry*, Allison et al., pp. 757–758.

page 54

"Not that I would not":

James, *The Principles of Psychology*, pp. 309–310.

page 55

"toy with his own":

This material is drawn from Farber's article "On Jealousy" in *Commentary*, October 1973, pp. 50–58. The specific material quoted can be found on p. 56 and p. 57.

page 55

"two me's":

Bowlby, *Loss*, p. 227.

page 56

"who glittered when he walked":

These quotations are from the poem "Richard Cory" by Edwin Arlington Robinson, *Contemporary Trends*, Nelson and Cargill, eds., p. 669.

page 56

The true self:

This section is based on Winnicott's discussion of the true self and false self, found in *The Maturational Processes and the Facilitating Environment*, "Ego Distortion in Terms of True and False Self."

page 56

The as-if personality:

This section is based on Deutsch's discussion of the as-if personality found in *Neuroses and Character Types*, "Some Forms of Emotional Disturbance and Their Relationship to Schizophrenia." The quoted material appears on p. 265.

page 57

The borderline personality:

Otto Kernberg's *Borderline Conditions and Pathological Narcissism* provides a full discussion of the borderline personality. See also the third edition of the *Diagnostic and Statistical Manual of Mental Disorders*, the American Psychiatric Association, code 301.83.

page 57

"actively cutting off":

Kernberg, *Borderline Conditions and Pathological Narcissism*, p. 165.

page 58

Freud said that the love:

See Freud's discussion in the *Standard Edition*, Vol. 14, "On Narcissism: An Introduction."

page 58

Narcissism, says Kohut:

My discussion of narcissism is based primarily on the fascinating and somewhat controversial theories of Heinz Kohut as presented in his two books, *The Analysis of the Self* and *The Restoration of the Self*. Kohut describes two separate side-by-side lines of development, one leading to love of others (object love) and one leading to higher, healthy forms of self-love (narcissism). In Kohut's view, the development of narcissism begins with a state of primary narcissism, when self and mother form a perfect oneness, and continues after separation with the child trying to restore that lost perfection by creating (a) an exhibitionistic "grandiose self" on which all power and goodness can be concentrated, and (b) an "idealized parent imago," in whose great power and goodness he can participate.

In time, says Kohut, these two poles of self will be modified into realistic ambitions and ideals and we will possess a steady but not excessive narcissism. But first we must pass through a normal phase during which our parents function as parts of ourself, as "self-objects," to confirm and support our grandiosity and idealizations. This developmental phase begins approximately at the period between the end of symbiosis and the early stages of separation-individuation (*Kohut, The Analysis of the Self*, p. 220).

page 59

to function as that mirror:

When the parent (usually the mother) functions as a "mirroring self-object" who enjoys and admires her child, the child receives confirmation of "his tentatively established, yet still vulnerable, creative-productive-active self" (Kohut, *The Restoration of the Self*, p. 76).

page 59

to function as that ideal:

When the parent (usually the father) functions as an "idealized self-object" who permits and enjoys his child's idealization of him and merger with him, the child feels enlarged and augmented (Kohut, *The Restoration of the Self*, p. 185).

page 59

And supplied with these vital ingredients:

Kohut writes that while traces of ambitions and ideals are beginning to be acquired in early infancy, most of our grandiosity consolidates into core ambitions around the second, third and fourth years, while most of our core ideals are acquired in later childhood, around the fourth, fifth and sixth years (Kohut, *The Restoration of the Self*, p. 179). Kohut also notes that if there is failure in the development of either our grandiose or idealizing aspect we can compensate by the especially strong development of one or the other aspect. We have, therefore, two chances to make good—"self disturbances of pathological degree result only from the failure of both of these developmental opportunities" (Kohut, *The Restoration of the Self*, p. 185).

page 59

missing pieces of self:

Our relationships with others, says Kohut, can be understood in terms of whether we are actually loving them as others or loving them as parts of ourself, as self-objects. However, he writes, "I have no hesitation in claiming that there is no mature love in which the love object is not also a self-object. . . . There is no love relationship without mutual (self-esteem enhancing) mirroring and idealization" (Kohut, *The Restoration of the Self*, p. 122).

page 60
"not loved or admired":
Kohut, *The Analysis of the Self*, p. 45.

page 60
A composite portrait:
This composite draws from Kohut's writings, Kernberg's *Borderline Conditions and Pathological Narcissism* and Christopher Lasch's elegant, highly readable *The Culture of Narcissism*.

page 61
"considers himself to be":
Don Marquis, *archy and mehitabel*, p. 82.

page 61
"The question was raised":
Kohut, *The Analysis of the Self*, p. 149.

page 61
The trouble with grandiosity:
Kernberg, *Borderline Conditions and Pathological Narcissism*, discusses this vulnerability, pp. 310–311.

page 62
"All her substitute":
Miller, *Prisoners of Childhood*, p. 42.

page 62
"the total involvement":
Johnson, "A Temple of Last Resorts: Youth and Shared Narcissisms," p. 42. Her discussion of narcissism and cults is found in *The Narcissistic Condition*, Marie Coleman Nelson, ed.

page 62
"I painted a picture":
Cynthia Macdonald, "Accomplishments," *A Geography of Poets*, Edward Field, ed., pp. 332–333.

page 63
Such narcissistic parents:
Miller's *Prisoners of Childhood* discusses narcissistic parents.

page 64
the pathological narcissist:
According to Kohut, people may deal with defects in their self by developing "defensive structures" to cover the damaged parts and "compensatory structures" to strengthen the healthy parts (Kohut, *The Restoration of the Self*, p. 3).

page 64
a sense of identity:
Useful discussions of identity can be found in Heinz Lichtenstein's "The Dilemma of Human Identity: Notes on Self-Transformation, Self-Objectivation and Metamorphosis," the *Journal of the American Psychoanalytic Association*, Vol. 11, No. 1,

pp. 173–223; Hans Loewald's "On the Therapeutic Action of Psychoanalysis," *International Journal of Psycho-Analysis*, Vol. 41, Part 1, pp. 16–33; "Problems of Identity," panel, David Rubinfine, reporter, *Journal of the American Psychoanalytic Association*, Vol. 6, No. 1, pp. 131–142; and Erik Erikson's *Identity: Youth and Crisis*.

page 65
Our mother helps us fulfill:
See Loewald, "On the Therapeutic Action of Psychoanalysis," *The International Journal of Psycho-Analysis*, Vol. 41, Part 1, pp. 16–33. This paper discusses the mother's crucial role as her baby's organizer or mediator: "The bodily handling of and concern with the child, the manner in which the child is fed, touched, cleaned, the way it is looked at, talked to, called by name, recognized and rerecognized—all these and many other ways of communicating with the child, and communicating to him his identity, sameness, unity and individuality, shape and mould him so that he can begin to identify himself, to feel and recognize himself as one and as separate from others yet with others. The child begins to experience himself as a centered unit by being centered upon" (p. 20).

CHAPTER FIVE   LESSONS IN LOVE

page 66
Our mother loves without limits:
In "Love for the Mother and Mother-Love," *International Journal of Psycho-Analysis*, Vol. 30, pp. 251–259, Alice Balint discusses unconditional love.

page 66
if a mother is good enough:
In *Collected Papers*, "Mind and Its Relation to the Psyche-Soma," Winnicott writes: *"The ordinary good mother is good enough*. If she is *good enough* the infant becomes able to allow for her deficiencies by mental activity. . . . The mental activity of the infant turns a *good-enough* environment into a perfect environment. . . ." (p. 245).

page 67
the wish to undo that separation:
The wish to undo separation by being in love is discussed by Robert Bak in "Being in Love and Object Loss," *International Journal of Psycho-Analysis*, Vol. 54, Part 1, pp. 1–7.

page 67
"The more I give":
The line is from Shakespeare's *Romeo and Juliet*, Act 2, Scene 2.

page 67
"Infantile love follows":
Fromm, *The Art of Loving*, pp. 40–41.

page 68
"With the exception":
S. Freud, *Standard Edition*, Vol. 14, "Thoughts for the Times on War and Death," p. 298.

page 68
"Ah, I have loved":

The quoted material is from Racine's *Andromache*, Act Two.

page 68

Winnicott lists eighteen reasons:

The list appears in Winnicott's *Collected Papers*, "Hate in the Countertransference,"
p. 201.

page 68

"it contains a denial":

Ibid, p. 202.

page 69

"He will just do nothing at all":

This poem appears in Karl Menninger's *Love Against Hate*, pp. 19–20, credited to
The New Yorker, July 1, 1939.

page 69

"We'll eat you up":

The phrase quoted is from Maurice Sendak's *Where the Wild Things Are*, unpaged.

page 69

"It is indeed foreign":

S. Freud, *Standard Edition*, Vol. 14, "Thoughts for the Times on War and Death,"
p. 299.

page 70

we are all still murderers:

Ibid., p. 297. "And so, if we are to be judged by our unconscious wishful impulses,
we ourselves are, like primaeval man, a gang of murderers."

page 70

the daimonic:

For May's discussion of the daimonic see his *Love and Will*, Chapters 5 and 6.

page 70

"the urge in every being":

Ibid., p. 122.

page 70

"If my devils":

Ibid., p. 121.

page 70

Liv Ullmann:

These paragraphs are based on my interview with Liv Ullmann, supplemented by
material from her book *Changing*, pp. 96–97.

page 71

"This nasty stuff":

Many argue, however, that the aggressive drive isn't exclusively "nasty stuff."
Although Freud presented aggression as a destructive force linked to the death
instinct, others talk about constructive aggression as well: the urge for mastery, for
achievement, for power, for obstacles to overcome. There is a good survey of current
thinking about aggression in Justin Krent's "Some Thoughts on Aggression," *Journal of the American Psychoanalytic Association*, Vol. 26, No. 1, pp. 185–232.

page 71

our "second other":

The phrase and much useful material on early fathering can be found in Stanley
Greenspan's " 'The Second Other'—The Role of the Father in Early Personality
Formation and in the Dyadic-Phallic Phase of Development," found in *Anthology
on Fatherhood*, S. Cath, A. Gurwitt, J. Ross, eds.

page 72
"the father's role":
Michael Yogman, "Development of the Father-Infant Relationship," *Theory and Research in Behavioral Pediatrics*, Vol. 1, Fitzgerald, Lester, Yogman, eds., p. 221. In this fascinating chapter, Yogman reviews historical, cross-cultural, phylogenetic and anthropological studies of the father-infant relationship, seeking to understand paternity in *biological* terms as well as psychological ones. He also reviews recent studies of the father-infant relationship from birth to two years of age. Some of his major points include:

—With the recent increased interest by and involvement of fathers in child care there has been a legitimization, in the last ten years, of father-infant research. Earlier studies of attachment focused almost entirely on the mother in the infant's first year of life.

—Infants are biologically adapted to elicit caregiving from adults and thus insure their survival. They can elicit this care from both male and female adults.

—Interactions between fathers and infants are characterized by accentuated shifts from peaks of maximal attention to valleys of minimal attention. Interactions between mothers and infants are characterized by more gradual and modulated shifts.

—Fathers do not evoke a more excited response in babies because they are more novel. There are qualitative differences in care even when they are the primary caretaker.

—Mothers spend more time with their babies than fathers do; the studies Yogman cites "have been based on the assumption that the quality of the father-infant relationship is more important than the quantity, given some yet-to-be-defined lower limit" (p. 256).

—Fathers as well as mothers undergo psychological changes during pregnancy (and even some physical ones) and experience parenthood as a psychosocial crisis—generativity versus self-absorption, in Erikson's terms.

page 72
"provide conclusive evidence":
Ibid., p. 253.

page 72
"qualitatively different":
Ibid., p. 259.

page 73
the "biological component":
Ibid., p. 270.

page 73
"We're not very happy today":
Greene, *Good Morning, Merry Sunshine*, pp. 102–103.

page 73
"no known society":
Alice Rossi, "A Biosocial Perspective on Parenting," *Daedalus*, Spring 1977, pp. 1–31. The statement appears on p. 5.

page 73
"A biosocial perspective":
Ibid., p. 4.

page 74
This isn't meant to suggest that fathers aren't important:

For further discussion of the father's role see: Cath, Gurwitt, Ross, *Father and Child;* John Munder Ross's "Fathering: A Review of Some Psychoanalytic Contributions on Paternity," *The International Journal of Psycho-Analysis*, Vol. 60, Part 3, pp. 317–327; J. O. Wisdom's "The Role of the Father in the Mind of Parents, in Psychoanalytic Theory and in the Life of the Infant," *The International Review of Psychoanalysis*, Vol. 3, Part 2, pp. 231–239; "The Role of the Father in the Preoedipal Years," reported by Robert Prall, *Journal of the American Psychoanalytic Association*, Vol. 26, No. 1, pp. 143–161; and *The Role of the Father in Child Development*, Michael Lamb, ed.

page 75

Liv Ullmann:

These paragraphs are based on my interview with Liv Ullmann supplemented by material from her book *Changing*, pp. 11–12.

page 76

the repetition compulsion:

The compulsion to repeat is first discussed by Freud in *Standard Edition*, Vol. 12, "Remembering, Repeating and Working-Through." He notes that events we cannot remember are reproduced as actions and that this "repetition is a transference of the forgotten past . . ." onto the present (p. 151). In *Standard Edition*, Vol. 18, "Beyond the Pleasure Principle," Freud asserts the universality of the repetition compulsion and relates it to the death instinct (see note "the death instinct," p. 79, below). Anna Freud clarifies the relationship between the repetition compulsion and transference in *The Ego and the Mechanisms of Defense:* "By transference we mean all those impulses . . . which are not newly created . . . but have their source in early—indeed, the very earliest—object relations and are now merely revived under the influence of the repetition compulsion" (p. 18). She also notes (p. 19) that the repetition compulsion extends not only to former impulses but also to former defensive measures against them.

page 77

For many men the denial of dependency:

Analyst Otto Kernberg describes a promiscuous patient of his, a smart and successful man in his early thirties, who found himself again and again engaged in short-lived sexual encounters: pursuing women, taking them to bed, and then moving on before he could form a relationship. His mother had chronically frustrated him, withdrawing from him both physically and emotionally. She possessed such treasures, he felt, but she would not share them. He remembered trying to cling to her while she coldly rejected his love and his demands upon her. And through his promiscuity, he enacted one version of that early history, taking a woman's treasures and—by loving and leaving—denying how much he needed her. (See *Object-Relations Theory and Clinical Psychoanalysis*, pp. 191–195.)

page 77

"Out of boredom":

K. Snow, *Willo*, pp. 96–97.

page 78

Benjamin Spock:

This material is based on my interviews with Dr. Spock and Mary Morgan in 1983.

page 78

the woman described by Freud:

S. Freud, *Standard Edition*, Vol. 18, "Beyond the Pleasure Principle," p. 22.

page 79

the woman who disdained her parents' . . . marriage:
Miller describes this case in her book *Prisoners of Childhood*, pp. 60–61.
    page 79
    "pursued by a malignant fate":
S. Freud, *Standard Edition*, Vol. 18, "Beyond the Pleasure Principle," p. 21.
    page 79
    transference love:
In Freud's *Standard Edition*, Vol. 12, "Observations on Transference-Love," he notes
that "love consists of new editions of old traits and that it repeats infantile reactions. But this is the essential character of being in love. There is no such state
which does not reproduce infantile prototypes" (p. 168).
    page 79
    the death instinct:
Freud presents his controversial theory of the death instinct in *Standard Edition*,
Vol. 18, "Beyond the Pleasure Principle," and develops it in subsequent publications. Taking the sexual and aggressive instincts back one step, he establishes the
ultimate polarity—the life instinct and the death instinct. The life instinct—Eros
—is the sexual drive operating in us to preserve life, reproduce it, bring it together.
The death instinct—sometimes called Thanatos—is the aggressive drive operating
in us to destroy through killing and through dying.
    Freud attributes the urge to restore an earlier state of things, manifested as the
repetition compulsion, to the death instinct, which seeks to return to the "quies-
cence of the inorganic world" (p. 62). However, many analysts hold that all behavior (and not just that which is attributed to the death instinct) is in part under the
sway of the repetition compulsion. Furthermore, many analysts who accept Freud's
sex-aggression duality reject the concept of a death instinct.
    page 79
    to undo—rewrite—the past:
In *Standard Edition*, Vol. 20, "Inhibitions, Symptoms and Anxiety," Freud offers
this explanation for the compulsion to repeat. He writes: "When anything has not
happened in the desired way, it is undone by being repeated in a different way" (p.
120).
    page 80
    "Only connect!":
Forster, *Howards End*, p. 186.
    page 80
    we try to love:
In *Love and Will* May describes four kinds of love: *libido*, *eros*, *philia* and *caritas* (p.
37).
    page 80
    "Man is gifted":
Fromm, *The Art of Loving*, p. 8.

    CHAPTER SIX   WHEN ARE YOU TAKING THAT NEW KID BACK TO THE
    HOSPITAL?

    page 84
    "I thought. That question":
Hayward, *Haywire*, pp. 123–124.

page 84
"A small child":
S. Freud, *Standard Edition*, Vol. 15, "Introductory Lectures on Psycho-Analysis, Parts I and II," p. 204.

page 85
Symbiosis was strictly mama and me:
I am arguing here that every child experiences himself as his mother's only child during the symbiotic phase and thus all children (not only the oldest) suffer the loss of an exclusive mother-child relationship. (This is not to deny, of course, the unique displacement of the oldest child who in fact as well as in symbiotic delusion has had his mother to himself.)

page 86
"And the Lord had respect":
Holy Bible, Genesis.

page 86
inside our head:
Levy's *Studies in Sibling Rivalry* gives us a glimpse of some of these murderous sibling fantasies. He presents cases based on a series of play-technique experiments in which children with younger siblings were shown a mother doll, a nursing baby doll and an older brother or sister doll and invited to express the feelings of the older doll-sibling. The children responded by crushing, piercing, hammering, smashing and tearing apart the baby doll nursing at the mother doll's breast.

page 86
"extreme jealousy and competitiveness":
A. Freud, *Normality and Pathology in Childhood*, p. 176.

page 86
threatens vast anxiety:
In *Standard Edition*, Vol. 20, "Inhibitions, Symptoms and Anxiety," pp. 77–175, Freud states that human beings develop automatic anxiety when confronted with situations so overwhelming that they are rendered helpless. In the course of development we learn to anticipate these overwhelming situations—these traumatic situations—and to experience a diminished form of anxiety—signal anxiety—*before* the trauma occurs. Signal anxiety, then, is an internal warning signal whose function is to mobilize our defenses so that we can avert traumatic situations.

page 86
our dangerous and now unwanted impulse:
These dangerous and unwanted impulses stem from the part of our psyche called the id—seat of our unconscious primitive wishes. But another part of our psyche, the ego, is perpetually engaged in unconscious defensive operations against our id, providing us with both the warning of danger (through signal anxiety) and the means of protecting ourselves from these dangers (through our defense mechanisms).

page 86
a feared or actual loss:
In *Standard Edition*, Vol. 20, "Inhibitions, Symptoms and Anxiety," Freud describes a series of typical danger situations where the anxiety that threatens us is attendant upon an unendurable loss: The loss of the person we love. The loss of that loved person's love. The loss of some beloved body part—i.e., castration. And the loss of

the loving approval of our conscience, of our own internal judge. Each of these danger situations corresponds to a particular developmental phase, and each is liable to precipitate a traumatic experience. Freud says that the original danger situation—the prototype of absolute helplessness in the face of overwhelming stimuli—is birth.

page 87
our common everyday mechanisms of defense:
See A. Freud's *The Ego and the Mechanisms of Defense*, and Brenner's lucid discussion of defense in *An Elementary Textbook of Psychoanalysis*, pp. 79–96. Different theorists differ about what they would include on their list of "mechanisms of defense." They agree, however, that defenses sometimes lead to healthy adaptation and sometimes to neurotic symptoms. For instance, a person who regularly uses isolation as a defense may become cut off from his emotional life, feeling nothing very much about anything. Or a person who relies on projection may, by attributing all of his hostile feelings to others, become a paranoid who believes "they're all out to get me." On the other hand, identification may lead to self-enrichment through the acquisition of valuable characteristics, reaction formation may sometimes help establish useful and humane qualities, and sublimation, at its best, may produce great art.

page 88
almost anything can serve as a defense mechanism:
In *An Elementary Textbook of Psychoanalysis*, Brenner states that "the ego can and does use all the processes of normal ego formation and ego function for defensive purposes at one time or another" (p. 80).

page 88
"de-identification":
For a discussion of de-identification and split-parent identification, see "Sibling Deidentification and Split-Parent Identification: A Family Tetrad," by Frances Fuchs Schachter, pp. 123–151, in *Sibling Relationships: Their Nature and Significance Across the Lifespan*, Michael E. Lamb and Brian Sutton-Smith, eds.

page 88
Each could even feel superior:
Ibid. Schachter notes that these feelings of superiority suggest that de-identification may be a muted way of maintaining the benefits of sibling rivalry while minimizing the costs.

page 89
half of a whole human being:
An interesting problem with role polarization is discussed in "A Survey of Learning Difficulties in Children" by Gerald Pearson, *The Psychoanalytic Study of the Child*, Vol. 7. Pearson describes a thirteen-year-old girl who was interested in her school work to the exclusion of all else, in marked contrast to her older sister who was an indifferent student, a party girl, intensely sociable, etc. "Learning, for her, became a way of establishing her individuality, a way of expressing her rivalry with her sister, a way of obtaining her parents' love in a field that would not arouse her sister's jealousy and a method of avoiding her sister's jealous hostility" (p. 345).

page 89
"My mother used to characterize Margo":
Fishel, *Sisters*, p. 108.

page 90
"he will become a fighting child":
Adler, *Problems of Neurosis*, p. 98.

page 91
interesting work on adult sibling rivalry:
H. Ross and J. Milgram, "Important Variables in Adult Sibling Relationships: A Qualitative Study," *Sibling Relationships: Their Nature and Significance Across the Lifespan*, Lamb and Sutton-Smith, eds. Ross and Milgram describe three types of adult sibling rivalry: simple sibling rivalry, which involves one sib's resentment of another's greater strengths in one or more areas; reciprocal sibling rivalry, with each sib having certain strengths and weaknesses and resenting the strengths the other sib possesses; and sex-linked sibling rivalry, where the privileges granted for being a male or a female are resented—sometimes for a lifetime—by the one who isn't getting them.

Why the secrecy about this rivalry? Ross and Milgram speculate that it may have to do, first, with the fear that an admission of rivalrous feelings is akin to an admission of maladjustment. There may also be a concern that such disclosure would do permanent damage to the relationship. "Furthermore," they write, "to reveal feelings of rivalry to a brother or sister who is perceived as being stronger or as having the upper hand in the relationship increases one's vulnerability in an already unsafe situation" (pp. 236–237).

page 91
Henry and . . . William James:
The quoted material about and from Henry and William can be found in Edel's *Henry James*, Vol. 5, p. 295, p. 301, p. 300 and p. 298. Edel perceives them as a Jacob and Esau battling over their birthright.

page 91
Olivia de Havilland and Joan Fontaine:
From Joan Fontaine's autobiography, *No Bed of Roses*, "were not encouraged . . ." p. 102; "Now what had I done . . ." pp. 145–146.

page 92
Billy Carter . . . Jimmy Carter:
The material on the Carter brothers comes from Bank and Kahn, *The Sibling Bond*, pp. 229–231.

page 92
"for the favor of parents":
Cited in Arnstein, *Brothers and Sisters/Sisters and Brothers*, p. 3.

page 92
"is always breathing down my neck":
Ibid., pp. 3–4.

page 93
"I later discovered":
Ibid, p. 4.

page 93
"The nature and quality":
S. Freud, *Standard Edition*, Vol. 13, "Some Reflections on Schoolboy Psychology," p. 243.

page 94
"she had been the younger":

This case is discussed in Josephine Hilgard's "Sibling Rivalry and Social Hered-ity," *Psychiatry*, Vol. 14, No. 4, pp. 375–385. The quoted material appears on p. 380.

page 94

"My mom says I'm her sugarplum":

Viorst, *If I Were in Charge of the World, and Other Worries*, "Some Things Don't Make Any Sense At All," p. 8.

page 95

family order of birth:

Theories abound, and often conflict, on the relationship of order of birth to person-ality, but there seems to be agreement on some of the advantages and disadvan-tages of being the firstborn child. See Bank and Kahn, *The Sibling Bond*, for discussion of firstborn advantages and disadvantages, pp. 205–206, and for refer-ences to birth-order research, pp. 6–7. For the first serious effort to correlate birth order and personality, see Adler, *Problems of Neurosis*, Chapter 7. Arnstein's *Broth-ers and Sisters/Sisters and Brothers* mentions a study which showed that a majority of the members of Congress in a randomly selected sample were firstborns, but so were 31 out of a sample of 35 stripteasers. "It was suggested that both . . . have marked needs for recognition, attention and appreciation. Certainly both expose themselves in one way or another to public view" (p. 87).

page 95

"Apparently his mother":

Frisch, *I'm Not Stiller*, pp. 285–286.

page 95

"rotten bad influence":

E. O'Neill, *Long Day's Journey into Night*, p. 165.

page 96

Hansels and Gretels:

Hansels and Gretels are discussed in *The Sibling Bond*, Bank and Kahn, Chapter 5. The Jerome quotes can be found on p. 117. The authors point out that the develop-ment of these intense loyalties requires the presence of some loving figure in early life.

page 98

"one can conceive of rivalry":

Cicirelli discusses the sibling tie in "Sibling Influence Throughout the Lifespan," from *Sibling Relationships: Their Nature and Significance Across the Lifespan*, Lamb and Sutton-Smith, eds. The quoted material appears on p. 278.

page 98

"Sisters, while they are growing up":

Mead, *Blackberry Winter*, p. 70.

CHAPTER SEVEN   PASSIONATE TRIANGLES

page 101

from mouth to anus to genitals:

The first full discussion of sexuality in children is found in Freud, *Standard Edition*, Vol. 7, "Three Essays on the Theory of Sexuality." Freud describes the stages of psychosexual development and the successively central erogenous zones as follows:

From zero to one and a half years old—the oral phase—the zone is the mouth, and sucking and biting the pleasure.

From one and a half to three years old—the anal phase—the zone is the anus, and expelling and holding the pleasure.

From three to five or six years old—the phallic phase—the zone is the genital organs, and masturbation the pleasure.

And after a phase of relative calm, called latency, we enter—at puberty—into the genital phase.

The oral, anal and phallic phases of childhood described by Freud overlap and never completely vanish. Instead they become component parts of adult genital sexuality. In addition, there are other manifestations of the sexual instinct in childhood—a wish to look, a wish to exhibit, urethral erotism (sensual pleasure connected with urinating and the urethra) and sensual pleasure connected with hearing or smelling. Some of these, to varying degrees, may also become part of adult sexuality. A strong and persistent emotional investment in infantile modes (sucking, for instance) or objects (mother, for instance) of sexual gratification is called a fixation. A turning back to an earlier mode or object of gratification is called a regression.

page 101
"decisive encounters":

Erikson, *Childhood and Society*, p. 71. He also notes that "the optimum total situation implied in the baby's readiness to get what is given is his mutual regulation with a mother who will permit him to develop and co-ordinate his means of getting as she develops and co-ordinates her means of giving. There is a high premium of libidinal pleasure on this co-ordination . . ." (pp. 75–76). For further discussion, see his chapter on "The Theory of Infantile Sexuality."

While Erikson—in his amplification of Freud's psychosexual stages—emphasizes the links between erogenous zones and interpersonal relationships, Kernberg—in his amplification—focusses on *internalized* object relations (the mental representations of relationships). He states in *Object Relations Theory and Clinical Psychoanalysis* that "internalized object relations are a major organizer of instinctual development in man" (p. 186).

page 101
It was Sigmund Freud who discovered and described the Oedipus complex:

Freud's writings on the Oedipus complex include, all from the *Standard Edition*, "The Interpretation of Dreams" (Vol. 4), "Introductory Lectures on Psycho-Analysis" (Vol. 16), "The Ego and the Id," "The Dissolution of the Oedipus Complex" and "Some Psychical Consequences of the Anatomical Distinction Between the Sexes" (Vol. 19).

When Freud talks about incestuous wishes, he is talking about a child's unconscious wish to engage in sexual activities with his or her parent, though the fantasies of exactly what these sexual activities are may be quite inaccurate and bizarre. When Freud talks about murderous wishes, he is talking about a child's unconscious wish to kill his or her parent, though a child may not know that death is a permanent state.

The destiny of Oedipus moves us, writes Freud in "The Interpretation of Dreams," "only because it might have been ours—because the oracle laid the same curse upon us before our birth as upon him. It is the fate of all of us, perhaps, to direct our first sexual impulse towards our mother and our first hatred and our first murderous wish against our father" (p. 262).

page 102
our unconscious fear of damage:

This damage, according to Freud, is—for a boy—castration, untechnically defined as the loss of his beloved sex organ, his penis. (His observation that there actually are certain human beings who lack a penis persuades him that the loss of his is possible.) For a girl this fear of damage is much more vaguely defined by Freud and his followers. (Fear of genital injury through intercourse with her father is one suggestion.)

page 103
"an injured third party":

Freud, *Standard Edition*, Vol. 11, "A Special Type of Choice of Object Made By Men," p. 166.

page 104
"that the injured third party":

Ibid., p. 169.

page 104
Hamlet's famous procrastination as oedipal:

E. Jones, *Hamlet and Oedipus*. The quoted material appears on p. 51 and p. 100. Freud makes the same point in "The Interpretation of Dreams" when he writes: "Hamlet is able to do anything—except take vengeance on the man who did away with his father and took that father's place with his mother, the man who shows him the repressed wishes of his own childhood realized" (p. 265).

page 105
Or whether we're ready to deal with them:

There are many adults, and many patients in therapy, whose emotional life has not reached the level of oedipal conflict. Instead of being concerned with triangular issues of sexual love and competition, they are still struggling with whether they and others exist as whole and separate selves, with whether or not they can survive separateness or with a narcissistic perception of others as nothing more than extensions of themself.

page 105
"The forces of conscience":

Freud, *Standard Edition*, Vol. 14, "Some Character-Types Met with in Psycho-Analytic Work," p. 331. See also an excellent article on the success neurosis by Bryce Nelson called "Self-Sabotage in Careers—A Common Trap," *The New York Times*, February 15, 1983.

The success neurosis, by the way, can be generated in love as well as in work. Oedipal victors—people who symbolically (or actually) succeed in winning the sexually yearned-for parent—may also suffer from a success neurosis.

page 106
the *negative* Oedipus complex:

Freud's writings on the negative Oedipus complex include, in the *Standard Edition*, Vol. 19, "The Ego and the Id," "The Dissolution of the Oedipus Complex" and "Some Psychical Consequences of the Anatomical Distinction Between the Sexes."

Some writings seem to suggest that the negative Oedipus complex is a more well-defined phase—preceding the positive Oedipus complex—in girls than in boys. Boys do, however, have strong negative oedipal wishes to take their mother's place with their father. They relinquish this wish for the same reason they ultimately relinquish their sexual wish for their mother—castration anxiety. "For both of them entail . . . the loss of his penis—the masculine [way of obtaining satisfaction]

...as a resulting punishment and the feminine one as a precondition" ("The Dissolution of the Oedipus Complex," p. 176).

page 107

Little girls must submit their first love to a sex change:

See Freud, *Standard Edition*, Vol. 21, "Female Sexuality," where he writes that "a woman's strong dependence on her father merely takes over the heritage of an equally strong attachment to her mother...." (p. 227). See also J. Lampl-De Groot's "The Evolution of the Oedipus Complex in Women," *The International Journal of Psycho-Analysis*, Vol. 9 (pp. 332–345). These papers argue that little girls give up their mother as a sex object because they blame her for making them incomplete—i.e., for failing to give them a penis, which they covet and envy. Thus, while castration concerns put an *end* to the boy's positive Oedipus complex, they *are the beginning* of a girl's positive Oedipus complex, turning her angrily against her mother and sending her to her father with fantasies that through him she will receive a penis substitute—a baby. Many analysts today reject penis envy as a reason for the girl's shift from mother to father, though—as we will see in the next chapter—penis envy (along with womb envy and other kinds of envy) may play an important part in our mental life.

page 107

significantly reflect our human environment:

In *The Collected Papers of Otto Fenichel*, "Specific Forms of the Oedipus Complex," Fenichel discusses the influence of various environmental factors on oedipal conflicts.

For instance, he notes that our brothers and our sisters "are, above all, objects of jealousy, and, according to the individual circumstances, they may either increase the hatred directed in the Oedipus complex against one parent or they may deflect it and so diminish it" (p. 212). However, he says they can serve as love objects too.

He also makes the point that the Oedipus complex in children "is in part stimulated also by the corresponding attitude in their parents: the father loves the daughter and the mother the son. This unconscious sexual attachment to the children becomes specially strong wherever the parents' real sexual gratification leaves them unsatisfied" (p. 212).

Further material on environmental factors can be found in Lidz's *Hamlet's Enemy*, Chapter 17, "The Oedipal Transition: An Existential Interpretation." See also Peter Neubauer's "The One-Parent Child and His Oedipal Development" in *The Psychoanalytic Study of the Child*, Vol. 15.

page 107

"just a case of the kid":

Personal communication from Dr. Louis Breger.

page 108

"transitional space":

This discussion of the family, transitional space and incest comes from Dr. Winer's paper "Incest" (unpublished).

page 108

"After her mother died":

Fitzgerald, *Tender Is the Night*, p. 129.

page 108

"rigidness of her shocked body":

Morrison, *The Bluest Eye*, p. 128.

page 109
"I have blotted out":
Fields, *Like Father, Like Daughter*, pp. 161–162.

page 109
"incestuous fantasies may be realized":
Winer, "Incest" (unpublished).

page 109
motherly incest fantasies:
Feldman, "On Romance," *Bulletin of the Philadelphia Association for Psychoanalysis*, Vol. 19, No. 3, pp. 153–157.

page 110
the child doesn't wind up walking away with the parent:
In her book *The Magic Years*, Selma Fraiberg talks about the ways in which "we create the feeling in the child that his parents' relationship . . . must be respected. A child, dearly loved as he is, may not intrude upon this intimate relationship, cannot share the intimacies of his parents' lives, and cannot obtain the exclusive love of a parent. If the child has fantasies about marrying the parent of his choice, fantasies about a more intimate and exclusive love, the fantasy remains a fantasy, for we do nothing to encourage it, and without encouragement the fantasy will be given up" (p. 225).

page 110
At dinner a four-year-old girl:
Sweet, "The Electra Complex," *Ms.*, May 1984, pp. 148–149. The quoted material appears on p. 149.

page 111
One woman, who lived with a man she loved:
Fenichel describes this case in *The Collected Papers of Otto Fenichel*, "Specific Forms of the Oedipus Complex," pp. 213–214.

page 111
Linda Bird Francke's "The Sons of Divorce":
Francke's survey of studies on the impact of divorce on boys, "The Sons of Divorce," appeared in *The New York Times Magazine*, May 22, 1983, pp. 40–41, 54–57. Her article is the source of the quotations from Dr. Livingston and the three "divorced" sons.

page 112
We will struggle with oedipal conflicts all our life:
Loewald makes this point in a beautiful paper called "The Waning of the Oedipus Complex," *Journal of the American Psychoanalytic Association*, Vol. 27, No. 4. He writes that "no matter how resolutely the ego turns away from it and what the relative proportions of repression, sublimation, 'destruction' might be, in adolescence the Oedipus complex rears its head again, and it does during later periods in life. . . . It repeatedly requires repression, internalization, transformation, sublimation, in short, some forms of mastery in the course of life" (p. 753).

page 113
an inner law-enforcement agency:
The taking in of our parents' moral standards provides us with an inner ally in our struggle to repudiate our dangerous oedipal wishes. This inner ally, our superego, is thus—in Freud's words—the "heir" of the Oedipus complex.

page 113
the Oedipus complex "has taken its name from failure":
Mead's statement on oedipal failure and success appears in *Male and Female*, p. 108.

page 113
"Aha! a traitor in the camp":
Ibid., pp. 108–109. In a footnote Mead provides the complete text of Eugene Field's poem "To a Usurper."

CHAPTER EIGHT   ANATOMY AND DESTINY

page 115
our wish to do so may be "one of the deepest tendencies":
See Lawrence Kubie's "The Drive to Become Both Sexes," *The Psychoanalytic Quarterly*, Vol. 43, No. 3, pp. 349–426. The passage quoted appears on p. 370.

page 115
Orlando:
See Virginia Woolf's novel *Orlando*.

page 115
gender identity:
According to analyst Robert Stoller, gender identity is fairly irreversibly established between eighteen months and three years. His research persuasively challenges Freud's theory that while males have a primary masculinity, a little girl's femininity is a later development which occurs after the traumatic discovery that she lacks a penis. Rejecting the notion of a primary femininity, Freud describes the little girl as masculine in her sexuality until the recognition of the differences between boys and girls, which—he says—leads to feelings of being castrated, and penis envy. As a result of this penis envy, her self-love is mortified, she renounces masturbatory satisfaction (because her equipment—her clitoris—is so inferior), she blames her mother for failing to equip her properly and she perceives her, and all penisless women, as debased. At this point she turns from her mother to her father, a shift that initiates the female Oedipus complex and also initiates the development of femininity.

Stoller, in "A Different View of Oedipal Conflict," *The Course of Life*, Vol. 1, Greenspan and Pollock, eds., argues for a primary femininity—an early "unquestioned, unconflicted, egosyntonic acceptance of oneself as female" (p. 595). In another paper, "Primary Femininity," *Journal of the American Psychoanalytic Association*, Vol. 24, No. 5, he discusses "core gender identity," which he defines as "the sense we have of our sex—of maleness in males and femaleness in females" (p. 61). It is around this core that our gender identity, a broader term including masculinity and femininity and various sex-linked roles and relationships, gradually forms. Stoller says core gender identity is the result of five factors: (1) a biological "force"—the effect of sex hormones on the fetus; (2) sex assignment at birth; (3) parental attitudes toward the sex assignment, reflected back onto the infant; (4) "biopsychic" phenomena—the effects of patterns of handling, conditioning, imprinting; (5) bodily sensations, especially from the genitals.

James Kleeman, same journal, notes in his paper "Freud's Views on Early Female Sexuality in the Light of Direct Child Observation" that an important key to early gender identity is the child's conscious and not-so-conscious labeling of him or her self as a boy or a girl. This labeling "serves as the primary and basic organizer for subsequent gender experience" (p. 15).

page 116

three feminist writers:

Viorst, "Are Men and Women Different?" *Redbook*, November 1978. See pp. 46–50 for responses from Gould, Steinem, Jong, etc.

page 117

Sigmund Freud would have answered:

Freud, *Standard Edition*, Vol. 22, "New Introductory Lectures on Psycho-Analysis," offers this characterization of women in his lecture on "Femininity."

page 117

"certainly incomplete and fragmentary":

Ibid., p. 135.

page 117

Two Stanford psychologists:

Maccoby and Jacklin summarize and comment on patterns of difference and similarity in Chapter 10 of *The Psychology of Sex Differences*, pp. 349–374.

page 118

"I think hormones":

Viorst, "Are Men and Women Different?" *Redbook*, November 1978, p. 48.

page 119

"Here it was—The Cinderella Complex":

Dowling, *The Cinderella Complex*, p. 64. There is also a stirring exposition of this theme in Vivian Gornick's "Toward a Definition of the Female Sensibility" in *The Village Voice*, May 31, 1973.

She writes: "The subjection of women, in my view, lies most deeply in the ingrained conviction—shared by both men and women—that for women marriage is the pivotal experience. It is this conviction, primarily, that reduces and ultimately destroys in women that flow of psychic energy that is fed in men from birth by the anxious knowledge given them that one is alone in this world; that one is never taken care of; that life is a naked battle between fear and desire, and that fear is kept in abeyance only through the recurrent urge of desire; that desire is whetted only if it is reinforced by the capacity to experience oneself; that the capacity to experience oneself is everything."

She continues: "It is the re-creation in women of the experiencing self that is the business of contemporary feminism: the absence of that self is the slave that must be squeezed out drop by drop. Vast internal changes must occur in women. . . . A new kind of journey into the interior must be taken, one in which the terms of internal conflict are re-defined. It is a journey of unimaginable pain and loneliness, this journey, a battle all the way, one in which the same inch of emotional ground must be fought for over and over again, alone and without allies, the only soldier in the army the struggling self. But on the other side lies freedom: self-possession" (pp. 21–22).

page 120

"mature dependence":

The phrase is Fairbairn's, from *Psychoanalytic Studies of the Personality*. He notes that he prefers the term "mature dependence" to "independence" because "a capacity for relationships necessarily implies dependence of some sort" (p. 145).

page 120
"male and female voices":
Gilligan, *In a Different Voice*, p. 156.

page 120
women's concern with relationships:
In Gilligan's thought-provoking *In a Different Voice* she refers to a study on adult fantasies of power showing that "women are more concerned than men with both sides of an interdependent relationship" and "quicker to recognize their own interdependence." The study also found that "while men represent powerful activity as assertion and aggression, women in contrast portray acts of nurturance as acts of strength" (pp. 167–168).

page 120
"By yourself":
Ibid., p. 160.

page 121
"What I had to learn":
Scarf, *Unfinished Business*, p. 89.

page 121
"we are never so defenseless":
Freud, *Standard Edition*, Vol. 21, "Civilization and Its Discontents," p. 82.

page 121
depression when important love relationships are through:
See Maggie Scarf's fine book, *Unfinished Business*, which relates depression in women to "the loss of an important, self-defining, powerful and binding emotional relationship" (p. 86). Scarf reports that depression is suffered by an estimated three to six times as many women as men.

In further support of her point, see Erik Erikson's *Identity: Youth and Crisis*, where his clinical experience leads him to conclude: "Emptiness is the female form of perdition. . . . To be left, for her, means to be left empty, to be drained of the blood of the body, the warmth of the heart, the sap of life" (p. 278).

page 121
they *do* do it differently:
In Mead's *Male and Female*, for instance, she notes that in a two-sex world "we find that there are certain biological regularities" (p. 147). These include the fact that the mother nurses both boys and girls, which means that "the female child's earliest experience is one of closeness to her own nature" while the little boy must "begin to differentiate himself from this person closest to him" (p. 148). Mead adds, however, that this biological regularity would vanish if men shared equally in child care, a point that is eloquently elaborated on in Dorothy Dinnerstein's difficult and elegant book, *The Mermaid and the Minotaur*.

For a full discussion of the developmental differences between boys and girls in establishing their gender identity, see Tyson, "A Developmental Line of Gender Identity, Gender Role and Choice of Love Object," *Journal of the American Psychoanalytic Association*, Vol. 30, No. 1, pp. 61–86.

page 122
Boys, to be boys:
See Stoller and Herdt, "The Development of Masculinity: A Cross-Cultural Contribution," in the *Journal of the American Psychoanalytic Association*, Vol. 30, No. 1. Here the authors hypothesize that the earliest stage of masculine development is a "protofemininity, a condition induced through the merging that occurs in the

mother-infant symbiosis." To develop masculinity, the boy must erect an inner barrier, a protective shield against the urge "to maintain the blissful sense of being one with mother" (pp. 32–33).

page 122
"until it seemed we were one":
L. Michaels, *The Men's Club*, p. 161.

page 124
"This renunciation":
L. Altman, "Some Vicissitudes of Love," *Journal of the American Psychoanalytic Association*, Vol. 25, No. 1, p. 48.

page 124
For a girl to give up her mother:
In "Some Thoughts on the Nature of Woman," *Bulletin of the Philadelphia Association for Psychoanalysis*, Vol. 20, Louis Kaplan writes: "Penis envy then does not arise from the chance observation that her brother or her father are better endowed but rather from the realization that they can and she can't achieve ultimate reunion with mother" (p. 324).

page 124
"to be discontent":
This Webster dictionary definition of envy is used by Daniel Jaffe to explore womb envy in "The Masculine Envy of Woman's Procreative Function," *Journal of the American Psychoanalytic Association*, Vol. 16, No. 3, pp. 521–548.

page 124
"source of all comforts":
Hanna Segal, *Introduction to the Work of Melanie Klein*, p. 40. See Chapter Four of her book for further discussion of breast envy.

page 124
creating new life:
There is an interesting discussion of creativity and gender in Greenacre's book *Emotional Growth*, Vol. 2, "Woman as Artist." And Mead notes in *Male and Female* that it is civilization's problem to define a role for men that will give them a sense of "irreversible achievement" comparable to that which women achieve through childbearing (p. 160).

page 125
And some puberty rites:
Bettelheim, *Symbolic Wounds*. The quoted material is found respectively on p. 262 and p. 264.

page 125
Felix Boehm wrote of the male's intense envy:
Boehm, "The Femininity-Complex in Men," *The International Journal of Psycho-Analysis*, Vol. 11, Part 4, pp. 444–469. The quoted material is found respectively on p. 456 and p. 457.

page 126
"remember that every son":
Piercy, *Circles on the Water*, "Doing It Differently," p. 113.

page 126
working woman's version of penis envy:
See Applegarth's "Some Observations on Work Inhibitions in Women," *Journal of the American Psychoanalytic Association*, Vol. 24, No. 5, pp. 251–268.

page 126

In a recent study:

Carol Tavris, with Dr. Alice Baumgartner, reports on this study in "How Would Your Life Be Different If You'd Been Born a Boy?" *Redbook*, February 1983, pp. 92–95. Dr. Baumgartner and her colleagues at the University of Colorado's Institute for Equality in Education surveyed nearly 2,000 schoolchildren in Colorado and found that both sexes still think that boys have it better.

page 127

that "something" a penis has come to represent:

One analyst says, "My experience with women patients has shown me that penis envy is not an end in itself, but rather the expression of a desire to triumph over the . . . mother through the possession of the organ the mother lacks. . . ." (Chasse-guet-Smirgel, "Freud and Female Sexuality: The Consideration of Some Blind Spots in the Exploration of the 'Dark Continent,'" *The International Journal of Psycho-Analysis*, Vol. 57, Part 3, p. 285.)

Another analyst says that penis envy may sometimes be "the wish to have something personally satisfying to lessen dependence on men. . . ." (Moore, B., "Freud and Female Sexuality: A Current View," from above-mentioned journal, p. 296.)

See also Grossman and Stewart, "Penis Envy: From Childhood Wish to Developmental Metaphor," *Journal of the American Psychoanalytic Association*, Vol. 24, No. 5, pp. 193–212.

page 127

"cut short of something":

In Freud's *Standard Edition*, Vol. 14, "Some Character-Types Met With in Psycho-Analytic Work," he wrote about men and women who secretly feel that life has done them wrong and who therefore feel entitled to special treatment and exemptions. He says that we all have our buried, or maybe not so buried, grievances and that "we all demand reparation for early wounds to our narcissism, our self-love." But some people, says Freud, people whom he labeled "the exceptions," actually live as if they are exceptions: Demanding special treatment. Believing that the rules don't apply to them. And some people—women!—he says, because they feel "undeservedly cut short of something and unfairly treated" believe themselves deserving of exemptions from "many of the importunities of life" (p. 315). His point seems to be that women think that they ought to be spared because they have suffered enough, that the absence of a penis makes women feel entitled to claim special treatment.

page 128

Thus the discovery:

According to all the latest research—and contrary to Freud's assumptions—penis envy, along with castration anxiety and a wish for a baby, can occur well before the oedipal phase.

page 128

castration anxiety:

In "Comments on Penis Envy and Orgasm in Women," *The Psychoanalytic Study of the Child*, Vol. 32, K. R. Eissler compares male and female psychosexual processes and concludes that, because of male castration anxiety, men have a harder developmental task than women do. While a woman "runs the risk of being plagued for the rest of her life by envy . . . a man may have to expect to be haunted by the anxiety that he will be deprived of his penis. It stands to reason that envy is far more easy to bear and far less painful than such a terrible anxiety" (p. 65).

page 128
"Daddy, I love you!":
Tyson, "A Developmental Line of Gender Identity, Gender Role and Choice of Love Object," *Journal of the American Psychoanalytic Association*, Vol. 30, No. 1, p. 69.

page 129
we identify with our other parent too:
Analyst Albert Solnit notes: "It is the child's bisexuality that enables him to identify with both parents, to acquire a maternal as well as a *paternal* psychological capacity. . . ." See "Psychoanalytic Perspectives on Children One–Three Years of Age," *The Course of Life*, Vol. 1, Greenspan and Pollock, eds. (p. 512).

page 129
"The potter who works with clay":
Mead, "Male and Female," p. 19.

CHAPTER NINE   GOOD AS GUILT

page 130
the price we pay for civilization:
In his *Standard Edition*, Vol. 21, "Civilization and Its Discontents," Freud discusses the limits we must place upon ourselves in order to live as civilized members of a society. He says that it is his intention "to represent the sense of guilt as the most important problem in the development of civilization and to show that the price we pay for our advance in civilization is a loss of happiness through the heightening of the sense of guilt" (p. 134).

page 131
True guilt:
Whether or not we have feelings of guilt before we have a conscience or superego (I am using the words interchangeably) has been the subject of much psychoanalytic debate, the answers to which depend on how broadly or narrowly the concept of guilt is defined. In "Civilization and Its Discontents," see note above, Freud takes both positions, saying (p. 136) that guilt is in existence before conscience, after having said (p. 125) that it is not until the establishment of the superego "that we should speak of . . . a sense of guilt." In "On the Concept of Superego," *The Psychoanalytic Study of the Child*, Vol. 15, analyst Joseph Sandler supports this second view, writing that what we are displaying in the preoedipal years is an "undergraduate superego which only works under the supervision of the parents. . . . It has not yet gained a license for independent practice. . . ." Thus, he argues, when this undergraduate superego sends us a warning signal of impending punishment or loss of love, that signal "does not yet deserve the name of guilt, though the affective state it produces in the ego may be identical with that which we refer to as guilt, later in the child's development" (pp. 152–153).

page 131
our parents installed in our mind:
It has been observed, however, that sometimes the child of lenient or tolerant parents develops a very harsh and punitive superego. Why? Because some children have more innate aggression than others and because in the process of controlling this aggression they turn a portion of it back against themselves. Nevertheless, as

Freud notes in "Civilization and Its Discontents," see the first note for this chapter, a severe upbringing "does also exert a strong influence on the formation of the child's superego. What it amounts to is that in the formation of the superego . . . innate constitutional factors and influences from the real environment act in combination" (p. 130).

page 131

the stages of our moral reasoning:

Kohlberg's six stages of moral thought are divided into three major levels—preconventional, conventional and postconventional or autonomous—and there are two stages within each level. (See Kohlberg and Gilligan's "The Adolescent as a Philosopher: The Discovery of the Self in a Postconventional World," *Daedalus*, pp. 1066–1068.)

Kohlberg's work builds on Piaget, who describes the following sequence of logical and cognitive development from the egocentrism of infancy—where thought is tied to action—to the capacity for abstract thought: Ages 0 to two, the era of sensorimotor intelligence; ages two to five, the era of symbolic, intuitive or prelogical thought; ages six to ten, the era of concrete operational thought; and ages eleven to adult, the era of formal-operational thought. (See p. 1063 of above-mentioned paper.)

Kohlberg relates the stage of our moral reasoning to the level of cognitive development we attain—though he notes that "cognitive maturity is a necessary but not a sufficient condition for moral judgment maturity" (p. 1071, same paper). Underscoring this relationship between cognitive and moral development, some researchers observe that guilt requires the ability to mentally reverse an act and consider alternative possibilities. They note that this ability belongs to the concrete-operational level of thought, which—they further note—is achieved around the end of the oedipal phase.

Both Kohlberg and Piaget see the stages they describe as an unvariable progression from less to more complex, although not everyone reaches Piaget's cognitive stage of formal operational thought or Kohlberg's fifth or sixth moral stages.

For full discussions of these ideas, see Kohlberg and Gilligan's paper, pp. 1051–1086. See also Kohlberg and Kramer, "Continuities and Discontinuities in Childhood and Adult Moral Development," *Human Development* 12, pp. 93–120. An excellent synthesis of theories of conscience formation and cognitive and moral development can be found in Chapter 8 of Louis Breger's *From Instinct to Identity*.

page 131

inner submission to human law:

Just to remind you: According to Freud, the superego comes into existence as a way of resolving the Oedipus complex. Impelled by the fear of castration (or, in girls, some less specific injury) and the fear of losing our parents' love, we become like our parents in repudiating our wishes to kill one parent and to possess the other one sexually. These primal prohibitions are the foundation of our superego, our conscience.

Thus the superego is regarded as a structure in the human personality which comes into being at a certain stage in our development. Our preoedipal experiences, however, strongly influence the character of our superego and many of the elements that go into the formation of our superego—called "superego precursors"—are present in the preoedipal years.

The superego which emerges in the fifth or sixth year, however, does not become stable until age nine or ten, does not become independent of outside authority until the end of adolescence and may be subject to some alteration throughout life.

Freud also asserted, by the way, that the female superego is weaker, less inexorable, less impersonal than the male's because the threat to female anatomy, being less drastic than the threat of castration, is less likely to motivate her to as full a resolution of her Oedipus complex. Carol Gilligan's *In a Different Voice* also finds differences between male and female moral reasoning—with women emphasizing connectedness and care and men emphasizing personal integrity. But, she argues, one is not superior to the other. Rather, they represent two modes of experience and interpretation which together could enable us to "arrive at a more complex rendition of human experience" (p. 174).

page 132

This excessive punishing guilt:

The more primitive parts of our mind still believe in talion law, which demands that a criminal's punishment be the same injury he inflicted on his victim—"an eye for an eye, a tooth for a tooth." Some of us guilt-ridden people, however, may go even further than talion law by insisting on imposing upon ourself capital punishments for misdemeanors.

page 133

A rabbi:

H. Kushner, *When Bad Things Happen to Good People*, p. 91.

page 133

"But the neurotic conscience":

Fraiberg, *The Magic Years*, p. 247.

page 134

"I think, in general":

Dr. Louis Breger, personal communication.

page 134

"Can't smoke, hardly drink":

Roth, *Portnoy's Complaint*, pp. 124–125.

page 135

"Ellie and Marvin":

J. Viorst, *How Did I Get to Be Forty and Other Atrocities*, "Secret Meetings," pp. 26–27.

page 137

"In such instances":

Freud, *Standard Edition*, Vol. 19, "The Economic Problem of Masochism," p. 166. See also, from the same volume, "The Ego and the Id," pp. 49–50, for more on the unconscious sense of guilt.

page 137

deficiencies in our capacity for guilt:

In his *Standard Edition*, Vol. 22, "New Introductory Lectures on Psycho-Analysis," Freud writes: "Following a well-known pronouncement of Kant's which couples the conscience within us with the starry Heavens, a pious man might well be tempted to honour these two things as the masterpieces of creation. The stars are indeed magnificent, but as regards conscience God has done an uneven and careless piece of work, for a large majority of men have brought along with them only a modest amount of it, or scarcely enough to be worth mentioning" (p. 61).

page 138
to punish, not to prevent:
Jacobson refers, in her book *The Self and the Object World*, to "the type of patients who constantly act out impulsively and then pay for their sins with depressive conditions and the destructive results of their actions; persons whose superego is punitive but, in spite of this, never serves either as a moral preventive or as a moral incentive. Fundamentally, their moral conflict appears to survive and to remain unchanged from one depression and one impulsive action to the next" (p. 134).

page 138
to expiate unconscious guilt:
Freud, *Standard Edition*, Vol. 14, "Some Character-Types Met With in Psycho-Analytic Work," writes about people who "might justly be described as criminals from a sense of guilt," whose misdeeds do not precede, but follow, their feelings of guilt and whose guilty acts actually serve to relieve their oppressive and free-floating guilt feelings because now the "guilt was at least attached to something" (p. 332).

page 138
psychopathic personalities:
In a troubling and fascinating book, *The Mask of Sanity*, Hervey Cleckley presents case after case of these psychopathic personalities. Although the book is marred by freewheeling assaults on a variety of ideas and people, it is a riveting account of a group of men and women who seem to have no sense of guilt or remorse, conscious or unconscious.

page 138
In a famous experiment:
The experiment is described in Milgram's book *Obedience to Authority*. The quotes appear on p. 10 and p. 5.

page 139
The philosopher Martin Buber:
Buber, "Guilt and Guilt Feelings," *Psychiatry*, Vol. 20, No. 2, p. 119, p. 118, p. 121, p. 128.

page 140
our conscience also contains our ego ideal:
In his *Standard Edition*, Vol. 22, "New Introductory Lectures on Psycho-Analysis," Freud writes that another important function of the superego is as "the vehicle of the ego ideal, by which the ego measures itself . . . and whose demand for ever greater perfection it strives to fulfill" (pp. 64–65). See also Schafer, "The Loving and Beloved Superego in Freud's Structural Theory," *The Psychoanalytic Study of the Child*, Vol. 15, pp. 163–188.

page 140
our lost narcissism lives on—in our ego ideal:
In Hartmann and Lowenstein's "Notes on the Superego," *The Psychoanalytic Study of the Child*, Vol. 17, the authors write that "the ego ideal can be considered a rescue operation for narcissism" (p. 61). And in *The Self and the Object World* Jacobson writes that by means of the ego ideal, "the superego, this unique human acquisition, becomes the one area in the psychic organization where . . . the child's grandiose wishful fantasies can find a safe refuge and can be maintained forever to the profit of the ego" (p. 94).

Jacobson also notes that because the ego ideal has a "double face," because it is a unification of idealized parents and idealized self, it also gratifies "the infantile longing . . . to be one with the love object. Even our never-ending struggle for oneness between ego and ego ideal reflects the enduring persistence of this desire" (p. 96). Joseph Sandler, in his "On the Concept of Superego," *The Psychoanalytic Study of the Child*, Vol. 15, makes a similar point when, speaking of the superego, he writes that "although it is often the agent of pain and destruction, its existence appears to be brought about by the child's attempt to transform paradise lost into paradise regained" (p. 159).

CHAPTER TEN   CHILDHOOD'S END

page 142
"I'm getting sick of this":
One version of this wonderful story, attributed to *The New Yorker*, appears in Fraiberg's *The Magic Years*, p. 250.

page 143
Freud labeled "latency":
Freud's *Standard Edition*, Vol. 7, "Three Essays on the Theory of Sexuality," introduced the concept of latency back in 1905. Much of the material on which I am basing the latency section of this chapter comes from a series of recent papers found in *The Course of Life*, Vol. 2, Greenspan and Pollock, eds.

In these discussions latency is seen, not as an absence of sexuality, but as a stage of relative calm between two more intense phases of sexual development. There is some debate about whether this relative calm is due to diminished instinctual urges or to increased coping mechanisms, but whatever the reason, our ego—at latency—seems to have more power vis-a-vis our id. During latency our sexual (and aggressive) urges are partly repressed (pushed out of consciousness) and partly sublimated (redirected) toward other activities—scholarly, social and athletic. In addition to the defenses of repression and sublimation, there is also the defense of reaction-formation where, by replacing unacceptable impulses with their opposites, we develop socially acceptable virtues, like—for example—cleanliness and modesty.

Interesting sidelight: Most of us come to latency having forgotten large portions of our pre-latency life—a family vacation, a former neighbor, a once extremely beloved baby-sitter. The reason is that, in repressing the passions of our oedipal stage, we repress the events surrounding those passions, too. And although we cannot obliterate them, we can bury them so deep that they are unavailable to our consciousness. The result is a universal condition called infantile amnesia, the loss of a part of ourself, the loss of our past. It is the psychological equivalent, you might say, of throwing out the baby with the bath water.

page 143
our latency phase may be linked to a biological clock:
It has been argued that the changes in neurobiological and cognitive development which occur at around age seven provide latency with many of its characteristics. These changes include the refinement of perceptual and motor skills; a maturing of our time and space orientation; the brain's development of feedback systems allowing for longer attention spans; and the development of the brain's frontal lobe, which seems to have a bearing on socialization. Among the cognitive changes of this period is the ability to perform what Piaget calls concrete operations, which

permits us—among other things—to form categories and to see a sameness despite apparent differences. These operations help us proceed from an egocentric to a more objective view by enabling us to see that what we know about Y can also apply to Z, thus helping us put ourself in another's shoes. As I discussed in a back-note for Chapter 9 (page 360), researchers have found a correlation between logical and moral reasoning. For a full discussion of the cognitive and physiological under-pinnings of latency, see Shapiro and Perry's "Latency Revisited," *The Psychoanalytic Study of the Child*, Vol. 31, pp. 79–105.

page 143

trouble taking on these tasks:

Learning difficulties, behavior difficulties, troubles with peer relationships, school phobias and homesickness are characteristic problems of latency children. So, because of the harshness of our new superego, is a hypersensitivity to criticism and an unreasonable demand on ourself for perfection. Indeed, at this age, we often project our harsh conscience onto somebody else and complain of a teacher or parent, "She's always picking on me," when in fact the person who is always picking on us is no one but us. A successful latency requires some modification of the strictness of our conscience and a capacity to live, at least some of the time, by the spirit instead of the letter of the law.

page 143

that parents are fallible:

In addition to realistically perceiving our parents as fallible and imperfect, many of us at latency develop a fantasy known as the "family romance." In this typical latency fantasy we imagine that we have been adopted, that we are not our parents' biological child and that our true biological parents are far more exalted, aristo-cratic people. In other words, though mom and dad are clods, I am by birth and blood a prince or princess.

page 144

"Eight Ages of Man":

In Erikson's *Childhood and Society*, his chapter entitled "Eight Ages of Man" describes a stage-by-stage series of critical points in human psychosocial development when there are "moments of decision between progress and regression, integration and retardation" (pp. 270–271). The issues to be determined at each of these ages are: basic trust versus basic mistrust, autonomy versus shame and doubt, initiative versus guilt, industry versus inferiority, identity versus role confusion, intimacy versus isolation, generativity versus stagnation and ego integrity versus despair.

Erikson notes that what he is speaking of here are not absolute achievements but "favorable ratios" of positive to negative, with the negatives remaining a "dynamic counterpart" throughout our life (p. 274).

page 144

"sooner or later, become dissatisfied":

Erikson, *Identity: Youth and Crisis*, p. 123.

page 144

Joseph Conrad:

In Conrad's *Heart of Darkness* Marlow says: "I don't like work,—no man does—but I like what is in the work,—the chance to find yourself. Your own reality—for yourself, not for others—what no other man can ever know" (p. 41).

page 144

flame-kindling grownup:

In Erikson's *Identity: Youth and Crisis* he writes: "Again and again in interviews with especially gifted and inspired people, one is told spontaneously and with a special glow that *one* teacher can be credited with having kindled the flame of hidden talent" (p. 125).

page 145
"And as I was green and carefree":
Thomas, "Fern Hill," *The Norton Anthology of Poetry*, Allison et al., eds., pp. 1166–1167.

page 146
"transition from barrenness to fertility":
The phrase is derived from Kestenberg's paper "Eleven, Twelve, Thirteen: Years of Transition from the Barrenness of Childhood to the Fertility of Adolescence" in *The Course of Life*, Vol. 2, Greenspan and Pollock, eds.

page 147
"My mother's always talking":
Blume, *Are You There God? It's Me, Margaret*, p. 25.

page 147
"Are you there God?":
Ibid., p. 37.

page 147
"that extended period of rage":
Roth, *Portnoy's Complaint*, pp. 40–41.

page 148
"that the assumption of responsibility":
Growing up as a form of homicide is discussed by analyst Hans Loewald in "The Waning of the Oedipus Complex," *Journal of the American Psychoanalytic Association*, Vol. 27, No. 4, pp. 751–775. The quoted material appears on p. 757. Later Loewald notes that "Parricide, if the child convincingly develops as an individual, is more than symbolic. . . . Not to shrink from blunt language, in our role as children of our parents, by genuine emancipation we do kill something vital in them—not all in one blow and not in all respects, but contributing to their dying" (p. 764). See also Modell's discussion of separation guilt in "On Having the Right to a Life: An Aspect of the Superego's Development," *The International Journal of Psycho-Analysis*, Vol. 46, part 3, pp. 323–331.

page 148
Zapped by hormones:
Girls generally mature two years before boys, though there are both early and late bloomers of both sexes. For most girls the onset of menstruation (menarche) has occurred by age fourteen. A good discussion of physical changes at puberty and the psychological reactions to them can be found in Morris Sklansky's "The Pubescent Years: Eleven to Fourteen," in *The Course of Life*, Vol. 2, Greenspan and Pollock, eds., pp. 265–292.

page 149
"If you are a girl":
Ephron, *Teenage Romance*, p. 115.

page 149
"to be different":
Esman quoting Schoenfeld in "Mid-Adolescence—Foundations for Later Psychopathology," in *The Course of Life*, Vol. 2, Greenspan and Pollock, eds., p. 421.

page 149

anorexia nervosa:

It has been found that girls suffering from anorexia nervosa have a near-delusional perception of themselves—even when down to skin and bones—as too fat, that "fat" is sometimes equated unconsciously with "pregnant" and that sexual features like breasts or menstruation may be a source of powerful shame and guilt. All these elements may intermingle with earlier disturbances in separation-individuation, and with an actual inability to recognize the body signal of "hunger," and with a fearful need to control a body which—in the spurts and explosions of puberty— seems to have gone utterly out of control. See Bruch's "The Sleeping Beauty: Escape From Change," in *The Course of Life*, Vol. 2, Greenspan and Pollock, eds., pp. 431–444.

page 150

so restless and twitchy and awkward:

"The rapidity of the growth spurt is in itself disturbing to the body image and may explain the physical awkwardness of some adolescents." See Sklansky, "The Pubescent Years: Eleven to Fourteen," in *The Course of Life*, Vol. 2, Greenspan and Pollock, eds., p. 272.

page 150

sex on the brain:

"Pubescence is usually followed by an onset or increase in genital masturbation." Ibid., p. 269.

page 150

agony to ecstasy:

Adolescents ". . . are subject to the variations in mood which result from unstable self-definition. Compensatory grandiosity in fantasy and behavior alternates with periods of low self-esteem and a sense of fragility." Ibid., p. 276.

page 150

capable of abstract logical thinking:

Jean Piaget writes that "the great novelty that characterizes adolescent thought and that starts around the age of 11 to 12, but does not reach its point of equilibrium until the age of 14 or 15—this novelty consists in detaching the concrete logic from the objects themselves, so that it can function on verbal or symbolic statements without other support. . . . The great novelty that results consists in the possibility of manipulating ideas in themselves and no longer in merely manipulating objects." See Piaget's "The Intellectual Development of the Adolescent," in *Adolescence: Psychosocial Perspectives*, Caplan and Lebovici, eds., p. 23.

page 150

parents as merely fallible:

"For most adolescents this deidealization is in the service of ego development and autonomy. . . . That the deidealization serves an intrapsychic growth process, rather than being simply an accurate assessment of the reality of the parent, is evident from the frequent exaggeration of their faults and the amount of affect that accompanies the faultfinding. Of course, parents naturally do not react amiably to this process. . . ." See Sklansky, "The Pubescent Years: Eleven to Fourteen," in *The Course of Life*, Vol. 2, Greenspan and Pollock, eds., p. 277.

page 150

"that it is normal for an adolescent":

Anna Freud, "Adolescence," *The Psychoanalytic Study of the Child*, Vol. 13, p. 275. While this paper (pp. 255–278) asserts the universality of turmoil in adolescence, a study of a group of normal adolescents whose progression through adolescence was apparently untumultuous is described by Offer in his paper "Adolescent Development: A Normative Perspective," *The Course of Life*, Vol. 2, Greenspan and Pollock, eds., pp. 357–372. However, it seems widely agreed that some turmoil is inevitable and universal, whether or not it is accompanied by overt disruptions.

page 151
the sexual stew of adolescence:
The intensification of sexual urges at puberty reactivates the old oedipal triangle, with young adolescents experiencing erotic fantasies and feelings about their parents which are sometimes quite conscious and explicit, evoking anxiety or shame or guilt. (Because of these reawakened oedipal stirrings, for instance, adolescent girls do not feel comfortable being hugged by daddy or sitting on his lap, while adolescent boys feel a similar uneasiness with their mothers.) However, in contrast to the earlier resolution of oedipal struggles, when sexual impulses were more or less repressed, adolescents must manage the tricky task of renouncing incestuous sexual wishes without renouncing sexual wishes in general.

page 151
"develop the prerequisites":
Erikson, *Identity: Youth and Crisis*, p. 91.

page 152
toning down of our conscience's harshness:
Analyst Aaron Esman writes that "adolescence affords an opportunity for the reshaping of the ego ideal and a readjustment of the superego." The ego ideal, he says, is "more closely attuned to current reality, closer to consciousness and normally less peremptory in nature . . ." while the superego "loses its categorical all or nothing quality. . . ." From "Mid-Adolescence—Foundations for Later Psychopathology," *The Course of Life*, Vol. 2, Greenspan and Pollock, eds., p. 427.

page 153
There is a course to adolescence:
Different researchers may place some of these struggles at different points in the stages of adolescence, but all seem to agree that dealing with pubertal changes is the focus of the first stage of adolescence and that separation is a pervasive issue.

page 153
"an intensity of grief":
In Martha Wolfenstein's "How Is Mourning Possible?" found in *The Psychoanalytic Study of the Child*, Vol. 21, pp. 93–123, she quotes Jacobson on the intensity of grief in adolescence (p. 114) and A. E. Housman's poem about the land of lost content (p. 115).

page 154
College-bound Roger:
Dr. Cheryl Kurash, in her paper "The Transition to College: A Study of Separation-Individuation in Late Adolescence" (unpublished), divides this transition into three subphases: anticipatory, leavetaking, and settling in. During the anticipatory subphase, she writes, "adolescents renew their efforts to further distance themselves from their parents. . . . Perhaps most notable is the increased expression of aggression toward both parents" (pp. 71–72).

page 154
"All through senior year":
Ibid., p. 1.

page 154
depression, breakdowns, suicide:
This is not to say that such adolescent problems are always the result of separation difficulties. See Noshpitz's "Disturbances in Early Adolescent Development," *The Course of Life*, Vol. 2, Greenspan and Pollock, eds., pp. 309–356, for an excellent review of the developmental problems of adolescence.

page 155
the rate of suicide:
The suicide statistics are from the National Center for Health Statistics.

page 155
"Don't ever tell anybody":
Salinger, *The Catcher in the Rye*, p. 214.

page 155
Henry David Thoreau:
See Edel, *Stuff of Sleep and Dreams*, "The Mystery of Walden Pond," pp. 47–65. The "buckle on your knapsack" and "methinks" material appears on p. 54, and Edel's comment about "Thoreau, shut up in his childhood" appears on p. 62.

page 155
"Adolescent individuation":
Blos, *On Adolescence*, p. 12.

page 156
"I keep picturing":
Salinger, *The Catcher in the Rye*, p. 173.

page 157
"warn of the utterly destructive consequences":
Bettelheim, *Freud and Man's Soul*, p. 25.

page 157
"There is no guilt, my man":
MacLeish, *J. B.*, p. 123.

page 158
"The two Greek goddesses":
Blos, *On Adolescence*, p. 195.

CHAPTER ELEVEN   DREAMS AND REALITIES

page 161
dearest megalomaniacal dreams:
Blos, in his book *On Adolescence*, writes: "Adolescent individuation . . . brings some of the dearest megalomaniacal dreams of childhood to an irrevocable end. They must now be relegated entirely to fantasy: their fulfillments can never again be considered seriously" (p. 12).

page 161
they press themselves upon us in sneaky ways:
According to psychoanalytic theory, conflicts over repressed impulses may result in neurotic symptoms; and slips of the tongue, lapses of memory, accidents and other similar mishaps do not occur by chance but are intentional acts unconsciously motivated. (For instance, a mishap like spilling the borscht may occur

when a hostile impulse—get that rival!—escapes from repression.) See, in the *Standard Edition*, "Introductory Lectures on Psycho-Analysis," Freud's discussion of The Paths to the Formation of Symptoms (Vol. 16) and Parapraxes (Vol. 15).

page 164

the omnipotence of thoughts:

In Freud's *Standard Edition*, Vol. 17, "The Uncanny," he discusses "the old, animistic conception of the universe" characterized "by the subject's narcissistic overvaluation of his own mental processes; by the belief in the omnipotence of thoughts. . . ." He says that "each one of us has been through a phase of individual development corresponding to this animistic stage in primitive man, that none of us has passed through it without preserving certain residues and traces of it" (p. 240).

page 164

"It is as though":

Ibid., p. 248.

page 165

the vibrant, secret language of our unconscious:

This language is different from, and alien to, the orderly ways we consciously use our mind. It relies on what is called "primary-process thinking." This is the mode of "thought" we use before we learn to think with logic and reason, before we achieve the capacity for grown-up "secondary-process thinking." There is a beautiful description of primary-process thinking in Ann and Barry Ulanov's book *Religion and the Unconscious*, pp. 26–32. See also Brenner's lucid book for the general reader, *An Elementary Textbook of Psychoanalysis*, pp. 45–53. But the original discussion of primary-process thinking is found in Freud's *Standard Edition*, Vols. 4 and 5, "The Interpretation of Dreams," a dazzling exploration into the mysteries of unconscious mental functioning.

page 166

"My mother was speaking":

Altman, *The Dream in Psychoanalysis*, p. 10, provides this fine example of condensation.

page 166

"I was standing":

Ibid., p. 13, provides this example of displacement.

page 166

A woman dreams of a German officer:

Psychoanalyst Justin Frank (private communication) provided this example.

page 166

This dream that we recall:

In "The Interpretation of Dreams" (see note above, "the vibrant . . . unconscious"), Freud discusses the process by which our unconscious dream thoughts and wishes (the *latent content*) are transformed into the dream we recall upon waking (the *manifest content*).

Freud also says that dreams are given their shape by two forces, one of which constructs a wish and the other of which censors the expression of that wish. The bizarre and distorted qualities of the manifest dream are thus reflections of its primary-process nature, of the secondary revision and of the further distortions imposed on it by its need to be acceptable to the dream censorship.

page 166

Hugo's dream:

Altman presents and discusses Hugo's dream in *The Dream in Psychoanalysis*, pp. 126–128.

page 167

Freud says every dream contains a wish:

Although the forbidden wishes of our childhood arise from the part of our psyche called the id, a dream is not *merely* the expression of id wishes, for even during dreaming our ego's intentions and our superego's constraints make themselves felt, insist on having their say. Our dreams, then, are a compromise that is reached between these three conflicting forces—id, ego, and superego.

It also should be noted that many students of dreams today are less single-minded than Freud about perceiving the dream's *only* function as wish fulfillment. Erikson writes, for instance, that dreams "not only fulfill naked wishes of sexual license, of unlimited dominance and of unrestricted destructiveness; . . . they also lift the dreamer's isolation, appease his conscience and preserve his identity, each in specific and instructive ways" (p. 55, reference follows). For material on post-Freudian dream theory, see Erikson's "The Dream Specimen of Psychoanalysis," *Journal of the American Psychoanalytic Association*, Vol. 2, No. 1, pp. 5–56; Rycroft's *The Innocence of Dreams;* and *The Dream in Clinical Practice*, Joseph Natterson, ed. In this last volume, however, Samuel Eisenstein notes in his "The Dream in Psychoanalysis" that most analysts still subscribe to Freud's view of "the central role of wish fulfillment in the dream" (p. 362).

page 167

waking or sleeping fantasies:

Freud writes eloquently of fantasy—which his translators spell "phantasy"—in *Standard Edition*, Vol. 16, "Introductory Lectures on Psycho-Analysis (Part 3)." He states: "Every desire takes before long the form of picturing its own fulfillment; there is no doubt that dwelling upon imaginary wish-fulfillments brings satisfaction with it. . . . The creation of the mental realm of phantasy finds a perfect parallel in the establishment of 'reservations' or 'nature reserves' in places where the requirements of agriculture, communications and industry threaten to bring about changes in the original face of the earth. . . . A nature reserve preserves its original state. . . . Everything, including what is useless and even what is noxious, can grow and proliferate there as it pleases. The mental realm of phantasy is just such a reservation withdrawn from the reality principle."

Freud notes that while the "best-known productions of phantasy are the so-called 'day-dreams,' " the "night-dream is at bottom nothing other than a day-dream that has been made utilizable owing to the liberation of the instinctual impulses at night, and that has been distorted by the form assumed by mental activity at night." He also notes "that there are unconscious [as well as conscious] day-dreams" (pp. 372–373).

page 167

"healthy adult":

My description of the "healthy adult" draws heavily from McGlashan and Miller's "The Goals of Psychoanalysis and Psychoanalytic Psychotherapy," *Archives of General Psychiatry*, Vol. 39, pp. 377–388. The authors note that many of the aims discussed in their paper "are synonymous with general mental health and emotional maturity" (p. 378).

page 168

"reality testing":

A discussion of reality-testing can be found in Freud's *Standard Edition*, Vol. 14, "A Metapsychological Supplement to the Theory of Dreams," pp. 230–234.

CHAPTER TWELVE   CONVENIENCE FRIENDS . . .

page 172
the curse of ambivalence:

In Freud's *Standard Edition*, Vol. 13, "Totem and Taboo," he writes: "In almost every case where there is an intense emotional attachment to a particular person we find that behind the tender love there is a concealed hostility in the unconscious. This is the classical example, the prototype, of the ambivalence of human emotions. This ambivalence is present to a greater or less amount in the innate disposition of everyone" (p. 60). In the same volume, "Some Reflections on Schoolboy Psychology," Freud writes that ambivalent feelings in later life have their origins in early childhood, when the child's love/hate feelings toward his parents and siblings become fixed. "All those whom he gets to know later become substitute figures for these first objects of his feelings. . . . His later acquaintances are thus obliged to take over a kind of emotional heritage" (p. 243).

page 172
Dinah, wife and mother:

Robb Forman Dew, *Dale Loves Sophie to Death*, p. 132, p. 131, p. 134.

page 172
Freud argued that all love relationships:

In Freud's *Standard Edition*, Vol. 18, "Group Psychology and the Analysis of the Ego," he writes: "The nucleus of what we mean by love naturally consists . . . in sexual love with sexual union as its aim. But we do not separate from this . . . on the one hand, self-love, and on the other, love for parents and children, friendship and love for humanity. . . . Our justification lies in the fact that psycho-analytic research has taught us that all these tendencies are an expression of the same instinctual impulses; in relations between the sexes these impulses force their way towards sexual union, but in other circumstances they are diverted from this aim or are prevented from reaching it" (p. 90).

page 173
"no individual is limited":

Freud, *Standard Edition*, Vol. 23, "An Outline of Psychoanalysis," p. 188. Some of Freud's other discussions of bisexuality appear in *Standard Edition*, Vol. 7, "Three Essays on the Theory of Sexuality," pp. 141–148, and Vol. 21, "Civilization and Its Discontents," pp. 105–106 (footnote). A footnote in Vol. 19, "The Ego and the Id," points out that in writing about bisexuality to his friend Wilhelm Fliess, Freud commented: "I am accustoming myself to regarding every sexual act as an event between four individuals" (p. 33).

page 174
having "sexual feelings toward someone of the same sex":

Group for the Advancement of Psychiatry, *Friends and Lovers in the College Years*, p. 88. For a discussion of homosexual relationships, see Chapter 7.

page 174

"There need not be":

Shere Hite, *The Hite Report*, p. 365.

page 174

"much as pink":

Leo Rangell, "On Friendship," *Journal of the American Psychoanalytic Association*, Vol. 11, No. 1, p. 5. Rangell is quoting Hart, who has this to say about Freud's discussion of friendship: "Friendliness and friendship are referred to as if they were dilute editions of love, much as pink is regarded as a dilution of red."

page 174

"differ from one's main relationship":

James McMahon, "Intimacy Among Friends and Lovers," *Intimacy*, Fisher and Stricker, eds., p. 302.

page 175

"no man or woman can be all things to another":

Ibid., p. 304. See also anthropologist Robert Brain's *Friends and Lovers*, where he, too, vigorously denies "that the needs of a man and a woman for love and friendship can be satisfied by one single partnership. . . . The man who drinks with his friends every night often loves them as much as he loves his wife—in a different way. And his wife loves her friend next door, who comes in and watches television with her every afternoon" (pp. 262–263).

page 175

"If I told my wife":

Wagenvoord and Bailey (producers), *Men: A Book for Women*, p. 277.

page 175

men friends to be less open and intimate:

In Robert Bell's *Worlds of Friendship* he writes: "The evidence clearly indicates that female patterns of friendship are much more revealing and intimate than those found among men" (p. 62). In his interviews with 101 women and 65 men, Bell found that their response to his question about how many friends they had averaged 4.7 for women and 3.2 for men (p. 63). He writes: "The fact that men are trapped within themselves has come through in our interviews. Women overwhelmingly reveal many of their fears, anxieties and insecurities to their best friends, while men overwhelmingly do not" (p. 80). For further discussion of female friendships and male friendships, see chapters 3 and 4 of Bell's book.

page 175

"There are some things":

Ibid., pp. 81–82.

page 176

"I love my women friends":

Ibid., p. 63.

page 176

the celebrated friendships of myth and folklore:

Ibid. Bell writes: "The great friendships recorded in history have been between men. In the past when friendships among men have been romanticized and eulogized, they have been friendships reflecting bravery, valor and physical sacrifice in coming to the aid of another. . . . But rarely have the recollections been to celebrate interpersonal relationships of feeling, understanding and compassion of one male for another" (p. 75).

page 177

"men are for friendships":
Ibid., p. 104.
    page 177
    In one study:
Ibid. Both interviews appear on p. 111.
    page 177
    Lucy, a married woman:
The interview with Lucy appears on p. 38 of Judith Viorst's "Friends, Good Friends
—and Such Good Friends," *Redbook*, October 1977, pp. 31–32, 38.
    page 177
    one of the following categories:
See Rangell's discussion of the three categories of friendship in "On Friendship,"
Journal of the American Psychoanalytic Association, Vol. 11, No. 1, pp. 30–31.
    page 178
    "not quite a 'friendship' ":
Ibid., p. 40.
    page 178
    both lovers and best friends:
In Bell's *Worlds of Friendship* he writes that in his research "about one-half of the
women named their husbands as a very close friend. About 60 percent of the married men named their wives as a very close friend" (p. 125). He points out, however,
that these figures also show, of course, that about half of all married people do *not*
consider their spouses a close friend.
    page 178
    "a little bit of sex":
In Bell's *Worlds of Friendship* he cites a *Psychology Today* reader survey which found
"that about three-fourths of the respondents felt that friendships with someone of
the opposite sex were different from same-sex friendships. A major reason given for
the difference was that sexual tensions complicated the relationship" (pp. 98–99).
    page 178
    Friendship, like civilization, is bought at the price:
In his paper "On Friendship," *Journal of the American Psychoanalytic Association*,
Vol. 11, No. 1, Rangell writes: "True friendship is a human trait which goes along
with, and makes possible, civilization. Both are at the expense of instincts" (p. 49).
    page 179
    the following categories of friendship:
These categories and interviews are adapted from J. Viorst, "Friends, Good Friends
—and Such Good Friends," *Redbook*, October 1977, pp. 31–32, 38.
    page 180
    "To be her friend":
Jane Howard, *Families*, p. 263.
    page 181
    "growth demands relatedness":
James McMahon, "Intimacy Among Friends and Lovers," *Intimacy*, Fisher and
Stricker, eds., p. 297.
    page 181
    He quotes philosopher Martin Buber:
Ibid.
    page 181

"Rosie is my friend":
J. Viorst, *Rosie and Michael*, unpaged.
    page 183
    "On Friendship":
Cicero, "On Friendship," *The Harvard Classics*, Vol. 9, *Letters of Marcus Tullius Cicero and Letters of Gaius Plinius Caecilius Secundus*, Charles Eliot, ed., p. 15 ("how can life . . ." and "a complete accord . . . ") and p. 29 ("stainless" and "There must be complete harmony . . .").
    page 183
    "may be more likely":
Bell, *Worlds of Friendship*, p. 122. He is describing the ideas of sociologist Georg Simmel, who contrasted the friendship ideal of the past—"total psychological intimacy"—with our modern, partial, differentiated friendships.
    page 183
    "If Rosie told me a secret":
J. Viorst, *Rosie and Michael*, unpaged.
    page 184
    "sacred and miraculous":
The lovely description of friendship as "sacred and miraculous" appears in Jane Howard's *Families*, p. 265.

CHAPTER THIRTEEN   LOVE AND HATE IN THE MARRIED STATE

    page 185
    "normal, crucial beginning":
Kernberg, "Adolescent Sexuality in the Light of Group Process," *The Psychoanalytic Quarterly*, Vol. 49, No. 1, p. 46.
    page 186
    "Last night, ah, yesternight":
This verse is from Ernest Dowson's poem "Non sum qualis eram bonae sub regno Cynarae," *The Norton Anthology of Poetry*, Allison et al., eds., pp. 937–938.
    page 186
    In Freud's discussions of love:
See Hitschmann's paper on "Freud's Conception of Love," *The International Journal of Psycho-Analysis*, Vol. 33, Part 4, pp. 421–428. See also Freud's discussion of Being in Love and Hypnosis in *Standard Edition*, Vol. 18, "Group Psychology and the Analysis of the Ego."
    page 186
    "The silken texture":
Howells, *The Rise of Silas Lapham*, p. 43.
    page 186
    "One person, without any hostility":
The statement comes from University of Pennsylvania sociologist Otto Pollak and is quoted on p. 5 of Israel Charny's paper "Marital Love and Hate," *Family Process*, Vol. 8, No. 1, pp. 1–24.
    page 186
    Psychologist Israel Charny:

I. Charny, "Marital Love and Hate," *Family Process*, Vol. 8, No. 1. "The myth . . ." p. 3; "empirically it cannot . . ." p. 3; "a wise balancing . . ." pp. 2–3.

    page 187

    "So they were married":

Louis MacNeice, "Les Sylphides," *Modern Poetry*, Mack, Dean, Frost, eds., p. 296.

    page 187

    a doctor's wife named Emma:

Gustave Flaubert, *Madame Bovary*. The "marvelous realm . . ." appears on p. 140. "Her too lofty . . ." and "the sole object" appear on p. 94. "That marvelous passion . . ." appears on p. 34.

    page 188

    "Marriage," writes anthropologist Bronislaw Malinowski:

The Malinowski quote appears in Nena O'Neill's book *The Marriage Premise*, p. 36.

    page 188

    "The true man or woman":

Kathrin Perutz, *Marriage Is Hell*, pp. 96–97. Both anecdotal and research material support this contention: See, for instance, Masters and Johnson's book *The Pleasure Bond*, where the sex therapists state, "Sex in a warm, emotionally committed relationship may change in character, and sexual response may become diffused after a while. It may not always reach the peaks of excitement that are sometimes experienced by a man and woman in their early, experimental encounters" (p. 99). And a married woman writing to me from Pennsylvania voices a frequently heard complaint: "Expectation: No matter what else happens in your lives, the sex part will always stay fresh and exciting. . . . The truth is . . . there is the sheer problem of boredom. I defy any couple married more than ten years or so to say this hasn't been the case."

    page 189

    "I bring the children":

J. Viorst, *It's Hard to Be Hip Over Thirty and Other Tragedies of Married Life*, "Sex Is Not So Sexy Anymore," p. 63.

    page 190

    "multiple forms of transcendence":

O. Kernberg, "Boundaries and Structure in Love Relations," *Journal of the American Psychoanalytic Association*, Vol. 25, No. 1, p. 99. See his entire section on Sexual Passion and the Crossing of Boundaries in Love Relations, pp. 93–104.

    page 190

    "I have sought love":

B. Russell, *The Autobiography of Bertrand Russell, 1872–1914*, p. 3.

    page 190

    "haven in a heartless world":

The phrase is the title of Christopher Lasch's book *Haven in a Heartless World*.

    page 191

    "intimate enemies":

The phrase derives from Bach and Wyden's book on how to fight fair in love and marriage, *The Intimate Enemy*.

    page 191

    Listen to Millie:

J. Viorst, "Sometimes I Hate My Husband," *Redbook*, November 1976, pp. 73–74. The interview with Millie appears on p. 73.

page 192
"to distinguish between their conscious":
The Kubie quote appears on pp. 119–120 of Jessie Bernard's book *The Future of Marriage.*

page 192
"complementary marriages":
For a discussion of marital complementarity, see Bela Mittelmann's "Complementary Neurotic Reactions in Intimate Relationships," *The Psychoanalytic Quarterly,* Vol. 13, No. 4, pp. 479–491. He concludes: "Because of the continuous and intimate nature of marriage, every neurosis in a married person is strongly anchored in the marriage relationship. The presence of a complementary neurotic reaction in the marriage partner is an important aspect of the married patient's neurosis" (p. 491). See also Henry Dicks's classic work, *Marital Tensions.* Other references to complementarity can be found in Jessie Bernard's *The Future of Marriage,* where she refers to Robert Ryder's twenty-one different patterns of mating and Robert Winch's "fourfold classification of matings: an Ibsenite mating, in which the husband is dominant and nurturant, the wife the opposite; a Thurberian mating, in which the husband is submissive and nurturant rather than the wife; a Master-Servant Girl mating, in which the husband is dominant and the wife receptive; and a Mother-Son mating, in which the husband is submissive and receptive" (p. 119).

page 193
"couples in collusion":
The phrase, and (with some modifications) the preceding discussion of shared assumptions in marriage, derive from Jurg Willi's book *Couples in Collusion.*

page 193
projective identification:
This definition and an excellent discussion of projective identification can be found in Thomas Ogden's book *Projective Identification and Psychotherapeutic Technique.* I am also indebted to therapist Anne Stephansky for a beautifully lucid explanation of this difficult concept.

page 194
"If a woman has been taught":
See "What Qualities Do Women Most Value in Husbands?" *Viewpoints,* Vol. 16, No. 5, pp. 77–90. Harriet Lerner's comments appear on p. 89.

page 194
A mid-thirties wife:
See Giovachinni's paper "Characterological Aspects of Marital Interaction" and the discussants' comments in *The Psychoanalytic Forum,* Vol. 2, No. 1, pp. 7–29. The quoted phrases appear on p. 9.

page 195
Ironically, the thrust of human development:
In Kernberg's "Boundaries and Structure in Love Relations," *Journal of the American Psychoanalytic Association,* Vol. 25, No. 1, pp. 81–114, he writes that in his analysis of love relations he was "forced to conclude that emotional maturity is no guarantee for a couple's nonconflictual stability. The very capacity for loving in depth and for realistically appreciating another person over the years . . . may both reconfirm and deepen the relationship or lead it to disillusionment and termination. The complication is that both individuals and couples change, and that . . . developing maturity may open new degrees of freedom in the couple's re-examining realistically the basis of their life together" (p. 84).

page 195
"introduce[d] us to the human situation":
Dinnerstein, *The Mermaid and the Minotaur*, p. 234.

page 196
"while much of our pleasure":
Ibid., pp. 5–6. While conceding that there are, of course, many exceptions to the rule, Dinnerstein mobilizes arguments to show "how female-dominated child care guarantees male insistence upon, and female compliance with, a double standard of sexual behavior"; how "it guarantees that women and men will regard each other, respectively, as silly overgrown children"; and how "it guarantees certain forms of antagonism—rampant in men, and largely shared by women as well—against women," including the conviction that women are defective, untrustworthy and malevolent (p. 36). Regarding this antagonism, Dinnerstein notes that there is no purpose in reproaching men "for a hatred they are bound to feel; when they claim—in many cases sincerely—not to feel it, there is no reason at all to believe them; when they recognize and deplore it in themselves, there is no sense at all in trusting them to keep it under control" (p. 90).

page 196
"So long as the first parent":
Ibid., pp. 111–112.

page 196
in the process of forming their gender identity:
See the discussion of gender-identity formation in this book, Chapter Eight, "Anatomy and Destiny."

page 197
"intimate strangers":
The phrase is the title of Dr. Rubin's book *Intimate Strangers*, which argues the nurture, not nature, theory of male-female psychological differences. Like Dorothy Dinnerstein in *The Mermaid and the Minotaur*, Dr. Rubin believes that men would have less trouble with intimacy, and girls would have less trouble with autonomy, if fathers were as involved as mothers with child-rearing.

page 197
"The whole goddam business":
Rubin, *Intimate Strangers*, p. 66.

page 198
"more wives than husbands report marital frustration":
Bernard, *The Future of Marriage*, pp. 26–27.

page 199
"conform more to husbands' expectations":
Ibid., p. 39.

page 199
"There are two marriages":
Ibid., p. 14.

page 199
"demonstrate this need":
Ibid., p. 53.

page 199
"the demands men and women make":
Ibid., "the demands . . ." p. 289; "will continue . . ." p. 289; "intrinsically tragic . . ." pp. 265–266.

page 200
"cat and dog" marriages:
Dicks, in *Marital Tensions*, refers to cat and dog relationships on p. 52 and p. 69, and discusses those unions where there is "perpetual sunshine without a shadow" on p. 73. In Bowlby's *Loss*, pp. 209–210, there is reference to Cat and Dog marriages and Babes in the Wood marriages, the first characterized by perpetual conflict and the second by resolute denial of conflict.

page 200
Rachel's feelings:
J. Viorst, "Sometimes I Hate My Husband," *Redbook*, November 1976, pp. 73–74. The interview with Rachel appears on p. 74.

page 200
Connie, a gentle woman:
Ibid. The interview with Connie appears on p. 74.

page 201
Perhaps, says psychoanalyst Leon Altman:
In Altman's discussion of love in "Some Vicissitudes of Love," *Journal of the American Psychoanalytic Association*, Vol. 25, No. 1, pp. 35–52, he writes: "All the clinical evidence we have, including our own personal experience, will testify to the presence of aggression and hate in the midst of what may seem the most perfect love affair. . . . The need to disown hate might even be the root cause of our need to place so much emphasis on love, to ask so much of it. . . . Perhaps man could love more if he could also hate cheerfully" (p. 43).

page 201
No aggression; no love:
See Lorenz's book *On Aggression*, particularly Chapter 11, "The Bond." Citing evidence from animal studies, he concludes that "aggression can certainly exist without its counterpart, love, but conversely there is no love without aggression" (p. 217).

page 201
"transforms a deep love relation":
See Kernberg's "Love, the Couple and the Group: A Psychoanalytic Frame," *The Psychoanalytic Quarterly*, Vol. 49, No. 1, pp. 78–108. The quote is on p. 83. Dicks, in *Marital Tensions*, is in agreement when he writes: "The opposite to love is not hate. These two always co-exist so long as there is a live relationship. The opposite to love is indifference" (p. 133).

page 201
"an attempt to arrive":
Erikson, *Childhood and Society*, p. 262.

page 201
"identity searching":
Ibid., p. 264.

page 202
open us to gratitude:
For a discussion of gratitude and other aspects of love, see Martin Bergmann's wide-ranging paper, "On the Intrapsychic Function of Falling in Love," *The Psychoanalytic Quarterly*, Vol. 49, No. 1, pp. 56–77.

page 202
"All human relationships must end":

O. Kernberg, *Object Relations Theory and Clinical Psychoanalysis*, p. 238.

page 202

"And down by the brimming river":

These verses are from Auden's poem "As I Walked Out One Evening," found in *Modern Poetry*, Mack, Dean, Frost, eds., pp. 184–185.

page 204

beloved enemies:

The phrase is from Altman's paper "Marriage—Dream and Reality," summarized in the "Bertram D. Lewin Memorial Symposium: Psychoanalytic Perspectives on Love and Marriage," *Journal of the Philadelphia Association for Psychoanalysis*, Vol. 2, 1975, pp. 191–201. "Even the most devoted mate, he states, can be one's beloved enemy and the marriage is the opportunity for a state of siege or battle in full array" (p. 193).

page 204

"love forever; hate never":

The phrase is from Benedek's paper "Ambivalence, Passion and Love," *Journal of the American Psychoanalytic Association*, Vol. 25, No. 1, pp. 53–79. "The ethos of marriage demands a great deal, probably the impossible," she writes; "love forever, hate never" (p. 77).

CHAPTER FOURTEEN   SAVING THE CHILDREN

page 206

"she felt this thing that she called life":

Virginia Woolf, *To the Lighthouse*, p. 92.

page 206

The World According to Garp:

In John Irving's novel, Garp and Helen warn their children, Duncan and Walt, about the undertow. One day, watching Walt at the water's edge peering uneasily into the waves, they ask what he's looking for. "I'm trying to see the Under Toad," he replies. And, "Long after the monster was clarified for Walt, ('Under*tow*, dummy, not Under Toad!' Duncan had howled), Garp and Helen evoked the beast as a way of referring to their own sense of danger" (p. 341).

page 207

One father says:

J. Viorst, "Letting Go: Why It's Hard to Let Children Grow Up," *Redbook*, May 1980, pp. 42, 44. This interview appears on p. 44.

page 207

"A man who cannot stand":

Louis Simpson, "The Goodnight," *Sound and Sense*, Laurence Perrine, ed., pp. 133–134.

page 207

"It only recently":

J. Viorst, "Letting Go: Why It's Hard to Let Children Grow Up," *Redbook*, May 1980, pp. 42, 44. This interview appears on p. 44.

page 208

Consider this mother:
Ibid., p. 42.
page 208
Selena who, as a child:
Ibid. This interview appears on p. 42.
page 208
the "too-good" mother:
In a paper called "The Too-Good Mother," *The International Journal of Psycho-Analysis*, Vol. 45, Part 1, pp. 85–88, Robert Shields takes off from Winnicott's concept of the good-enough mother and discusses the mother who sees herself "only as the supplier of infinite satisfactions."
page 209
"had from early on":
H. Kohut, *The Restoration of the Self*, p. 146. See his discussion of "The Psychoanalyst's Child," pp. 146–151. Kohut calls such insights "distorted empathy," because while these parents' "empathic grasp of certain details . . . was often quite accurate," they were "out of tune with their children's maturational needs" (p. 150).
page 209
I am told of a mother:
J. Viorst, "Letting Go: Why It's Hard to Let Children Grow Up," *Redbook*, May 1980, pp. 42, 44. This interview appears on p. 44.
page 209
"a mother might need to give up the fantasy":
T. Berry Brazelton and Catherine Buttenwieser, "Early Intervention in a Pediatric Multidisciplinary Clinic," *Infants and Parents*, Sally Provence, ed., p. 13.
page 210
"In erotic love":
E. Fromm, *The Art of Loving*, p. 51.
page 211
"goodness of fit":
A good discussion of mother-child "fit" can be found in "Infants, Mothers and Their Interaction: A Quantitative Clinical Approach to Developmental Assessment" by Stanley Greenspan and Alicia Lieberman, *The Course of Life*, Vol. 1, pp. 271–312, Greenspan and Pollock, eds. A detailed assessment of "goodness of fit" based on four sets of samples of mother-child interactions begins on p. 289.
page 211
"The mother's love":
Winnicott, *Collected Papers*, "Psychoses and Child Care," p. 223.
page 211
stop being that all-accommodating mother:
Ibid. In Winnicott's *Collected Papers*, "Mind and Its Relation to the Psyche-Soma," p. 246, he calls this a "graduated failure of adaptation."
page 211
"primary maternal preoccupation":
Winnicott relates the special intensity of the mother-child bond to what he calls "primary maternal preoccupation," described as "a very special psychiatric condition of the mother" which "gradually develops and becomes a state of heightened sensitivity" toward the end of pregnancy and for a few weeks after birth. The mother's state of profound attachment to, and identification with, her baby allows

her "to adapt delicately and sensitively to the infant's needs at the very beginning," and is, in Winnicott's view, a normal sickness from which mothers eventually recover (p. 302). See his *Collected Papers*, "Primary Maternal Preoccupation."

See Winnicott's *The Maturational Processes and the Facilitating Environment*, "The Theory of the Parent-Infant Relationship," for the statements beginning "to let go . . ." (p. 53) and "a difficult thing . . ." (p. 54).

page 211

"the emotional growth of the mother":

M. Mahler, *The Psychological Birth of the Human Infant*, p. 79. Mahler comments on the various reactions the mothers in her study had to their children's separation-individuation. One mother, for instance, could accept her little boy "only as a symbiotic part of herself and . . . actively interfered with his attempts to move away" (p. 67). Still other mothers "liked the closeness of the symbiotic phase but once this phase was over they would have liked their children to be 'grown up' already" (p. 66). Other mothers, who had been very anxious in the early phases of mothering, were "greatly relieved when their children became less fragile and vulnerable and somewhat more independent" (p. 66).

page 212

The good-enough mother, Winnicott writes:

Winnicott, *Collected Papers*, "Paediatrics and Psychiatry," pp. 160–161, offers this list of "the following things about a mother [which] stand out as vitally important."

page 212

"The loving mother teaches her child":

In *The Psychological Birth of the Human Infant*, Mahler credits E. J. Anthony with discovering this illustrative passage by Kierkegaard (pp. 72–73).

page 212

And we will renegotiate our relationship:

See the discussion of stages of parenthood in "The Experience of Separation-Individuation in Infancy and Its Reverberations Through the Course of Life: Maturity, Senescence and Sociological Implications," Irving Sternschein (reporter), *Journal of the American Psychoanalytic Association*, Vol. 21, No. 3, pp. 633–645.

page 212

"Each transition":

J. Kestenberg, "The Effect on Parents of the Child's Transition into and out of Latency," *Parenthood: Its Psychology and Psychopathology*, E. James Anthony and Therese Benedek, eds., p. 290.

page 213

"Not one of us":

Haim Ginott, *Between Parent and Child*, p. 92.

page 213

"I'd vowed to be rational":

This statement, from a mother of two girls now grown, appears in Shirley Radl's book *Mother's Day Is Over*, p. 128.

page 214

"tendency of adults to replay old fears and conflicts":

Group for the Advancement of Psychiatry, *The Joys and Sorrows of Parenthood*, p. 41. The book offers this example: "A physician's eldest daughter was sensitive, high-strung and emotional, like her grandfather. Her father had always hated and feared his father's volatility and temper tantrums, which he regarded as evil and self-centered. He had coped with his father's emotional demands by being a hard worker and helper and by a keen sensitivity to his moods. He could forestall his father's rage by anticipating his demands and being a model son. His attitude toward his daughter was suspicious and critical. Although he tried at times to appease her, he more often showed the resentment and anger that had been buried because of his fear" (p. 41).

page 214

"still there is only one image":

Jane Lazarre, from the preface of *The Mother Knot*, pp. vii–viii.

page 215

"The baby is an interference":

D. W. Winnicott, *Collected Papers*, "Hate in the Countertransference," p. 201.

page 215

"I am angry with my baby":

Jane Lazarre, *The Mother Knot*, p. 59.

page 216

the True Dilemma Theory of Parenthood:

See Group for the Advancement of Psychiatry, *The Joys and Sorrows of Parenthood*, pp. 43–44.

page 216

babies are born with specific temperaments:

See Chess and Alexander, "Temperament in the Normal Infant," *Individual Differences in Children*, Jack Westman, ed., for their discussion of temperamental individuality.

page 217

"the importance of innate (constitutional) factors":

In Freud's *Standard Edition*, Vol. 12, "The Dynamics of Transference," this footnote appears on p. 99: "I take this opportunity of defending myself against the mistaken charge of having denied the importance of innate (constitutional) factors because I have stressed that of infantile impressions. A charge such as this arises from the restricted nature of what men look for in the field of causation; in contrast to what ordinarily holds good in the real world, people prefer to be satisfied with a single causative factor. Psychoanalysis has talked a lot about the accidental factors in aetiology and little about the constitutional ones; but that is only because it was able to contribute something fresh to the former, while, to begin with, it knew no more than was commonly known about the latter. We refuse to posit any contrast in principle between two sets of aetiological factors; on the contrary, we assume that the two sets regularly act jointly in bringing about the observed result. [Endowment and Chance] determine a man's fate—rarely or never one of these powers alone."

page 217

And sometimes a bad fit:

For more on fit, see Daniel Stern's book *The First Relationship*, particularly Chapter 8, "Missteps in the Dance."

page 217

Psychoanalyst Stanley Greenspan:

Personal communication.

page 218

"we could get the baby through":

Ibid.

page 218
hypersensitive to sound:

See Greenspan's excellent book, *Psychopathology and Adaptation in Infancy and Early Childhood: Principles of Clinical Diagnosis and Preventive Intervention*, for his case history of Hilda, who—in her mother's presence—became rigid and cried most of the time. It was discovered that Hilda had a special sensitivity to sound that made her mother's high-pitched voice a particular irritant. Her mother was taught to speak in a low-pitched, rhythmic voice, to soothe Hilda with rhythmic rocking motions, and to distract her from the upsetting sounds by presenting her with interesting visual stimuli. For further case histories of infant-parent interventions, see *Infants and Parents*, Sally Provence, ed.

page 220
Freud originally believed:

In Freud's *Standard Edition*, Vol. 20, "An Autobiographical Study," pp. 33–34, he discusses his abandonment of the seduction theory and his conclusion that "neurotic symptoms were not related directly to actual events but to wishful phantasies" (p. 34).

page 221
"soul-destroying" experiences:

See Shengold's eloquent paper "Child Abuse and Deprivation: Soul Murder," *Journal of the American Psychoanalytic Association*, Vol. 27, No. 3, pp. 533–559 for his discussion of soul-destroying experiences. The quotation appears on p. 550.

page 221
"Human beings are mysteriously resourceful":

Ibid., pp. 549–550.

page 221
"that as far as the neurosis was concerned":

Freud, *Standard Edition*, Vol. 20, "An Autobiographical Study," p. 34.

page 221
link between early experience and future emotional health is currently being challenged:

Spokesmen for this view include University of Chicago psychologist Bertram Cohler and Harvard's Jerome Kagan. See also Rudolph Schaffer's book *Mothering*, in which he challenges the persistent faith, among parents and professionals, in the permanent formative effects of early childhood experiences.

page 221
what happens in childhood matters enormously:

In Kliman and Rosenfeld's useful book *Responsible Parenthood*, they cite a number of studies (see pp. 243–244) supporting the view that what happens to a person in early childhood strongly affects his later emotional life. They concede that what they dub the Childhood-Doesn't-Matter Movement has some value in reminding us that there is no *necessary* connection between a disadvantaged childhood and a troubled adulthood—"inadequate parenting does not condemn a child to failure or unhappiness"; and that parents need not always take the blame when children, by whatever standard, "have turned out badly" (p. 240). They also concede that the movement has value in making the crucial point that childhood damage is surely not irreversible. "But such reversal," the authors note, "is achieved at great cost, and only with great effort. Prevention is so much better" (p. 244).

Dr. Sally Provence addresses the does-childhood-matter question in her foreword to Stanley Greenspan's book *Psychopathology and Adaptation in Infancy and Early Childhood: Principles of Clinical Diagnosis and Preventive Intervention*: "It is true that in some instances infants with vulnerabilities and maladaptive behavior in the first year of life may improve in functioning without intervention, or, at least, without the sort of intervention that we can identify specifically. The fact that this occurs, that many infants are resilient and that many parents improve as nurturers, leads some to discount the importance of providing help early in the life of the child. And yet, other infants and parents fare far less well: Early dysfunctions may crystallize into maladaptive, psychopathological patterns that not only interfere with current development and parent-infant relationships, but exert long-lasting adverse effects as well" (p. xii). Dr. Provence agrees, however, that studies predicting future development and adaptive capacities have been frequently unreliable, in part because there is still much to be learned about those factors that promote *healthy* development and in part because earlier studies failed to reflect the fact that many factors—not one—determine human behavior.

page 222
"of ancient, fabulous forests":
V. Nabokov, *Speak, Memory*, p. 297.

page 222
"Who said that tenderness":
Louis Simpson, "The Goodnight," *Sound and Sense*, Laurence Perrine, ed., pp. 133–134.

CHAPTER FIFTEEN   FAMILY FEELINGS

page 224
family myths—unspoken or spoken themes:
Family themes (I am using the words "theme" and "myth" interchangeably) are discussed on pp. 17–19 of Robert Hess and Gerald Handel's "The Family as a Psychosocial Organization," *The Psychosocial Interior of the Family*, Gerald Handel, ed.

page 224
"corporate characteristic":
The concept of "corporate characteristics" is discussed in the introduction to *The Psychosocial Interior of the Family*, Gerald Handel, ed., p. 5.

page 224
But many family myths distort reality:
See Antonio Ferreira's "Family Myth and Homeostasis," *Archives of General Psychiatry*, Vol. 9, pp. 457–463. The quoted phrase appears on p. 462. See also Dennis Bagarozzi and Steven Anderson on "The Evolution of Family Mythological Systems: Considerations for Meaning, Clinical Assessment and Treatment," *The Journal of Psychoanalytic Anthropology*, 5:1, pp. 71–90. And see Lynn Wikler's *"Folie à Famille*: A Family Therapist's Perspective," *Family Process*, Vol. 19–3, pp. 257–268, for her discussion of shared familial delusions. Wikler describes a hypothetical continuum of family beliefs ranging from *folie à famille* to family myths to incongruous shared concepts to shared idiosyncratic reality.

page 225
"We are all peaceful":
See "Pseudo-Mutuality in the Family Relations of Schizophrenics," by Lyman Wynne, Irving Ryckoff, Juliana Day and Stanley Hirsch, in *The Psychosocial Interior of the Family*, George Handel, ed., p. 451.

page 225
"pseudo-mutuality":
Ibid. The concept of pseudo-mutuality is defined on pp. 444–449.

page 225
"intense and enduring":
Ibid., p. 447.

page 226
even before we were actually born:
In his paper on "The Role of Family Life in Child Development," *The International Journal of Psycho-Analysis*, Vol. 57, Part 4, pp. 385–395, Horst-Eberhard Richter writes: "Frequently, even before the child is born, parents entertain fairly detailed fantasies concerning the position the child is to take in the family. . . . The more burdened the parents are by their own inner conflicts . . . the more rigidly and compulsively their educational behavior is governed by these fantasies. . . . In this perspective the development of the child is seen as his lasting attempt to come to terms with the role that one or both parents have prescribed for him" (p. 387).

page 226
"like mother, dumb and stupid":
Ferreira, "Family Myth and Homeostasis," *General Archives of Psychiatry*, Vol. 9, p. 463.

page 226
There are all kinds of roles:
See Richter (two notes above), pp. 387–388, for a discussion of these four roles. For an interesting further look at the scapegoat role, see innovative family therapist Nathan Ackerman's chapter on "Rescuing the Scapegoat" in his book *Treating the Troubled Family*.

page 226
"It is often assumed":
Peter Lomas, "Family Role and Identity Formation," *The International Journal of Psycho-Analysis*, Vol. 42, Parts 4–5, p. 379.

page 226
Death of a Salesman:
Arthur Miller, *Death of a Salesman*, p. 54 ("can't take hold . . ."), p. 132 ("I am not . . ."), p. 133 ("Pop . . . happens").

page 227
The allotment of roles:
In "The Role of Family Life in Child Development," *The International Journal of Psycho-Analysis*, Vol. 57, Part 4, Richter writes: "Studies of families carried out over a number of years show that children understand exactly the role which the parental unconscious seeks to allot to them, and that many of their reactions may be interpreted partly as identifications and partly as protests against the directives unconsciously imposed upon them" (p. 388).

page 227
"Our subjective experience":

Roger Gould, "Transformational Tasks in Adulthood," *The Course of Life*, Vol. 3, Greenspan and Pollock, eds., p. 58.

page 228

"Parents continue to monitor":

Ibid., p. 69.

page 229

We begin to recognize our identifications:

Gould (see above) writes: "During our twenties, our knowledge of these identifications had to be suppressed so we could believe in the illusion of our complete independence from parental influence. Now, in order to avoid blind repetition of their patterns and in order not to forfeit the piece of self underlying the parental identification, we must first acknowledge the presence of this mysterious, slightly foreign inner self."

But not all identifications are either an exact duplication or a complete repudiation of a parental quality. "The final solution to a successful processing of identifications comes when we find we have a *similarity* to a parent but are *not identical*. We may share the stem of a value but not the ramifications. We may share a temperament characteristic but use it for different purposes. Hostility might be spunk; niggardliness may be prudence. But only after the identification similarity is admitted can the necessary discriminations be made and the self attached to that characteristic allowed to live," (p. 73).

page 230

Parenthood can be a constructive developmental phase:

See Therese Benedek's "Parenthood as a Developmental Phase," *Journal of the American Psychoanalytic Association*, Vol. 7, pp. 389–417, where she argues that at each successive stage of a child's development his parents are afforded another chance to work through, or reinforce, solutions to conflicts arising at a comparable stage of their own childhood. She notes that each child "stirs up through his own phasic development the corresponding unconscious developmental conflict of the parent . . . [and] . . . the parent cannot help but deal with his own conflict unconsciously, while consciously he tries to help the child achieve his developmental goal" (pp. 404–405). "We assume that while parents thus deliberately manipulate the behavior of the child and their current relationship with him, unconsciously they also modify their own intrapsychic processes" (p. 408).

page 231

"Grandparenthood," writes psychoanalyst Therese Benedek:

T. Benedek. This material is an addendum to "Parenthood as a Developmental Phase" and appears on p. 406 of her *Psychoanalytic Investigations: Selected Papers*.

page 233

"my friends are much more interested":

Featherstone, "Family Matters," *Harvard Educational Review*, Vol. 49, No. 1, pp. 29–30.

page 233

And we often discover secrets:

For a discussion of family secrets, see Theodore Jacobs' "Secrets, Alliances and Family Fictions: Some Psychoanalytic Observations," *Journal of the American Psychoanalytic Association*, Vol. 28, No. 1, pp. 21–42.

page 234

"I remember why skating":

Herbert Gold, *Fathers*, pp. 199–200.
    page 234
    "struck again and again":
Featherstone, "Family Matters," *Harvard Educational Review*, Vol. 49, No. 1, p. 51.

    CHAPTER SIXTEEN   LOVE AND MOURNING

    page 237
    "a lifelong human condition":
Rochlin, "The Dread of Abandonment," *The Psychoanalytic Study of the Child*, Vol. 16, p. 452.
    page 237
    "In what, now":
Freud, *Standard Edition*, Vol. 14, "Mourning and Melancholia," p. 244.
    page 238
    phases of mourning:
The Institute of Medicine's exhaustive survey of bereavement research—*Bereavement: Reactions, Consequences, and Care*, Marian Osterweis, Frederic Solomon and Morris Green, eds.—notes that "most observers . . . speak of clusters of reactions or 'phases' of bereavement that change over time. Although observers divide the process into various numbers of phases and use different terminology to label them, there is general agreement about the nature of reactions over time. Clinicians also agree that there is substantial individual variation in terms of specific manifestations of grief and in the speed with which people move through the process" (p. 48).
    page 238
    "sorrow . . . turns out to be":
C. S. Lewis, *A Grief Observed*, p. 68.
    page 238
    "shock, numbness and a sense of disbelief":
Institute of Medicine, *Bereavement: Reactions, Consequences, and Care*, p. 49.
    page 238
    Mark Twain:
Clemens, *The Autobiography of Mark Twain*, p. 324 ("our wonder and our worship") and p. 323 ("It is one of the . . .").
    page 239
    "anticipatory mourning":
Many studies of bereavement take note of the phenomenon of "anticipatory mourning" or "mourning before the fact." In George Pollock's "Mourning and Adaptation," *The International Journal of Psycho-Analysis*, Vol. 42, Parts 4–5, pp. 341–361, he writes: "In instances where death is anticipated as a result of a long-standing debilitation, acute mourning reactions may occur prior to the actual death. In several patients, whose parents were dying of malignant conditions, the shock response came when the patients first heard of the hopeless malignant diagnosis, and only very slightly when the actual death occurred" (p. 346). Pollock notes, however, that after the death has in fact occurred, "mourning work is still required" (p. 349).

page 239
"An elderly woman":
This clinical illustration was presented by Channing Lipson in "Denial and Mourning," *The Interpretation of Death*, p. 269.

page 240
physical complaints:
According to the Institute of Medicine's *Bereavement: Reactions, Consequences, and Care*, "acute grief is associated with a variety of physical complaints, including pain, gastrointestinal disturbances and the very 'vegetative' symptoms that, at another time, might signal the presence of a depressive disorder (e.g., sleep disturbance, appetite disturbance, loss of energy)" (p. 51).

page 240
regression (to a needier, "Help me!" stage):
In *Death and the Family*, social worker Lily Pincus discusses (pp. 41–43) the importance of being allowed, as part of mourning, to regress. She cites "one widow who, after an initial period of sleeplessness, could happily go to sleep cuddling a bolster, just like a baby who needs a teddy bear to go to sleep without his mother. Why not acknowledge and satisfy without shame the baby needs stirred up by bereavement?" (pp. 114–115). Pincus later notes: "The three year old who starts wetting and soiling again after the birth of a rival sibling is asking for extra care and attention. Both the small child who wants to be a baby again and the adult in pain learn to use regression in their new situation to gain comfort and love. If the desired response is forthcoming, the toddler can move on and make a step toward growth. . . . Regression in grief must be seen and supported as a means toward adaptation and health" (pp. 122–123).

page 240
"how I hated the world":
Raphael, *The Anatomy of Bereavement*, p. 49.

page 240
"Your logic, my friend, is perfect":
These are verses nine and ten of James Russell Lowell's "After the Burial," *The Complete Poetical Works of James Russell Lowell*, pp. 308–309, written after his child's death.

page 240
anger—toward others, and also toward the dead:
Bowlby, in *Loss*, citing corroborating research, affirms the place of anger in normal mourning: "There can in fact be no doubt that in normal mourning anger expressed towards one target or another is the rule. . . . [N]either the occurrence nor the frequency of anger can be regarded any longer as at issue" (p. 29).

page 241
Guilty feelings too—:
In *The Anatomy of Bereavement*, psychiatrist Beverley Raphael, who has done extensive work with, and research on, bereaved people, notes that in mourning: "Guilt is frequent: it relates to the imperfection of human relationships. During the reviewing process of mourning, one may recall the love that was not given, the care that was not provided—the 'sins' of omission. Or, one may remember the hatred he felt for the dead person, the resentment, the violence that was fantasized—the 'sins' of commission. Where the relationship was basically loving, such guilt is transient; where ambivalence was high, it creates greater stress in the working through process. Relief may also be felt—relief that the illness is over, that the

painful relationship is finished, that one did not die oneself—and this may be accepted or become a further cause of guilt" (p. 45).

page 241

"Missing him now":

These words by Frances Gunther appear in John Gunther's memoir of their son, *Death Be Not Proud*, p. 258, p. 259.

page 242

Canonizing—idealizing—the dead:

In Freud's *Standard Edition*, Vol. 14, "Thoughts for the Times on War and Death," he describes the way we idealize our dead: "We suspend criticism of him, overlook his possible misdeeds, declare that *de mortuis nil nisi bonum* [of the dead nothing but good], and think it justifiable to set out all that is most favourable to his memory in the funeral oration and upon the tombstone. Consideration for the dead, who, after all, no longer need it, is more important to us than the truth" (p. 290).

page 242

"the greatest little woman":

Raphael, *The Anatomy of Bereavement*, p. 207.

page 242

"He could say nothing negative":

Ibid.

page 242

"On the one hand":

Bowlby, *Loss*, p. 87. See searching discussion, pp. 87–90.

page 243

". . . I went to find you":

Anne Philipe, *No Longer Than a Sigh*, pp. 90–91.

page 243

A father dreams of his son:

This dream of Samuel Palmer was described by Bowlby in *Loss*, p. 112.

page 243

A mother dreams of her daughter:

This dream was described to me by a woman whose daughter died of cancer.

page 243

A woman dreams of her sister:

This dream was described by Geoffrey Gorer in *Death, Grief, and Mourning*, p. 53.

page 243

A daughter (Simone de Beauvoir) dreams of her mother:

This dream was described by de Beauvoir in *A Very Easy Death*, pp. 102–103.

page 244

A son dreams of his father:

This dream, from a man in his twenties who had a very *unpeaceful* relationship with his father, was described to me by his psychiatrist.

page 244

A son dreams of his mother:

These dreams were described to me by a man who had greatly idealized his mother after her death.

page 244

A daughter dreams of her father:

Gorer, *Death, Grief, and Mourning*, p. 55.

page 244

A widow dreams of her husband:

This dream was described to me by a woman whose husband, a manic-depressive, shot himself when he was fifty and she forty-six.

page 244

And the writer Edmund Wilson:

Wilson, *The Thirties*, pp. 367, 368, 369.

page 245

we can begin to come to the end of mourning:

In George Pollock's "Mourning and Adaptation," *The International Journal of Psycho-Analysis*, Vol. 42, parts 4–5, pp. 341–361, he writes: "The ego's ability to perceive the reality of the loss; to appreciate the temporal and spatial permanence of the loss; to acknowledge the significance of the loss; to be able to deal with the acute sudden disruption following the loss with attendant fears of weakness, help-lessness, frustration, rage, pain and anger; to be able effectively to reinvest new objects or ideals with energy, and so re-establish different but satisfactory relation-ships, are the key factors in this process" (p. 355).

page 246

"one of the more universal forms":

Ibid., p. 345. See also Pollock's "The Mourning Process and Creative Organizational Change," *Journal of the American Psychoanalytic Association*, Vol. 25, No. 1, pp. 3–34.

page 246

". . . now I see what":

This is the final section of Linda Pastan's poem, "The Five Stages of Grief," from her book *The Five Stages of Grief*, p. 62.

page 246

"after the amputation":

Ibid., p. 61.

page 247

C. S. Lewis:

Both passages appear in Lewis's "A Grief Observed," p. 67.

page 247

"anniversary reactions":

See Pollock's "Anniversary Reactions, Trauma and Mourning," *The Psychoanalytic Quarterly*, Vol. 39, No. 3, pp. 347–371.

page 247

this record of a daughter's grieving testifies:

These selections from Toby Talbot's *A Book About My Mother* appear on the follow-ing pages: 10, 16, 33, 75, 120, 121, 154, 166, 172, 178–179.

page 248

"filled with her":

Ibid., p. 178.

page 248

It is by internalizing the dead:

Since some writers talk about *internalization* of the lost "object" and some talk about *identification* with it, let me distinguish between these two words. Internali-zation is most usefully defined as a general term for various processes (identifica-tion, incorporation, introjection, to name three) by which we transform our relationships and experiences with the outer world into inner relationships and experiences. Identification is the process of internalization by which we modify our self to become in some ways like this or that person out there.

In "Mourning and Melancholia" Freud argued that identification with the lost loved person only occurred when mourning was pathological, but he later (in "The Ego and the Id") took the position that identification is part of all mourning and is the means by which we are able to relinquish our relationship with the lost person.

page 249

The "loved object is not gone":

Abraham, *Selected Papers*, "A Short Study of the Development of the Libido, Viewed in the Light of Mental Disorders," p. 437.

page 249

One form of internalization:

See this book, Chapter Four, "The Private 'I'," pp. 52–54.

page 249

Therapist Lily Pincus describes:

Pincus gives these examples in her book *Death and the Family*, noting further that the dull wife who became witty after her husband's death also "told me that she had always been amused by her husband's patient peeling of the top of his boiled egg, while she used to cut it off. 'Now,' she said, 'I just cannot bring myself to cut the top off, I have to peel it off patiently' " (p. 121).

page 249

identifications can be pathological:

Pincus (see above reference) describes a woman who had deplored her husband's bad table manners during his life, then acquired those same bad manners after his death. Pincus suggests that this was an attempt at restitution for her nagging (pp. 122–123). Pathological identifications include identifying with, and actually developing, the symptoms of the dead person's last, fatal illness. Pathological identifications may also occur when there has been great ambivalence in the relationship. The mourner has feelings of anger and reproach toward the person who died but directs them, instead, against himself. (See Freud's "Mourning and Melancholia.")

page 250

"There is continued crying":

Raphael, *The Anatomy of Mourning*, p. 60.

page 250

"it is as though":

Ibid., p. 60.

page 250

"Grief fills the room up":

Shakespeare, *King John*, Act 3, Scene 4.

page 250

"mummification":

Gorer discusses mummification in *Death, Grief, and Mourning*, pp. 85–87.

page 251

Bowlby says there are many different clues:

See Bowlby's discussion of absence of conscious grieving in *Loss*, pp. 152–156.

page 251

"Give sorrow words":

Shakespeare, *Macbeth*, Act 4, Scene 3.

page 251
harmful effects on the mental and physical health:
For a full discussion of the health consequences following a loss through death, see Chapter 2 of the Institute of Medicine's *Bereavement: Reactions, Consequences, and Care*. Among the conclusions reported on pp. 39–40 are:

"Following bereavement there is a statistically significant increase in mortality for men under the age of 75. . . . There is no higher mortality in women in the first year; whether there is an increase in the second year is unclear.

"There is an increase in suicide in the first year of bereavement, particularly by older widowers and by single men who lose their mothers. There may be a slight increase in suicide by widows.

"Among widowers, there is an increase in the relative risk of death from accidents, cardiovascular disease and some infectious diseases. In widows, the relative risk of death from cirrhosis rises.

"All studies document increases in alcohol consumption and smoking and greater use of tranquilizers or hypnotic medication (or both) among the bereaved. For the most part, these increases occur in people who already are using these substances; however, some of the increase is attributable to new users.

"Depressive symptoms are very common in the first months of bereavement. Between 10 and 20 per cent of men and women who lose a spouse are still depressed a year later."

See also Chapter 6 of that book, "To a Biology of Grieving," which explores the impact of grief on our biological systems.

page 252
"The father, Hermann Castorp":
The Institute of Medicine's study of bereavement (see reference above) begins its report with this apt selection from Thomas Mann's novel *The Magic Mountain*. It appears on p. 19.

page 252
The statistics are these:
These figures come from the Institute of Medicine's bereavement study (see above reference, p. 4).

page 252
Here are some answers:
Ibid., pp. 35–41, and Chapter 5.

page 253
the losses of early childhood may continue:
See Chapter 5 of the Institute of Medicine's *Bereavement: Reactions, Consequences, and Care*, for a discussion of the immediate, intermediate and long-range reactions of children to loss.

page 253
The Danish writer Tove Ditlevsen:
Moffat's *In the Midst of Winter* introduced me to Ditlevsen's poem, translated from the Danish by Ann Freeman, and provided the biographical information about her on pp. 88–90. Ditlevsen's poems "Self-Portrait 1" and "Self-Portrait 2" can be found in *The Other Voice: Twentieth-Century Women's Poetry in Transition*, Bankier et al., eds., pp. 27–29.

page 254
no young child has the ego strength:

One of the more fatiguing debates among the experts is whether or not children are capable of mourning, with some (like Melanie Klein) claiming that even infants can mourn and others (like Martha Wolfenstein) claiming that mourning does not become possible until adolescence. Part of the confusion has to do with different definitions. But if complete mourning is defined not merely as the capacity to feel grief over the loss of someone you love but as the capacity to confront that loss and sustain that grief (and other emotions) and in time to internally detach yourself from the lost one, it seems likely that children find it harder than adults to mourn, and need more help from adults with the mourning process. In the Institute of Medicine's report (see earlier citation) it notes: "Generally it is agreed that prior to age 3 or 4 children are not able to achieve complete mourning and it is agreed that by adolescence youngsters can mourn but are still more vulnerable than adults because they are experiencing so many other losses and changes. The controversy centers on the years in between" (Chapter 5, pp. 2–3).

For more on this controversy, see Melanie Klein's "Mourning and Its Relation to Manic-Depressive States" in *The Interpretation of Death*, Hendrik Ruitenbeek, ed.; Martha Wolfenstein's "How is Mourning Possible?", in *The Psychoanalytic Study of the Child*, Vol. 21; Edna Furman's *A Child's Parent Dies;* and John Bowlby's *Loss.*

page 254
Bowlby and others:
See Bowlby's *Loss* for his discussion of the conditions under which mourning in children leads to healthy and to unhealthy outcomes. In *The Anatomy of Bereavement*, pp. 114–119, Raphael discusses a variety of family contexts in which a child experiences loss and death.

page 254
"Jessica was five":
Raphael, *The Anatomy of Bereavement*, p. 138.

page 256
grief for a dead grown child:
See pp. 121–126 of Gorer's *Death, Grief, and Mourning* for his discussion of parents' responses to the death of their children.

page 256
"They said it was nothing":
Raphael, *The Anatomy of Bereavement*, p. 236.

page 257
"then there was the empty room":
Ibid., pp. 251–252.

page 257
"may alter, forever":
Ibid., p. 281.

page 257
"Although we know that after such a loss":
This is from Freud's letter to Ludwig Binswanger, *The Letters of Sigmund Freud*, Ernst Freud, ed., p. 386.

page 258
"Our society is set up":
Caine, *Widow*, p. 1.

page 258

"her own life had no meaning":
Raphael, *The Anatomy of Bereavement*, p. 207.

page 258
"I was just as crazy":
The Hayes statement appears in Lynn Caine's *Widow*, pp. 75–76.

page 258
"God has moved me up":
This poignant line appears in Etty Hillesum's *An Interrupted Life*, p. 182.

page 259
that other marital death called divorce:
For a fuller discussion of this subject, see Gerald Jacobson's *The Multiple Crises of Marital Separation and Divorce*.

page 259
"There was once a man":
de Beauvoir, "The Woman Destroyed," from her collection also entitled *The Woman Destroyed*, pp. 207–208.

page 260
"the 'bereaved' must mourn":
Raphael, *The Anatomy of Bereavement*, p. 228.

page 260
"The world breaks everyone":
Hemingway, *A Farewell to Arms*, p. 186.

page 261
"When we found out what the disease would do":
This is all but the opening portion of Maxine Kumin's poem "The Man of Many L's," *Our Ground Time Here Will Be Brief*, pp. 30–31.

page 262
Jerome said Kaddish:
Many of the books mentioned in these notes discuss the great importance of such traditional rituals of mourning in facilitating the internal mourning process.

page 263
"You have grown wings of pain":
This is a portion of Linda Pastan's poem "Go Gentle," *PM/AM*, p. 41.

page 263
"I had grown very fond":
de Beauvoir, *A Very Easy Death*, p. 76.

page 263
"there is no loss":
Pincus, *Death and the Family*, p. 278.

page 264
"I am a more sensitive person":
Kushner, *When Bad Things Happen to Good People*, pp. 133–134.

CHAPTER SEVENTEEN   SHIFTING IMAGES

page 265
Confucius:
Daniel Levinson's book *The Seasons of a Man's Life* is the source for "the ages of

man" according to Confucius (p. 326), Solon (p. 326) and the Talmud (p. 325). From Confucius:

The Master said, At 15 I set my heart upon learning.

At 30, I had planted my feet firm upon the ground.

At 40, I no longer suffered from perplexities.

At 50, I knew what were the biddings of heaven.

At 60, I heard them with a docile ear.

At 70, I could follow the dictates of my own heart; for what I desired no longer overstepped the boundaries of right.

page 265

Solon:

0– 7	A boy at first is the man; unripe; then he casts his teeth; milk-teeth befitting the child he sheds in his seventh year.
7–14	Then to his seven years God adding another seven, signs of approaching manhood show in the bud.
14–21	Still, in the third of the sevens his limbs are growing; his chin touched with a fleecy down, the bloom of the cheek gone.
21–28	Now, in the fourth of the sevens ripen to greatest completeness the powers of the man, and his worth becomes plain to see.
28–35	In the fifth he bethinks him that this is the season for courting, bethinks him that sons will preserve and continue his line.
35–42	Now in the sixth his mind, ever open to virtue, broadens, and never inspires him to profitless deeds.
42–56	Seven times seven, and eight; the tongue and the mind for fourteen years together are now at their best.
56–63	Still in the ninth is he able, but never so nimble in speech and in wit as he was in the days of his prime.
63–70	Who to the tenth has attained, and has lived to complete it, has come to the time to depart on the ebb-tide of Death.

page 265

The Talmud:

5	years is the age for reading (Scripture);
10	for Mishnah (the laws);
13	for the Commandments (Bar Mitzvah, moral responsibility);
15	for Gemara (Talmudic discussions; abstract reasoning);
18	for Hupa (wedding canopy);
20	for seeking a livelihood (pursuing an occupation);
30	for attaining full strength ("Koah");
40	for understanding;
50	for giving counsel;
60	for becoming an elder (wisdom, old age);
70	for white hair;
80	for Gevurah (new, special strength of age);
90	for being bent under the weight of the years;
100	for being as if already dead and passed away from the world

page 265

Shakespeare:

From *As You Like It*, Act 2, Scene 7:

All the world's a stage,

And all the men and women merely players:

They have their exits, and their entrances;
And one man in his time plays many parts,—
His acts being seven ages. At first, the infant,
Mewling and puking in the nurse's arms:
Then the whining schoolboy, with his satchel,
And shining morning face, creeping like snail
Unwillingly to school: and then the lover,
Sighing like furnace, with a woeful ballad
Made to his mistress' eyebrow: Then a soldier,
Full of strange oaths, and bearded like a pard,
Jealous in honour, sudden and quick in quarrel,
Seeking the bubble Reputation
Even in the cannon's mouth: and then the justice,
In fair round belly, with good capon lin'd,
With eyes severe, and beard of formal cut,
Full of wise saws and modern instances,
And so he plays his part: The sixth age shifts
Into the lean and slipper'd pantaloon;
With spectacles on nose, and pouch on side
His youthful hose well sav'd, a world too wide
For his shrunk shank; and his big manly voice
Turning again toward childish treble, pipes
And whistles in his sound: Last scene of all,
That ends this strange eventful history,
Is second childishness, and mere oblivion;
Sans teeth, sans eyes, sans taste, sans—everything.

page 265
Erikson:

Erik Erikson's *Childhood and Society*, Chapter 7, describes "Eight Ages of Man," successive phases of the life cycle during which crucial turning-point decisions are made between:

basic trust versus basic mistrust
autonomy versus shame and doubt
initiative versus guilt
industry versus inferiority
identity versus role confusion
intimacy versus isolation
generativity versus stagnation
ego integrity versus despair.

page 265
Sheehy:

Gail Sheehy's *Passages* focuses on stages of adult development between what she calls "The Trying Twenties" and the "Deadline Decade" of mid-life.

page 265
Jaques:

Elliott Jaques' "The Midlife Crisis," *The Course of Life*, Vol. 3, Greenspan and Pollock, eds., describes the following developmental stages: "*infancy:* the critical first year of life terminated by what might be termed the *depressive crisis* . . .; *early childhood:* the period of emergence of organized conscious ego functioning and language, separated by the *oedipal crisis* from the *latency stage* of development which in turn is ended by the *crisis of puberty and adolescence*. There then emerges the stage of *early adulthood*, from roughly the late teens to the middle thirties; in the middle and late thirties occur the *midlife crisis* and the transition to *mature adulthood* which runs from around forty to the middle or late fifties. There then occurs what I would term the *late adult crisis*, leading into *late adulthood*, the period of the sixties and seventies. There is some evidence . . . that there is a further maturational step at around the age of eighty if senility does not step in, but we leave this possibility as an open question" (p. 2).

    page 265
    Gould:
Roger Gould's *Transformations* presents a series of false assumptions which, in sequential stages between adolescence and mid-life, must be challenged. These will be discussed later in this chapter.

    page 265
    Levinson:
Daniel Levinson's *The Seasons of a Man's Life* is based on his intensive study of the lives of forty men representing four different occupations—industrial workers, business executives, university biologists and novelists—between the ages of thirty-five and forty-five. Generalizing from in-depth biographical interviews, Levinson and his colleagues have formulated a developmental theory of men in the years between their entry into adulthood and mid-life. The life cycle is viewed as a sequence of partially overlapping eras:

    0–22   childhood and adolescence;
    17–45   early adulthood;
    40–65   middle adulthood;
    60–?   late adulthood.

The transition from one era to the next takes place over several years; the zone of overlap between eras is the transition period. Thus the Early Adult Transition extends from seventeen to twenty-two; the Mid-Life Transition extends from forty to forty-five; the Late Adult Transition extends from sixty to sixty-five. The eras, according to Levinson, are further subdivided into developmental periods (to be discussed in the text of this chapter).

    page 265
    normal predictable stages of adult development:
Freud's work emphasized the developmental stages of childhood. In recent years, however, much attention has been paid to adult stages of development. The father of these adult developmental studies, in the view of Levinson and others, is Freud's disciple Carl Jung, who later split with Freud and founded his own school of "analytical psychology." Jung wrote forcefully of change and development in the second half of life, the "afternoon of life." See, for instance, his "The Stages of Life" in *The Portable Jung*, Joseph Campbell, ed.

    page 266
    "is an ending":
Levinson, *The Seasons of a Man's Life*, p. 50, p. 51.

    page 266
    "In the course of these changes":
This paragraph is based on Levinson's divisions of the developmental periods between early adulthood and mid-life: Early Adult Transition; Entering the Adult

World; Age Thirty Transition; Settling Down and Becoming One's Own Man; Mid-Life Transition and Entering Middle Adulthood (p. 68). Although his research is on men only, the general time frames seem applicable—to some extent—to both sexes.

page 266

"What am I doing with a mid-life crisis":

J. Viorst, *How Did I Get to Be Forty and Other Atrocities*, "Mid-Life Crisis," p. 17.

page 267

"When I was young and miserable and pretty":

These lines are from Randall Jarrell's poem, "Next Day," quoted by Charles Simmons in "The Age of Maturity," *The New York Times Magazine*, Dec. 11, 1983, p. 114.

page 268

Quoting that poem in a wistful essay:

Charles Simmons, "The Age of Maturity," *The New York Times Magazine*, Dec. 11, 1983, p. 114.

page 268

"Being physically attractive":

Susan Sontag, "The Double Standard of Aging," *Saturday Review*, Oct. 1972, pp. 29–38. The statements quoted appear on p. 31.

page 269

"Most men experience getting older":

Ibid., p. 34.

page 270

empty nests have advantages:

Many women will attest to the pleasures of the empty nest: the new neatness and quiet of the house, the freedom to eat, sleep and make love on their own schedule, the freedom from anxiety which comes from not knowing, on any given blizzardy night, whether or not their children are out in a car. Indeed, Lillian Rubin's book, *Women of a Certain Age*, challenges the concept of an empty-nest syndrome of sadness, loneliness and depression. "Almost all the women I spoke with," she writes, "respond to the departure of their children, whether actual or impending, with a decided sense of relief" (p. 15). Almost all of the women *I* spoke with, however, felt both the relief and a sense of sadness, particularly in the period just following departure. And with the departure of the last child, they note, all the friends of that child also vanish from the household. The loss, then, is not only of their own children—but of children's presence in their daily life.

page 271

"renunciation of what has been inexorably outlived":

Dinnerstein, *The Mermaid and the Minotaur*, p. 140.

page 272

"the one major institution in our society":

Gutmann, "Psychoanalysis and Aging: A Developmental View," *The Course of Life*, Vol. 3, Greenspan and Pollock, eds., p. 513.

page 272

"I've finished six pillows":

Judith Viorst, *How Did I Get to Be Forty and Other Atrocities*, "Self-Improvement Program," p. 45.

page 273

"our ground time here":

Our Ground Time Here Will Be Brief is the title and title poem of a book of poetry by Maxine Kumin.

page 274
"a dark wood":
Many of those who have written about the mid-life crisis find it most movingly rendered in the opening lines of Dante's *The Divine Comedy:* "Midway in the journey of our life I found myself in a dark wood, for the straight way was lost. Ah, how hard it is to tell what that wood was, wild, rugged, harsh; the very thought of it renews the fear! It is so bitter that death is hardly more so" (p. 3).

page 274
"God ordains":
Jaques quotes Shaw in "The Midlife Crisis," *The Course of Life*, Vol. 3, Greenspan and Pollock, eds., p. 4.

page 276
"The old conspiracies":
Gould, *Transformations*, p. 291.

page 278
"I might as well have a roommate":
Mary Bralove, "Husband's Hazard," *The Wall Street Journal*, Nov. 9, 1981. See p. 1 for headline and quote about roommate.

page 278
"out of phase":
Ibid., p. 24.

page 278
what psychologist Gilligan calls both "voices":
See Carol Gilligan's book *In a Different Voice.*

page 278
masculine autonomy is far more valued:
Gilligan takes issue in Chapter 6 of *In a Different Voice* with studies of adult development (like Levinson's and George Vaillant's) "that convey a view of adulthood where relationships are subordinated to the ongoing process of individuation and achievement" (p. 154).

page 278
"the chronic emergency of parenthood":
Gutmann, "Psychoanalysis and Aging: A Developmental View," *The Course of Life*, Vol. 3, Greenspan and Pollock, eds., p. 499.

page 279
"During the active and critical period":
Ibid., p. 500.

page 279
"Thus, men begin to live out directly":
Ibid., p. 502.

page 279
creativeness/destructiveness duality:
This duality is one of four sets of polarities discussed by Levinson in *The Seasons of a Man's Life* (pp. 197–198, pp. 209–244). According to Levinson, the four polarities, "whose resolution is the principal task of mid-life individuation, are: (1) Young/Old, (2) Destruction/Creation, (3) Masculine/Feminine and (4) Attachment/Separateness" (p. 197).

page 279
"childhood consciousness":
Gould, *Transformations*, see Section I, "Childhood Consciousness vs. Adult Consciousness."
page 280
four assumptions:
These four false assumptions are described in Gould's "Transformational Tasks in Adulthood," *The Course of Life*, Vol. 3, Greenspan and Pollock, eds., p. 66.
page 280
"our darker, mysterious center":
Gould, *Transformations*, p. 294.
page 281
"the madness of unbridled rationality":
Loewald, *Psychoanalysis and the History of the Individual*, p. 56.
page 281
connecting "with the insane in us":
Gould, *Transformations*, p. 305.
page 281
Analyst Elliott Jaques:
See Jaques, "The Midlife Crisis," *The Course of Life*, Vol. 3, Greenspan and Pollock, eds. The quoted material appears on p. 6, p. 8, p. 9 and p. 9 again.
page 282
"The Mid-Life Transition":
Levinson, *The Seasons of a Man's Life*, p. 197.

CHAPTER EIGHTEEN   I GROW OLD . . . I GROW OLD

The Boston Society for Gerontologic Psychiatry produced three books which I found invaluable background reading for this chapter: *Normal Psychology of the Aging Process*, Zinberg and Kaufman, eds.; *Geriatric Psychiatry: Grief, Loss and Emotional Disorders in the Aging Process*, Berezin and Cath, eds.; and *Psychodynamic Studies on Aging: Creativity, Reminiscing and Dying*, Levin and Kahana, eds.
page 284
"creative freedoms":
George Pollock, "Aging or Aged: Development or Pathology," *The Course of Life*, Vol. 3, Greenspan and Pollock, eds., p. 573.
page 285
"How hard and painful":
de Beauvoir, *The Coming of Age*, p. 92.
page 285
From Ovid:
Ibid., p. 121.
page 285
From Montaigne:
Ibid., p. 159.

page 285
From Chateaubriand:
Ibid., p. 299.
page 285
From Gide:
Ibid., p. 460.
page 285
"Old age," says de Beauvoir:
Ibid., p. 539.
page 286
"Eighty years old! No eyes left":
Ibid., p. 303. Although de Beauvoir's book emphasizes the miseries of age, she does —from time to time—present some spokesmen for a more positive view of aging.
page 286
"body preoccupation" and "body transcendence":
See Robert Peck, "Psychological Developments in the Second Half of Life," *Middle Age and Aging*, Bernice Neugarten, ed., pp. 90–91, for a discussion of body transcendence vs. body preoccupation.
page 286
(a health pessimist):
See Ethel Shanas, et al., "The Psychology of Health," *Middle Age and Aging*, Bernice Neugarten, ed., for a discussion of health optimists, pessimists and realists.
page 287
"all the boring physical symptoms":
Fisher, *Sister Age*, p. 237.
page 287
"We who are old":
Florida Scott-Maxwell, *The Measure of My Days*, p. 5, p. 36.
page 287
Although aging is not an illness:
A helpful discussion of mental and physical changes with normal aging can be found in Chapters 6 through 12 of *Aging*, Woodruff and Birren, eds.
page 287
Malcolm Cowley writes:
Cowley, *The View from 80*, pp. 3–4.
page 288
"Put cotton in your ears":
Ibid., p. 5.
page 288
For although in today's America:
These statistics, obtained from the National Institute on Aging, were the latest available as of August 1984.
page 288
"Old age in America is often a tragedy":
Butler, *Why Survive?*, p. xi.
page 289
"We start by growing old":
Cowley, *The View From 80*, p. 5.
page 289

"should an old person":

Blythe, *The View in Winter*, p. 80. See also de Beauvoir's discussion of sex and the elderly in *The Coming of Age*, pp. 317–351.

page 289

"I was depressed":

Ibid., p. 220.

page 290

"while we unburden'd":

Shakespeare, *King Lear*, Act 1, Scene 1.

page 290

"of rule, interest of territory":

Ibid., Act 1, Scene 1.

page 291

"I'll resume the shape":

Ibid., Act 1, Scene 5.

page 291

a "mounting distaste":

Blythe, *The View in Winter*, p. 22, p. 73.

page 291

"profound, underlying problem":

Ibid., p. 13. Blythe is quoting geriatrician Paul Tournier.

page 291

For we live in a society:

In Butler's *Why Survive?* he passionately documents our present society's responsibilities for much of the suffering of the elderly, arguing that America "is extremely harsh to live in when one is old" (p. 2). He urges humane reforms that would assure the elderly adequate incomes, decent housing, appropriate medical care, community support systems, useful roles, workable transportation, available recreation, diverse companionship and physical safety.

For a discussion of different societies' treatment of the elderly, see de Beauvoir's *The Coming of Age*. See also Gutmann's discussion of the psychosocial function of the elderly in his fine paper "Psychoanalysis and Aging: A Developmental View," *The Course of Life*, Vol. 3, Greenspan and Pollock, eds., pp. 489–517.

page 291

"this absurdity . . . this caricature":

Yeats, *The Collected Poems of W. B. Yeats*, from "The Tower," pp. 192–197. These lines appear on p. 192.

page 292

My friend Irene:

J. Viorst, "In Praise of Older Women," *Redbook*, September 1980, pp. 42, 44. A longer version of the interview with Irene appears on p. 42.

page 292

the English professor:

Personal communication.

page 293

"nothing is too late":

Longfellow, "Morituri Salutamus," *The Complete Poetical Works of Henry Wadsworth Longfellow*. The full poem appears on pp. 310–314, these lines on p. 313.

page 293

Hear the miner's mother:
Blythe, *The View in Winter*, p. 167.
    page 293
    Hear the artist Goya:
Cowley, *The View From 80*, pp. 16–17.
    page 293
    Hear the Montessori teacher:
Blythe, *The View in Winter*, p. 200.
    page 293
    Hear the student:
This man, who had left the business world at the age of sixty-five, also told me, "I didn't retire. I turned the page."
    page 294
    And hear Lady Thelma:
Blythe, *The View in Winter*, p. 232.
    page 294
    I must mention one more woman:
J. Viorst, "In Praise of Older Women," *Redbook*, September 1980, pp. 42, 44. This material appears on p. 44.
    page 295
    People age well in many different modes:
Two opposing theories of aging have related "optimal aging" to (1) high activity levels and (2) disengagement from activity. However, in Bernice Neugarten, Robert Havighurst, and Sheldon Tobin's "Personality and Patterns of Aging," *Middle Age and Aging*, Bernice Neugarten, ed., the authors argue that neither the activity nor the disengagement theory is adequate and that different patterns of optimal aging characterize different personality types. They describe a study in which they measured life satisfaction against different patterns of aging in a group of seventy-year-olds.

Among the so-called "integrated" personalities in this group, there were three different types, distinguished by their different approaches to aging: the high-activity reorganizers, the medium-activity focused and the low-activity disengaged. All three types measured high in life satisfaction.

The study also reported on the aging patterns of the "armored" or "defended" personalities in this group, for whom there was a need for tight controls and strong defenses against the anxiety evoked by the threat of aging. Two patterns were perceived: a high-activity "holding on" to former ways of doing things and a low-activity "constricted" retreat from any new experiences. Both types of these "defended" personalities measured high to medium in life satisfaction.

A third category—"passive dependent" personalities—had strong needs for someone on whom they could lean. Those who were "succorance-seeking" had a medium activity level, looked for someone to meet their emotional needs, and if successful, measured medium in life satisfaction. Those who were "apathetic" had a low activity level, were immobilized by their passivity and measured low in life satisfaction.

In a fourth category were the "unintegrated" personalities, who displayed severe defects in psychological functions, loss of emotional control and deterioration in thought process. They were low both in activity and in life satisfaction.
    page 296

"for social initiative":
Butler, *Why Survive?*, p. 341. The Gray Panthers, started by Maggie Kuhn at age sixty-seven, is an organization of retired older persons committed to social change.
    page 296
    "When I am an old woman I shall wear purple":
This is the first verse of Jenny Joseph's poem "Warning" in *The Oxford Book of Twentieth Century English Verse*, Philip Larkin, ed., pp. 609–610.
    page 296
    "ego transcendence":
See Robert Peck, "Psychological Developments in the Second Half of Life," *Middle Age and Aging*, Bernice Neugarten, ed., pp. 91–92, for a discussion of ego transcendence vs. ego preoccupation. See also Gutmann, "Psychoanalysis and Aging: A Developmental View," *The Course of Life*, Vol. 3, Greenspan and Pollock, eds., where he is surely describing ego transcendence in his reference to a capacity for the "cathexis of otherness"—the "capacity to cathect [invest intensely in] and to make real those agencies which do not in any direct way bear on the security and priorities of the self" (p. 492).
    page 297
    "a sense of presentness":
Butler, *Why Survive?*, p. 410.
    page 297
    "when the sound of a child's laugh":
Fisher, *Sister Age*, p. 237.
    page 297
    "vanished geography":
Blythe, *The View in Winter*, p. 82, p. 87.
    page 297
    "the life review":
See Butler's "The Life Review: An Interpretation of Reminiscence in the Aged," *Psychiatry*, Vol. 26, No. 1, pp. 65–76, in which he postulates "the universal occurrence in older people of an inner experience or mental process of reviewing one's life," sometimes leading to depression and sometimes leading to "candor, serenity and wisdom" (p. 65).
    page 297
    "one and only life cycle":
Erikson, *Identity: Youth and Crisis*, p. 139.
    page 297
    "the fact that one's life":
Ibid., p. 139.
    page 298
    "How can you expect us":
Blythe, *The View in Winter*, p. 23.
    page 298
    "denigrates their humanness":
Butler, *Why Survive?*, p. 414.
    page 298
    "have made and—continue to make":
Ibid., p. 414.
    page 298
    "bright souls":

Fisher, *Sister Age*, pp. 234–235.

page 298

"a wide range of social and biological changes":

Neugarten, Havighurst, Tobin, "Personality and Patterns of Aging," *Middle Age and Aging*, Bernice Neugarten, ed., pp. 176–177.

page 299

new opportunities for change:

See Colarusso and Nemiroff, *Adult Development*, Chapters 4 and 12, for a useful discussion of development and change in adult life.

page 299

"All is uncharted and uncertain":

Scott-Maxwell, *The Measure of My Days*, pp. 139–140.

page 299

Benjamin Spock:

This discussion is based on several interviews with Dr. Spock in person, by phone and through the mails during 1983.

page 302

But age itself may also call forth new strengths:

In Scott-Maxwell's *The Measure of My Days*, she writes: "Age can seem a debacle, a rout of all one most needs, but that is not the whole truth. What of the part of us, the nameless, boundless part who experienced the rout, the witness who saw so much go, who remains undaunted and knows with clear conviction that there is more to us than age? Part of that which is outside age has been created by age, so there is gain as well as loss. If we have suffered defeat we are somewhere, somehow beyond the battle" (pp. 140–141).

page 303

though Sigmund Freud said otherwise:

Freud and others have argued that treatment of older people is contraindicated because they become more rigid and inflexible with age. Analysts working with older patients, however, have found that they can be as flexible and as well-motivated for change as younger patients.

page 303

the emotional problems that the coming of age may initiate:

Among the elderly, depression is the most prevalent of the mental health disorders. In addition, depression—as well as the risk of suicide—is more prevalent among the elderly than it is in any other age group. See *Physicians' Guide to the Diagnosis and Treatment of Depression in the Elderly*, Crook and Cohen, eds.

page 303

"The basic insight is that parts of self":

Pollock, "Aging or Aged: Development or Pathology," *The Course of Life*, Vol. 3, Greenspan and Pollock, eds., p. 579.

page 303

Psychoanalysts report that psychoanalysis with the elderly:

Panel Report: "The Psychoanalysis of the Older Patient," reported by Nancy Miller. For *Journal of the American Psychoanalytic Association* (in press).

page 303

Why, a seventy-six-year-old woman was asked:

This vignette is described by analyst Martin Berezin in "Psychotherapy of the Elderly," *Aspects of Aging*, No. 4, unpaged.

page 304

"Though he has watched a decent age pass by":
Sophocles, "Oedipus at Colonus," *Sophocles I*, Grene and Lattimore, eds., p. 134.

CHAPTER NINETEEN   THE ABC OF DYING

page 306
"Death is the mother of beauty":
This line is from Stevens' poem "Sunday Morning," *The Norton Anthology of Poetry*, Allison et al., eds., pp. 968–970. The line appears on p. 970.

page 306
"Life without death is meaningless":
See Lisl Marburg Goodman's *Death and the Creative Life*, where she interviews eminent artists and scientists on death. The interview with Wheeler appears on pp. 76–83; the quoted line appears on p. 78.

page 306
"And if one is not able to die":
See Tillich's "The Eternal Now" in *The Meaning of Death*, Herman Feifel, ed., p. 32.

page 306
"If I had my life over again":
Spark, *Memento Mori*, p. 149.

page 307
Why were we born:
In *The Broken Connection*, Robert Jay Lifton quotes Ionesco's poignant line: "Why was I born if it wasn't forever?" (p. 70).

page 307
"to every thing there is a season":
Holy Bible, Ecclesiastes 3:1, 2.

page 308
arrange with cryonics companies to be deep-frozen:
The theory of cryonics is that if a dead body is frozen and preserved, it then can be thawed and revived sometime in the future, when a cure has been found for whatever has been the cause of the death. Several cryonics companies now are freezing the dead bodies of people who have made prior arrangements for such preservation.

page 308
perhaps to eternity:
In his foreword to John A. Mann's *Secrets of Life Extension*, Saul Kent notes that "pioneering 'longevists' . . . have embarked upon a fantastic journey that could, eventually, lead to the achievement of physical immortality" (p. xi). And in Salholz and Smith's article in *Newsweek*, March 26, 1984, on life-extension practitioners Durk Pearson and Sandy Shaw, they are described as believing "that ultimately the only causes of death will be suicide, murder or accident" (p. 81).

page 308
a dread of abandonment:
See Gregory Rochlin's "The Dread of Abandonment: A Contribution to the Etiology of the Loss Complex and to Depression," *The Psychoanalytic Study of the Child*, Vol. 16, where he discusses the "two great inseparable fears of man . . . the fear of not

surviving or death, and . . . the dread of abandonment" (p. 460). He further argues that what he calls the "paradise myth" (p. 467) is an effort to transform the meaning of death and abandonment from separation to reunion—a joining with others.

page 308

"The Death of Ivan Ilych":

These lines and passages from Tolstoy's "The Death of Ivan Ilych " are found in *Great Short Works of Leo Tolstoy* on the following pages: "something terrible, new . . ." p. 274; "My God . . ." p. 278; "It is impossible . . ." p. 279; "the syllogism . . ." p. 280; "It cannot be . . ." p. 280; "stand before him . . ." p. 281; "alone with It . . ." p. 282; "Why, and for what . . ." p. 296; "Agony, death . . ." p. 298.

page 310

"This deception tortured him":

Ibid., p. 285.

page 310

On Death and Dying:

Kübler-Ross's book *On Death and Dying* arose out of a seminar on death, which she originated and conducted at the University of Chicago. In this seminar, students of medicine, sociology, psychology and theology listened to the terminally ill discussing their wants and fears. Kübler-Ross maintains that all terminally ill patients are "aware of the seriousness of their illness whether they are told or not" (p. 233). She says that although they may be initially glad that their doctors and relatives (because of their own anxieties) don't want to discuss it, there comes a time when the dying have a need for an understanding person with whom to share some of their feelings and concerns, with whom "to lift the mask, to face reality" and with whom to talk about their impending death (p. 234). Kübler-Ross notes, however, that even very realistic patients will leave "the possibility open for some cure" and that it is important—without telling lies—to "share with them the hope that something unforeseen may happen" (p. 123).

Although Kübler-Ross believes that doctors and family should make themselves available to talk frankly about death, she also makes the important point "that we do not always state explicitly that the patient is actually terminally ill. We attempt to elicit the patients' needs first . . . and look for overt or hidden communications to determine how much a patient wants to face reality at a given moment" (p. 41).

Some doctors say that there will always be certain patients who don't want to know, and should never be told, that they are dying. Eissler discusses such a patient (case three) in his book *The Psychiatrist and the Dying Patient.* For more on the subject of telling patients about their fatal illnesses, see Payne's "The Physician and His Patient Who Is Dying," *Psychodynamic Studies of the Aging: Creativity, Reminiscing, Dying,* Levin and Kahana, eds., pp. 135–139.

page 310

Denial:

In Kübler-Ross's *On Death and Dying* she notes that after an initial state of shock, patients respond to news that they are terminally ill with denial. She says that complete denial is rarely maintained until the end although partial denial is used by almost all patients from time to time. Patients, she says, "may briefly talk about the reality of their situation, and suddenly indicate their inability to look at it realistically any longer" (pp. 36–37). Later, she says, they may use the defense of isolation rather than denial, and thus talk about health and illness, mortality and immortality, death and hope, as if there were no inherent contradictions.

There is also a good discussion of denial in Payne's "The Physician and His Patient Who Is Dying," see note above, pp. 131–135.

page 310

Anger:

Kübler-Ross notes that the anger and resentment of the dying about having to die may be redirected—displaced onto—family and friends and hospital staff and procedures. She also notes that this anger may be quite rational (having to do, say, with insensitive and incompetent treatment) as well as irrational ("Why couldn't it have been, instead of me, that old and useless fellow down the street?")

page 310

Bargaining:

Kübler-Ross is describing (*On Death and Dying*, p. 73) the bargaining strategy of one of her patients. She notes that such bargaining includes the implicit promise (to the doctor, to God) that if this postponement is granted the patient will not ask for further postponements. She says that none of the patients that she has worked with have kept this promise.

page 310

Depression:

Kübler-Ross distinguishes between two kinds of depression—reactive and preparatory. She says that depression over past losses (reactive depression) may involve sorrows a listener can help to alleviate, whether it is reassurance of a mastectomy patient's continuing femininity or offers of assistance with the management of a household when a patient can no longer manage it him- or herself. However, she says, depression over one's death (preparatory depression) does not call for encouragements and reassurances. She writes: "The patient is in the process of losing everything and everybody he loves. If he is allowed to express his sorrow he will find a final acceptance much easier, and he will be grateful to those who can sit with him during this stage of depression without constantly telling him not to be sad" (*On Death and Dying*, p. 77).

page 310

Acceptance:

Ibid., p. 99, p. 100.

page 311

"against the dying of the light":

In Thomas's "Do Not Go Gentle into That Good Night," *Sound and Sense*, Laurence Perrine, ed., pp. 345–346, his first stanza tells us:

> Do not go gentle into that good night,
> Old age should burn and rave at close of day;
> Rage, rage against the dying of the light.

page 311

And some critics fear:

Another criticism of Kübler-Ross, though it has no bearing on the validity of *On Death and Dying,* has been her subsequent interest in supernatural post-death communication.

page 311

Dr. Edwin Shneidman:

Shneidman, *Voices of Death,* "my own . . ." p. 108; ". . . I reject . . ." p. 108, p. 109; "natural law . . ." p. 109.

page 311
allowed to be a baby again:
See Payne's "The Physician and His Patient Who Is Dying," *Psychodynamic Studies of the Aging: Creativity, Reminiscing, Dying*, Levin and Kahana, eds., pp. 141–143, for his discussion of regression. In *The Interpretation of Death*, Ruitenbeek, ed., Ruitenbeek quotes from a tender letter written by a therapist to a girl dying of cancer: "Above all do not be ashamed of being a baby. We all regress into childhood when we are in deep discomfort and physical pain" (pp. 3–4). And in Tolstoy's "The Death of Ivan Ilych" the dying man speaks of his longing to regress: "At certain moments after prolonged suffering he wished most of all (though he would have been ashamed to confess it) for someone to pity him as a sick child is pitied. He longed to be petted and comforted. He knew that he was an important functionary, that he had a beard turning gray and that therefore what he longed for was impossible, but still he longed for it" (p. 286).

page 312
they will teach us:
In addition to Payne (see previous note), several other writings offer valuable discussions of work with the dying: Eissler, *The Psychiatrist and the Dying Patient;* Feifel, "Attitudes toward Death in Some Normal and Mentally Ill Populations," *The Meaning of Death*, Feifel, ed.; Tor-Bjorn Hagglund's *Dying;* and in *The Interpretation of Death*, Ruitenbeek, ed., Janice Norton's "Treatment of a Dying Patient," Hattie Rosenthal's "Psychotherapy for the Dying" and Lawrence and Eda LeShan's "Psychotherapy and the Patient with a Limited Life-Span."

page 313
In videotapes about a thirty-nine-year-old doctor:
This material about Dr. Gary Leinbach appears in "A Fatally Ill Doctor's Reaction to Dying," by Lawrence Altman, *The New York Times*, July 22, 1974, p. 1, p. 26. The story notes that "there are many other dying patients who, like Dr. Leinbach, put up a fight to the very last." According to the story the therapy called hyperalimentation (feeding a patient, through a vein in the neck, a sugar and protein-rich solution) is usually a temporary post-operative procedure. But when the doctors hesitated about continuing the hyperalimentation, Dr. Leinbach pressed them to keep it going, asking them, "How can I live without it?" (p. 26).

page 314
"the condemned cheats the executioner":
Eissler, *The Psychiatrist and the Dying Patient*, p. 66.

page 314
In 1982, for instance:
These are the latest available statistics from the National Center for Health Statistics. The actual suicide rate may be considerably higher; many probable suicides —from overdoses, for instance—may be officially listed as "natural causes."

page 315
Thus Cecil and Julia Saunders:
The story of the Saunderses and of other elderly and terminally ill suicides appears in "Some Elderly Choose Suicide Over Lonely, Dependent Life," by Andrew Malcolm, *The New York Times*, September 24, 1984, p. 1, p. B6. The Saunderses' letter appears on p. B6.

page 315
to reach out a rescuing hand:

In Eissler's *The Psychiatrist and the Dying Patient* he discusses his efforts to dissuade a dying patient from suicide, pp. 186–194.

page 315

"Who knows how he may be tempted":

This quote from Robert Burton's *Anatomy of Melancholy*, a study of suicide published in 1621, is cited in A. Alvarez's *The Savage God*, p. 167. In addition to Alvarez, I found useful discussions of suicide in *Suicide in America*, by Herbert Hendin; and Lifton's *The Broken Connection*, pp. 239–280.

page 316

"care, grief [and] perplexity":

Clemens, *The Autobiography of Mark Twain*, p. 249.

page 316

"Men must endure":

Shakespeare, *King Lear*, Act 5, Scene 2.

page 316

"When I catch myself resenting":

Arnold J. Toynbee, "Why and How I Work," *Saturday Review*, p. 15, April 5, 1969.

page 316

"Without regret for father":

Philippe Ariès quotes these lines from Marguerite de Navarre in his book *The Hour of Our Death*, p. 309.

page 316

"Thou shalt lie down":

William Cullen Bryant, "Thanatopsis," *A Treasury of the World's Best Loved Poems*, pp. 161–163. The lines quoted appear on p. 162.

page 317

"And does it not seem hard to you":

Robert Louis Stevenson, *A Child's Garden of Verses*, "Bed in Summer," p. 9.

page 317

"makes all the difference":

Kaufmann, "Existentialism and Death," *The Meaning of Death*, Herman Feifel, ed., p. 62.

page 318

"A single summer grant me":

This translation, by Kaufmann, of Holderlin's poem appears in Kaufmann's "Existentialism and Death" (see above reference), p. 59.

page 318

"in the face of death":

Ibid., p. 59.

page 318

it "is the person who is convinced":

Rosenthal, "Psychotherapy for the Dying," *The Interpretation of Death*, Ruitenbeek, ed., p. 94.

page 318

die the way we live:

"They died as they lived," writes Daniel Cappon of some twenty patients dying in a general hospital in "The Psychology of Dying," *The Interpretation of Death*, Ruitenbeek, ed. "The hostile became more hostile, the fearful more fearful, the weak weaker" (pp. 62–63). Shneidman, in his *Voices of Death*, agrees, arguing that "each individual tends to die as he or she has lived, especially as he or she has previously reacted in periods of threat, stress, failure, challenge, shock and loss" (p. 110).

page 318

"the knowledge or the vague feeling":

Eissler, *The Psychiatrist and the Dying Patient*, p. 53.

page 319

"a last step forward":

Ibid., p. 54.

page 319

the "perfect death" that is described by Lily Pincus:

Pincus, *Death and the Family*, pp. 6–8.

page 319

"The full awareness of each step":

Eissler, *The Psychiatrist and the Dying Patient*, p. 57.

page 320

rather not be there when it happens:

This is a play on Woody Allen's famous crack: "I'm not afraid to die. I just don't want to be there when it happens."

page 320

"corresponds exactly":

Ariès, *The Hour of Our Death*, p. 587.

page 320

hospice movement:

See the Institute of Medicine's *Cancer Today: Origins, Prevention and Treatment*, "Alternative Care for the Dying: American Hospices," pp. 103–116. On a personal note, I was tremendously impressed with the kindness and competence of the hospice people in their home treatment of my sister during her last days.

page 320

"avoid looking it":

La Rochefoucauld, *The Maxims of the Duc de la Rochefoucauld*, p. 128.

page 321

modes of immortality:

See Lifton's *The Broken Connection*, pp. 13–35, where he discusses the five general modes in which a sense of immortality may be expressed.

page 321

"derived from a more-than-natural source":

Ibid., p. 21.

page 321

"death-transcending truths":

Ibid., p. 20.

page 321

"exorcise the terrors":

Freud, *Standard Edition*, Vol. 21, "The Future of an Illusion," p. 18. In arguing that men can do without "the consolation of the religious illusion," he states that "surely infantilism is destined to be surmounted. Men cannot remain children for ever" (p. 49).

page 321

We can agree with Robert Lifton:

Lifton, *The Broken Connection*, p. 18. Lifton is talking about symbolic—not literal —immortality.

page 321

". . . Earth, that nourished thee, shall claim":

William Cullen Bryant, "Thanatopsis," *A Treasury of the World's Best Loved Poems*, pp. 161–163. The quoted lines appear on p. 162.

page 322

"Life is atrocious":

Yourcenar, *Memoirs of Hadrian*, p. 293.

page 322

a broader—"biosocial"—image of living on:

Lifton notes in *The Broken Connection* that "the biosocial mode of immortality can be extended outward from family to tribe, organization, subculture, people, nation, or even species. . . . An encompassing vision of biosocial immortality . . . would provide each individual anticipating death with the image: 'I live on in human-kind' " (pp. 19–20).

page 323

"an indissoluble bond":

Freud, *Standard Edition*, Vol. 21, "Civilization and Its Discontents," p. 65. Freud is paraphrasing a letter from Romain Rolland, who wrote about his "oceanic" feelings.

page 323

"I cannot discover":

Ibid., p. 65. Freud argues that Rolland's feelings of oneness with the universe can be traced back to babyhood's blurred-boundaries stage. Lifton, however, says that these oneness experiences should not be viewed as merely regressive, for the redis-covery of the harmony, the inner unity, of early childhood is occurring now within an adult framework. See his chapter "The Experience of Transcendence" in *The Broken Connection*, pp. 24–35.

page 323

"Whether you think of it":

de Beauvoir, *A Very Easy Death*, p. 92.

page 323

"I don't want to gain immortality":

Mr. Allen confirms having made this statement, but neither I nor his office have been able to establish where it originally appeared.

page 323

"Not unless I be aware":

In Karen Snow's novel *Willo*, p. 98, her heroine recalls this exchange between the dying Flavian and his friend Marius in the novel *Marius the Epicurean*.

page 323

"a corollary of the knowledge of death":

Lifton, *The Broken Connection*, p. 17.

page 324

"The sunlight on the garden":

MacNeice, "The Sunlight on the Garden," *The Norton Anthology of Poetry*, Allison et al., eds., p. 1127.

Bibliography

Abraham, Karl. 1927. *Selected Papers of Karl Abraham.* New York: Basic Books, Inc.

Ackerman, Nathan. 1966. *Treating the Troubled Family.* New York: Basic Books, Inc.

Adler, Alfred. 1929. *Problems of Neurosis.* London: Kegan Paul, Trench, Trubner & Co., Ltd.

Albee, Edward. 1978. *Who's Afraid of Virginia Woolf?.* New York: Atheneum. (paperback)

Allison, Alexander; Barrows, Herbert; Blake, Caesar; Carr, Arthur; Eastman, Arthur; English, Hubert. 1970, 1975. *The Norton Anthology of Poetry.* New York: W. W. Norton & Co., Inc. (paperback)

Altman, Lawrence. July 22, 1974. "A Fatally Ill Doctor's Reactions to Dying." *The New York Times*, p. 1, p. 26.

Altman, Leon. 1969. *The Dream in Psychoanalysis.* New York: International Universities Press, Inc.

———. 1977. "Some Vicissitudes of Love." *Journal of the American Psychoanalytic Association*, Vol. 25, No. 1, pp. 35–52.

Alvarez, A. 1970, 1971, 1972. *The Savage God.* New York: Random House.

American Psychiatric Association. 1980. *Diagnostic and Statistical Manual of Mental Disorders*, Third Edition. Washington, D.C.: American Psychiatric Association.

Applegarth, Adrienne. 1976. "Some Observations on Work Inhibitions in Women." *Journal of the American Psychoanalytic Association*, Vol. 24, No. 5, pp. 251–268.

Ariès, Philippe. 1962. *Centuries of Childhood.* New York: Alfred A. Knopf.

———. 1981. *The Hour of Our Death.* New York: Alfred A. Knopf.

Arnstein, Helene. 1979. *Brothers and Sisters/Sisters and Brothers.* New York: E. P. Dutton.

Auden, W. H. 1950. "As I Walked Out One Evening." *Modern Poetry*, Mack, Dean, Frost, eds. New York: Prentice-Hall, Inc.

———. 1979. "September 1, 1939." *Selected Poems*, Edward Mendelson, ed. New York: Vintage Books. (paperback)

Bach, George, and Wyden, Peter. 1969. *The Intimate Enemy.* New York: William Morrow and Company, Inc.

Bagarozzi, Dennis, and Anderson, Steven. Winter 1982. "The Evolution of Family Mythological Systems: Considerations for Meaning, Clinical Assessment and Treatment." *The Journal of Psychoanalytic Anthropology*, 5:1, pp. 71–90.

Bak, Robert. 1973. "Being in Love and Object Loss." *The International Journal of Psycho-Analysis*, Vol. 54, Part 1, pp. 1–7.

Balint, Alice. 1949. "Love for the Mother and Mother-Love." *The International Journal of Psycho-Analysis*, Vol. 30, pp. 251–259.

Balint, Michael. 1968. *The Basic Fault.* London: Tavistock Publications.

Bank, Stephen, and Kahn, Michael. 1982. *The Sibling Bond.* New York: Basic Books, Inc.

Bankier, Joanna; Cosman, Carol; Earnshaw, Doris; Keefe, Joan; Lashgari, Deirdre; Weaver, Kathleen. 1976. *The Other Voice: Twentieth-Century Women's Poetry in Transition*. New York: W. W. Norton & Co., Inc.

Becker, Ernest. 1973. *The Denial of Death*. New York: The Free Press. (paperback)

Bell, Robert. 1981. *Worlds of Friendship*. Beverly Hills: Sage Publications.

Benedek, Therese. 1959. "Parenthood as a Developmental Phase." *Journal of the American Psychoanalytic Association*, Vol. 7, pp. 389–417.

———. 1973. *Psychoanalytic Investigations: Selected Papers*. New York: Quadrangle/ New York Times.

———. 1977. "Ambivalence, Passion and Love." *Journal of the American Psychoanalytic Association*, Vol. 25, No. 1, pp. 53–79.

Berezin, Martin. 1984. "Psychotherapy of the Elderly." *Aspects of Aging*, No. 4. Philadelphia: SmithKline Beckman Corporation. (unpaged)

Berezin, Martin, and Cath, Stanley, eds. 1965. *Geriatric Psychiatry: Grief, Loss and Emotional Disorders in the Aging Process*. New York: International Universities Press, Inc.

Bergmann, Martin. 1980. "On the Intrapsychic Function of Falling in Love." *The Psychoanalytic Quarterly*, Vol. 49, No. 1, pp. 56–77.

Bernard, Jessie. 1982. *The Future of Marriage*. New Haven and London: Yale University Press. (paperback)

Bettelheim, Bruno. 1954. *Symbolic Wounds*. Glencoe, Illinois: The Free Press.

———. 1983. *Freud and Man's Soul*. New York: Alfred A. Knopf.

Blos, Peter. 1962. *On Adolescence*. New York: The Free Press.

Blume, Judy. 1970. *Are You There, God? It's Me, Margaret*. New York: Dell Publishing Co., Inc. (paperback)

Blythe, Ronald. 1979. *The View in Winter*. New York and London: Harcourt Brace Jovanovich.

Boehm, Felix. October 1930. "The Femininity-Complex in Men." *The International Journal of Psycho-Analysis*, Vol. 11, Part 4, pp. 444–469.

Bowlby, John. 1969. *Attachment*. New York: Basic Books, Inc.

———. 1973. *Separation*. New York: Basic Books, Inc.

———. 1980. *Loss*. New York: Basic Books, Inc.

Brain, Robert. 1976. *Friends and Lovers*. New York: Basic Books, Inc.

Bralove, Mary. Nov. 9, 1981. "Husband's Hazard." *The Wall Street Journal*, pp. 1, 24.

Breger, Louis. 1974. *From Instinct to Identity*. Englewood Cliffs, New Jersey: Prentice-Hall, Inc.

Brenner, Charles. 1974. *An Elementary Textbook of Psychoanalysis*. New York: Anchor Books. (paperback)

Bruch, Hilde. 1980. "The Sleeping Beauty: Escape from Change." *The Course of Life*, Vol. 2, Greenspan and Pollock, eds.

Bryant, William Cullen. 1961. "Thanatopsis." *A Treasury of the World's Best Loved Poetry*. New York: Avenel Books.

Buber, Martin. May 1957. "Guilt and Guilt Feelings." *Psychiatry*, Vol. 20, No. 2, pp. 114–129.

Busse, Ewald, and Feiffer, Eric. 1969. *Behavior and Adaptation in Late Life*. Boston: Little, Brown and Company.

Butler, Robert. February 1963. "The Life Review: An Interpretation of Reminiscence in the Aged." *Psychiatry*, Vol. 26, No. 1, pp. 65–76.

———. 1975. *Why Survive?*. New York: Harper & Row.

Caine, Lynn. 1974. *Widow*. New York: Bantam Books. (paperback)

Cappon, Daniel. 1969, 1973. "The Psychology of Dying." *The Interpretation of Death*, Hendrik Ruitenbeek, ed. New York: Jason Aronson.

Cath, Stanley, Gurwitt, Alan, and Ross, John Munder. 1982. *Father and Child*. Boston: Little, Brown and Company.

Charny, Israel. March 1969. "Marital Love and Hate." *Family Process*, Vol. 8, No. 1, pp. 1–24.

Chasseguet-Smirgel, Janine. 1976. "Freud and Female Sexuality: The Consideration of Some Blind Spots in the Exploration of the 'Dark Continent.' " *The International Journal of Psycho-Analysis*, Vol. 57, Part 3, pp. 275–286.

Chess, Stella, and Thomas, Alexander. 1973. "Temperament in the Normal Infant." *Individual Differences in Children*, Jack Westman, ed. New York: John Wiley & Sons.

Cicero, Marcus Tullius. 1909. "On Friendship." *The Harvard Classics*, Vol. 9, *Letters of Marcus Tullius Cicero and Letters of Gaius Plinius Caecilius Secundus*, Charles Eliot, ed. New York: P. F. Collier & Son.

Cicirelli, Victor. 1982. "Sibling Influence Throughout the Lifespan." *Sibling Relationships: Their Nature and Significance Across the Lifespan*, Michael Lamb and Brian Sutton-Smith, eds. Hillsdale, New Jersey: Lawrence Erlbaum Associates.

Cleckley, Hervey. 1964. *The Mask of Sanity*. Saint Louis: The C. V. Mosby Company.

Clemens, Samuel. 1959. *The Autobiography of Mark Twain*, arranged and edited by Charles Neider. New York: Harper.

Colarusso, Calvin, and Nemiroff, Robert. 1981. *Adult Development*. New York and London: Plenum Press.

Conrad, Joseph. 1902. *Heart of Darkness*. Great Britain: Penguin Books. (paperback)

Cowley, Malcolm. 1980. *The View from 80*. New York: The Viking Press.

Crook, Thomas, and Cohen, Gene. 1983. *Physicians' Guide to the Diagnosis and Treatment of Depression in the Elderly*. New Canaan: Mark Powley Associates, Inc.

Dante Alighieri. 1980. *The Divine Comedy*, Charles Singleton, translator. Princeton: Princeton University Press. (paperback)

de Beauvoir, Simone. 1966. *A Very Easy Death* (originally published in 1964). New York: G. P. Putnam's Sons.

———. 1971. *The Woman Destroyed*. Great Britain: Fontana/Collins. (paperback)

———. 1972. *The Coming of Age*. New York: G. P. Putnam's Sons.

Deutsch, Helene. 1965. *Neuroses and Character Types*. New York: International Universities Press, Inc.

Dew, Robb Forman. 1979, 1981. *Dale Loves Sophie to Death*. New York: Penguin Books. (paperback)

Dicks, Henry. 1967. *Marital Tensions*. New York: Basic Books.

Dillard, Annie. 1974. *Pilgrim at Tinker Creek*. New York: Harper's Magazine Press.

———. 1982. *Teaching a Stone to Talk*. New York: Harper & Row.

Dinnerstein, Dorothy. 1977. *The Mermaid and the Minotaur*. New York: Harper & Row. (paperback)

Dowling, Colette. 1982. *The Cinderella Complex*. New York: Pocket Books. (paperback)

Dowson, Ernest. 1970, 1975. "Non sum qualis eram bonae subregno Cynarae." *The Norton Anthology of Poetry*, Allison et al., eds. (paperback)

Edel, Leon. 1972. *Henry James, The Master: 1901–1916*. Vol. 5. New York: Avon Books. (paperback)
———. 1982. *Stuff of Sleep and Dreams*. New York: Avon Books. (paperback)
Eissler, K. R. 1955. *The Psychiatrist and the Dying Patient*. New York: International Universities Press, Inc. (paperback)
———. 1977. "Comments on Penis Envy and Orgasm in Women." *The Psychoanalytic Study of the Child*, Vol. 32. New York: International Universities Press, Inc.
Ephron, Delia. 1981. *Teenage Romance*. New York: Ballantine Books. (paperback)
Erikson, Erik. 1950, 1963. *Childhood and Society*. New York: W. W. Norton & Co., Inc. (paperback)
———. January 1954. "The Dream Specimen of Psychoanalysis." *Journal of the American Psychoanalytic Association*, Vol. 2, No. 1, pp. 5–56.
———. 1968. *Identity: Youth and Crisis*. New York: W. W. Norton & Co., Inc.
Esman, Aaron. 1980. "Mid-Adolescence—Foundations for Later Psychopathology." *The Course of Life*, Vol. 2, Greenspan and Pollock, eds.
Fairbairn, W. R. D. 1952. *Psychoanalytic Studies of the Personality*. London: Tavistock Publications Limited.
———. 1954. *An Object-Relations Theory of the Personality*. New York: Basic Books, Inc.
Farber, Leslie. October 1973. "On Jealousy." *Commentary*, pp. 50–58.
Featherstone, Joseph. February 1979. "Family Matters." *Harvard Educational Review*, Vol. 49, No. 1, pp. 20–52.
Feifel, Herman. 1959. "Attitudes Toward Death in Some Normal and Mentally Ill Populations." *The Meaning of Death*, Herman Feifel, ed. New York: McGraw-Hill Book Company, Inc.
———, ed. 1959. *The Meaning of Death*. New York: McGraw-Hill Book Company, Inc.
Feldman, Sandor. September 1969. "On Romance." *Bulletin of the Philadelphia Association for Psychoanalysis*, Vol. 19, No. 3, pp. 153–157.
Fenichel, Otto. 1953. *The Collected Papers of Otto Fenichel*. New York: W. W. Norton & Co., Inc.
Ferenczi, Sandor. 1950. *Sex in Psychoanalysis*. New York: Basic Books, Inc.
Ferreira, Antonio. November 1963. "Family Myth and Homeostasis." *Archives of General Psychiatry*, Vol. 9, pp. 457–463.
Fields, Suzanne. 1983. *Like Father, Like Daughter*. Boston: Little, Brown and Company.
Fishel, Elizabeth. 1979. *Sisters*. New York: William Morrow and Co., Inc.
Fisher, M. F. K. 1983. *Sister Age*. New York: Alfred A. Knopf.
Fitzgerald, F. Scott. 1933. *Tender Is the Night*. New York: Charles Scribner's Sons. (paperback)
Flaubert, Gustave. 1981. *Madame Bovary* (originally published in 1857). New York, Toronto, London: Bantam Books. (paperback)
Fontaine, Joan. 1978. *No Bed of Roses*. New York: William Morrow & Company, Inc.
Forster, E. M. 1921. *Howards End*. New York: Vintage Books.
The Foster Care Monitoring Committee. 1984. *Foster Care 1984: A Report on the Implementation of the Recommendations of the Mayor's Task Force on Foster Care*.
Fraiberg, Selma. 1959. *The Magic Years*. New York: Charles Scribner's Sons.
———. 1969. "Libidinal Object Constancy and Mental Representation." *The Psy-*

choanalytic Study of the Child, Vol. 24. New York: International Universities Press, Inc.

———. 1977. *Every Child's Birthright.* New York: Basic Books, Inc.

Francke, Linda Bird. May 22, 1983. "The Sons of Divorce." *The New York Times Magazine,* pp. 40–41, 54–57.

Freud, Anna. 1952. "A Connection Between the States of Negativism and of Emotional Surrender." *The International Journal of Psycho-Analysis,* Vol. 33, Part 3, p. 265.

———. 1958. "Adolescence." *The Psychoanalytic Study of the Child,* Vol. 13. New York: International Universities Press, Inc.

———. 1965. *Normality and Pathology in Childhood.* New York: International Universities Press, Inc.

———. 1966. *The Ego and the Mechanisms of Defense.* New York: International Universities Press, Inc. (paperback)

Freud, Anna, and Burlingham, Dorothy. 1943. *War and Children.* New York: International Universities Press, Inc.

Freud, Anna, and Burlingham, Dorothy. 1944. *Infants Without Families.* New York: International Universities Press, Inc.

Freud, Ernst, ed. 1960, 1975. *The Letters of Sigmund Freud.* New York: Basic Books, Inc. (paperback)

Freud, Sigmund. 1953. "The Interpretation of Dreams" (originally published in 1900). *Standard Edition,* Vols. 4 and 5, James Strachey, ed. London: The Hogarth Press.

———. 1953. "Some Reflections on Schoolboy Psychology" (originally published in 1914). *Standard Edition,* Vol. 13, James Strachey, ed. London: The Hogarth Press.

———. 1953. "Three Essays on the Theory of Sexuality" (originally published in 1905). *Standard Edition,* Vol. 7, James Strachey, ed. London: The Hogarth Press.

———. 1953. "Totem and Taboo" (originally published in 1913 [1912–1913]). *Standard Edition,* Vol. 13, James Strachey, ed. London: The Hogarth Press.

———. 1955. "Beyond the Pleasure Principle" (originally published in 1920). *Standard Edition,* Vol. 18, James Strachey, ed. London: The Hogarth Press.

———. 1955. "Group Psychology and the Analysis of the Ego" (originally published in 1921). *Standard Edition,* Vol. 18, James Strachey, ed. London: The Hogarth Press.

———. 1957. "A Metapsychological Supplement to the Theory of Dreams" (originally published in 1917 [1915]). *Standard Edition,* Vol. 14, James Strachey, ed. London: The Hogarth Press.

———. 1957. "Mourning and Melancholia" (originally published in 1917 [1915]). *Standard Edition,* Vol. 14, James Strachey, ed. London: The Hogarth Press.

———. 1957. "On Narcissism: An Introduction" (originally published in 1914). *Standard Edition,* Vol. 14, James Strachey, ed. London: The Hogarth Press.

———. 1957. "Some Character-Types Met With in Psycho-Analytic Work" (originally published in 1916). *Standard Edition,* Vol. 14, James Strachey, ed. London: The Hogarth Press.

———. 1957. "A Special Type of Choice of Object Made By Men" (originally published in 1910). *Standard Edition,* Vol. 11, James Strachey, ed. London: The Hogarth Press.

———. 1957. "Thoughts for the Times on War and Death" (originally published in

1915). *Standard Edition*, Vol. 14, James Strachey, ed. London: The Hogarth Press.

———. 1958. "The Dynamics of Transference" (originally published in 1912). *Standard Edition*, Vol. 12, James Strachey, ed. London: The Hogarth Press.

———. 1958. "Observations on Transference-Love" (originally published in 1915 [1914]). *Standard Edition*, Vol. 12, James Strachey, ed. London: The Hogarth Press.

———. 1958. "Remembering, Repeating and Working-Through" (originally published in 1914). *Standard Edition*, Vol. 12, James Strachey, ed. London: The Hogarth Press.

———. 1959. "An Autobiographical Study" (originally published in 1925 [1924]). *Standard Edition*, Vol. 20. James Strachey, ed. London: The Hogarth Press.

———. 1959. "Inhibitions, Symptoms and Anxiety" (originally published in 1926 [1925]). *Standard Edition*, Vol. 20, James Strachey, ed. London: The Hogarth Press.

———. 1961. "Civilization and Its Discontents" (originally published in 1930 [1929]). *Standard Edition*, Vol. 21, James Strachey, ed. London: The Hogarth Press.

———. 1961. "The Dissolution of the Oedipus Complex" (originally published in 1924). *Standard Edition*, Vol. 19, James Strachey, ed. London: The Hogarth Press.

———. 1961. "The Economic Problem of Masochism" (originally published in 1924). *Standard Edition*, Vol. 19, James Strachey, ed. London: The Hogarth Press.

———. 1961. "The Ego and the Id" (originally published in 1923). *Standard Edition*, Vol. 19, James Strachey, ed. London: The Hogarth Press.

———. 1961. "Female Sexuality" (originally published in 1931). *Standard Edition*, Vol. 21, James Strachey, ed. London: The Hogarth Press.

———. 1961. "The Future of an Illusion" (originally published in 1927). *Standard Edition*, Vol. 21, James Strachey, ed. London: The Hogarth Press.

———. 1961. "Introductory Lectures on Psycho-Analysis, Parts I and II" (originally published in 1916–1917 [1915–1917]). *Standard Edition*, Vol. 15, James Strachey, ed. London: The Hogarth Press.

———. 1961. "Some Psychical Consequences of the Anatomical Distinction Between the Sexes" (originally published in 1925). *Standard Edition*, Vol. 19, James Strachey, ed. London: The Hogarth Press.

———. 1963. "Introductory Lectures on Psycho-Analysis, Part III" (originally published in 1916–1917 [1915–1917]). *Standard Edition*, Vol. 16, James Strachey, ed. London: The Hogarth Press.

———. 1964. "New Introductory Lectures on Psycho-Analysis" (originally published in 1933 [1932]). *Standard Edition*, Vol. 22, James Strachey, ed. London: The Hogarth Press.

———. 1964. "An Outline of Psycho-Analysis" (originally published in 1940 [1938]). *Standard Edition*, Vol. 23, James Strachey, ed. London: The Hogarth Press.

Frisch, Max. 1958. *I'm Not Stiller*. New York: Vintage Books. (paperback)

Fromm, Erich. 1956. *The Art of Loving*. New York: Harper & Brothers.

Furman, Edna. 1974. *A Child's Parent Dies*. New Haven and London: Yale University Press.

Gilligan, Carol. 1982. *In a Different Voice*. Cambridge, Mass.: Harvard University Press. (paperback)

Ginott, Haim. 1965. *Between Parent and Child*. New York: The Macmillan Company.

Giovacchini, Peter. Spring 1967. "Characterological Aspects of Marital Interaction." *The Psychoanalytic Forum*, Vol. 2, No. 1, pp. 7–29.

Gold, Herbert. 1968. *Fathers*. Greenwich, Conn.: Fawcett Publications, Inc. (paperback)

Goldstein, Joseph; Freud, Anna; Solnit, Albert J. 1973, 1979. *Beyond the Best Interests of the Child*. New York: The Free Press. (paperback)

Goodman, Lisl. 1981, 1983. *Death and the Creative Life*. New York: Penguin Books. (paperback)

Gorer, Geoffrey. 1965. *Death, Grief, and Mourning*. New York: Doubleday & Company, Inc.

Gornick, Vivian. May 31, 1973. "Toward a Definition of a Female Sensibility." *The Village Voice*.

Gould, Roger. 1978. *Transformations*. New York: Simon and Schuster. (paperback)

———. 1981. "Transformational Tasks in Adulthood." *The Course of Life*, Vol. 3, Greenspan and Pollock, eds., pp. 55–89.

Greenacre, Phyllis. 1971. *Emotional Growth*, Vol. 2. New York: International Universities Press, Inc.

Greene, Bob. 1985. *Good Morning, Merry Sunshine*. New York: Penguin Books. (paperback)

Greenspan, Stanley. 1981. *Psychopathology and Adaptation in Infancy and Early Childhood*. New York: International Universities Press, Inc.

———. 1982. " 'The Second Other'—The Role of the Father in Early Personality Formation and in the Dyadic-Phallic Phase of Development." *Anthology on Fatherhood*, S. Cath, A. Gurwitt, J. Ross, eds. Boston: Little, Brown and Company.

Greenspan, Stanley, and Lieberman, Alicia. 1980. "Infants, Mothers and Their Interaction: A Quantitative Clinical Approach to Developmental Assessment." *The Course of Life*, Vol. 1, Greenspan and Pollock, eds.

Greenspan, Stanley, and Pollock, George, eds. 1980. *The Course of Life*, Vol. 1: *Infancy and Early Childhood*. Washington, D.C.: Government Printing Office. DHHS Pub. No. (ADM) 80–786.

———. 1980. *The Course of Life*, Vol. 2: *Latency, Adolescence and Youth*. Washington, D.C.: Government Printing Office. DHHS Pub. No. (ADM) 80–999.

———. 1981. *The Course of Life*, Vol. 3: *Adulthood and the Aging Process*. Washington, D.C.: Government Printing Office. DHHS Pub. No. (ADM) 81–1000.

Grene, David, and Lattimore, Richmond, eds. 1954. *Sophocles I*. Chicago and London: The University of Chicago Press. (paperback)

Grossman, William, and Stewart, Walter. 1976. "Penis Envy: From Childhood Wish to Developmental Metaphor." *Journal of the American Psychoanalytic Association*, Vol. 24, No. 5, pp. 193–212.

Group for the Advancement of Psychiatry. 1973. *The Joys and Sorrows of Parenthood*. New York: Charles Scribner's Sons.

———. 1983. *Friends and Lovers in the College Years*. New York: Mental Health Materials Center. (paperback)

Gunther, John. 1949. *Death Be Not Proud*. New York: Harper & Brothers.

Gutmann, David. 1981. "Psychoanalysis and Aging: A Developmental View." *The Course of Life*, Vol. 3, Greenspan and Pollock, eds.

Hagglund, Tor-Bjorn. 1978. *Dying*. New York: International Universities Press, Inc.

Handel, Gerald, ed. 1967. *The Psychosocial Interior of the Family*. Chicago: Aldine Atherton.

Hartmann, Heinz, and Loewenstein, R. M. 1962. "Notes on the Superego." *The Psychoanalytic Study of the Child*, Vol. 17. New York: International Universities Press, Inc.

Hayward, Brooke. 1978. *Haywire*. New York: Bantam Books. (paperback)

Heinicke, Christoph, and Westheimer, Ilse. 1965. *Brief Separations*. New York: International Universities Press, Inc.

Hemingway, Ernest. 1929. *A Farewell to Arms*. New York: Bantam Books. (paperback)

Hendin, Herbert. 1982. *Suicide in America*. New York: W. W. Norton & Co.

Hess, Robert, and Handel, Gerald. 1967. "The Family as a Psychosocial Organization." *The Psychosocial Interior of the Family*, Gerald Handel, ed.

Hilgard, Josephine. 1951. "Sibling Rivalry and Social Heredity." *Psychiatry*, Vol. 14, No. 4, pp. 375–385.

Hillesum, Etty. 1981, 1983. *An Interrupted Life*. New York: Pantheon Books.

Hite, Shere. 1976. *The Hite Report*. New York: Macmillan Publishing Co., Inc.

Hitschmann, Edward. 1952. "Freud's Conception of Love." *The International Journal of Psycho-Analysis*, Vol. 33, Part 4, pp. 421–428.

Holy Bible

Howard, Jane. 1978. *Families*. New York: Simon and Schuster.

Howells, William Dean. 1951 (originally published in 1885). *The Rise of Silas Lapham*. New York: Random House, Inc.

Institute of Medicine, Marian Osterweis, Fredric Solomon and Morris Green, eds. 1984. *Bereavement: Reactions, Consequences, and Care*. Washington, D.C.: National Academy Press.

Institute of Medicine. 1984. *Cancer Today: Origins, Prevention and Treatment*. Washington, D.C.: National Academy Press. (paperback)

Irving, John. 1976, 1977, 1978. *The World According to Garp*. New York: E. P. Dutton.

Jacobs, Theodore. 1980. "Secrets, Alliances and Family Fictions: Some Psychoanalytic Observations." *Journal of the American Psychoanalytic Association*, Vol. 28, No. 1, pp. 21–42.

Jacobson, Edith. 1964. *The Self and the Object World*. New York: International Universities Press, Inc.

Jacobson, Gerald. 1983. *The Multiple Crises of Marital Separation and Divorce*. New York: Grune & Stratton.

Jaffe, Daniel. 1968. "The Masculine Envy of Woman's Procreative Function." *Journal of the American Psychoanalytic Association*, Vol. 16, No. 3, pp. 521–548.

James, William. 1950. *The Principles of Psychology* (originally published in 1890). New York: Dover Publications, Inc.

———. 1961. *The Varieties of Religious Experience*. New York: Collier Books. (paperback)

Jaques, Elliott. 1981. "The Midlife Crisis." *The Course of Life*, Vol. 3, Greenspan and Pollock, eds.

Johnson, Ann Braden. 1977. "A Temple of Last Resorts: Youth and Shared Narcissisms." *The Narcissistic Condition*, Marie Coleman Nelson, ed. New York: Human Science Press.

Jones, Ernest. 1955. *Hamlet and Oedipus*. New York: Doubleday Anchor Books. (paperback)

Joseph, Jenny. 1973. "Warning." *The Oxford Book of Twentieth Century English Verse*, Philip Larkin, ed. London: Oxford University Press.

Jung, Carl. 1971. *The Portable Jung*, Joseph Campbell, ed. New York: The Viking Press. (paperback)

Kagan, Jerome; Kearsley, Richard B., and Zelazo, Philip R. 1978. *Infancy*. Cambridge, Massachusetts and London: Harvard University Press.

Kaplan, Louis. 1970. "Some Thoughts on the Nature of Women." *Bulletin of the Philadelphia Association for Psychoanalysis*, Vol. 20, pp. 319–328.

Kaufmann, Walter. 1959. "Existentialism and Death." *The Meaning of Death*, Herman Feifel, ed. New York: McGraw-Hill Book Company, Inc.

Kernberg, Otto. 1975. *Borderline Conditions and Pathological Narcissism*. New York: Jason Aronson, Inc.

———. 1976. *Object-Relations Theory and Clinical Psychoanalysis*. New York: Jason Aronson, Inc.

———. 1977. "Boundaries and Structure in Love Relations." *Journal of the American Psychoanalytic Association*, Vol. 25, No. 1, pp. 81–114.

———. 1980. "Adolescent Sexuality in the Light of Group Process." *The Psychoanalytic Quarterly*, Vol. 49, No. 1, pp. 26–47.

———. 1980. "Love, the Couple and the Group: A Psychoanalytic Frame." *The Psychoanalytic Quarterly*, Vol. 49, No. 1, pp. 78–108.

Kestenberg, Judith. 1970. "The Effect on Parents of the Child's Transition Into and Out of Latency." *Parenthood: Its Psychology and Psychopathology*. E. James Anthony and Therese Benedek, eds. Boston: Little, Brown and Company.

———. 1980. "Eleven, Twelve, Thirteen: Years of Transition From the Barrenness of Childhood to the Fertility of Adolescence." *The Course of Life*, Vol. 2, Greenspan and Pollock, eds.

Kleeman, James. 1976. "Freud's Views on Early Female Sexuality in the Light of Direct Child Observation." *Journal of the American Psychoanalytic Association*, Vol. 24, No. 5, pp. 3–27.

Klein, Melanie. 1969, 1973. "Mourning and Its Relation to Manic-Depressive States." *The Interpretation of Death*, Hendrik Ruitenbeek, ed. New York: Jason Aronson, Inc.

Kliman, Gilbert, and Rosenfeld, Albert. 1980. *Responsible Parenthood*. New York: Holt, Rinehart and Winston.

Kohlberg, Lawrence, and Gilligan, Carol. 1971. "The Adolescent as a Philosopher: The Discovery of the Self in a Postconventional World." *Daedalus* 100, pp. 1051–1086.

Kohlberg, L., and Kramer, R. 1969. "Continuities and Discontinuities in Child and Adult Moral Development." *Human Development* 12, pp. 93–120.

Kohut, Heinz. 1971. *The Analysis of the Self*. New York: International Universities Press, Inc.

———. 1977. *The Restoration of the Self*. New York: International Universities Press, Inc.

Krent, Justin. 1978. "Some Thoughts on Aggression." *Journal of the American Psychoanalytic Association*, Vol. 26, No. 1, pp. 185–232.

Kris, Ernst. 1975. *Selected Papers of Ernst Kris*. New Haven and London: Yale University Press.

Kubie, Lawrence. 1939. "A Critical Analysis of the Concept of a Repetition Compulsion." *The International Journal of Psycho-Analysis*, Vol. 20, Parts 3 and 4, pp. 390–402.

———. 1974. "The Drive to Become Both Sexes." *The Psychoanalytic Quarterly*, Vol. 43, No. 3, pp. 349–426.

Kübler-Ross, Elisabeth. 1969. *On Death and Dying*. London: Collier-Macmillan Ltd.

Kumin, Maxine. 1982. *Our Ground Time Here Will Be Brief*. New York: Penguin Books. (paperback)

Kushner, Harold. 1981. *When Bad Things Happen to Good People*. New York: Schocken Books.

Lamb, Michael, ed. 1976. *The Role of the Father in Child Development*. New York: John Wiley and Sons.

Lamb, Michael E., and Sutton-Smith, Brian, eds. 1982. *Sibling Relationships: Their Nature and Significance Across the Lifespan*. Hillsdale, New Jersey: Lawrence Erlbaum Associates.

Lampl-De Groot, J. 1928. "The Evolution of the Oedipus Complex in Women." *The International Journal of Psycho-Analysis*, Vol. 9, pp. 332–345.

Larkin, Philip, ed. 1973. *The Oxford Book of Twentieth Century English Verse*. London: Oxford University Press.

La Rochefoucauld, François, Duc de. 1957. *The Maxims of the Duc de la Rochefoucauld*. London: Allan Wingate.

Lasch, Christopher. 1977. *Haven in a Heartless World*. New York: Basic Books, Inc.

———. 1978. *The Culture of Narcissism*. New York: W. W. Norton & Co., Inc.

Lawrence, D. H. 1957. *Lady Chatterley's Lover*. New York: Grove Press, Inc.

Lazarre, Jane. 1976. *The Mother Knot*. New York: McGraw-Hill.

LeShan, Lawrence, and LeShan, Eda. 1969, 1973. "Psychotherapy and the Patient with a Limited Lifespan." *The Interpretation of Death*, Hendrik Ruitenbeek, ed. New York: Jason Aronson, Inc., Publishers.

Levin, Sidney, and Kahana, Ralph, eds. 1967. *Psychodynamic Studies on Aging: Creativity, Reminiscing and Dying*. New York: International Universities Press, Inc.

Levinson, Daniel. 1978. *The Seasons of a Man's Life*. New York: Ballantine Books. (paperback)

Levy, David. 1937. *Studies in Sibling Rivalry*. American Orthopsychiatric Association.

Lewis, C. S. 1963. *A Grief Observed*. New York: Bantam Books. (paperback)

Lichtenstein, Heinz. 1963. "The Dilemma of Human Identity: Notes on Self-Transformation, Self-Objectivation and Metamorphosis." *Journal of the American Psychoanalytic Association*, Vol. 11, No. 1, pp. 173–223.

Lidz, Theodore. 1975. *Hamlet's Enemy*. New York: Basic Books, Inc.

Lifton, Robert Jay. 1979. *The Broken Connection*. New York: Simon and Schuster.

Lipson, Channing. 1969, 1973. "Denial and Mourning." *The Interpretation of Death*, Hendrik Ruitenbeek, ed. New York: Jason Aronson, Inc.

Loewald, Hans. 1960. "On the Therapeutic Action of Psychoanalysis." *The International Journal of Psycho-Analysis*, Vol. 41, Part 1, pp. 16–33.

———. 1978. "Instinct Theory, Object Relations and Psychic-Structure Formation." *Journal of the American Psychoanalytic Association*, Vol. 26, No. 3, pp. 493–506.

———. 1978. *Psychoanalysis and the History of the Individual*. New Haven and London: Yale University Press.

———. 1979. "The Waning of the Oedipus Complex." *Journal of the American Psychoanalytic Association*, Vol. 27, No. 4, pp. 751–775.

Lomas, Peter. 1961. "Family Role and Identity Formation." *The International Journal of Psycho-Analysis*, Vol. 42, Parts 4–5, pp. 371–380.

Longfellow, Henry Wadsworth. 1893. "Morituri Salutamus." *The Complete Poetical Works of Henry Wadsworth Longfellow.* Boston: Houghton Mifflin Company.

Lorenz, Konrad. 1974. *On Aggression.* New York and London: Harcourt Brace Jovanovich, Publishers. (paperback)

Lowell, James Russell. 1925. *The Complete Poetical Works of James Russell Lowell.* Cambridge: The Riverside Press.

Maccoby, Eleanor, and Jacklin, Carol. 1974. *The Psychology of Sex Differences.* Stanford, California: Stanford University Press.

Macdonald, Cynthia. 1979. "Accomplishments." *A Geography of Poets,* Edward Field, ed. New York: Bantam Books.

Mack, Maynard; Dean, Leonard; Frost, William, eds. 1950. *Modern Poetry.* New York: Prentice-Hall, Inc.

MacLeish, Archibald. 1956. *J.B.* Cambridge, Mass.: The Riverside Press.

MacNeice, Louis. 1950. "Les Sylphides." *Modern Poetry,* Mack, Dean, Frost, eds. New York: Prentice-Hall, Inc.

———. 1970, 1975. "The Sunlight on the Garden." *The Norton Anthology of Poetry,* Allison et al., eds. New York: W. W. Norton & Company. (paperback)

Mahler, Margaret. 1968. *On Human Symbiosis and the Vicissitudes of Individuation,* Vol. I. New York: International Universities Press, Inc.

Mahler, Margaret, and McDevitt, John. 1980. "The Separation-Individuation Process and Identity Formation." *The Course of Life,* Vol. 1, Greenspan and Pollock, eds.

Mahler, Margaret; Pine, Fred; and Bergman, Anni. 1975. *The Psychological Birth of the Human Infant.* New York: Basic Books, Inc.

Malcolm, Andrew. September 24, 1984. "Some Elderly Choose Suicide Over Lonely, Dependent Life." *The New York Times,* pp. 1, B6.

Mann, John. 1980, 1982. *Secrets of Life Extension.* New York: Bantam Books. (paperback)

Mann, Thomas. 1969. *The Magic Mountain* (originally published in German, 1924, and in English, 1927). New York: Random House. (Vintage Books paperback)

Marquis, Don. 1927. *archy and mehitabel.* New York: Doubleday & Co., Inc.

Masters, William, and Johnson, Virginia, in association with Robert Levin. 1976. *The Pleasure Bond.* Toronto/New York/London: Bantam Books. (paperback)

May, Rollo. 1969. *Love and Will.* New York: Dell Publishing Co., Inc.

McDevitt, John. 1979. "The Role of Internalization in the Development of Object Relations During the Separation-Individuation Phase." *Journal of the American Psychoanalytic Association,* Vol. 27, No. 2, pp. 327–343.

McDevitt, John, and Mahler, Margaret. 1980. "Object Constancy, Individuality and Internalization." *The Course of Life,* Vol. 1, Greenspan and Pollock, eds.

McGlashan, Thomas, and Miller, Glenn. April 1982. "The Goals of Psychoanalysis and Psychoanalytic Psychotherapy." *Archives of General Psychiatry,* Vol. 39.

McMahon, James. 1982. "Intimacy Among Friends and Lovers." *Intimacy,* Martin Fisher and George Stricker, eds. New York: Plenum Press.

Mead, Margaret. 1972. *Blackberry Winter.* New York: William Morrow & Co., Inc.

———. 1975. *Male and Female* (originally published in 1949). New York: William Morrow & Co., Inc. (paperback)

Menninger, Karl. 1942. *Love Against Hate.* New York: Harcourt, Brace and Co.

Michaels, Leonard. 1978. *The Men's Club.* New York: Farrar Straus Giroux.

Milgram, Stanley. 1974. *Obedience to Authority.* New York: Harper & Row.

Miller, Alice. *Prisoners of Childhood.* 1981. New York: Basic Books, Inc.

Miller, Arthur. 1958. *Death of a Salesman.* New York: The Viking Press. (paperback)

Mittelmann, Bela. 1944. "Complementary Neurotic Reactions in Intimate Relationships." *The Psychoanalytic Quarterly,* Vol. 13, No. 4, pp. 479–491.

Modell, Arnold. 1965. "On Having the Right to a Life: An Aspect of the Superego's Development." *The International Journal of Psycho-Analysis,* Vol. 46, Part 3, pp. 323–331.

———. 1975. "The Ego and the Id: Fifty Years Later." *The International Journal of Psycho-Analysis,* Vol. 56, Part 1, pp. 57–68.

Moffat, Mary Jane, ed. 1982. *In the Midst of Winter: Selections from the Literature of Mourning.* New York: Random House.

Moore, Burness. 1976. "Freud and Female Sexuality: A Current View." *The International Journal of Psycho-Analysis,* Vol. 57, Part 3, pp. 287–300.

Morrison, Toni. 1972. *The Bluest Eye.* New York: Pocket Books. (paperback)

Nabokov, Vladimir. 1966. *Speak, Memory.* New York: G. P. Putnam's Sons.

Nacht, Sacha, and Viderman, S. 1960. "The Pre-Object Universe in the Transference Situation." *The International Journal of Psycho-Analysis,* Vol. 41, Parts 4–5, pp. 385–388.

Natterson, Joseph, ed. 1980. *The Dream in Clinical Practice.* New York: Jason Aronson.

Nelson, Bryce. February 15, 1983. "Self-Sabotage in Careers—A Common Trap." *The New York Times.*

Nelson, John, and Cargill, Oscar, eds. 1949. *Contemporary Trends.* New York: The Macmillan Company.

Neubauer, Peter. 1960. "The One-Parent Child and His Oedipal Development." *The Psychoanalytic Study of the Child,* Vol. 15. New York: International Universities Press, Inc.

Neugarten, Bernice; Havighurst, Robert; and Tobin, Sheldon. 1968. "Personality and Patterns of Aging." *Middle Age and Aging,* Bernice Neugarten, ed. Chicago and London: The University of Chicago Press.

Neugarten, Bernice, ed. 1968. *Middle Age and Aging.* Chicago and London: The University of Chicago Press.

Norton, Janice. 1969, 1973. "Treatment of a Dying Patient." *The Interpretation of Death,* Hendrik Ruitenbeek, ed. New York: Jason Aronson.

Noshpitz, Joseph. 1980. "Disturbances in Early Adolescent Development." *The Course of Life,* Vol. 2, Greenspan and Pollock, eds.

Offer, Daniel. 1980. "Adolescent Development: A Normative Perspective." *The Course of Life,* Vol. 2, Greenspan and Pollock, eds.

Ogden, Thomas. 1982. *Projective Identification and Psychotherapeutic Technique.* New York and London: Jason Aronson.

O'Neill, Eugene. 1955. *Long Day's Journey Into Night.* New Haven and London: Yale University Press. (paperback)

O'Neill, Nena. 1978. *The Marriage Premise.* New York: Bantam Books. (paperback)

Panel, David Rubinfine, reporter. 1958. "Problems of Identity." *Journal of the American Psychoanalytic Association,* Vol. 6, No. 1, pp. 131–142.

Panel, Irving Sternschein, reporter. 1973. "The Experience of Separation-Individuation in Infancy and Its Reverberations Through the Course of Life: Maturity, Senescence, and Sociological Implications." *Journal of the American Psychoanalytic Association,* Vol. 21, No. 3, pp. 633–645.

Panel. 1975. "Bertram D. Lewin Memorial Symposium: Psychoanalytic Perspectives on Love and Marriage." *Journal of the Philadelphia Association for Psychoanalysis*, Vol. 2, pp. 191–201.

Panel, Robert C. Prall, reporter. 1978. "The Role of the Father in the Preoedipal Years." *Journal of the American Psychoanalytic Association*, Vol. 26, No. 1, pp. 143–161.

Panel. May 1982. "What Qualities Do Women Most Value in Husbands?" *Viewpoints*, Vol. 16, No. 5, pp. 77–90.

Panel, Nancy Miller, reporter. (in press). "The Psychoanalysis of the Older Patient." For *Journal of the American Psychoanalytic Association*.

Pastan, Linda. 1978. *The Five Stages of Grief*. New York: W. W. Norton. (paperback)

———. 1982. *PM/AM*. New York: W. W. Norton. (paperback)

Payne, Edmund. "The Physician and His Patient Who Is Dying." *Psychodynamic Studies of Aging: Creativity, Reminiscing and Dying*, Sidney Levin and Ralph Kahana, eds. New York: International Universities Press, Inc.

Pearson, Gerald. 1952. "A Survey of Learning Difficulties in Children." *The Psychoanalytic Study of the Child*, Vol. 7. New York: International Universities Press, Inc.

Peck, Robert. 1968. "Psychological Developments in the Second Half of Life." *Middle Age and Aging*, Bernice Neugarten, ed. Chicago and London: The University of Chicago Press.

Perrine, Laurence, ed. 1956, 1963, 1969, 1973, 1977. *Sound and Sense*. New York: Harcourt Brace Jovanovich, Inc. (paperback)

Perutz, Kathrin. 1972. *Marriage Is Hell*. New York: William Morrow & Company, Inc.

Philipe, Anne. 1964. *No Longer Than a Sigh*. New York: Atheneum.

Piaget, Jean. 1969. "The Intellectual Development of the Adolescent." *Adolescence: Psychosocial Perspectives*, Caplan and Lebovici, eds. New York: Basic Books.

Piercy, Marge. 1982. *Circles on the Water*. "Doing It Differently." New York: Alfred A. Knopf. (paperback)

Pincus, Lily. 1974. *Death and the Family*. New York: Random House. (Vintage Books paperback)

Pollock, George. July–October 1961. "Mourning and Adaptation." *The International Journal of Psycho-Analysis*, Vol. 42, Parts 4–5, pp. 341–361.

———. 1964. "On Symbiosis and Symbiotic Neurosis." *The International Journal of Psycho-Analysis*, Vol. 45, Part 1, pp. 1–30.

———. 1970. "Anniversary Reactions, Trauma, and Mourning." *The Psychoanalytic Quarterly*, Vol. 39, No. 3, pp. 347–371.

———. 1977. "The Mourning Process and Creative Organizational Change." *Journal of the American Psychoanalytic Association*, Vol. 25, No. 1, pp. 3–34.

———. 1981. "Aging or Aged: Development or Pathology." *The Course of Life*, Vol. 3, Greenspan and Pollock, eds.

Provence, Sally, ed. 1983. *Infants and Parents*. New York: International Universities Press, Inc.

Racine, Jean. 1961. *Three Plays of Racine* (originally presented in 1667). George Dillon, translator. Chicago: University of Chicago Press.

Radl, Shirley. 1973. *Mother's Day Is Over*. New York: Charterhouse.

Rangell, Leo. 1963. "On Friendship." *Journal of the American Psychoanalytic Association*, Vol. 11, No. 1, pp. 3–54.

Rank, Otto. 1952. *The Trauma of Birth*. New York: Robert Brunner.

Raphael, Beverley. 1983. *The Anatomy of Bereavement*. New York: Basic Books, Inc.

Richter, Horst-Eberhard. 1976. "The Role of Family Life in Child Development." *The International Journal of Psycho-Analysis*, Vol. 57, Part 4, pp. 385–395.

Robinson, Edwin Arlington. 1949. "Richard Cory" (originally published in 1897). *Contemporary Trends*, John Nelson and Oscar Cargill, eds. New York: The Macmillan Co.

Robinson, Marilynne. 1982. *Housekeeping*. New York: Bantam Books. (paperback)

Rochlin, Gregory. 1961. "The Dread of Abandonment: A Contribution to the Etiology of the Loss Complex and to Depression." *The Psychoanalytic Study of the Child*, Vol. 16. New York: International Universities Press, Inc.

Rosenthal, Hattie. 1969, 1973. "Psychotherapy for the Dying." *The Interpretation of Death*, Hendrik Ruitenbeek, ed. New York: Jason Aronson.

Ross, Helgola, and Milgram, Joel. 1982. "Important Variables in Adult Sibling Relationships: A Qualitative Study." *Sibling Relationships: Their Nature and Significance Across the Life-Span*, Lamb and Sutton-Smith, eds.

Ross, John Munder. 1979. "Fathering: A Review of Some Psychoanalytic Contributions on Paternity." *The International Journal of Psycho-Analysis*, Vol. 60, Part 3, pp. 317–327.

Rossi, Alice. Spring 1977. "A Biosocial Perspective on Parenting." *Daedalus*, pp. 1–31.

Roth, Philip. 1967, 1968, 1969. *Portnoy's Complaint*. New York: Random House.

Rubin, Lillian. 1979. *Women of a Certain Age*. New York: Harper & Row. (paperback)

———. 1983. *Intimate Strangers*. New York: Harper & Row.

Ruitenbeek, Hendrik, ed. 1969, 1973. *The Interpretation of Death*. New York: Jason Aronson.

Russell, Bertrand. 1967. *The Autobiography of Bertrand Russell, 1872–1914*. London: Allen & Unwin.

Rycroft, Charles. 1979. *The Innocence of Dreams*. New York: Pantheon.

Salholz, Eloise, with Jennifer Smith. March 26, 1984. "How to Live Forever." *Newsweek*, p. 81.

Salinger, J. D. 1945, 1946, 1951. *The Catcher in the Rye*. New York: Bantam Books. (paperback)

Sandler, Joseph. 1960. "On the Concept of Superego." *The Psychoanalytic Study of the Child*, Vol. 15. New York: International Universities Press, Inc., pp. 128–162.

Sass, Louis. August 22, 1982. "The Borderline Personality." *The New York Times Magazine*, pp. 12–15, 66–67.

Scarf, Maggie. 1980. *Unfinished Business*. New York: Doubleday & Co.

Schachter, Frances Fuchs. 1982. "Sibling Deidentification and Split-Parent Identification: A Family Tetrad." *Sibling Relationships: Their Nature and Significance Across the Lifespan*. Michael Lamb and Brian Sutton-Smith, eds. Hillsdale, New Jersey: Lawrence Erlbaum Associates.

Schafer, Roy. 1960. "The Loving and Beloved Superego in Freud's Structural Theory." *The Psychoanalytic Study of the Child*, Vol. 15. New York: International Universities Press, Inc.

———. 1968. *Aspects of Internalization*. New York: International Universities Press, Inc.

Schaffer, Rudolph. 1977. *Mothering.* Cambridge, Mass.: Harvard University Press.

Scott-Maxwell, Florida. 1979. *The Measure of My Days.* New York: Penguin Books. (paperback)

Searles, Harold. 1979. *Countertransference.* New York: International Universities Press, Inc.

Segal, Hanna. 1964, 1973. *Introduction to the Works of Melanie Klein.* New York: Basic Books, Inc.

Sendak, Maurice. 1963. *Where the Wild Things Are.* New York: Harper & Row.

——. 1970. *In the Night Kitchen.* New York: Harper & Row.

Shakespeare, William. *As You Like It.*

——. *King John.*

——. *King Lear.*

——. *Macbeth.*

——. *Romeo and Juliet.*

Shanas, Ethel; Townsend, Peter; Wedderburn, Dorothy; Friis, Hennig; Milhoj, Poul; and Stehouwer, Jan. 1968. "The Psychology of Health." *Middle Age and Aging,* Bernice Neugarten, ed. Chicago and London: The University of Chicago Press.

Shapiro, Theodore, and Perry, Richard. 1976. "Latency Revisited." *The Psychoanalytic Study of the Child,* Vol. 31, pp. 79–105.

Sheehy, Gail. 1974, 1976. *Passages.* New York: E. P. Dutton & Co., Inc.

Shengold, Leonard. 1979. "Child Abuse and Deprivation: Soul Murder." *Journal of the American Psychoanalytic Association,* Vol. 27, No. 3, pp. 533–559.

Shields, Robert. 1964. "The Too-Good Mother." *The International Journal of Psycho-Analysis,* Vol. 45, Part 1, pp. 85–88.

Shneidman, Edwin. 1980, 1982. *Voices of Death.* New York: Bantam Books. (paperback)

Silverman, Lloyd; Lachmann, Frank; Milich, Robert. 1982. *The Search for Oneness.* New York: International Universities Press, Inc.

Simmons, Charles. Dec. 11, 1984. "The Age of Maturity." *The New York Times Magazine,* p. 114.

Simpson, Louis. 1956, 1963, 1969, 1973, 1977. "The Goodnight." *Sound and Sense,* Laurence Perrine, ed. New York: Harcourt Brace Jovanovich. (paperback)

Sklansky, Morris. 1980. "The Pubescent Years: Eleven to Fourteen." *The Course of Life,* Vol. 2, Greenspan and Pollock, eds.

Smith, Sydney. 1977. "The Golden Fantasy: A Regressive Reaction to Separation Anxiety." *The International Journal of Psycho-Analysis,* Vol. 58, Part 3, pp. 311–324.

Snow, Karen. 1976. *Willo.* Ann Arbor: Street Fiction Press, Inc.

Solnit, Albert. 1980. "Psychoanalytic Perspectives on Children One–Three Years of Age." *The Course of Life,* Vol. 1, Greenspan and Pollock, eds.

Sontag, Susan. October 1972. "The Double Standard of Aging." *Saturday Review,* pp. 29–38.

Sophocles. 1954. "Oedipus at Colonus." *Sophocles I,* Grene and Lattimore, eds. Chicago and London: The University of Chicago Press. (paperback)

——. 1954. "Oedipus the King." *Sophocles I,* Grene and Lattimore, eds. Chicago and London: The University of Chicago Press. (paperback)

Spark, Muriel. 1966. *Memento Mori.* New York: The Modern Library.

Spitz, René. 1945. "Hospitalism." *The Psychoanalytic Study of the Child,* Vol. 1. New York: International Universities Press, Inc.

————. 1965. *The First Year of Life*. New York: International Universities Press, Inc.

Stern, Daniel. 1977. *The First Relationship*. Cambridge, Mass.: Harvard University Press.

Stevens, Wallace. 1970, 1975. "Sunday Morning." *The Norton Anthology of Poetry*, Allison et al., eds. New York: W. W. Norton & Company. (paperback)

Stevenson, Robert Louis. 1885. *A Child's Garden of Verses*. "Bed in Summer." London: George C. Harrap and Company Ltd.

Stoller, Robert. 1976. "Primary Femininity." *Journal of the American Psychoanalytic Association*, Vol. 24, No. 5, pp. 59–78.

————. 1980. "A Different View of Oedipal Conflict." *The Course of Life*, Vol. 1, Greenspan and Pollock, eds.

Stoller, Robert, and Herdt, Gilbert. 1982. "The Development of Masculinity: A Cross-Cultural Contribution." *Journal of the American Psychoanalytic Association*, Vol. 30, No. 1, pp. 29–59.

Sutherland, John D. 1980. "The British Object Relations Theorists: Balint, Winnicott, Fairbairn, Guntrip." *Journal of the American Psychoanalytic Association*, Vol. 28, No. 4, pp. 829–860.

Suttie, Ian. 1935. *The Origins of Love and Hate*. London: Kegan Paul, Trench, Trubner & Co., Ltd.

Sweet, Ellen. May 1984. "The Electra Complex: How Can I Be Jealous of My Four-Year-Old Daughter?" *Ms.*, pp. 148–149.

Talbot, Toby. 1980. *A Book About My Mother*. New York: Farrar, Straus and Giroux.

Tavris, Carol, with Dr. Alice Baumgartner. February 1983. "How Would Your Life Be Different If You'd Been Born a Boy?" *Redbook*, pp. 92–95.

Teicholz, Judith Guss. 1978. "A Selective Review of the Psychoanalytic Literature on Theoretical Conceptualizations of Narcissism." *Journal of the American Psychoanalytic Association*, Vol. 26, No. 4, pp. 831–861.

Tennyson, Alfred, Lord. 1970, 1975. "Ulysses." (originally published 1833, 1842.) *The Norton Anthology of Poetry*, Allison et al., eds. New York: W. W. Norton. (paperback)

Thomas, Dylan. 1970, 1975. "Fern Hill." *The Norton Anthology of Poetry*, Allison et al., eds. New York: W. W. Norton. (paperback)

————. 1977. "Do Not Go Gentle into That Good Night." *Sound and Sense*, Laurence Perrine, ed. New York: Harcourt Brace Jovanovich, Inc. (paperback)

Tillich, Paul. 1959. "The Eternal Now." *The Meaning of Death*, Herman Feifel, ed. New York: McGraw-Hill.

Tolstoy, Leo. 1967. *Great Short Works of Leo Tolstoy*. "The Death of Ivan Ilych." New York: Harper & Row. (paperback).

Toynbee, Arnold J. April 5, 1969. "Why and How I Work," *Saturday Review*, pp. 22–27, 62.

Tyson, Phyllis. 1982. "A Developmental Line of Gender Identity, Gender Role and Choice of Love Object." *Journal of the American Psychoanalytic Association*, Vol. 30, No. 1, pp. 61–86.

Ulanov, Ann and Barry. 1975. *Religion and the Unconscious*. Philadelphia: The Westminster Press.

Ullmann, Liv. 1977. *Changing*. New York: Alfred A. Knopf.

Viorst, Judith. 1968. *It's Hard to Be Hip Over Thirty and Other Tragedies of Married Life*. New York and Cleveland: World Publishing Company.

————. 1973, 1974, 1976. *How Did I Get To Be Forty and Other Atrocities*. New York: Simon and Schuster.

————. 1974. *Rosie and Michael*. New York: Atheneum.

————. November 1976. "Sometimes I Hate My Husband." *Redbook*, pp. 73–74.

————. February 1977. "The Hospital That Has Patience for Its Patients: A Look at Children's Hospital, in Washington, D.C." *Redbook*, pp. 48–54.

————. October 1977. "Friends, Good Friends—and Such Good Friends." *Redbook*, pp. 31–32, 38.

————. November 1978. "Are Men and Women Different?" *Redbook*, pp. 46–50.

————. May 1980. "Letting Go: Why It's Hard to Let Children Grow Up." *Redbook*, pp. 42, 44.

————. September 1980. "In Praise of Older Women." *Redbook*, pp. 42, 44.

————. 1981. *If I Were in Charge of the World and Other Worries*. New York: Atheneum.

Wagenvoord, James, and Bailey, Peyton. 1978. *Men: A Book for Women*. New York: Avon. (paperback)

White, E. B. *Poems and Sketches of E. B. White*. 1981. New York: Harper & Row.

Wikler, Lynn. 1980. "Folie à Famille: A Family Therapist's Perspective." *Family Process*, Vol. 19:3, pp. 257–268.

Wilbur, Richard. 1970, 1975. "Seed Leaves" (originally published in 1969). *The Norton Anthology of Poetry*, Allison et al., eds. New York: W. W. Norton. (paperback)

Willi, Jurg. 1982. *Couples in Collusion*. New York and London: Jason Aronson.

Wilson, Edmund. 1980. *The Thirties*. New York: Farrar, Straus and Giroux.

Winnicott, D. W. 1958. *Collected Papers*. New York: Basic Books, Inc.

————. 1965. *The Maturational Processes and the Facilitating Environment*. New York: International Universities Press, Inc.

Wisdom, J. O. 1976. "The Role of the Father in the Mind of Parents, in Psychoanalytic Theory and in the Life of the Infant." *The International Review of Psychoanalysis*, Vol. 3, Part 2, pp. 231–239.

Wolfenstein, Martha. 1966. "How Is Mourning Possible?" *The Psychoanalytic Study of the Child*, Vol. 21. New York: International Universities Press, Inc.

Woodruff, Diana, and Birren, James. 1975. *Aging*. New York: D. Van Nostrand Company.

Woolf, Virginia. 1927. *To the Lighthouse*. New York: Harcourt, Brace and World, Inc. (paperback)

————. 1928, 1956. *Orlando*. New York and London: Harcourt Brace Jovanovich. (paperback)

Wynne, Lyman; Ryckoff, Irving; Day, Juliana; and Hirsch, Stanley. 1967. "Pseudo-Mutuality in the Family Relations of Schizophrenics." *The Psychosocial Interior of the Family*, Gerald Handel, ed. Chicago: Aldine.

Yeats, W. B. 1956. *The Collected Poems of W. B. Yeats*. New York: Macmillan Publishing Co., Inc.

Yogman, Michael. 1982. "Development of the Father-Infant Relationship." Fitzgerald, Lester, Yogman, eds. *Theory and Research in Behavioral Pediatrics*, Vol. 1. New York: Plenum Publishing Corporation.

Yourcenar, Marguerite. 1954. *Memoirs of Hadrian*. New York: Farrar, Straus and Giroux. (paperback)

Zinberg, Norman, and Kaufman, Irving, eds. 1963. *Normal Psychology of the Aging Process*. New York: International Universities Press, Inc.

Index

Mourning (*cont.*)
  search for dead and, 242–45
  for sibling, 260–62
  for spouse's death, 247, 257–59
  stress and, 252
"Mourning and Melancholia," 237
"Mummification" of dead (morbid
    preservation of all
    possessions), 250
Murder
  of self. *See* Suicide.
  sibling, 85–86
Murderous feelings, 163
  toward parent, 102, 104, 147–
    148
Mysterious center, 280, 281

Nabokov, Vladimir, 222
Narcissism, 55, 58–64
  adolescence and, 151, 152, 201
  depression and, 62
  ego ideal and, 140
  Freud on, 58
  grandiosity and, 59, 61, 62, 64
  Kohut on, 58, 60
  loss of, 140
  parental, 63
  practicing stage and, 45
  primary vs. secondary, 58
  self-objects, 60, 62
Nature
  immortality and, 321
  oneness (harmony) with, 35, 36
Neurosis
  external vs. internal events and,
    218–22
  guilt and, 133–34
  marriage and, 192–95
  success, 105–6
  symbiotic, 38

Obedience vs. conscience, 138–39
Object constancy, 49–50
Occupation
  female vs. male expectations for,
    120
  mid-life crisis and, 277–78
  Oedipus complex and, 105–6
  retirement from, 289–90

sibling rivalry and, 90
success neurosis and, 105–6
working wives, changing
    attitudes toward, 277–78
Oceanic feeling, 37, 323
Oedipus, 100, 107, 157
Oedipus complex, 100–114
  adaptability and, 123–24
  adolescence and, 151
  castration anxiety and, 128
  central thesis of, 101–2
  compulsion for married men
    and, 103
  compulsion for older mate and,
    102–3
  death of parent and, 111
  divorce and, 111–12
  Freud on, 101–2, 103–4, 105
  Hamlet and, 104
  incest and, 102, 107–10
  negative, 106–7
  professional life and, 105
  reality and, 220
  resolution of, 112–14
  seductive parent and, 108–10
  success neurosis and, 105–6
  "victories" and, 111–12
Old age, 284–304. *See also* Aging.
O'Neill, Eugene, 95
"On Friendship," 183
Oneness, 34–42, 322–23
  separateness conflict with, 43–
    44, 46
Opposites, merger of, 326–27
Oral phase, 101
Orgasm, 36, 37–38, 188, 189
"Out-of-phase" problem, marital,
    278
Ovid, 285

Parent(s). *See also* Father; Mother.
  beliefs and, 227
  biosocial perspective on, 73–74
  chronic emergency of, 278–79
  death of, 262–63
  dependency of, 270
  developmental phase of, 230
  emotional separateness of child
    from, 208–9

About the Author

Judith Viorst, the author of numerous books of poetry and prose and a contributing editor to *Redbook* magazine, graduated from the Washington Psychoanalytic Institute in 1981 after six years of study. Mrs. Viorst lives in Washington, D.C., with her husband, Milton Viorst, the political writer. They have three sons—Anthony, Nicholas and Alexander.